RUSSIAN ORTHODOXY RESURGENT

For our friends in the Russian Orthodox faith, with admiration and best wishes)

Carol Garrard

John Garrard (6/22/09)

RUSSIAN ORTHODOXY RESURGENT

Faith
and
Power
in the
New
Russia

John Garrard & Carol Garrard

PRINCETON UNIVERSITY PRESS

PRINCETON AND OXFORD

Library of Congress Cataloging-in-Publication Data

Garrard, John Gordon.
Russian Orthodoxy resurgent : faith and power in the new Russia /
John Garrard and Carol Garrard.
p.   cm.
Includes bibliographical references (p.   ) and index.
ISBN 978-0-691-12573-2 (cloth : alk. paper)   1. Religion and politics—Russia
(Federation)—History—20th century.   2. Religion and politics—Russia (Federation)—
History—21st century.   3. Russkaia pravoslavnaia tserkov'—Influence.   4. Russkaia
pravoslavnaia tserkov'.   5. Aleksii II, Patriarch of Moscow and All Russia, 1929–   I. Garrard,
Carol.   II. Title.
BL65.P7G37 2008
281.9'47090511—dc22   2008005415

British Library Cataloging-in-Publication Data is available

This book has been composed in Electra
Printed on acid-free paper. ∞
press.princeton.edu

Printed in the United States of America
1   3   5   7   9   10   8   6   4   2

To the memory of

John Simmons and Sir Julian Bullard

Patriots and Scholars

The three most importantly innovative and transformative political developments of the last twenty years [have been] the rise of the Christian right in America, the explosion of Islamic fundamentalism in Iran, and the collapse of Communism in the Soviet Union.

James Billington, Librarian of Congress,
from the 1997 *Templeton Lecture*

Contents

Illustrations

Preface

The official dissolution of the USSR on December 25, 1991, occasioned self-congratulation among some in the West but provoked an agony of conscience and recrimination within Russia itself. With huge sections of the country poisoned by chemicals, fresh evidence mounting of the contempt with which the Soviet government treated its own citizens, and the list of those who died in the Gulag growing by millions, Russians faced a period of disorienting turmoil as they saw their truncated country plummet from superpower status. The almost instantaneous disintegration of the Soviet system and the Communist Party that ran it left a vacuum once occupied by the official ideology of "scientific atheism."

The Russian Orthodox Church (ROC) is filling this vacuum and reconstituting a national belief system in its own image. Believers are replacing party members. The story of the Russians' recovery of their sense of themselves as a great nation (*derzhava*) is still in progress; its events are being recorded in newspaper headlines and television bulletins. Whatever the outcome, the key role played by the ROC has already recast the country we once thought we knew into a power whose motivations we understand very little. Orthodox believers now constitute the largest volunteer movement inside the Russian Federation during the "zero years"—the Russians' own term for the period since 2000. Two powerful trends are converging: one emanates up from the grass roots, and the other is directed down from the Moscow Patriarchate. In an important switch from the situation obtaining in the late tsarist period, those attracted to the church include not only the stereotypical kerchiefed little old ladies (*babushki*, "grandmothers") but also the Russian military and the political, scientific, cultural, and financial elites.

We backed into this critically important topic while editing *World War 2 and the Soviet People* (1993) and researching and writing *The Bones of Berdichev: The Life and Fate of Vasily Grossman* (1996). In 1992 we landed at Sheremetievo Airport laden with more than twenty crates of medical aid assembled by the congregation of Our Saviour's Lutheran Church in Tucson, Arizona, and the donations of many other ecumenical groups. We intended to distribute this aid both to those Jews who wished to leave Russia and to an ROC congregation and school that we had learned about from the librarian at our daughters' elementary school. Our two girls had also led a drive to collect toys, school supplies, and other items for the church children. Thanks to American Airlines and Lufthansa, we flew to Moscow without paying any overweight penalty. It took so long to get the enormous containers of aid through Russian customs that the cavernous waiting room was almost empty when we entered, shepherding a long line of metal trolleys lumbering unsteadily beneath their loads. In one corner waited a greeting committee from "Operation Exodus"—a huddle of young men in keppas from Moscow University's newly established Hillel (a student group). They kept casting sidelong glances to the other corner of the waiting room—an equally mystified and tense circle comprised of a Russian Orthodox priest (Father Sergy Romanov) with a luxuriant black beard, several deacons, and a few young Orthodox nuns. Over the anxious and puzzled heads of both groups hung the unspoken question, "Can they be waiting for the same people we are?" It was a window into the stresses pulling at the substrata of the new Russia.

As we helped this Orthodox congregation restore an eighteenth-century Russian Orthodox Church building, our research began to segue from the Holocaust in the occupied Soviet Union to the revival of Orthodoxy. Indeed, the history of this single church and its courageous priest, Father Sergy Romanov (no relation to the tsarist family), informs the whole subject. This personal engagement led Carol Garrard to publish an article, "Religion: From Official Atheism to Freedom of Choice," in an anthology *Re-Emerging Russia: Search for Identity* (1995), sponsored by Older Americans Service and Information System (OASIS), an innovative and imaginative organization headquartered in St. Louis. The anthology was the basis for a ten-part forum taught in dozens of cities and towns nationwide.

In spite of lively interest from the public, most Western academics, with important exceptions, neglected the church's resurgence. Political scientists and historians prefer to study the new Russia through the traditional secular lens of economics, politics, demography, and other social sciences. Orthodox theologians here in the West, or the memoirs of believers who suffered mistreatment, can hardly be objective. There are, however, distinguished historians in the West, led by James Billington, the librarian of Congress, who have written perceptively in this field. Billington's *The Icon and the Axe: An Interpretive History of Russian Culture* (New York: Knopf, 1966) is essential background to any work on this subject. Further, through an amazing coincidence, he happened to be in Moscow when the August 19–21, 1991 coup by KGB and party hard-liners was attempted. His memoir, *Russia Transformed: Breakthrough to Hope*, is a first-person account that should not be missed. William Brumfield, professor at Tulane University, has produced a magisterial *History of Russian Architecture*, which contains photographs of literally thousands of Russian Orthodox churches, together with his uniquely informed commentary. The

J. M. Dawson Institute of Church-State Studies at Baylor University and the Kennan Institute of the Woodrow Wilson International Center for Scholars in Washington, D.C., supervise innovative research and organize excellent conferences on the Orthodox faith and civic life in Russia. Baylor University Professor Wallace Daniels's *The Orthodox Church and Civil Society in Russia* (2006) offers an in-depth perspective focused on individual parishes and priests as they sought to revitalize Orthodox life.

Once people had asked us, since we are not Jewish, why were we so interested in the tragedy of Soviet Jewry. Now, both the Orthodox congregation we befriended and other scholars asked why we were interested in the church's revival since we are not members of the Russian Orthodox Church. For those who concern themselves with such things, John Garrard was baptized in the Church of England but is not a member of any organized religion; Carol Garrard is a practicing Lutheran. We do not write from the perspective of faith, and we do not belong to a particular political party. We believe that religious tolerance is what this planet needs, in the twenty-first century more than ever. Before being seconded to British Intelligence as an officer-cadet, John Garrard served as a private in the Royal Inniskilling Fusiliers in Northern Ireland. He was posted at Omagh and saw what religious hatred can lead human beings to do to one another.

We plunge into our subject *in medias res* at the Feast of the Transfiguration (Preobrazhensky Post), as it was co-celebrated on August 19, 1987, by the patriarch of the Russian Church, Pimen, and the patriarch of Constantinople, Demetrios I, who was the first patriarch of Constantinople to visit Moscow in four hundred years. Though change had been bubbling beneath the surface for decades, this emotional and beautiful service was the first signal on the national stage that the president of the USSR, Mikhail Gorbachev, planned to extend glasnost and perestroika into the area of faith. The consequences of this switch in policy would be both far-reaching and unanticipated—by Gorbachev himself, by the Communist Party, by Western observers, and perhaps by the Russian Orthodox Church hierarchy. They certainly were unforeseen by us at that moment, even though we were eyewitnesses to this impressive service.

The leitmotif of our book is the career of Pimen's successor as patriarch of Moscow and All Russia, the former Aleksey Ridiger, a man born and brought up in Estonia. He served as metropolitan of Leningrad (now once again St. Petersburg) prior to being enthroned as Patriarch Aleksy II on June 10, 1990. It was Aleksy who intervened at the crisis of the coup by party hardliners the following year: his "address" (*obrashchenie*) threatened excommunication for anyone who took up arms against civilians and closed with a direct plea to the "Mother of God" (Mater Bozhia) to help the Russians reconcile themselves to "one another, to the truth, and to God." It was read over Soviet radio and television at 1:42 A.M. on August 21, 1991. The order for the tanks to advance and seize Boris Yeltsin, elected president of the Russian Republic in June, and members of the Parliament holed up in the Russian White House, was expected just eighteen minutes later; 2:00 A.M. was the KGB's favorite "zero hour" for attack. Instead, at 3:00 A.M., Vladimir Kryuchkov, head of the KGB and leader of the coup, called Yeltsin to say there would be no assault "that night." "That night" became "never" when the tanks turned around at dawn. Since then, Aleksy II has led the resurgence of the Orthodox faith.

This book is not, however, a hagiography, but an examination of the ways in which an institution once despised and rejected by the vast majority of the citizenry has come to reshape post-Soviet Russia. Ours is a "warts and all" portrait of both man and institution. Thus we have been told we will be "cursed" for acknowledging in print what has been known by insiders since the early 1990s—namely, that Ridiger had served in the KGB for more than thirty years prior to his enthronement as patriarch. However, we argue that his KGB experience helped him defeat the 1991 coup, outwit the extreme radicals in the church itself, make a crucial alliance with the Russian military, and reach a modus vivendi with President Putin, another KGB alumnus. The collapse of the Soviet Union was neither accompanied nor followed by large-scale neighbor-on-neighbor violence, such as the pogroms that blighted Russian life under the last two tsars, and for that, Russians can credit Patriarch Aleksy II more than any other person.

The church's revitalization presented a blizzard of moral, intellectual, emotional, and financial problems, some the legacy of the Soviet past and others the detritus of the tsars. Each chapter takes up one of these daunting challenges and shows how Aleksy and his supporters have dealt with it. The topics are not watertight—characters and events recur, viewed from different angles. For example, the account of Nicholas and Alexandra's insistence upon the canonization of the hermit Seraphim of Sarov in 1903 is first treated in chapter 2 as we analyze the skillful use the new patriarch made of the motif of new life for the church and rebirth for Russia in 1991, when he recovered Seraphim's bones from the KGB's closet of stolen relics. The Seraphim saga resurfaces in chapter 4, now intertwined with the debate over canonizing the murdered imperial family, anti-Semitism, and the forged *Protocols of the Elders of Zion.* Thus, the narrative does not unfold in strict chronological time. Rather, we show how, under Aleksy II, ancient symbols from Orthodoxy's thousand-year history have become vibrantly alive in a contemporary kaleidoscope of policies, threats, and countermoves.

This focus has necessarily excluded some important topics. The other branches of the Russian Orthodox Church—the émigrés, the Old Believers, the sister churches in Eastern Orthodoxy, notably the Patriarchate of Constantinople (modern Istanbul)—are discussed only when their story intersects that of the Moscow Patriarchate. There are also interesting developments taking place outside the capital, but these are for the most part heavily influenced by decisions made in Moscow. Moscow is where the KGB and party hard-liners attempted their coup and where the defeat of that coup changed history.

This book has its heroes, but they remain profoundly human, not divine. First and foremost must be the ordinary Russian Orthodox believer—persecuted, reviled, imprisoned, exiled. These stalwarts kept their faith through the most sustained attack on religion in recorded history. Such individuals as Father Sergy Romanov and his congregation of St. Vladimir's Russian Orthodox Church are representative of such people; their courage and commitment refused to ever give way to despair. We know the history of believers under Soviet oppression chiefly thanks to the Keston Institute in Oxford, England. It was founded in 1969 by the Reverend Canon Michael Bourdeaux and maintained with funds from the Templeton Prize, which he was awarded in 1984 to study religion's fate in the Soviet Union under the official ideology of "scientific atheism."

Since the Feast of the Transfiguration celebrated on August 19, 1987, twenty years have passed. The world has changed, but twenty years of wars dotted around the globe have continued. The strife in the Balkans; the ebb and flow of the guerrilla war in Chechnya; the agony of Lebanon; the bitter struggle between the Israelis and Palestinians; the defeat of the Red Army in Afghanistan by the mujaheddin; the morphing of the mujaheddin into the amoeba-like Al-Qaeda; the war between the Hutu and the Tutsi in Rwanda; the genocide in the Darfur region of Sudan; the open-ended "war on terror" provoked by the attack of September 11, 2001; the religious war between the Sunni and Shia of Iraq, which began in earnest in February 2006 with the blowing up of the Askariya shrine, the famous golden-domed mosque in Samarra—all these conflicts have resulted in horrific casualties. All seem to be never-ending. All have taken a toll in human suffering that is almost incalculable.

But there was one war that did not happen. The Soviet Union was born in civil war; most Russians expected it to die in a similar bloodbath. That it did not is something for which everyone on this planet must be grateful. This is where our story begins.

Finally, is there a conclusion to be drawn from this study? We believe so, but it is not one from which we in the West can take much comfort. However industrialized Russia is, however contemporary Russians appear—laden as they are with cell phones, computers, and the other paraphernalia of modernity—Russia is not "Western" and most likely cannot be. Russia is trying to achieve its own version of "democracy," that is, free elections with more than one candidate on the ballot. But Russia is unlikely to become "Western" because the original East-West divide is the one that split Christianity in 1054. That fault line has contoured history ever since. During the Cold War, the Warsaw Pact laid down an artificial border, largely marking the line the Red Army had reached when Nazi Germany surrendered in Berlin on May 9, 1945. That line has been erased, and the original East-West dividing line between Western Christianity (Catholicism and its Protestant offshoots) and Orthodoxy has reappeared. Wars may draw borders; the end of wars can redraw them. The divisions of faith, because they live on in the minds of men and women, seem impervious to cartography.

Acknowledgments

We have incurred many debts in the course of our research for this book. First and foremost is to the Woodrow Wilson International Center for Scholars in Washington, D.C., for offering John the opportunity to be a Woodrow Wilson Fellow in 2004–5. The incomparable resources of the Wilson Center, ably directed by Lee Hamilton, a true statesman, provided a perfect setting. Janet Spikes, the center's librarian, and her colleagues were invariably helpful. The center provided two remarkably gifted research assistants, Jennifer Murray and Nana Tchibuchian. The Kennan Institute, under its director Blair Ruble, assisted by Margaret Paxson, supported our research in many ways. We thank them all.

The essential source for work on the revival of the Russian Orthodox Church is the Keston Archive of the Keston Institute. During the years of our research, Keston Institute was affiliated with Oxford University in Oxford, England. Canon Michael Bourdeaux, founder and president of Keston Institute, and Malcolm Walker, the archive librarian, were indispensable.

This book would never have happened without the support and encouragement from John's colleagues at the University of Arizona, chiefly Terry Polowy, head of the Department of Russian and Slavic Studies, and Charles Tatum, dean of the College of Humanities. They provided a generous research leave and much needed travel grants. The International Studies Office further supplemented the dean's and department's grants.

Carol Garrard thanks the OASIS Institute (Older Americans Service & Information System) for sponsoring an anthology, *Re-Emerging Russia: Search for Identity*, edited by Max J. Okenfuss and Cheryl D. Roberts (Needham Heights, Mass.: Simon & Schuster, 1995), to which she contributed the article "Religion from Official Atheism to Freedom of Choice." The OASIS Institute in headquartered in St. Louis, Missouri, and has satellites in many cities and towns. The Tucson Campus, directed by Prindle Gorman-Oomens, has allowed Carol to teach on this subject for more than ten years.

We are also indebted to many colleagues on the other side of the pond. St. Antony's College, Oxford, gave John a most-welcome Senior Associate Member status for the Trinity Term of 2005. We especially thank Archie Brown, Alex Pravda, and Robert Service, all Fellows of the College, for sharing their knowledge and expertise. We are also grateful to Vanessa Hack, Antonian network and public relations officer, and to Kärin Leighton-Barrett, accommodation co-ordinator, for their kind assistance.

Many other people have contributed their time and expertise to this endeavor. We thank Sir Rodric Braithwaite, British ambassador to the Soviet Union and subsequently the Russian Federation from 1988 to 1992, for allowing us to quote from his personal diary. Dr. William Miller, former U.S. ambassador to Ukraine, and Dr. Igor Glazin, former member of the Russian Parliament and subsequently member of the Parliament of Estonia, also provided in-depth and personal information about world-changing events. All three men were Fellows of the Woodrow Wilson International Center for Scholars during John's tenure there.

Research opportunities at Oxford University also were invaluable. Bishop Kallistos, the former Timothy Ware, shared with us his encyclopedic personal and professional knowledge of the Orthodox faith; his seminar on the Russian Orthodox Church at All Souls College, Oxford University, was extremely helpful. Dr. Ann Shukman shared her remarkable knowledge of the St. Seraphim cult and the issue of the church's relationship with Soviet power. The manciple of All Souls College, Paul Gardner, made each of our stays comfortable. The Fellows and warden of Merton College, Dame Jessica Rawson, welcomed John (an old Mertonian from the class of '54) warmly, and the college librarian, Dr. Julia Walworth, helped us with rare items.

We thank the Sourozh Diocese, which acknowledges the authority of the Moscow Patriarchate, for allowing us to attend its Diocesan Conference held at Headington, Oxford, May 28–31, 2004. Many Orthodox theologians and priests, most especially Matthew Steenburg of Oxford University and Father Stephen Platt, answered our questions with limitless patience.

Research trips to the British Library in London were made much more pleasurable by the opportunity to stay at John's club, the Athenaeum, where the hospitality of the club secretary, Jonathan Ford, made our many visits memorable. The wonderful library of the Athenaeum and its helpful staff assisted as well.

England lost one of its finest diplomats, Sir Julian Bullard, Fellow of All Souls, formerly of the British Foreign Office, in 2006. We met Sir Julian and his gracious wife, Margaret, Lady Bullard, as we began work on this book. Another Fellow of All Souls College, the former Slavonic librarian of the Codrington Library, the late John Simmons, also gave of his time and unparalleled knowledge. We were honored to know both Sir Julian and John Simmons as scholars and friends, and their loss will be deeply felt by anyone interested in Russia.

Our personal interest in this topic first came about in 1992 when we led a mission of mercy carrying medical supplies and other aid to St. Vladimir's Russian Orthodox Church. The congregation of Carol's church, Our

Saviour's Lutheran Church of Tucson, Arizona, sponsored them, but many other people outside the church contributed. Joyce and Roger Stewart, Tucson philanthropists, donated much needed medical supplies, as well as packing the crates at their company, AGM Controls. Many hospitals, especially Kino Community Hospital and its head cardiologist, Dr. Brendan Phibbs, were amazingly charitable. The children of Sunrise Elementary School, led by their energetic librarian Mimi Crowley, conducted their own drive to garner toys, school supplies, and personal items.

Our debts to Russians are of a special kind. Father Sergy Romanov of St. Vladimir's Church in Moscow and his parishioners, most notably Olga Lugovaya and Tatiana Kiselyova, are people for whom we have unbounded admiration. We have known this congregation for more than fifteen years; its phenomenal energy and faith in the face of countless difficulties are truly amazing. It must be noted that none of the conclusions we draw in this book are from them. Father Sergy and his entire congregation remain completely and unquestioningly devoted to the Moscow Patriarchate. We also thank Liudmila Kiselyova, head of the Rare Book Division of the Academy of Sciences' library in St. Petersburg, who shared with us her photographs and helped us locate hard-to-obtain items.

We also thank Fred Appel, our editor at Princeton University Press, for his perceptive support. The two anonymous outside readers of our initial draft made a great many incisive criticisms, all of which were constructive in the best sense of the word. Any errors that remain are our own responsibility.

Finally a special debt of gratitude is due to Rose Hamersen, Carol's mother. She died a few days after we arrived in Oxford for our final trip to the Keston Archive. She left a last message with Carol's father, Clarence, that we were not to return until our research was finished. Her selflessness allowed us to complete this book; the Keston Archive was in the process of being packed as we worked. As this book goes to press, it is now awaiting reopening at its new home, the J. M. Dawson Institute of Church-State Studies of Baylor University in Waco, Texas.

Carol Garrard, Tucson, Arizona and
John Garrard, Professor of Russian Studies,
University of Arizona (November 7, 2007)

Note on Transliteration

Translating Russian letters into English (chiefly for names or special terms) presents an unavoidable problem because the Russian or Cyrillic alphabet contains thirty-two letters and our own alphabet only twenty-six. In addition, the letters stand for sounds that are occasionally unique to each language. Therefore, our chief concern has been readability for the English-speaking audience rather than systematic letter-to-letter equivalence. Anyone who knows Russian should have no problem in restoring the original Russian, or in discerning the exceptions we have employed. All transliterations and translations, unless otherwise noted, are by John Garrard.

RUSSIAN ORTHODOXY RESURGENT

Sergiev Posad: Russian Orthodoxy Resurgent

And after six days Jesus taketh Peter, James, and John his
brother, and bringeth them up into an high mountain [Mount
Tabor] apart, And was transfigured before them: and his face
did shine as the sun, and his raiment was white as the light.
—*Matthew 17:1–2*

ON AUGUST 19, 1987, Pimen, the patriarch of Moscow and All Russia,
and Demetrios I, the ecumenical patriarch of Constantinople, jointly celebrated the Divine Liturgy for the Feast of the Transfiguration at the Cathedral of the Dormition in the Trinity–St. Sergius Monastery, which is located a few miles northeast of Moscow (see figure P.1). It was the first visit
of a patriarch of Constantinople to Russia in almost four hundred years. In
January 1589 Patriarch Jeremias II visited Moscow to elevate the status of
the Moscow metropolitan to patriarch. No longer the daughter, the Church
of Russia would be the sister to the Orthodox Church of Constantinople,
which was obviously hoping for support from the rising power of Orthodox
Russia.[1] On the way back to his see, Jeremias II died. His death symbolized
Constantinople's declining influence, which had been shrinking since 1453
when the Ottoman Turks captured the city and renamed it Istanbul. The
Orthodox congregation of the premier patriarchate dwindled further over
the ensuing centuries. By 1987 the patriarch of Constantinople, a courtesy
title permitted by the Turks, was shepherd to only about two thousand souls.
Meanwhile, the Russian Orthodox Church (ROC), which Jeremias had officially raised to patriarchal status, continued to grow in power and prestige
until it suffered its own hostile takeover by militantly atheist Bolsheviks after
the October Revolution of 1917.

The 1987 co-celebration, in ways unanticipated by anyone, including the
celebrants themselves, also heralded fundamental change for the church. It
signaled a perestroika in faith a full four years before the formal dissolution
of the Soviet Union on December 25, 1991.

1

Figure P.1 Russians stream toward the entrance of the Holy Trinity St. Sergius Monastery to witness co-celebration of the Feast of Transfiguration by Patriarch Pimen and Patriarch of Constantinople, Demetrios I, August 19, 1987. (Photo credit: John Garrard)

Although the invitation had been issued in the name of Patriarch Pimen, everyone knew that Mikhail Gorbachev, president of the Soviet Union and general secretary of the Communist Party of the Soviet Union (CPSU) since March 1985, made the decision. Gorbachev thought the church might become an ally in his campaign to modernize the country, to make it work more efficiently, and to raise the moral tone, thus bringing about a decline in the widespread corruption that characterized Soviet society. According to the *Journal of the Moscow Patriarchate*, the ROC hoped that Demetrios's visit would promote "inter-Christian dialogues, participation in the World Council of Churches and the ecumenical movement as a whole," and "closer cooperation" between the two churches in "their efforts to establish on Earth a just and lasting peace."[2] Neither Gorbachev nor the ROC achieved hoped-for objectives. In fact, even after accepting an invitation, Demetrios I failed to attend the 1988 celebration to mark the thousand-year anniversary of the Christianization of the Eastern Slavs, or, as the Russians call it, "the Baptism of Rus" (Kreshchenie Rusi).

The 1987 service conducted jointly by the two patriarchs took place in what is known as Sergiev Posad, literally "Sergy's Abode." During Soviet times, the monastery complex disappeared from the map; it was simply renamed "Zagorsk." Sergy of Radonezh (1314–92), the future St. Sergius (canonized 1422) founded it in 1337 while still a young man. In a great explosion of monastic expansion in the fourteenth and fifteenth centuries, it hived off other communities organized according to his standards and rules. The mother house itself became the seat of icon painting and the spiritual heart of Russia.

In 1380 Sergiev Posad witnessed one of the great turning points of Russian history. The account written by monks in the medieval Chronicles retains its emotional impact to this day:

> A rumor spread that Khan Mamay was raising a large army as a punishment for our sins and that with all his heathen Tatar hordes he would invade Russian soil.... The puissant and reigning prince, who held the scepter of all Russia, great Dmitri [Prince Dmitry Ivanovich Donskoy, 1350–89], having a great faith in the saint [Sergius], came to ask him if he counseled him to go against the heathen. The saint, bestowing on him his blessing, and strengthened by prayer, said to him:
>
> "It behooveth you, lord, to have a care for the lives of the flock committed to you by God. Go forth against the heathen; and upheld by the strong arm of God, conquer; and return to your country sound in health, and glorify God with loud praise."
>
> Dmitri and all his armies were filled with a spirit of temerity and went into battle against the pagans. They fought; many fell; but God was with them, and helped the great and invincible Dmitri, who vanquished the ungodly Tatars.... The Grand Duke Dmitri returned to his country with great joy in his heart, and hastened to visit holy, venerable Sergius. Rendering thanks for the prayers of the saint and of the brotherhood, he gave a rich offering to the monastery.[3]

Russians credit Donskoy's 1380 victory at Kulikovo over Khan Mamay as a watershed in Russian history, marking the beginning of their release from the long years of the "Tatar yoke" (*Tatarskoe igo*). The victory gave rise to the proverbial saying that separate forces from principalities northeast of Rus (the ancient name for Russia) came to the battlefield of Kulikovo, but they left a united Russian people (*yediny russky narod*). Kulikovo took on the same associations as the Battle of Gettysburg did for the United States, sacred ground whose memory, in the words of Lincoln's Gettysburg Address, should "not perish from the earth."

Grand Prince Dmitry's victory at Kulikovo also marks the beginning of the rise to dominance of Muscovy. For his crucial role in encouraging the grand prince (he even sent two monks into the battle), Sergius would become known as the "godfather of Muscovy." So deeply embedded was this story in the Russian memory that Stalin resurrected it during the darkest days of World War II. With the Wehrmacht literally at the gates of Moscow, he allowed the metropolitan of Leningrad to stir the deep patriotism of his audience by retelling the tale. Once the Germans were defeated, however, the Soviet authorities once again erased Orthodoxy from Russia's history. Donskoy's triumph over Mamay remained part of the state curriculum but was taught without its religious frame of reference. By 1987 the churches within the monastery gates were occupied by the Theological Academy of Orthodoxy, and the Cathedral of the Dormition had not seen the liturgy performed for decades.

As the "cultural lecturers" for the 1987 University of Arizona Alumni tour, we expected to shepherd our charges around virtually empty grounds of Sergiev Posad, dotted by the occasional elderly *babushka* communing alone. Instead, the buses parked not far from a row of black Chaika ("Seagull") limousines. This meant that the occupant was very important indeed. A huge crowd of Russians streamed toward the entrance of the Cathedral of the Dormition. A continuous torrent of people—old, young, middle-aged—swept toward the double doors. Inside, the cathedral was packed to the rafters. The atmosphere was electric, akin to the charged emotion of a Billy Graham "Crusade for Christ" in a Texas convention center. The cathedral itself glowed. Orthodoxy's message is that it is the "light of the world," and light was the immaterial substance disposed through the sanctuary. To squeeze into the space was effectively to walk into and through light refracting all around. The effect was both immediate and physiological. As the eye adjusted, it began to play tricks. The walls of the cathedral gleamed a warm gold as the light reflected off the painted frescoes. The gold began to take on a rosy tint, as if it had been overlaid with a luminous pink. And the sky, which could just be glimpsed through the tiny windows, became suffused with a purplish glow. The windows had not been treated; it was the phenomenon of

Figure P.2 Russians pack the Cathedral of the Dormition as Patriarch Pimen of the Russian Orthodox Church and Patriarch Demetrios of the Church of Constantinople co-celebrate the liturgy August 19, 1987, for the first time in 398 years. (Photo credit: John Garrard)

complementary retinal adjustment, for the sky was still blue. These optical effects were evanescent, mutable, though the eye needed time to adjust in order to see clearly. To be forced in this way to confront one's physicality and by extension, one's mortality, heightened the sense of being in an otherworldly space (see figure P.2).

The iconostasis (the screen inset with icons that separates the altar from the nave and blocks the congregation's view of the altar) shone in the flickering tapers held by the audience, and a gold, red, and blue rainbow refracted throughout the sanctuary. The original builders of the cathedral had carefully placed the slit windows for maximum light, and sickles of brightness curved through the air illuminating individual icons. The Slavic school of icon painting had perfected the technique of applying layers of translucent washes, one on top of the other, each composed of a mixture of egg yolk and water or vinegar, which served as the medium to bind the pigments. Light passing through these glazes would reflect from the background gesso. The iconostasis must have recently been restored; the once murky panels of brown figures on dark backgrounds shone in their original subtle, luminous colors, and the brush strokes of pure white flashed out.

To the believer, icons (from the Greek, "image") are more than art; they are portals into the spiritual world. The Orthodox hold that as they look at the icon, the icon gazes back. Believers talk to them, and the icons answer. Indeed, Orthodox believers pray with their eyes open, and they need an icon to focus their gaze as they do so. They are not praying "to" the icon, but "through" it to the divine world it depicts in gesso and tempura. Such communication is both intimate and interactive. The cleft between the celestial and the terrestrial dissolves, and the believer participates in an image of heaven itself. With the atmosphere inside the Cathedral of the Dormition altered to pink, satiny indigo, and warm gold, the air itself seemed charged. All around were standing Russians (there are no pews), moving in regular rapid rhythm, bowing and crossing themselves, with an expression on their faces difficult to describe. Russians cross themselves using two fingers and a thumb pressed against the third and fourth finger, not just two fingers, and from right shoulder to left, not left to right, as do Catholics. Some people were on their knees, bowing and kissing the floor, alternating between adoration and penitence.

For seventy years the official ideology of the USSR was "scientific atheism," carefully termed "Marxism-Leninism" for Western consumption. Lenin and Stalin were equal opportunity haters of all religions, but Russian Orthodoxy, state faith of the tsarist empire, was their special target. Khrushchev, who passed as a reformer in the West, confidently predicted that "the last remaining priest would be exhibited at a museum twenty years hence."[4] He did not specify if this cleric would be stuffed or live, but his point was clear. Though Khrushchev fell from power October 1964, the anti-Orthodox campaign did not let up. And yet, on this August afternoon in 1987, it looked as if the sun shone over a service that had been running continually since 1917. The packed cathedral, the icons, the ecstatic believers, the beautiful liturgy, and the exquisite robes of the two patriarchs seemed as if nothing had changed. Only the artificial bright lights of the Soviet television crew and its huge black boom and cameras betrayed the date.

Even for those who were not Orthodox, the sheer beauty of the experience was overwhelming. The sound of the melodious voices singing with no musical instrument as accompaniment, the gaze of the icons, the crackle of the tapers, the continual bowing and crossing, which energizes the breathing— all of these elements synthesized into a total mind-body experience powerfully communicating an ineffable sense of the divine. When both patriarchs censed the congregation (from a theological point of view, they were recognizing the divine spark in every human), an indescribable fragrance wafted through the air. Non-Orthodox who had not fasted could not partake of the consecrated bread and wine, but all were invited to come forward for a piece of the *prosfora*, the leavened bread blessed but not consecrated by the priest.

Men shape buildings as the embodiment of their spiritual vision. Russian Orthodox Church interiors synthesize this truth, for they are coded as visible "texts" of its liturgy, as Archpriest Lev Lebedev explained early in the run up to the millennial celebration of the Baptism of Rus: "A Russian Orthodox Church is not merely a place for prayer, it above all is the image of the Kingdom of Heaven in everything from the symbols of the architectural forms and its inner tripartite division, to the decoration of the icons, especially the iconostasis."[5] Here Lebedev puts his finger on a crucial feature of the faith: "In Russian Orthodoxy the personal spiritual life of the faithful, domestic life, family relations, economic and all other activity consciously aspire to the 'embodiment,' the reflection of the Heavenly in the earthly, which is the chief means of transforming the earthly, of spiritualizing and bringing it closer to the Heavenly." Thus Russian Orthodox architecture proclaims that the image of paradise is visible in the sanctuary's structure. Orthodoxy does not pretend that the believer has been magically transported into the empyrean. Rather, the liturgy as text and the coded space of the sanctuary as context together give a mystical foretaste of the eternal heaven. Each part of the church is a form of worship itself, synchronous with specific elements of the liturgy.

Soviet officials commonly referred to churches as "prayer buildings." Indeed, Soviet law, based on Lenin's decree of January 20, 1918, misleadingly titled "On the Separation of Church and State," made performing church rites the sole function permitted the ROC. Furthermore, it was a crime to perform the liturgy outside a licensed "prayer building." Theologians defined the Russian Orthodox Church as more than a building and a service; rather, it was the people of God who make up the Body of Christ active in the world today. Lenin had forestalled that; his decree of 1918 stated that religious congregations (*obshchiny*) did not enjoy the rights of a legal entity. According to the Soviet legal code, outside the performance of the liturgy the church did not legally exist. Seizing churches would prevent the liturgy from being performed. No liturgy—*ergo*, no faith.

But, however small the number of churches, however dilapidated and desecrated their interior, the liturgy itself survived. The Soviet authorities never insisted that it be changed. The liturgy was performed in OCS—Old Church Slavonic, the liturgical language derived from the alphabet invented by Cyril and Methodius, two monks sent in the ninth century from Constantinople to

Moravia (the modern Czech Republic and Slovak Republic) to Christianize the Slavs.[6] Perhaps the party, thoroughly secularized in its worldview, thought the archaic nature of the language would drain the liturgy of its power. Unwittingly, they allowed the ROC to continue the most compelling element of its confession. For however antiquated the words, no other liturgy in all Christianity is more elaborate or more awe-inspiring. St. Nicholas Cabasilas, a fourteenth-century theologian, in *The Life of Christ* called the liturgy of the Orthodox Church the final and greatest of the mysteries "since it is not possible to go beyond it or add anything to it. After the liturgy there is nowhere to go. There all must stand, and try to examine the means by which we may preserve the treasure to the end. For in it we obtain God himself, and God is united with us in the most perfect union."[7] Judaism can be carried in the arms of a single man: the Torah scrolls transported the faith during the two thousand years of the Diaspora to every continent. Similarly, Protestantism is Bible-based; a Bible in the vernacular can function as a miniature church, enabling a missionary to take the Gospel anywhere, or a believer to stay connected to his faith. But to a great extent, Russian Orthodoxy exists for its believers in its liturgy, the power of whose beauty the party underestimated.

The centrality of the Orthodox liturgy for the Russians was attested to from the moment of their conversion. When, in the tenth century, the envoys of Grand Prince Vladimir of Kiev arrived in Constantinople to inquire about the Christian faith, they were not offered a verbal explanation. Rather, they were taken to the Church of the Holy Wisdom (St. Sophia) to witness the celebration of the liturgy. So dazzling was this experience that it converted them, though they could not understand the words, which were being sung in Greek. Soon translated into Old Church Slavonic (understood by Russians more easily than Latin in the West), this liturgy became the centerpiece of their faith for almost a thousand years. The experience was so profound that they were convinced that here they could meet God.[8] In retrospect, Communist planners would have been better advised to allow the Orthodox to do charity, teach the catechism, print Bibles, and open seminaries—anything but perform their liturgy. Instead, like the fox in *Uncle Remus* who threw tarry Br'er Rabbit into the briar patch, they outwitted themselves.

On August 19, 1987, for the first time in almost seventy years, this vital liturgy was being performed in the Cathedral of the Dormition, restored to a semblance of its former stunning beauty and opulence.[9] Even from far in the back, the "royal doors," which stand in the center of the iconostasis and open into the sanctuary, glowed with renewed luminescence. Representing the doors to paradise, their shape (the two upper panels rounded at the top) and their message had been codified centuries ago. The original doors were modeled on the pair in the monastery's Trinity Cathedral. Those had been seized by the Soviet state and placed in the Sergiev Posad Museum. They were painted by an artist from the circle of the greatest icon painter of them all, Andrey Rublyov. On those doors the Annunciation was painted in the upper panels, and the Four Evangelists writing their Gospels appeared below. These images had once interrelated with the frescoes in the eastern part of the church, where the Annunciation had appeared on the altar columns, officiating bishops on the walls of the apse, and the Evangelists on the pendentives of the domes. The whitewash that had once covered these frescoes was gone. Painted in 1684 under the guidance of the Yaroslavl master Dmitry Grigoriev in the amazing space of three months, they had not been seen for almost seventy years.[10] Now they sparkled with their original brilliance. Once again the whole eucharistic rite as a reenactment of the life of Christ from his incarnation to his ascension into heaven and the promise of his coming again could be seen interacting with the fabric of the building.

Time itself could be traced on the iconostasis; it showed figures known to history, such as St. Sergius, as well as people known only through the Bible, such as St. Elijah and St. Ezekiel. The timeline could be followed up to the very last moment of the future, when linear time itself will dissolve, at the Second Coming, the Parousia, predicted by Christ in Matthew 25:31–33:

> When the Son of Man comes in His glory and all His angels with Him, then He will sit on the Throne of His glory.
>
> And all the nations will gather around Him. And He will divide one from the other, just as the shepherd separates the sheep from the goats. . . .
>
> To the saved He will invite, "Come, ye blessed of my Father, inherit the kingdom prepared for you from the foundation of the world." (Matthew 25:34)

Inside the Cathedral of the Dormition, eyes traveled up to the ceiling. Overhead was a blue dome: the visual equivalent of the vault of heaven. There in a crescendo of visual glory sat Christ, looking directly at the viewer. But this was not Christ on the cross. The throne he sat on was magnificent, and the angels swarming around him hovered and jostled, wing to wing. The entire fabric of the dome seemed to vibrate; the gaze of the Savior did not appear to come from a great height, but trembled as a face-to-face encounter. This was the gaze of Christ Pantocrator (Vsederzhitel, that is, "All Powerful" or "Almighty"), judge of all nations at the end of time itself. This was not the ebb and flow of human history but God's plan. The message

9

was palpable: each individual was going to have eternal life, whether one wished for it or not. These theological principles were no longer abstract but vividly, physically present that day.

Reinforcing the imagery of the Last Days was the occasion itself. The two patriarchs were celebrating one of the twelve great "feasts" of the Orthodox calendar: the Transfiguration. On that day, according to the New Testament, Jesus took three of the disciples up to Mount Tabor. There he rose into the air, between Moses and Elijah, and he was "transfigured before them: and his face did shine as the sun, and his raiment was white as the light" (Matthew 17:2; see also Mark 9:2–8 and Luke 9:28–36). Orthodox believers hold that through prayer and meditation they too can see the celestial light that shone around Christ on the mountain. They petition in the feast's hymn stanza (*troparion*):

> Thou [wast] transfigured on the
> Mountain, O Christ God, showing to Thy Disciples
> Thy glory as each one could endure. May Thy
> Eternal light shine forth upon us sinners, through
> The prayers of the Theotokos (the "God-Bearer," i.e., Mary)
> Light Bestower, glory to Thee.[11]

The Transfiguration prefigures the glorified body that Christ will assume after the Resurrection, and by extension reveals the wondrous body that the faithful will put on at the Day of Judgment. Thus, its importance extends beyond its pairing with Christ's Ascension on the Mount of Olives. The Eucharist, the heart of the Orthodox liturgy, links the Transfiguration as described in the Gospels and the calling of the blessed at the end of time: "come ye blessed of my Father, inherit the kingdom." For the believer, this is not a spectacle but a reality mystically "made present again." While the communion rite reenacts the life of Christ from the Incarnation through the Ascension, simultaneously the believer is carried from sin to salvation. Through partaking of the "Holy Gifts," he or she enters liturgical time, all of whose cycles are depicted in a consecrated Orthodox sanctuary.

As non-Orthodox, our experience of this liturgy was not that of the believers who surrounded us. We looked for down-to-earth explanations as to why this service was being allowed now, at this moment in time. Around us were people who were not analyzing at all: they were praying and petitioning the saints and the Theotokos for help in the quest to save their souls. St. Nicholas Cabasilas quoted earlier also states a core principle of Orthodoxy: rationality alone cannot capture the mystery of the divine. Specific portions of the liturgy depict two events that are beyond human comprehension, Christ's incarnation and sacrifice, with the aim

> that we might not reason with the mind alone, but indeed should see in some fashion with our eyes the great poverty of the one who is rich, the dwelling within us of him who inhabits every place, the reproaches suffered by the blessed one, the sufferings of the impassible one; how much he was hated, how much he loved; being so great, how much he abased himself; and what he suffered and what he accomplished to spread this table (i.e., the Eucharist) before us.[12]

The wonder stamped on the Russians' faces demonstrated the human longing to sense and touch mystery. The power of this appeal was especially forceful given the drab background of grungy and soulless Soviet life outside the cathedral.

The fervor of the crowd was reminiscent of the Muslim Shia's yearly reenactment of the grief of the original followers of Ali, the Prophet's son-in-law, at the murder of his son Hussein and seventy-two of his followers. They were massacred at Karbala, in the desert of southern Iraq, after challenging the authority of Islam's Sunni caliph, Yazid. The Orthodox were not ritually flagellating themselves with chains, but the same sense was palpable that an event that took place long ago (Hussein's martyrdom occurred in 680) was being experienced in the present. The individual is not hallucinating but experiencing an epiphany: the collapse of the past, the present, and the future into a single moment, what T. S. Eliot called the "still point of the turning world." In Western Christianity, the parallel impact would be the medieval passion play. Those actors who represented Roman soldiers were advised to nail Jesus to the cross immediately lest the audience rush the stage to stop them. Then they should run in case the audience tried to attack them physically. The boundary between the mythic time of the event and the present moment of its staging was erased. The audience no longer watched the past; it participated in events occurring in a mystical, eternal present.

Every element of this celebration of the Feast of the Transfiguration reinforced the message that Christ's Passion was being made present again. Both patriarchs were wearing a robe we had never seen before outside of a museum case: the *sakkos*, an episcopal garment whose shape derived from the costume worn by Byzantine emperors. Each *sakkos* was densely embroidered with images drawn from the life of Christ. Was Patriarch Pimen's *sakkos* a new replica of the famous one made in Constantinople and sent to Moscow as a gift to commemorate the 1339 canonization of Metropolitan Peter, who made the momentous decision to move the Orthodox see of the Rus from Kiev?[13] The back of that garment pairs the Transfiguration and Ascension, each embroidered in gold and silver thread so dense the cloth resembles a huge cloisonné enamel. The original had been seized by the Soviet state and transferred to the Kremlin Armory in 1920. Its pearls were cut off. But Pimen looked to be wearing something equally gorgeous.

Once outside in the blinding white light of the monastery grounds, we rejoined the Soviet world. The militantly Communist guides supplied by Intourist had not entered the cathedral, but smoked in the buses, as if crossing its threshold might infect them with some contagious disease. Yet even though the service had ended, more Russians were still crowding inside. One of the University of Arizona's elderly alumna got caught in the doorway with people on one side pushing in, and people on the other coming out. The horizontal crosscurrents pinioned her and she bobbled, an unwilling cork, for several minutes. Had she gone down, she could easily have been trampled, a victim to the power of a crowd to act as an undertow.

But to adduce to this experience a cosmic significance seemed self-indulgent. In spite of the elaborate service, it was unlikely anything would fundamentally change inside the Soviet Union. Though Gorbachev had become the CPSU's general secretary in March 1985, in September *Pravda* stated that the forthcoming millennial anniversary of the Baptism of the Rus meant that atheistic propaganda should show "particular vigilance." The new party program adopted in 1986 included a paragraph on the necessity for "atheistic education." On November 24, 1986, Gorbachev made a speech in Tashkent, capital of the Uzbek Republic, calling for "an uncompromising struggle against religious manifestations."[14]

Yet in retrospect, the celebration of the Feast of the Transfiguration at Zagorsk (soon to be once again Sergiev Posad) on August 19, 1987, played its part in history. Four years to the day after Pimen and Demetrios were inside its Cathedral of the Dormition, another Feast of the Transfiguration would be celebrated by a new patriarch, Aleksy II, in the Cathedral of the Assumption inside the *Kremlin* walls in Moscow. This too would be a "first" in Soviet times. At that moment, KGB and party hard-liners attempted a coup in Moscow. It failed by the morning of August 21, 1991. When the tanks encircling the Russian Parliament Building, called the "White House," turned around, Soviet power itself evaporated. The country began a transformation that continues to this day.

Orthodox believers, who assert we live in liturgical time, interpret the 1987 Feast of the Transfiguration as the hand of God active in their affairs. Less divinely, it can be seen it as proof of the law of unintended consequences.

Gorbachev made the startling admission to a journalist in Paris that his mother had been a believer and he had been baptized.[15] But he did not attend the co-celebration at Sergiev Posad. Had he done so, he might have realized that, like the Sorcerer's Apprentice, he was unleashing forces he would not be able to control.

To understand the energies reshaping life in the Russian Federation, we in the West must make a journey of the imagination across the centuries and into an alien landscape. The roots of the Russian religious tradition lie in a past with which most westerners are unfamiliar. In 1054, when Christianity split into Eastern and Western halves, and rival prelates anathematized each other, Orthodoxy ceased evolving theologically. The fact that the East did not pass through a Reformation means that Western scholars of religion frequently bypass the Byzantine tradition altogether. In his important 2003 book *The Reformation* Diarmaid MacCullough declares that he will not deal with the Orthodox story, except where it is intertwined "with that of the Latin West. There is a simple reason for this: so far the Orthodox Churches have not experienced a Reformation."[16] It is vital to understand that the Orthodox regard this as a virtue, because they believe the three forces that remade Western Europe—the Renaissance, the Reformation, and the Counter-Reformation—represent a falling away from the true faith, the church of Christ and the Apostles. Believers in Orthodoxy are called *pravoslavnye*, that is, "true believers." The word itself constitutes a value judgment: any non-Orthodox faith, such as Catholicism and its spin-off, Protestantism, must to some degree be false. Thus, as Russia tries to move forward to a prosperous and stable future, it must look back upon a thousand-year past that has never been free of religious tension with the West.

We in the West should not underestimate the significance of the resurgence of a faith unchanged in a thousand years liturgically and theologically, over a landmass extending almost one-sixth of the planet's surface, in a country that controls vast reservoirs of oil and mineral resources. The fall of the Communist Party of the Soviet Union shifted history's tectonic plates. We must give up the thinking and lexicon of the Cold War. Once we knew the Soviet Union. Now we face the Russian Federation, a country that is neither Cold War adversary nor World War II ally. The vocabulary, heroes, villains, and myths of their mind's eye are linked to medieval history. This may seem disconcerting, given that Russia is a heavily industrialized state, which sent the first man into space and whose military arsenal includes some of the most advanced weapons in the world. But an attempt must be made to understand the memory of Russia's thousand years of Orthodoxy, for it is the hidden mainstream coloring Russian domestic behavior and shaping Russian policies abroad.

13

ONE

The End of the Atheist Empire

Every person who raises arms against his neighbor,
against unarmed civilians, will be taking upon his soul
a very profound sin which will separate him from the
Church and from God.

—*Patriarch Aleksy's address to the nation, 1:42 A.M., August 21, 1991*

ON AUGUST 19, 1991, SOVIET KGB and party hard-liners returned from their dachas and summer vacations to Moscow, determined to suppress the democratic movement born when Boris Yeltsin had been elected president of the Russian Republic just two months earlier. He was the first popularly elected leader in the thousand-year history of the Russian people. Yeltsin threatened to exercise the Russian Republic's legal right under the country's constitution to withdraw from the multinational state. The Soviet system, always officially proclaimed a voluntary union, was in danger of being hoist by its own petard. The junta, led by Vladimir Kryuchkov, head of the KGB, seized television and radio stations and, with the majestic music of *Swan Lake* as background, announced on the airwaves that it had formed a "State Emergency Committee" and was "taking supreme power in the USSR." Earlier on the previous evening of August 18 just before 5:00 P.M., it had taken captive, in the government dacha in Yalta on the Black Sea, the president of the USSR, Mikhail Gorbachev. His chief of staff played the Judas, accompanied by Politburo member Oleg Shenin and a small clutch of party myrmidons. They demanded he either sign a decree declaring a state of emergency or resign. Courageously, Gorbachev refused to do either. Nevertheless, the traitors confiscated the codes needed to launch the Soviet nuclear arsenal and confined him and his family to house arrest. He was now nowhere to be seen. The KGB plotters made just one mistake: they missed taking prisoner Boris Yeltsin.

The CPSU and KGB hard-liners had worried about glasnost and perestroika when Gorbachev announced them as policies after he became general secretary of the CPSU in March 1985. But he first provoked a sharp reaction on March 8, 1991, when he unveiled the draft of a new, conciliatory union treaty. It proposed a new name for the country omitting the words "Socialist" and "Soviet." Even though the republics were offered much greater autonomy, allowing them to control their own economic development, sign international treaties, and establish separate diplomatic missions, only nine of the fifteen Soviet republics participated in the referendum. While Gorbachev continued to work on a draft treaty acceptable to all, the KGB and party bosses knew there could be no compromise. They recalled only too well the earlier loss of central control when Gorbachev had released a little nugget of glasnost to the Baltic States. In a radio address on the fiftieth anniversary of the signing of the Nazi-Soviet Non-Aggression Pact of August 23, 1939, Gorbachev admitted that Lithuania, Estonia, and Latvia had been forcibly incorporated into the USSR. Western historians knew this perfectly well, having read the pact's secret protocols, but the Soviet population had been fed the party line that the Baltic States had "volunteered" for the privilege. Backing and filling, Gorbachev had immediately argued that a "common destiny" had been forged for all republics, so everyone should still stay together. But countless numbers of protesters linked hands to form human chains spanning the borders of the three Baltic satellites.

Even worse for the party and KGB sclerotics, shortly thereafter on September 10, 1989, Austria took down twelve and a half miles of the border fence with Hungary. East German families, who were legally free to travel to Hungary, now saw a safe, though circuitous escape route to West Germany. They loaded their cars and set off. The party's East German satrap, Erich Honecker, implored Gorbachev to order the Red Army (which was still deployed in Hungary) to forcibly put the barrier back up and open fire on the caravans. He refused, and the floodgates stayed open. The last person shot trying to make it over the Berlin Wall died in February 1989. Within six months, he could have strolled across unchallenged. East Germany itself, the jewel of the Warsaw Pact crown, was no more. Honecker, once all-powerful dictator, suddenly became a fugitive, not knowing whether he would be arrested or shot on sight. After all, that was the treatment he had meted out in the past to innocent citizens.

At this critical hour, Gorbachev's passive response to Yeltsin's challenge threatened the existence of the Union of Soviet Socialist Republics itself. Yeltsin wanted to sign a new union treaty that would loosen the bonds of the country to a far great extent than Gorbachev had proposed. The plotters very much doubted that anything acceptable to Yeltsin would preserve the party as the country's leading force, and the KGB as the party's "sword and shield."

They feared that they too would soon be perestroika-ed right out of their jobs and privileges. And so it came to pass, but the decisive challenge emerged from a totally unexpected source.

With Gorbachev safely tucked away at Yalta, the plotters wrestled with the problem of Yeltsin, now holed up in the Russian Parliament, a multistory office building called the "Russian White House." He and his staff still had access to fax and telephone, and later to radio and television. He summoned the ordinary citizens of Moscow to defend the democracy—that is, his election—that had just been born. He stood on one of the tanks at 1:00 P.M., August 19, audaciously defying the junta. In a few hours, a loudspeaker announced to the Muscovites forming human shields around the building that ten of the tanks had gone over to the defenders of the Russian White House.

By an extraordinary coincidence, the United States had an eyewitness and participant in these events who was also a distinguished Russian historian. James Billington, the librarian of Congress and founding director of the Woodrow Wilson International Center for Scholars, happened to be in Moscow for a library conference. When the conference broke up, Dr. Billington learned about the attempted takeover. He squeezed among the defenders and heard cries from the crowd: "A rhythmic chant of *mo-lod-tsy, mo-lod-tsy* [literally, "good guys, good guys"] was the crowd's response to this, the first of many communiqués that 'Radio White House' broadcast periodically."[1] As Billington notes, this was a "first announcement of an unprecedented change of allegiance by a military unit," and it inspired the crowd ringing the parliament.

The unit comprised only ten tanks with their commanding officer, but the fact that Radio White House could broadcast this news at all came as a nasty shock to the plotters. In a critical move, the Russian Supreme Soviet radio service had circumvented the KGB's seizure of the radio and television stations. It began broadcasting from the Parliament Building itself on 1,500 kHz medium wave. Then the Echo of Moscow radio station, which had been forced off the air on the afternoon of August 19, resumed broadcasting on 1,206 kHz at 1:40 P.M. August 20.[2] Now the KGB was in the unfamiliar and unpleasant position of having its opponents able to get their message across to the mass of the Russian people. The junta had decreed, "Control shall be established over the mass media, for which a specially created organ of the Emergency Committee shall be responsible."[3] Already its orders were being flouted, a sign the junta had lost Leninist efficiency in controlling sources of information.

Yeltsin used the media to make a tough speech claiming that elements of three divisions of the troops sent to storm and occupy the Parliament had crossed over and were now supporting him. Then the elite Alpha Unit, paratroopers commanded by General Alexander Lebed, a hero of Afghanistan, refused to storm the White House. Yeltsin spoke from a podium where now Major General Kobiets stood in full uniform, acknowledging Yeltsin's pronouncement that he had been appointed the new defense minister. The defection of just ten tanks had pulled the thumb out of the KGB's dike, and the momentum was sucking others up the chain of command over to Yeltsin's side.

But the outcome was still very much in doubt. Yes, the rings of human shields around the Russian Parliament were increasing by the hour. But the defenders had ten tanks, whereas the party and the KGB commanded whole armored divisions. If they attacked, thousands would die in the carnage. Yeltsin fully expected a bloodbath and tried to get help. He first called the West. He telephoned President George Herbert Bush and also John Major, who had succeeded Mrs. Thatcher as the British prime minister in the fall of 1990. Perhaps Bush recalled that he had telephoned Gorbachev just weeks before to warn him that a coup was threatening. Apparently the general secretary never shared this foreboding with Yeltsin. Gorbachev ruefully recalled in a 1996 interview with Radio Free Europe and Radio Liberty, "Bush phoned me and I said, 'George, you can sleep soundly. Nothing's going to happen.' That's what I said." Now Bush—like Major—could offer only sympathy to the embattled Yeltsin. Stymied by the West, Yeltsin then took a fateful step.

He appealed to the new patriarch of the Russian Orthodox Church, the former Aleksey Ridiger, who had been elected in June the previous year by a meeting of bishops. He had taken the official name of Aleksy II. Yeltsin's words went out over the national radio, defying the junta's orders to silence him:

> The tragic events that have occurred throughout the night made me turn to you, to reach the nation through you.
>
> There is lawlessness inside the country—a group of corrupt Party members has organized an anti-constitutional revolution. Essentially, a state of emergency has been declared inside the country due to the extreme gravity of the situation, and the laws and constitution of the USSR and of the sovereign republics of the Union have been grossly violated.
>
> It is no coincidence that these events have taken place on the eve of the signing of a new Union Treaty, which would have paved the way to freedom, democracy, and progress and a resolution of the recent crisis.
>
> Our State has been violated and along with it the newly emerging democracy, and freedom of choice for the electorate. There is once again the shadow of disorder and chaos hanging over our country.

At this moment of tragedy for our Fatherland I turn to you, calling on your authority among all religious confessions and believers. The influence of the Church in our society is too great for the Church to stand aside during these events. This duty is directly related to the Church's mission, to which you have dedicated your life: serving people, caring for their hearts and souls. The Church, which has suffered through the times of totalitarianism, may once again experience disorder and lawlessness.

All believers, the Russian nation, and all Russia await your word![4]

They did not have long to wait. Within hours of this appeal, the patriarch demonstrated that he would not remain a bystander but would throw the full weight of his position as patriarch against the coup.

On August 19, as the tanks moved ominously into their staging area in Red Square, Aleksy was physically only yards away (see figure 1.1). Inside the redbrick walls of the Kremlin, he was presiding at the liturgy of the Feast of the Transfiguration in the Cathedral of the Assumption (Uspensky Sobor), not only the oldest cathedral within the Kremlin but also the most important Orthodox church in Russia, having been begun in 1326–28 at the behest of Metropolitan Peter, whose move of the Orthodox see from Kiev to Moscow ended Kiev's status as the center of the faith. Still unfinished, it collapsed in 1472. As with other Kremin cathedrals, architects imported from Italy, in part from the Ticino (an area in northern Italy and southern Switzerland), rebuilt it in its present form.

During the service Aleksy said nothing about the outside events but made an interesting change in the closing litany. Instead of remembering the "authorities" and "the army" as was customary, he prayed "for our country protected by God and its people."[5] Then he took a momentous decision. On August 20, only a day after Yeltsin's appeal to him, Aleksy faxed to the country and to selected sites around the world an "announcement" (*zayavlenie*), which challenged the junta's legality.[6] Aleksy had already identified this as the key weakness of the coup:

This situation [i.e., the departure of Gorbachev from power, and his disappearance] is troubling the consciences of millions of our fellow citizens, who are concerned about the legality of the newly formed State Emergency Committee.... In this connection we declare that it is essential that we hear without delay the voice of President Gorbachev and learn his attitude toward the events that have just taken place.

Notably, the patriarch made no mention of Yeltsin. Instead, he referred to Gorbachev, a reformer with whom he believed the church could do business, the

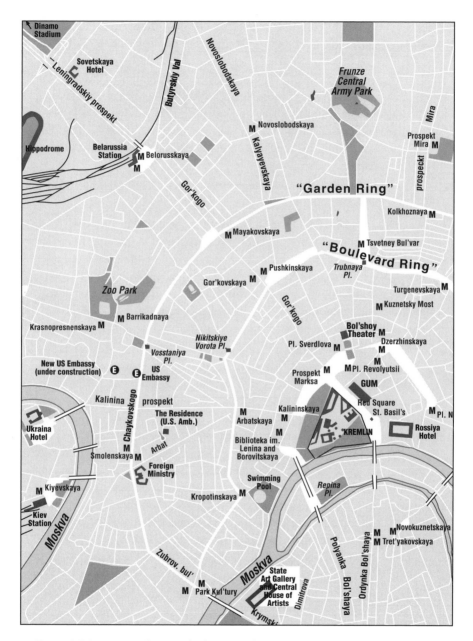

Figure 1.1 Soviet map showing the location of the Kremlin, cathedrals, Red Square, Metro stations, and the Lubyanka. (Photo credit: "Intourist" Map, Moscow, 1960)

same attitude once expressed by Margaret Thatcher. Now Aleksy repaid the ROC's debts to Gorbachev's reforms by calling for Gorbachev to be allowed to speak to the country. But this would not be the limit of his help.

The remainder of Aleksy's "announcement" demonstrated his political savvy: "We hope that the Supreme Soviet of the USSR will give careful consideration to what has taken place and will take decisive measures to bring about the stabilization of the situation in the country." That is, he called politely for action from the top government body in the country, notably *not* the party apparatus.

Next, he sought to isolate the plotters from two other national institutions, the church and the army:

> We call upon all parts of the Russian Orthodox Church, the whole of our people, and particularly our army at this critical moment for our nation to show support and not to permit the shedding of fraternal blood. We raise the heartfelt prayer to our Lord and summon all true believers in our Church to join this prayer begging Him to dispense peace to the peoples of our land so that they can in future build their homeland in accordance with freedom of choice and the accepted norms of morality and law.

Again, the patriarch touched delicately on the Achilles' heel of the coup, as he alluded to the "accepted norms of morality and *law*." Yeltsin had begun his radio appeal to the patriarch by referring to "lawlessness." Now the patriarch was reiterating the same idea to the nation, but associating legality with a "heartfelt prayer to our Lord" studded with the familiar language of the peace campaign—"peace" and "freedom"—turned back on the KGB.

Among the KGB generals directing the coup, a frisson of fear and righteous indignation must have taken hold. How dare Aleksey Ridiger, the very man they had put into power, speak out against them! The position of patriarch was on the KGB's *nomenklatura* list, meaning that the generals had the privilege of signing off on the occupant. And by 1991, Ridiger had been their man for thirty-three years. According to researchers at the Keston Institute in Oxford, who looked at all available documents, Ridiger had been "recruited by the Estonian KGB on 28 February 1958, just days after his 29th birthday." In February 1988, "exactly thirty years after his recruitment as an agent, Aleksy was given an award (*gramota*) by the KGB in recognition of his long service to them."[7] After handing him their equivalent of a thirty-year pin, surely they had a right to expect some gratitude. And if just now their *drozd* ("thrush" was his code name) did not want to sing the right tune from his gilded cage, then all he had to do was say nothing and go about his business of presiding at liturgies and other harmless religious services. His silence would give consent.

But Aleksy would not keep silent. Shortly after midnight on August 21, 1991, a column of tanks approached the barricades around the White House. Two young men were shot dead. Tank treads crushed another youth. Crowds swarmed the vehicles and set an armored personnel carrier on fire. Aleksy learned of this within moments, and now took a daring, virtually inconceivable step. At 1:30 A.M., only an hour after this carnage, and minutes before the order was expected for the general assault to storm the White House and seize Boris Yeltsin and the parliamentarians, he sent an extraordinary "address" (*obrashchenie*) to all "fellow-citizens." It was broadcast at 1:42 A.M. on national television and radio.

The patriarch began by addressing his listeners as "Brothers and Sisters." These were the same words Joseph Stalin, the former Russian Orthodox seminary student Joseph Dzugashvili, used when, two weeks after the German invasion of June 22, 1941, he called upon the Soviet citizenry to rise up and repel the invader. Now the patriarch appealed to his brothers and sisters to rise up and prevent *civil war*:

> The delicate civil peace of our society has been rent asunder. According to the latest information, open armed conflict and loss of life have begun [i.e., the death of three young men trying to block the tanks]. In these circumstances, my duty as Patriarch is to warn everybody for whom the word of the Church is dear and carries weight: Every person who raises arms against his neighbor, against unarmed civilians, will be taking upon his soul a very profound sin which will separate him from the Church and from God. It is appropriate to shed more tears and say more prayers for such people than for their victims.
>
> May God protect you from the terrible sin of fratricide. I solemnly warn all my fellow-citizens:
>
> The Church does not condone and cannot condone unlawful and violent acts and the shedding of blood.
>
> I ask all of you, my dear ones, to do everything possible to prevent the flame of civil war from bursting forth.
>
> Cease at once!
>
> I ask soldiers and their officers to remember that no one can set a price on human life and pay it [i.e., that price].
>
> I ask the Most Holy Mother of God, the Protector of our city, at this time of the Feast of the Transfiguration, not to withdraw Her protection from us, but to preserve all of us.

O Mother of God (Mater Bozhia), help us to reconcile ourselves to one another, to the truth, and to God! Aleksy II, Patriarch of Moscow and All Russia. [8]

The first of his interventions had been simply an announcement, but the address was both more personal and more magisterial. Once again there is the light touch on the theme of lawlessness, "the Church . . . cannot condone unlawful and violent acts." But there is more. The patriarch does not claim to speak "infallibly" as has the pope in Rome since the nineteenth century, but liturgical language has its own sonorous power, and Aleksy was cloaking himself in the aura of his position and the righteousness of his cause.

When Aleksey Ridiger was enthroned as patriarch June 10, 1990, he was free, like the pope, to select a new name. (Cardinal Joseph Ratzinger became Pope Benedict XVI when he succeeded John Paul II to the papacy in April of 2005.) "Aleksy II" recalled Aleksy I, who had become patriarch in 1945 at the end of World War II, after serving (as would Ridiger) as metropolitan of Leningrad and Novgorod. While metropolitan, the first Aleksy had also given a stirring address to the people of Moscow. It happened on August 10, 1941, almost exactly fifty years before the current crisis, and also at a moment when the state and the people's existence hung in the balance.

On August 10, 1941, the Red Army was retreating on all fronts, and German Panzers were racing toward Moscow. Desperate to rally the people, Stalin turned *not* to the party but to the ROC. He permitted Metropolitan Aleksy, one of the very few senior clerics to have survived the purge of the church hierarchy, to publicly address the people at the Epiphany (Bogoyavlensky) Cathedral in Moscow. The metropolitan appealed to their strongest motive:

Russian patriotism is known to the whole world. This deep and most fervent love of country is a particular characteristic of the Russian. It can only be compared to the love of one's mother, with the most tender care of her. It seems that in no other language is there exactly the same conception of "mother land" that we have. We do not simply say "native land," but "mother native land [i.e., *mat-rodina* or *rodina-mat*]."

In August 1941 the "mother native land" was under attack by "a strong enemy who dreams of crushing the whole world and barbarously sweeping from his path everything of value that has been built up during centuries of the progressive efforts of humanity." The metropolitan continued:

This struggle is not only a struggle for our native land, which is in great danger, but it can be said, for the whole civilized world over which the

22

sword of destruction is suspended. And just as the Russian people were called during the Napoleonic era to liberate the whole world from the madness of tyranny, so today has fallen to our people the high mission of delivering humanity from the villainies of fascism, of giving back freedom to the enslaved countries and of establishing everywhere peace, which has been so insolently destroyed by fascism.[9]

Then he called on the name of St. Prince Alexander Nevsky, who had declared "God is in Truth, not in Force" when he struck "terror in his enemies, the infamous ancestors of the present still more infamous fascist barbarians." That invasion was but the forerunner of this one, another in the long line of incursions by *religious* foes, who aimed to destroy the people and the faith of Russia. The metropolitan then went on to single out another hero—Prince Dmitry Donskoy of Moscow, who as described in the prologue sought the blessing of Sergius of Radonezh before setting out to battle the "savage Mamay," one of the Tatars who had oppressed "Russia for about three hundred years." And the "holy Sergius gave him not only solid advice, but also his blessing to confront Mamay, foretelling success in his undertaking and sending with him two of his monks—Peresvet and Oslyabya—two heroes as help for the warriors." As a result, Russians won the victory of Kulikovo in 1380, just as they defeated the Teutonic Knights in the famous Battle on the Ice of Lake Peipus in 1242. Both victories the metropolitan credits to divine intervention.

Metropolitan Aleksy assured the Muscovites that the same constellation of heroes and the same heavenly aid would come to their rescue:

> As in the time of Dmitry of the Don, of Holy Alexander Nevsky, as at the time of the Russian people's struggle with Napoleon, the victory of the Russian people is due not only to their patriotism, but also to their deep belief in God's aid to the righteous cause. Just as at that time the Russian army and the whole Russian people were shielded by the Blessed Mother of God, the warrior's patroness, and had the blessing of the saints, so too now we believe the whole heavenly host is with us.

The metropolitan's words turned out to be clairvoyant. The Russians would indeed halt the Wehrmacht in a magnificent stand; they then launched their counteroffensive on December 5, 1941. With the temperature minus 40 degrees Fahrenheit, oil in the sumps of the Wehrmacht's Panzers and trucks congealed to the consistency of tar, and the drag on the dynamos prevented even starting the engines. As their cylinder blocks split and axles refused to turn, the Germans' superiority in mobile warfare disappeared.[10] Siberian ski troops (transported across the country in record time) outmaneuvered a force now reduced to moving at the speed its inadequately clothed soldiers could slog through the snow. Military historians attribute the Red Army's halt of the German advance on Moscow to factors such as their unparalleled skill in mobilizing "General Winter," just as their deep knowledge of the ice had helped Nevsky defeat those "infamous ancestors," the Teutonic Knights. But Orthodox believers hold that in 1941 as in 1242 they were "shielded by the Blessed Mother of God." In 1991, almost exactly fifty years to the day after the Metropolitan of Leningrad had promised that the Theotokos would save Moscow, another Aleksy rewove the basic strands of that speech. And he too would call upon Mary to save the capital.

Now it was not foreign invasion but civil war that threatened. It was not German tanks but the Russians' own Red Army's armor poised to attack. The patriarch began by telling them that once again the "peace of our society has been rent asunder"—this time through the prospect of Russians killing one another. And, like his namesake, Metropolitan Aleksy, he exhorted Muscovites to turn to the most important weapon in their arsenal, "the most Holy Mother of God." He reminded his audience that she was "the Protector of our city, " and he pleaded with her "not to withdraw Her protection from us, but to preserve all of us."

These references to Mary as the "Protector of our city" tapped the deepest memory of the Russian people. For hundreds of years the Orthodox had believed that wonder-working icons of Mary protected them. Probably the most famous was the Vladimir icon of the Theotokos, the most sacred object in all of Russia and the inspiration for countless copies, several of which acquired wonder-working properties as well. The Vladimir icon shows Mary holding the Christ child in her right arm, with his cheek resting against hers.[11] The historian Vera Shevzov has studied this icon in detail and her account bears quoting at length:

> The life of the icon, which began outside the borders of Russia, was intimately tied to the history of the Russian nation. The icon belonged to that group of Marian images that have been attributed to the brush of the evangelist Luke. [That is, it was believed to have been painted from life.] According to the Vladimir icon's story, it was brought to Russia in the twelfth century as a gift from the patriarch of Constantinople, Lukas Chrysoberges, to the grand prince of Kiev, Yury Dolgoruky. It traveled with Yury's son, Prince Andrey, in the mid-twelfth century to northern Russia and became associated with the establishment of the principality of Moscow as Russia's center. Throughout the following centuries,

believers attributed the survival and welfare of the Russian state, especially during times of national crisis, to the protection of the Mother of
God through this icon.[12]

The icon was moved from Vladimir to Moscow in 1395, where it is credited
with protecting the city from the ravages of Tamerlane, also known as Timur
the Lame. There it was hung inside the Cathedral of the Assumption; Aleksy
had been celebrating the Feast of the Transfiguration before it at the moment
the tanks had moved into Red Square.

Russian believers are convinced that Mary continued protecting "Her" city
throughout the centuries. Tatars again besieged Moscow in 1451. Metropolitan Jonah organized a religious procession around the town's walls, with the
people following behind the Vladimir icon and other icons of the Theotokos.
According to the Chronicle, "Saint metropolitanate [sic] Jonah ordered all
the holy orders to sing prayers in all the town, and all the people to pray to
God and the Most Holy Theotokos ... and the Tatars on the same night ran
away from the town having heard the great noise in the town, thinking that
the Grand Prince had come with a big army."[13] Even if Soviet censorship
meant Russians had not been able to read this account for generations, that
memory had been preserved in famous icons. The Resurrection (Voskresenie)
Gates, which fronted on Red Square, had once had a chapel with its icon,
"Our Lady of the Gates." Recalling the same incident, a believer recounted
that the people prayed to the Theotokos to intercede and "The Tatars never
reached Moscow."[14] And one of her icons was considered to have wrought
a miracle at the beginning of the seventeenth century. This was held in the
Cathedral of the Kazan Icon of the Theotokos, outside the Kremlin walls.
It was considered to have saved the city from the invading Catholics of the
Polish-Lithuanian state during the Time of Troubles (1605–13), which followed the succession crisis after the death of Tsar Boris Godunov.

The Soviets had blown up many of the churches housing these miracle-
working icons. They dynamited the Cathedral of the Kazan Icon of the Theotokos, just as they reduced to rubble "Our Lady of the Gates." But the
image of the Mother of God as "Protector of our city" was still buried in
the deep recesses of the Russian mind. Metropolitan Aleksy of Leningrad
had been able to tap that past in 1941. He had promised that Mary would
again spread her protecting veil against the Wehrmacht's Panzers, and Russian
believers are convinced that she did so.

Now Patriarch Aleksy II closed his appeal to the "Mother of God" (Mater
Bozhia) in the form of a prayer-petition. It is shorter, but similar to the famous *troparion* written to the Kazan Icon of the Theotokos credited with

saving the city in the early seventeenth century: "Our zealous Intercessor, the Mother of God the Most High, pray to Your Son, Christ our God, asking for salvation of everybody, who come to your powerful protection. Protect all of us, Most Holy *Theotokos* [as we are in] sorrows and illnesses, burdened by many sins, praying to You with moved soul and humble heart."[15] Upon hearing Mater Bozhia, the Russian Orthodox believers in the crowd began crossing themselves and bowing, thus completing with their bodies a direct and dynamic relationship between the patriarch and his flock. Mary was being petitioned to save her city not from Tatars, Poles, or Lithuanians, but from the tanks and the soldiers of the Red Army. Would they obey the party and the KGB? Or would they be moved by this appeal to the Theotokos to help the patriarch and the Parliament?

Such an appeal, heard nationwide, was both powerful and dangerous. According to Orthodox thinking, if one's prayer is not answered, then in the eyes of the faithful, the petitioner has had insufficient faith. (This explains those otherwise surprising failures when the miracle is not granted.) Aleksy had asked for Mary's help to defeat the coup; if the coup succeeded, the KGB would order him rusticated to a distant church in eastern Siberia. Rustication would then be followed by his quiet liquidation, through either untreated pneumonia or the potions lining the KGB's medicine chest. The remaining hierarchy of the ROC would be assembled to enthrone a new patriarch, and the faithful would be told that Aleksy was not truly a man of God, for Mary had not interceded for him. Instead, she had "spread Her protecting veil" to preserve the Soviet state's apparatus. In short, if Mary did not answer positively, he was a dead man.

There is no doubting the courage required by the patriarch to make that petition. But it is fair to note that before he appealed to heaven, where, according to the New Testament, an army of "twelve legions of angels" musters (Matthew 26:53), Aleksy had been cultivating wingless allies with boots on the ground: the generals of the Red Army. The day before celebrating the Feast of the Transfiguration, he had been reburying the remains of the former patriarch Tikhon (who died in 1925, shortly after being released from stringent Soviet captivity) in the Moscow Monastery dedicated to "Our Lady of the Don." This church contains a copy of the wonder-working (*chudotvornaya*) icon credited with helping Grand Prince Dmitry Donskoy (later canonized) defeat the Horde at Kulikovo.[16] None other than the vice-president of the Russian Federation, Alexander Rutskoy, whose exploits in Afghanistan had made him a Hero of the Soviet Union, was in the crowd of worshipers.

On the evening of August 20, Rutskoy spoke in ringing tones against the coup, urging his fellow soldiers to "cross over to the side legally elected by the people, the organs of power, the president of the Russian Federation and the Council of Ministers of the Russian Federation of Soviet Socialist Republics." Rutskoy was defending his own election, but through his disavowal of the coup, he aligned himself with the new patriarch. The alliance between the patriarchate and the military that had existed in the catacombs was just beginning to surface into public view.[17]

And by 1:42 A.M. of August 21, even the KGB's own Praetorian Guard, the elite Alpha Unit of two hundred professionally trained killers, was leery of taking orders from the coup junta. As recounted earlier, on the afternoon of August 19 it had refused a direct order to storm the Parliament Building. Although this action did not occur on the public stage, it is highly likely that Aleksy, with his close contacts in the military, was apprised of it immediately. The refusal of the Alpha Unit to obey this command has puzzled Western Sovietologists, who paid virtually no attention to the fact that in January 1991 the patriarch had taken a very strong, public stand against Alpha's storming of the television station in Vilnius, Lithuania, at 2:00 A.M. More than twenty of the defenders died. Aleksy's response was forthright:

> The use of military force in Lithuania is a huge political mistake, or in church language, a sin. I ask Russians who are living in Lithuania not to consider these tragic days as "days of victory." ... As for those soldiers who are currently in Lithuanian cities, I want to remind you of the words John the Baptist used when replying to the soldiers who came to him for advice: "Rob no one by violence or by false accusation." (Luke 3:14)[18]

One Western diplomat stationed in Moscow at the time, however, did take surprised notice of Aleksy's open condemnation of the bloodshed. When the national newspaper *Izvestia* carried the patriarch's words all over the country, British embassy officials realized that the party's ability to declare media silence was cracking. Sir Rodric Braithwaite, then the ambassador to the USSR, sensed that real change was in the air:

> Such language from the traditionally sycophantic Orthodox Church was an unprecedented appeal to very profound Russian instincts.... for the first time since the October Revolution, a major Soviet crisis was conducted in the full glare of public opinion. No one could claim that he did not know what the issues were. A demonstration called by *Moscow News* on 20 January [i.e., of 1991] was attended by up to half a million people. Later estimates put the figure at 100,000—still a very large number.[19]

Party oligarchs were furious that Muscovites (Russians!) had turned out in thousands to support the perennially recalcitrant Lithuanians. They did not appreciate the irony that, in terms of their own ideology, this displayed "fraternal support" for another Socialist people. They also did not enjoy the spectacle of their man Aleksey Ridiger, only six months after his enthronement, breaking ranks with them. Thus, by August 1991 Aleksy had already demonstrated he was not afraid to oppose state authority, including Gorbachev himself, the same man whose hide he was now trying to save. In his January condemnation of the Alpha Unit's bloodshed in Vilnius, he used the highly charged language of John the Baptist and addressed soldiers of the Red Army as if face to face ("I want to remind you . . ."), speaking without the intermediary of the party.

Now, only eight months after the violence in Vilnius, he again spoke directly to soldiers and their officers. In his dramatic address, he warned that anyone who took up arms against innocent civilians was taking upon his soul a profound sin, which would "separate himself from the Church and from God." The threat of excommunication has not deterred Western armies for some time. But the patriarch was not appealing to a Western army. Instead, as Ambassador Braithwaite had recognized earlier, the patriarch knew precisely how to appeal to the "very profound Russian instincts" of the Red Army.

In hindsight, Aleksy's address to his "Brothers and Sisters!" was arguably the final nail in the coup's coffin. The immediate context was tense and fluid. By 1:42 A.M. on August 21, the young men in the tanks ringing the Parliament Building had themselves become the targets of believers pressing the New Testament on them. This itself was new to the Soviet Union, because the possession of the Bible in the Russian language had been deliberately restricted. But the Russian Bible Society had recently been reestablished — fortunately, four thousand new copies of the New Testament in vernacular Russian were available. Two thousand were distributed to the defenders. Even more importantly, two thousand new copies were pressed upon the tankers.[20] Priests had been performing baptisms in Red Square. The Committees of Soldiers' Mothers (Komitety soldatskikh materei), an important organization of more than fifty thousand mothers of serving Red Army officers and soldiers, had already issued a public plea calling on "all soldiers and seamen not to allow themselves to be turned into murderers and not to carry out criminal orders."[21]

And the composition of the crowd was leavened with many mothers and grandmothers (the famous and omnipresent *babushki*). Young men, shouting, pushing, and shoving, did not dominate. Had they done so, possibly the equally young men in the tanks might have felt their own testosterone kick in. The grandmothers especially, seen everywhere in the Soviet Union with their ubiquitous *avoska*, or "perhaps" string bag to do the family shopping, were a steadying and calming force. The KGB had not thought old women could be dangerous; they toddled to the derelict churches, but they were seen as harmless relics of a dusty past. The secret police had underestimated the willingness of these elderly women, believers all their lives, to now martyr themselves for their faith. And the young men in the tanks were faced with the prospect of being ordered to gun their engines and squash someone who looked much like their own *babushka*.

When Aleksy's *obrashchenie* was broadcast at 1:42 A.M., the young men in those tanks and armored personnel carriers covering the square in front of the Russian Parliament Building were themselves surrounded. Thousands of ordinary Muscovites had hastily thrown up barricades, which they had been energetically strengthening with pilfered material from construction sites around the city. In addition to the priests and grandmothers, there were members of the old Soviet elite. A year later, one middle-aged lady, the daughter of a famous Arctic explorer, reminisced in her elegant apartment about the exciting hours she had spent in front of the tanks wearing high heels.

And the crowd contained Afghan veterans as well. They put their frustration and anger at that failed campaign—and the shameful way they had been treated by the authorities—to use. These men, hardened to combat, would not scatter at the first gunning of the tanks' engines. With a charming sense of chivalry, they now began urging the *babushki* to leave, for they had begun counting down to 2:00 A.M., the KGB's favorite "zero hour" for assaults, when the body's circadian rhythms cycle adrenalin and testosterone to their lowest level. The Lithuanian attack, as Aleksy knew, had occurred precisely at that time.

Inside the building, the Parliament's defenders expected the attack within twenty minutes. Igor Glazin, former member of the Estonian Parliament, was with Yeltsin at that moment. He claims that in the wee hours of that critical August 21, Yeltsin told all present that he was releasing them from any commitment to stay. Those who remained would do so on a purely voluntary basis. Such was the cohesion among the Parliament members at this point that Glazin and the others—recalling the band of Gideon and the Spartans at Thermopylae—were firm that they would stand or perish. And outside in the crowd, the *babushki* astonished the Afghan veterans by declaring the same thing. The young tankers realized they would have to flatten real live Russians if they advanced. The deaths of the three young men—one crushed under tank treads, two shot—brought home to everyone that this could turn into a bloodbath and a savage civil war, like the one that followed the October Revolution of 1917.

It is impossible today to discover if an order to advance was ever issued. If it was, no members of the junta will now admit to it. Such is the desire among KGB officers to distance themselves from the actions of the coup that President Vladimir Putin publicly avows that he resigned from his beloved KGB that very August 20, though he had wanted to join since he was a boy and was by then a successful lieutenant-colonel.

However such ex post facto statements are evaluated, what is undeniable is that less than ninety minutes after the patriarch's address was heard, Vladimir Kryuchkov placed a fateful call to Yeltsin. At 3:00 A.M. in the morning of August 21, Kryuchkov told Yeltsin "there would be no assault that night."[22]

"That night"?

Not for all time.

Had Kryuchkov been able to issue an order that was obeyed by the tanks, they could have dispersed the crowd, blasted the Parliament Building, retaken the White House, and imprisoned or killed Yeltsin and his supporters in the resulting melee. Just two years earlier in 1989, China's market reforms did not prevent the Chinese Communist Party, headed by a similar group of aging reactionaries, from having its orders obeyed. There were delays, but the tanks did roll and fire on demonstrators in Tianenmen Square. Thousands died, but the party's septuagenarian ideologues still retain power in the People's Republic of China. There was certainly nothing sacrosanct about the Parliament Building, nor was it unthinkable to open fire on the deputies. Two years later in a startling reversal of roles, Yeltsin himself would order tanks to fire on a recalcitrant Russian Parliament, and they did so, leaving the building a burning, windowless shell with an enormous hole and many corpses in the hallways.[23] At that time, Aleksy made extensive but finally unsuccessful efforts to reconcile the two sides, hosting sessions in the Danilov Monastery, official headquarters of the patriarchate. Furthermore, Yeltsin did not hesitate to arrest his former colleague, Alexander Rutskoy, who had supported him during the attempted coup. But in the early hours of August 21, 1991, the KGB could not depend upon its order being carried out.

Though no one realized it yet, the "sword and shield" had failed to protect the party. Kryuchkov's coalition broke up with astonishing rapidity. One of the junta, Boris Pugo, minister of internal affairs, committed suicide that evening in his apartment, when Yeltsin sent police to arrest him. The others scrambled to get on planes and head down to Yalta to make their excuses to Gorbachev. Dmitry Yazov, Gorbachev's minister of defense and another of the coup's ringleaders, ordered the troops to withdraw just hours later. As a cold, drizzling dawn broke, the seemingly endless armored column turned around and left the city.

The patriarch himself lost no time in crediting the salvation of Russia to the Mother of God.[24] This statement had the virtue of modesty, while simultaneously recalling that he had ended his address with an appeal to her as the Protector of Moscow. By crediting Mary with the miraculous intervention that secured a virtually bloodless victory, the patriarch was reminding everyone that he had the ear of heaven. Once again the Theotokos had, in Orthodox language, "spread Her protecting veil" to save Moscow—and Aleksy himself.

Many Russians agreed with the patriarch that it was a miracle (*chudo*) and should be attributed to their faith. A much larger crowd than had manned the barricades and surrounded the tanks now headed to the nearby Lubyanka. There, in front of KGB headquarters, they pulled down the statue of Feliks Dzerzhinsky, founder of the Cheka, forefather of the Soviet secret police. CNN televised the event live, worldwide. But no Western broadcast showed what happened afterward. On the empty plinth, the crowd put up a homemade Orthodox cross, with its distinctive sidebar. The police removed it, but in a uniquely Russian compromise they left behind the graffiti painted in white on the black granite—*Sim pobedishi* (figure 1.2) Easily understood by any educated Russian, the words were written in Old Church Slavonic. They are the equivalent of the Latin *In hoc vinces*—"By this sign, [shalt thou] conquer." Constantine claimed to have seen these words in the heavens next to a celestial cross immediately before he won the crucial Battle of the Milvian Bridge in 312, the battle that led to his acclamation as sole emperor of the Romans.[25]

Constantine's vision ended what Christian historians call "The Great Persecution," the years of Diocletian's rule that saw believers fed to the lions in Roman stadiums across the Mediterranean world. Constantine's victory over his rival Maxentius paved the way for Christianity to become the state faith of the Roman Empire. Orthodoxy traces its roots directly to Constantine and to the city of Constantinople, which he founded on the banks of the Bosphorus as the "queen of Christendom." Orthodoxy not only sainted Constantine but elevated him to the special status of Ravnoapostolny, "Equal to the Apostles." For the crowd in front of the Lubyanka in 1991, the world was changing just as profoundly as it had in 312. The sufferings of Orthodox believers exceeded in scope if not in intensity those of the early Christian martyrs. Though not fed to the lions, for seventy years they were sent to "strict regime" camps, their church's priests and nuns were deported and killed, its property was pilfered,

Figure 1.2 The crowd that toppled Feliks Dzerzhinsky's statue on August 21, 1991, erected a homemade Orthodox cross on the pedestal and painted *Sim pobedishi*, the Old Church Slavonic equivalent of "By This Sign, Conquer," on the plinth. Though the police immediately removed the cross, the graffiti still proclaimed the victory of Orthodoxy over the secret police in March 1992. (Photo credit: John Garrard)

and its shrines were desecrated. *Sim pobedishi* paralleled two victories by the righteous over the evildoers separated by 1,679 years.

Today (2007), Dzerzhinsky's plinth and its white paint graffiti are gone. The square in front of the Lubyanka contains grass and flowerbeds. But Orthodox believers remain convinced that divine help, summoned by the patriarch, played a decisive role in defeating the coup. Seen from their perspective, the very suddenness of its collapse is part and parcel of how miracles work. Miracles are not just the record of the past. They are live events in a constant present, a déjà vu without end and without apology. On August 21, 1991, the Theotokos was in residence, again protecting "Her" city.

Aleksy quickly sold the "divine intervention by the Mother of God" theory to the Russian Parliament itself—that group of 150 or so men and women who had barricaded themselves in the White House with Yeltsin. On Monday, August 26, he conducted a requiem for the three young casualties of the coup inside the Cathedral of the Assumption. It was followed by the first parliamentary session following the coup.[26] The opening of the Parliament inside the Cathedral of the Assumption sent a powerful signal. Yeltsin publicly expressed his gratitude to the patriarch.

The Orthodox calendar itself played into Aleksy's hands. He had been conducting the service commemorating the Feast of the Transfiguration inside the Cathedral of the Assumption as the tanks rolled into Red Square. But the Transfiguration is followed at once by an equally important celebration in the liturgical calendar, the Assumption of Mary. The bodily assumption of Mary into heaven after her Dormition—that is, her falling asleep—is an article of faith for Russian Orthodoxy. (Mary's death is not related in the New Testament itself, unlike the Ascension of Jesus.) Once assumed into heaven, Mary becomes, in the words of James Billington, the "ultimate security policy" for the Russians.[27] The Feast of the Assumption occurs at the end of August. Thus, from the Orthodox viewpoint, the entire coup and its defeat takes place in liturgical time. In a merging of the secular and divine clocks, which the Orthodox read as "no accident," the world changed between the Feast of the Transfiguration and the Feast of the Assumption. When Yeltsin and his parliamentarians attended the patriarch's requiem inside the Cathedral of the Assumption immediately before opening the first post-Communist parliamentary session in history, the machinery of Russia's government meshed with Orthodox gears.

If Aleksy's interventions were important in the failure of the coup, then some might discern an additional element of meaning in an otherwise enigmatic statement by the current Russian president, Vladimir Putin. He is on record as having denied that a true popular revolution, that is, a revolution from below, took place August 19–21, 1991: "Let's proceed from reality. Democracy in Russia was in fact issued from above."[28] Putin's words have generally been interpreted to mean quite simply that it was Gorbachev who put into place opportunities for people to take charge of their own political destiny without facing immediate and certain arrest and execution. Kremlinologists, more eager to suggest that all statements are opaque, might conjecture that Putin's remark was a rueful accolade from one former KGB agent (Putin) to another (Ridiger). But Russian believers would be more likely to interpret Putin's "from above" in a spiritual rather than a political sense. Putin has certainly been ostentatious in his own profession of Russian Orthodoxy and has let it be known that he maintains a priest as his spiritual guide.

Western political scientists and historians, overwhelmingly secular in their outlook, rarely saw the hand of God active in human affairs of the twentieth century. They consider the claims of Russian Orthodox believers ludicrous.

For them the demise of the Soviet Union is a matter for roundtable discussions that focus on Marxism-Leninism, Gorbachev's policies, and the measurable impact of nascent capitalism, privatization, and commercialization on a lumbering Soviet economy. Indeed, in 2004 the *Slavic Review*, the premier journal of the field, devoted an entire issue to the discussion of the fall of the Soviet Union without once mentioning either the Russian Orthodox Church or the patriarch.[29] Right-wing Republicans claim that the collapse of the Soviet regime was nothing less than a victory over Communism won directly by Ronald Reagan—a view that Russians themselves find both risible and insulting.

No one would deny that Gorbachev's reforms, particularly the withdrawal of terror as the means of controlling the Russian and the East European populations, put into motion a chain of events that led people to think and to behave very differently than they had for the previous seventy years. But to deal with the question of the collapse of the August coup without mentioning the role played by the patriarch's interventions and the activities of priests and believers of the Orthodox Church around the Russian White House is to ignore facts on the ground.

The coup's failure set in motion the peaceful dissolution of the Soviet Union. Yeltsin's announcement that Russia would withdraw from the USSR made that process a certainty. Newly emboldened, on August 24, only seventy-two hours after the tanks had pulled back, the Ukrainian Republic announced that it too would exercise its right to withdraw from the Soviet Union. Other republics quickly followed suit. Finally, on December 25, 1991 (Christmas Day in the West), the heads of all the republics met in Minsk, the capital of Belarus, to sign an agreement dissolving the Union of Soviet Socialist Republics. They created in its place a Commonwealth of Independent States (CIS). This polite surrender of imperial power to former colonies echoes the British switch from empire to a commonwealth in the face of similar realities after World War II.

In retrospect, the election of Aleksey Ridiger as patriarch of the ROC turned out to be one of the turning points that marked the beginning of the end for Soviet power. Gorbachev's permission for the church to celebrate the Millennium of the Baptism of Rus, given in April 1987 to Patriarch Pimen, set the stage. But when the crisis came, it was Aleksy who publicly threw the whole weight of his office and his church against the coup, putting not just his career but also his life on the line. Would Pimen have had the strength to do so, had he lived on? The point is that Aleksy did, and from the moment the tanks turned around, a new period dawned for the Russian Orthodox Church.

How, then, had the men who planned the coup of August 19–21, 1991, come to make such a mistake in signing off on Aleksy's election as patriarch?

Kryuchkov and his junta were not buffoons. They were the nerve center of what had been the most successful secret police force in human history. Every day they sifted reports of what was happening inside a vast country. Their agents penetrated every Soviet enterprise. Their operation to seize Gorbachev in the Crimea went forward without a hitch. Yet they fatally underestimated the coalition of forces—the people, the army, and the church—that they would face in Moscow. That miscalculation says a great deal about the failings of the Soviet system itself.

TWO

A New Hope

The time has come for prophecy to be fulfilled.
— *Patriarch Aleksy II at the deposition of the relics of*
St. Seraphim at Diveyevo Convent, July 31, 1991

ALEKSEY RIDIGER WAS AN unlikely candidate to help save democracy during those critical days in August 1991. He had been one of the KGB's best and brightest operatives. That was why the KGB was so delighted at his election to the patriarchate on June 6–7, 1990, just over a year earlier. Few organizations can have been as disappointed by the performance of a former employee who had promised so much.

Ridiger's induction into the KGB at the age of twenty-nine marked a significant turning point in his life. He was born on February 23, 1929, and brought up in Estonia. The Soviet Union, while ostensibly a multinational state with equal rights for all, was Russo-centric and controlled from Moscow. Ridiger's class background was suspect: he had Baltic-German aristocratic roots. His mother was born in Revel, renamed Tallinn in Soviet times. From the perspective of the party, Ridiger came from an émigré pedigree. What is more, his father and mother were devout believers; indeed, his father, Mikhail, had finished the theological course in Tallinn in 1940 and later been ordained deacon and priest. His family took pilgrimages to the beautiful medieval monasteries on Lake Ladoga. When he was nine, they went to Valaam, then part of Finland, located at the northern end of the lake, about 120 miles north of Leningrad. He remembers that the peaceful scenery and pristine spirituality profoundly affected him. Finnish Valaam contrasted strikingly to the Soviet side of the lake, where the secret police, the NKVD, had thoroughly despoiled the church's property and driven out or murdered the monks. The KGB knew all this. In recruiting him, its headhunters were taking something of a gamble, but, then, they wanted the best and the brightest.

It is usually necessary to read between the lines of any official biography, and Ridiger's is no exception. Several lacunae stand out. After graduating from the Leningrad Seminary in 1949, he was ordained deacon and priest in April 1950. He then became the rector of the Church of the Epiphany in Tallinn. Ridiger initially entered the "white clergy" of the Orthodox Church. Orthodoxy requires its parish priests, or "white clergy" to marry. However, they do not rise within the church hierarchy, which is composed of the "black clergy," who are celibate. According to Dr. Igor Glazin, a former member of the Estonian Parliament, Ridiger did marry and fathered at least one child.[1] His official church biography makes no mention of marriage, children, or divorce, but then neither does it mention his recruitment by the Estonian KGB.

What is clear is that after being accepted into the KGB, Ridiger began to rocket up the ranks of the Russian Orthodox Church. Only one month later, the twenty-nine-year-old Ridiger was appointed dean of the Tartu-Vilyandi deanery of the Tallinn diocese. Five months after that he was elevated to the rank of archpriest. Then, on March 3, 1961, he entered the official "black clergy," which meant professing monastic vows of celibacy. Somewhere along the way, he shed wife and child. He continued to move up in rank and responsibility. At the earliest possible age of thirty-two, he became bishop of Tallinn, the only Orthodox bishop who spoke both Estonian and Russian. He wrote a dissertation, using original manuscript sources, on the Orthodox Church in Estonia; it remains the sole work on the subject.

He also demonstrated superb international skills from the outset. He was sent as a delegate to the Third Assembly of the World Council of Churches in New Delhi in 1961 and was elected a member of its Central Committee. His official curriculum vitae relates this with justifiable pride under the category, "work in the international field." However, Canon Michael Bourdeaux, president of Keston Institute at Oxford, has noted that precisely in 1961 party leader Khrushchev stepped up his violent persecution of the Russian Orthodox Church, imprisoning tens of thousands of believers and closing some two-thirds of its remaining twenty thousand churches, the majority of which had only opened during or after World War II. Bourdeaux argues that central to the KGB's success in concealing this outrage from the world was the willingness of the Orthodox hierarchy to collaborate in the cover-up. The key moment was "the permission the Kremlin gave to the Russian Orthodox Church to join the World Council of Churches at its New Delhi assembly in 1961. This inaugurated a campaign of misinformation which continued for a quarter of a century."[2] The KGB could congratulate itself on its vetting techniques: only three years earlier it had inducted a twenty-nine-year-old Estonian, and now he was placed within the heart of an organization through which the KGB would orchestrate one of its most successful international propaganda campaigns.

The CPSU suffered the existence of the Russian Orthodox Church because it had an important assignment in the Cold War. Its mission was to gain friends in the Third World and the West by portraying the Soviet Union as leading the world toward universal peace. The importance of this tactic may be judged by the contents of the *Journal of the Moscow Patriarchate* from 1970 (when it began publishing) through 1989. A sample issue fills at least one-third of its pages with various speeches, addresses, and communiqués under the heading "Peace movement." In cases of particularly "slow" issues, that is, when nothing at all is happening in the church domestically, the desperate editors resurrected minutes from old meetings of the peace movement. Thus, the sixth issue of 1987 juxtaposes the rather stale news of the "Meeting of the Working Presidium and Secretariat of the 1982 World [Peace] Conference" with the latest "Statement on Nuclear Disarmament," "Statement on Southern Africa," "Statement on Nicaragua," official communiqués "To the General Secretary of the CPSU Central Committee, M. S. Gorbachev," "To the President of the USA, R. Reagan," "To the UN Secretary-General, Dr. Javier Perez de Cuellar," and the minutes of the "5th International Round Table Conference of Religious Workers and Experts on 'Common Security and Moral-Ethical Values.'" A reader might conclude that the ROC existed "for export only," even though 1987 was supposed to be a year of glasnost and perestroika.

Aleksey Ridiger was the KGB's brightest star in marketing the peace campaign, which had nothing at all to do with the real Soviet "peace movement." That was formed by a small band of extraordinarily brave dissidents, lead by Andrey Sakharov, a member of the Soviet Academy of Sciences and world-famous scientist. The date was June 1982, after the USSR had signed the Helsinki Accords. According to international practice, the accords were supposed to be binding on the signatory states and would supersede national legislation should the two conflict. The Moscow Helsinki Group monitored to what degree the Soviet Union complied with its promises.

There is no record of Ridiger having said and done anything about the Moscow Helsinki Group's activities. Indeed, at the very moment the Moscow Helsinki Group was formed, he seemed to be one of the KGB's most loyal officers. He had moved smoothly up the ranks from sacristan as teenager to archbishop and member of the Holy Synod, and in 1982 he became chancellor of the Moscow Patriarchate.[3] In this position he scored an enormous success, one that scarcely registered in the West, but occasioned excited speculation within the Moscow intelligentsia. On May 25, 1983, he assumed the chairmanship of a new Russian Orthodox Executive Committee entitled intriguingly "For the *Reception* and Restoration of the Danilov

Monastery" (emphasis added). The single word "reception" was most puzzling. Even when the CPSU allowed the restoration of a derelict church,
the standard operating procedure was to turn its shell into a secular enterprise such as a factory, a prison, or a "museum of atheism." And the construction process itself was entrusted to a state committee on "architectural
and cultural monuments."

A month later the Soviet News Agency TASS made an even more startling
announcement: the government would carry out the request of the Moscow
Patriarchate and return the Danilov Monastery to the Russian Orthodox
Church. TASS referred to a petition written by the elderly Patriarch Pimen
to the president of the Council of Ministers of the USSR, Nikolai Tikhonov.[4]
Everyone knew that both Pimen and Tikhonov were figureheads. The real
decider was Yury Andropov, and he was notorious for his hatred of Orthodoxy.
Why had he authorized the return of the most important monastery of the
Moscow Patriarchate to the church? And did this really mean that services
could resume there?

For centuries, the Danilov Monastery had been the official headquarters of
the Moscow Patriarchate. Founded in 1282 by Prince Daniel of Moscow, the
youngest son of the great military hero Alexander Nevsky, the entire complex
had vital historical as well as religious significance. Prince Daniel elevated
Moscow to the status of capital of an expanding principality, making him the
acknowledged founder of the Muscovite state. He ordered himself tonsured
as a monk immediately before dying within its walls. This ancient and noble
history did not save the monastery from being seized by the Soviet regime. In
1931 an American purchased its bells and donated them to Harvard University
(for decades they composed its carillon). Subsequently the monastery was
used, among other things, as a detention center for the children of "enemies
of the people" (an Orwellian phrase that tarred those innocent of any crime),
then as a prison for juvenile delinquents, and later a factory to produce light
bulbs. In May 1983 its grounds were reduced to rubbish-strewn mud, its
frescoes plastered over, and its Holy Trinity Cathedral turned into a recreation center.

The Orthodox hierarchy, since 1937 squeezed into Moscow's Novodevichy
Monastery (which rather ominously contained Moscow's most famous cem-
etery), was delighted that Ridiger immediately embarked on its renovation
so that the Danilov could once again become Orthodoxy's Religious and
Administrative Center. Only six months after taking over as chairman for the
committee in September 1983, he gave his first report to the Holy Synod,
the church's ruling body. He had the architects and engineers engaged, the
plans drawn, a special bank account (about which more later) opened, and

donations flowing in. The complex would contain an official residence for the patriarch, some institutions for the Holy Synod, and a new conference hall "for religious and peace-making conferences."[5] For those few in the West reading these cheerful plans as detailed by the *Journal of the Moscow Patriarchate*, the reference to "peace-making" conferences seemed a trifle hollow. In that same September, Korean Airlines Flight 007 strayed unwittingly into Soviet airspace and was promptly shot down by the Soviet Air Force without any effort to make radio contact. In addition, the Moscow Helsinki Group announced that it would have to suspend its activities, as all members of the group had been either arrested or threatened. Chancellor Ridiger maintained a pristine silence on their fate.

And to make the situation within the USSR even bleaker, on September 13, 1983, the *Gazette of the Supreme Soviet of the USSR* published a new restrictive decree allowing the rearrest of prisoners without bothering for a new trial.[6] That was one week after the Madrid Helsinki review conference ended—and just before Ridiger made his first report to the Holy Synod on the Danilov restoration project with its new facilities for "peace-making" conferences. So far it seemed that Aleksey Ridiger was simply carrying out the directives of Yury Andropov, who had been head of the KGB before being selected by the Politburo as general secretary of the CPSU on November 12, 1982, only two days after the death of Leonid Brezhnev.

Andropov was a Cold War adversary of the old school, a grim secret police apparatchik who rose through the ranks by efficiently repressing the population. He had also organized the crushing of the Hungarian revolt in 1956 and the "Prague Spring" in 1968. Becoming head of the KGB in 1967, he suppressed the unsteady, nascent opposition, sending his victims to hard labor in prison camps or to be drugged in psychiatric hospitals, using techniques learned from the Nazi German doctors. From the outset of his career, he especially targeted Orthodox believers. In July 1938 *Yuny Kommunist* (*Young Communist*) featured an article by Andropov, then a mere twenty-three. Already he had made his mark as one of the "men of '38"—that ruthless gang of newcomers who vaulted over the corpses of the previous generation of party leaders purged by Stalin. As the chairman of the Yaroslavl provincial committee of the CPSU, he wrote an article entitled "Shielding Our Youth from the Destructive Influence of Clerics and Sectarians." Andropov reported that prerevolutionary Yaroslavl had once had 75 churches, and 1,125 had been scattered throughout the province, all supported through the "wretched" people forced to work for them. The "essential truth of religion" he claimed, was that it was a "weapon to enslave the working masses." (*orudie dlya zakreposhcheniya trudyashchikhsya mass*).[7] And, he warned ominously, religion was a far more dangerous enemy than his Komsomol friends naively believed. It was not yet dead; no, indeed, the party must vigorously continue the work against these relics of the prerevolutionary past. Fortunately, he reassured his readers, the great Stalin constitution of 1936 gives the party the power to crush them. In short, Andropov was proving himself "*plus royaliste que le roi même*," and "a kiss up, kick down" bureaucrat.

Throughout his years in the KGB, Andropov worked mightily to liquidate the church and its believers. When he became general secretary of the CPSU, it looked as though he would now finish the job he had started in 1938 when he supervised the destruction of Yaroslavl's 75 churches. Once Moscow had contained 1,600 working churches—a mystical number arrived at by multiplying 40 times 40 (*sorok sorokov*). By 1983 this figure had dwindled to 20. Even those who wished to attend services were harassed: on Easter Sunday, the most important day of the year in the Orthodox calendar, thugs on motorcycles zoomed up and down in front of the churches, nearly knocking over the tough little women carrying eggs to be blessed and making the service difficult to hear.[8] Andropov immediately initiated a new round of persecution against religious dissidents: the KGB searched their apartments, seized their Bibles, broke up their prayer meetings, and usually rounded off the evening by beating the miscreants. Then, four months after becoming general secretary, Andropov fell ill. Only a few top apparatchiks saw him; he ran the empire by pulling invisible strings.

Andropov was last seen in public August 18, 1983, when he met with a delegation of American senators. Pale, he needed help to stand up. Then he missed the obligatory November 7 parade, where the entire Politburo lined up on the top of the Lenin Mausoleum in identical overcoats and fedoras to review both the 9:00 A.M. *parad* (the missiles, troops, and tanks) and the 10:00 A.M. *demonstratsiya* (marching factory workers, gymnasts, etc.). At the end of December, Moscow buzzed with rumors that Andropov was indeed dying. He had just missed two more crucial occasions, the December 27 plenary session of the CPSU and the opening of the Supreme Soviet on December 29. This latter organization was a rubber stamp, but because it was part of the CPSU's "theater of democracy," the general secretary always showed up. Word began to circulate that Andropov planned on allowing the Danilov Monastery to resume its sacred identity, not just permit its carapace to be restored as an "architectural monument." Andropov had spent his career persecuting the faith, seizing its buildings, imprisoning its clergy, and spying on its believers. Now, like Ivan the Terrible, who ended his reign of murder and debauchery by ordering prayers for his victims and being tonsured as a monk,[9] it seemed he was thinking about eternity.

41

There is a less spiritual explanation. When juxtaposed with Ridiger's report to the Synod, it is probable that he had agreed with the chancellor's pitch that Moscow needed its own church showpiece to host meetings of the World Council of Churches. The restored Danilov would be a Potemkin monastery, where foreign delegates could see with their own eyes there was no religious persecution inside the people's paradise.

December was the same month Andropov was admitted to the Kuntsevo Hospital. He never emerged. Yet his bank of phones sent out orders making the country ever more Stalinist. He had earlier signed a law allowing the rearrest of prisoners simply because they had "violated the regime" of their previous incarceration. Now he changed the criminal code to make it an offense to pass practically any information, however innocent, to a foreigner.[10] Yet all the while Aleksey Ridiger proceeded apace restoring the Danilov. Andropov fell into a coma at the end of January 1984 and died without regaining consciousness on February 10. Not one single obituary in the Western media noticed his astonishing gesture of restoring the Danilov Monastery to the church, though Moscow itself was rife with speculation.

The Party Presidium elected ailing, colorless Konstantin Chernenko as a caretaker general secretary, but nothing slowed the meteoric speed at which the Danilov Monastery was being refurbished and repaired. Only three years after Ridiger became chairman of the committee for its "reception and restoration," Trinity Cathedral was sufficiently restored that a liturgy could be celebrated in it. On May 30, 1986, the primate of the Autocephalous Orthodox Church in America paid a visit and gave the father superior a reliquary "with a particle of the holy relics" [i.e., bones] of St. Daniel. He was then taken on a tour and was so impressed at the speed and quality of the work, he wrote in the Distinguished Visitors' Book: "I have seen with my own eyes truly the great historic and spiritual work that you have and are doing for the glory of God and the Holy Orthodox Church."[11]

Only Keston News Service, based in Moscow and Oxford, took note of the "how" of this achievement. On May 29, 1986 (just one day prior to the American primate's visit), Keston published a brief and innocuous paragraph describing an extraordinary privilege granted to the venture.[12] The bank account Ridiger had reported to the Holy Synod back in September 1983 turned out to be one of a kind. The KGB tightly controlled all financial transactions, especially in matters concerning foreign currency (*valyuta*), which by law no individual or organization could possess. Diplomats and the elite might own "coupons" that could be used in hard currency Beryozka stores. Otherwise *valyuta* given to an organization—such as the ROC—had to be converted into rubles at a special overseas trade bank (Vneshtorgbank). There the state took a large commission. But the party granted a special exemption to Ridiger's mission, though ostensibly in the name of the septuagenarian Patriarch Pimen. Early in 1986 Ridiger was permitted to expand his fundraising beyond the borders of the USSR. He could deposit the dollars, pounds, francs, and marks (up to a specified ceiling) into a special account in the Vneshtorgbank without conversion into rubles. Ridiger was thus in the exhilarating position of legally possessing foreign currency for his task—foreign currency from which the state had not bitten out a large chunk. The black market economy of the USSR was a dollar economy—and it worked far more efficiently than the state's. Ridiger had the funds to "encourage" Soviet builders to meet their deadlines and do work of the highest standard.

And to make these banking arrangements even more exceptional, just before Andropov slipped into unconsciousness he had signed another draconian amendment into law. This time it applied to the notorious Article 70 of the Criminal Code of the Russian Republic of the Soviet Union, which covered the many proscriptions against "anti-Soviet agitation and propaganda." As of February 1, 1984, the sentence could be up to ten years in jail with or without an additional five years of exile if such actions were deemed to be carried out "with the use of monies or other material goods received from foreign organizations or from persons acting in the interests of such organizations." In other words, if material aid of any kind from abroad—such as the foreign currency flowing into Ridiger's Vneshtorgbank account—were to be used for "anti-Soviet activities," such aid would be considered an aggravating circumstance.

Exactly how Ridiger managed to obtain foreign currency from abroad was itself a mystery. In August 1984 the Soviet agency handling parcels from overseas with duty prepaid for addressees in the USSR (Vneshposyltorg) officially served notice that no such packages would be allowed into the Soviet Union. However, Ridiger overcame all obstacles. The Danilov Monastery, from being in ruins—even the fortified walls were collapsing when the church got it back—was restored to new glory. Its walls gleamed a nacreous white; its turrets shone like a movie set of Camelot. The complex ended up containing, in the words of William Miller, the former U.S. ambassador to Ukraine who stayed in one of its luxurious suites, "a five-star hotel [with] nothing monastic about it."[13] Neither the Soviet press nor the *Journal of the Moscow Patriarchate* has ever referred to the monastery's Vneshtorgbank passbook, but it meant the CPSU was trusting Ridiger very far indeed.

Clearly, Ridiger was a sophisticated executive who knew how to manipulate the state system, influence important foreign guests, and raise the profile of the church. His success in restoring the monastery provided him with a golden parachute when he was removed from the post of Moscow chancellor in 1986. On Chernenko's death in March 1985, Mikhail Gorbachev took over as general secretary of the CPSU. He soon embarked upon his celebrated campaign of glasnost and perestroika. Then Ridiger made one of the few mistakes of his career: he took Gorbachev at his word. He wrote him expressing concern about the moral decline of the motherland. He urged that the state should allow the church to participate in the moral renewal of the citizenry. For once, his impeccable sense of timing betrayed him. The 27th Party Congress, held in the spring 1986, had just called for renewed vigor in promulgating "scientifically atheistic ideology for the overcoming of religious superstitions." And the program's section on "Atheistic Upbringing" equated the struggle against faith next to the overcoming of corruption, alcoholism, and theft.[14] So in 1986, no longer chancellor, Ridiger took up his next post: metropolitan of Leningrad and Novgorod and administrator of the diocese of Tallinn (his mother's birthplace).

Far from brooding, he plunged into these new duties with formidable energy. He began a meteoric rise in the Western European theater of the KGB's global peace campaign. He had already been successful in influencing the Conference of European Churches based in Geneva, Switzerland. He chaired many of its most important committees and was keynote speaker at many of its international conferences. He now worked his way up to be president of the organization and finally chairman, its most important position, in 1987.[15] Throughout his tenure he demonstrated consummate skill in fronting for the KGB's peace initiatives. The World Council of Churches attracted church and lay people from all over the globe. Gullible and devout pastors from the West attended its meetings and returned home convinced there was no religious persecution in the USSR—after all, they had just come back from a council meeting and met actual Orthodox priests who had testified to this! Indeed, Ridiger's success as the moderator of the panel at the First European Ecumenical Assembly on "Peace with Justice" Conference, which took place in Basel, Switzerland, from May 15 to 21 in 1989, can be said to mark the high point of the KGB's strategy to market the USSR as leading the world toward universal harmony and concord, while NATO countries regrettably engaged in saber rattling.

And if this were not enough to keep him busy, from September 1986 Metropolitan Ridiger chaired the subcommittee that did most of the groundwork for the celebration, scheduled for 1988, of the so-called "Baptism of Rus" (Kreshchenie Rusi), that is, the thousand-year anniversary of the adoption of Christianity by the grand prince of Kiev. In fact, according to his official church vita, Ridiger had been working on the 1988 celebrations since December 23,

1980, when he acted as vice-chairman for the "Preparatory Committee for the Millennium of the Christianization of the Eastern Slavs in Kiev."

Russians traditionally claimed the medieval Slavs of Kievan Rus (Kievskaya Rus) as their direct ancestors. Subsequently, Muscovite leaders, both tsarist and Soviet, had firmly incorporated Ukraine into the expanding Russian empire, which meant that Russians felt they owned it. Exactly how the 1980 committee spent its time may never be known. After a meeting between Gorbachev and Patriarch Pimen in the Kremlin in 1986, however, Gorbachev allowed him to "co-celebrate" with the patriarch of Constantinople the Feast of the Transfiguration at the Dormition Cathedral at St. Sergius Monastery on August 20, 1987 (see the description of this service in the prologue).

Plans for the millennial ceremonies mushroomed in scope and lavishness overnight. Ridiger's committee must have had a blueprint just waiting to be dusted off. Gorbachev certainly moved into these plans smoothly and seamlessly. He met Patriarch Pimen publicly in the Kremlin in April 1988 to mark the event. He then allowed the millennial anniversary to be celebrated with great pomp and circumstance. Soviet television broadcast gorgeous services, processions of the cross, chanting monks, and priests swinging censors and sprinkling holy water, and believers bowing and praying. These were extraordinary privileges. President and Mrs. Reagan visited the Danilov Monastery during the celebrations to show Western support. In June, Raisa Gorbachev was photographed attending the festivities perched between an Orthodox and a Western church prelate.[16] She looked very uncomfortable, which is understandable because she held a doctorate in Marxism-Leninism, that is, the "scientific atheism" whose *Weltanshauung* the 27th Party Congress had declared needed to be promulgated with special vigor at just this time.

Metropolitan Ridiger immediately took advantage of his new authority over Leningrad and the new *Zeitgeist*. He scored an enormous success by orchestrating the return to the church of the bones of St. Prince Alexander Nevsky (see figure 2.1). Nevsky had been prince of Novgorod, an extremely important medieval town, a center for Viking and Slavic commerce since the ninth century; indeed, it was the northernmost member of the Hanseatic League. Russians trace the beginnings of what would become the Muscovite state to Novgorod in 862 when it was still officially pagan. And St. Petersburg itself enjoyed a special connection with this famous hero. In 1240 Prince Alexander faced an invading army of Swedes. The two armies met on the banks of the Neva River. Fighting in the front lines, Alexander wounded the Swedish commander and the Russians routed the enemy. Alexander of Novgorod hence became better known by the honorific title Nevsky, that is, Alexander of the Neva.

Figure 2.1 St. Petersburg erected a new statue to its favorite son and Orthodox saint, Prince Alexander of Novgorod, who defeated the Swedes on the banks of the Neva River in 1240, thus earning the honorific Alexander Nevsky. (Photo credit: Liudmila Kiselyova)

When Peter the Great built his capital on those same banks, he ordered Nevsky's relics brought to the city and installed in the Holy Trinity Cathedral inside the Alexander Nevsky Lavra (i.e., Monastery). This complex anchors one end of the central artery of the city, the Nevsky Prospekt, which runs straight as a die from the Winter Palace out to the suburbs. It radiates out from the Admiralty, a landmark of neoclassical architecture that was once the headquarters of the Russian navy. It was at this very location that Peter built his shipyard, from whence his new fleet would set sail. The former shipyard is crowned with a spire, a compass needle pointing Russia toward the West. Peter announced the founding of St. Petersburg in 1703 as a fortress to hold the Swedes at bay. Naming the city's main thoroughfare was a shrewd move to connect his own victory over the Swedes at Poltava (1709) with the man who had first defeated them in 1240. Peter wanted simultaneously to subsume Nevsky's medieval glory and to reorient Russia toward modern Europe. Paradoxically then, the most westernized city of Russia claims a thirteenth-century prince and Orthodox saint (canonized in 1547) as its favorite son.

The Russian Orthodox Church reveres the bones of its saints with medieval fervor, and Nevsky's relics had made the Holy Trinity Cathedral a place of pilgrimage. Then, in 1922, armed Soviet Chekists (forerunners of the KGB) seized the bones. The relics passed sixty-seven years in the secret police's oubliette. On June 3, 1989, Metropolitan Aleksey Ridiger of Leningrad signed the documents that recovered them for the church; the minister of culture signed for the Russian Republic. The *Journal of the Moscow Patriarchate* reported the event in a short article, which includes three black-and-white photographs; Ridiger sits at a table with the Russian official surrounded by beaming prelates. The transfer took place in the "Museum of Atheism," known in pre-Soviet times as the Kazan Cathedral. This imposing neoclassical building, completed in 1811 and boasting a full 364 feet of curving colonnade, is barely half a mile from the Admiralty along the Nevsky Prospekt (see figure 2.2).

But what happened moments after the reliquary was physically handed over was equally significant. Ridiger marched to the spot in the cathedral where stands the marble tomb of Mikhail Kutuzov, one of only four people in Russian history to hold all four classes of the Order of St. George, and victor in 1812 over Napoleon in what the Russians call the "Patriotic War." Holding the reliquary, he announced to the startled crowd that he would lead them in singing "Eternal Memory." Furthermore, the rendition would be dedicated to every soldier who had fallen in the defense of the motherland. Soviet television carried the entire event live: a number of officers could be seen in full uniform standing in the enormous throng. The cameras record a visible wave of genuine emotion rippling through the crowd

Figure 2.2 The magnificent Cathedral of the Kazan Icon of the Mother of God, in Soviet times a "Museum of Atheism" but reconsecrated in 1991 as a jewel of Orthodoxy, dominates St. Petersburg's Nevsky Prospekt. (Photo credit: Liudmila Kiselyova)

as this unscheduled event occurred. There is nothing quite like the effect of Russian sacred music. The long, sustained notes in the lower voices sound like organ pedal tones, over which the upper voices dispatch a haunting melodic line. As the severely rich a cappella voices swelled inside the cathedral, the somber yet triumphant mood of this piece, the traditional Russian Orthodox burial hymn, came through powerfully. And no one in the crowd was more visibly affected than the officers and soldiers of the Red Army.

Ridiger's superb stage management of the handover ceremony proved to be a harbinger of the church's resurgence under his guidance. His selection of Alexander Nevsky's relics as the first to be recovered was itself no accident. Alexander Nevsky is not only a Russian Orthodox saint; he is also the most celebrated military leader in Russian history, honored even more than General Zhukov, the only Soviet general never to have lost a battle in World War II; or Kutuzov, victor over Napoleon's "Grande armée." Russian boys, like boys everywhere, love to play with toy soldiers. Their armies frequently contain more of Nevsky's miniature mailed and helmeted men-at-arms than Kutuzov's cavalry or the Red Army's Ivans.

But Nevsky's heroic glamour appeals not merely to children. Only two years after he had defeated the Swedes on the banks of the Neva, Nevsky rallied the Russians to rout a German invader. In 1242 Nevsky crushed the Teutonic Knights on the ice of Lake Peipus in modern day Estonia. The Russians believe that Nevsky's defeat of the Teutonic Knights shows divine purpose and prefigures the Red Army's 1945 victory over their descendants: the Wehrmacht. Hitler himself had initiated the parallel by code-naming his World War II invasion of the Soviet Union "Barbarossa" after the twelfth-century Holy Roman Emperor Frederick I, who tried to impose Roman Catholicism upon the Slavs with fire and the sword. Indeed, the largest crusader army ever assembled prior to the Fourth Crusade of 1202 was that of the "red beard" German emperor, who put together about twenty thousand knights and up to eighty thousand support personnel to attack the Russian Orthodox in Pskov and Novgorod.[17]

Stalin turned the Barbarossa parallel back on the Germans in his speech at the famous Red Square parade of November 7, 1941, arguably the darkest moment of the Russo-German war. After Metropolitan Aleksy of Leningrad's address to Muscovites on August 10, 1941 (as detailed in chapter 1), the Red Army rallied and fought on, even at the cost of losing 600,000 men (killed, wounded, and taken prisoner) at the twin battles of Vyazma-Bryansk on the approaches to Moscow. The way seemed paved for Panzers to capture the city. Stalin's speech ended with the stirring exhortation: "May the courageous image of our great forbears inspire you in this War; Alexander Nevsky, Dimitry

Donskoi, Kuzma Minin, Dimitry Pozharsky, Alexander Suvorov, Mikhail Kutuzov! May the victorious banner of great Lenin overshadow you!"[18] His catalog of Russia's greatest leaders opens with the name of Alexander Nevsky.

Although Stalin hated Russian Orthodoxy with the unique insider knowledge of a former seminarian, the dictator did create one military order on
the old tsarist model. In 1943, at the height of the Russo-German war, he
fashioned the Order of St. Prince Alexander Nevsky to reinforce the message
of the famous Eisenstein film. He had ordered Eisenstein's movie shelved in
1939 during the period of friendly cooperation with the Germans (i.e., the
Nazi-Soviet Non-Aggression Pact, signed August 23, 1939). Now he ordered
it screened throughout the country. It shows the heavily armored German
knights and their horses crashing through the ice of Lake Peipus, while the
more lightly clad Russians nimbly outmaneuver them. It made a visceral im-
pression on the Soviet population and the Red Army. When the Red Army
crossed into Germany, the soldiers celebrated their arrival with a sack of the
town of Hohensalza that began on January 20, 1944, and lasted three days.
On the pockmarked walls of its houses they painted this graffiti: "He who
comes to us with the sword, shall perish by the sword." The words are taken
directly from the movie's last scene, when Nevsky utters them to his troops.[19]

Ridiger had grown up in Estonia; his official vita from the Russian Orthodox Church emphasizes that he served as an altar boy at the Alexander Nevsky
Cathedral in Tallinn. He has publicly reminisced in interviews about that
time when he was a fifteen-year-old boy, and the Red Army retook Estonia
and reopened the cathedral of which he became the sexton. But even without
the personal interest, Nevsky's bones were a brilliant choice for the first set of
relics to be returned to the ROC. By 1989 the Red Army's stature had taken a
battering in Afghanistan. The Soviet Union had invaded December 26, 1979,
using as pretext that the Afghan satrap, Babrak Karmal, had requested "fraternal assistance." The ensuing civil war killed more than a million Afghan
civilians; the Red Army casualties totaled more than 13,000 soldiers dead and
a much larger number wounded. All the bloodshed came to naught when
Soviet troops began to leave in May 1988. The last divisions left February 15,
1989, that is, just a few months before the June 3 handover.

It is intriguing to speculate on how Ridiger persuaded the KGB to return
Nevsky's bones to the church. One can reasonably infer that the Red Army's
morale would be boosted (given its recent humiliations in Eastern Europe as
well) by saluting the memory of the country's greatest military hero. When
he led the cathedral audience in singing "Eternal Memory" at the tomb of
Kutuzov, pointedly dedicated to *all* soldiers "who had fallen in defense of the

Motherland," his gesture was immediately understood by the Red Army to be an accolade for its sacrifice in Afghanistan. In contrast, the party had resolutely ignored those casualties—indeed, it had purposely hidden the carnage from public view by concealing the wounded in East German hospitals.[20]

After the handover of the casket and the singing of "Eternal Memory," Ridiger led the procession of clergy out of the "Museum of Atheism" to the Holy Trinity Cathedral. The cameras kept rolling, filming the pageant all the way up to the iconostasis, where he celebrated the Divine Liturgy to honor the relics. With his own hands he placed the relics back in the exact spot where they had lain until 1922. Soviet television brought into millions of Russian apartments the spectacle of the immense crowd, the beautiful service, and the palpable connection between the medieval military commander and the contemporary Red Army. It was a huge success, all masterminded by Ridiger when he was still metropolitan of Leningrad, and at a moment (June 3, 1989) when, whatever reforms Gorbachev had promised, the writ of the CPSU still governed the country.

Already Ridiger sensed that the military could be his ally. At the time the KGB agreed to give the relics back, it could hardly have foreseen that the first link in a chain of "restorations" was being forged, a chain that would eventually help throttle the coup the KGB and party hard-liners attempted August 19–21, 1991. Orchestrating the return of the Nevsky relics would turn out to be the opening salvo in the future patriarch's successful campaign to forge a close relationship with the soldiers and officers of the Red Army, a relationship bypassing party control.

Patriarch Pimen, elderly and frail, could do little to follow up on these opportunities. But on June 6–7, 1990, shortly after Pimen's death, Aleksey Ridiger was elected his successor. According to Dimitry Pospielovsky, a respected Western scholar on the ROC, all diocesan bishops possessing Soviet citizenship who were at least forty years of age were eligible to become patriarch. On the first day, after several rounds of voting, the number of candidates was reduced to three. The next day, after two more rounds, Ridiger had more than 50 percent of the votes.[21] On June 10, 1990, he was enthroned Aleksy II, patriarch of Moscow and All Russia.

Aleksey Ridiger had shown that he was a loyal son of the KGB as well as a sophisticated diplomat in the Soviet Union's peace campaign. But one of the crucial weaknesses of the Soviet system was ideological blindness. It ignored the fact that people can, and do, change. As Aleksy II, Ridiger immediately enlarged the scope of his campaign to recover church property. Given the triumph of the recovery of the Nevsky relics, the newly minted patriarch wanted more bones back. And as a serving officer of the KGB for more than thirty years, he knew, quite literally, where in his own diocese of Leningrad the skeletons were buried.

With no hint of irony, the *Journal of the Moscow Patriarchate* makes the point that Aleksy's tenure as patriarch has witnessed an amazing number of rediscoveries of relics: his reign "has been marked by great events in the life of the Russian Orthodox Church. It turned out that the St. Petersburg Cathedral of the Kazan Icon of the Mother of God (formerly the Museum of Atheism) had for many years been the place where many Orthodox relics were hidden under a bushel."[22] But had it just "turned out" that way? The skeptical might take a more jaundiced view of this remarkable series of coincidences. While the Soviet state announced to the world and to Russian Orthodox believers that Orthodox bones were lost, the secret police of the USSR did not "lose" things. It considered as "state property" all items its myrmidons seized. This meant that they were carefully logged in and locked away in a secret closet. The KGB was particularly careful when "losing" human beings. Witness the decades of denial by the Soviet hierarchy that it knew anything about the death of Raoul Wallenberg, the Swedish diplomat who had saved thousands of Jews in Hungary at the end of World War II. The KGB arrested him in 1945, but the Soviet Union told the world that he had "disappeared" without a trace. And there matters stood for decades. Then, not long after he became general secretary of the CPSU, in a gesture to Sweden, Mikhail Gorbachev announced that, lo, the personal effects of Raoul Wallenberg had been found and would be handed over, along with a copy of the diplomat's death certificate issued in a KGB prison.

The sudden rediscovery of the personal effects (the modern equivalent of medieval relics) of Wallenberg should explain to the Western observer how it happened that, as soon as Aleksy became patriarch, the KGB's "closet" in Leningrad began to empty out its stolen Orthodox bones. Aleksy's stage management of the rediscovery of relics in his former bailiwick made scarcely a ripple in the Western press. But it illustrates a former KGB agent's masterful manipulation of proprietary knowledge. He knew the Cheka had carefully packed the relics of many Orthodox saints into the basement of the city's "Museum of Atheism." He had only to wait and gauge when the time was ripe to orchestrate their rediscovery. In the summer 1990 he was patriarch at the floodtide of Gorbachev's glasnost and perestroika: the moment had come for a series of miracles.

St. Prince Alexander Nevsky's relics had been a savvy choice as the first candidate. The next sets of bones "rediscovered" in the same basement were those of innocuous hermits of the Solovki ascetic tradition: Zosima, Savvaty, and Gherman.[23] By recovering the remains of the Solovki hermit saints, Aleksy sent the message that the Orthodox Church would no longer countenance the use of its property as part of the Soviet penal system. Solovki was the most northerly monastery on the planet. It had been founded in 1436, the furthest reach of a great explosion of monastic expansion that had begun under Sergius of Radonezh. Sergius's followers always moved north, as they could not expand to the west without encountering Catholicism; neither could they go east or south without encountering Islam. By 1397 they had monastic communities 300 miles north of Moscow and, with the founding of the great monastery of Solovki, they were 600 miles north of the city.[24] The Soviet state seized the complex in the 1920s and turned it into one of its earliest camps, even before the Gulag system got established under Stalin. Because of their remoteness, their fortifying walls, and their small cells, the secret police coveted Orthodox monasteries. Once seized, they turned out or murdered the nuns and priests, then converted the cells into units of the largest police state in the world. Ancient and lovely structures became penitentiaries, reformatories, jails, and holding pens, such as at Yaroslavl, where prisoners were immured before being formally sentenced to slave labor in the Siberian Gulag. At the height of the Stalinist terror, millions of unfortunates were incarcerated in these prison-monasteries.

Finally, Aleksy orchestrated the "miracle" of the rediscovery of the bones of the nineteenth-century hermit St. Seraphim of Sarov (born Prokhor Moshnin, 1755–1833). St. Seraphim was a celebrated member of the Russian ascetic movement, one of those extraordinary monks who spent years alone in silence. He finally emerged from fifteen years of total silence to become a spiritual guide to the convent of Diveyevo and agreed to meet with the stream of pilgrims at his door.

By 1990 St. Seraphim had become the most important saint in the ROC calendar after St. Sergius of Radonezh. He would play a special role in Aleksy's struggle with the monarchist elements in the ROC because he was canonized at the specific request of Tsar Nicholas II, whom the monarchists now wanted to canonize in turn.

Seraphim's fame in helping barren women to conceive—or mothers of daughters to give birth to sons—caught the attention of Nicholas II and his wife Alexandra. For ten years since their 1894 marriage, the tsarina had given birth only to daughters. Each was beautiful and healthy, but the tsar had no heir. Tsar Paul (d. 1801), who hated his mother, Catherine the Great, had changed the constitution so that no woman could inherit the throne— hence, the couple's desperate quest for a son. After the birth of their fourth daughter Anastasia, in 1900, the tsar and tsarina began to meet with a

French charlatan who styled himself Monsieur Philippe. Although Philippe had been prosecuted in France for practicing medicine without a license, he convinced the tsarina that she would become pregnant with an heir if she followed his instructions. (In one of her letters to the tsar, Alexandra confides that Father Philippe has given her a little bell that would ring when evil persons come near her.) In 1902 Alexandra believed she had conceived. She gained weight and her menses ceased.[25] The tsar refused to listen to agents of his own secret police, the Okhrana, who insisted that Philippe was an imposter. Indeed, as related in the diary of Grand Duke Konstantin Konstantinovich in August 1902, "politically unfavorable reports about Filippov [Philippe] were received from our main secret-police agent in Paris, and . . . the tsar ordered the dismissal of this agent within 24 hours, which left the whole of the Okhrana in a most difficult position, the agent apparently being in possession of all information relating to political criminals."[26] After Alexandra's menses restarted, doctors told the couple that there never had been a pregnancy. The circumspect doctors, who dared not diagnose "hysteria," attributed all the symptoms to "anaemia."

Father Philippe was packed off back to France, infuriating the tsarina. But before he left, he informed the couple that if she sought the intercession of "St. Seraphim of Sarov," then she would bear a son. The records of the Orthodox Church were canvassed—there was no such saint. But there had once been a monk at the monastery of Sarov who had taken the name "Seraphim" and was reputed to be able to perform miracles. Therefore, in 1903, the tsar and tsarina ordered him canonized. It was useless for the procurator of the Holy Synod to object on the grounds that when his bones were exhumed, neither the "local bishop, nor the Metropolitan of St. Petersburg confirmed their incorruption."[27] By 1903 Orthodoxy had become so completely the instrument of the state that the tsar could do, as the tsarina herself said, "anything."

The tsar, tsarina, and all four of their daughters attended the rites. The tsar carried the heavy solid silver reliquary containing the saint's bones throughout the three circumambulations of the cathedral—he refused to be relieved, though the much taller grand dukes each took only a single circuit. The empress stood throughout the entire three and a half hour service, despite her poor health. Their trust was confirmed when the longed for tsarevich, Aleksey Nikolayevich, was born a year later (July 30, 1904 old style [o.s.]).

After the canonization, tens of thousands of pilgrims flocked to the Diveyevo Convent to be cured of their ailments. Soon there were publicized a number of miracle cures—for barrenness, for lameness, for poor sight, and so on—which enhanced the reputation of the saint's relics for being "healing." The bulk of the Russian peasantry lived at that time with toothache, earache, rheumatism, arthritis, and the effects of malnutrition and poor hygiene. The lack of medical technology—few hospitals, no disinfectants, no antiseptics, few efficacious drugs—meant that most ordinary people saw a saint's relics as the best hope for relief from their ailments. They believed the power of relics came from heaven. Saints do not decay—their relics, which could be touched and venerated, were directly linked to heaven's incorruptibility. The tsar's diary entry affirming another "cure" as Seraphim's relics were processed attests to his conviction that relics can heal.

Because of their simultaneous link with the Romanov dynasty and the peasantry's faith, the Soviet regime had targeted Seraphim's relics very early. In December 1920 a commission headed by a Comrade Gudkov arrived at Diveyevo. His soldiers forcibly exhumed the saint's bones to show the "ignorant masses" (the phrase is Gudkov's, from his official report to the Cheka) that they were being cheated, for the saint's body was not "completely undecayed." Therefore the Orthodox phrase "incorruptible remains" (*netlennye moshchi*) was a lie. The monks protested to no avail that this was a "biased concept, [which] accuses[s] the representatives of the Orthodox Church of a crime which cannot be proved in any way."[28] The Communist Party Commission unceremoniously removed the skeleton from its reliquary and "uncovered" it to the populace. Stubbornly, the peasants clung to their faith in the healing power of bones (decayed or not). Indeed, the very next year they petitioned the local "executive committee" for permission to use them in a procession of the cross.[29] The party refused, with what disgust may well be imagined.

Given this level of recalcitrance among the "ignorant masses," more stringent efforts were necessary. If the peasantry still revered St. Seraphim's relics, the party would make them, the monastery, the nuns, and the priests disappear. In 1933 the entire Diveyevo Convent was seized by Stalin's government, its nuns driven out, and its physical riches—plate, icons, silver, relics—seized by armed soldiers. The monks were simply put on a barge in the nearby river, which was then sunk. As for the relics of St. Seraphim, they vanished. They were not seen again for seventy years, when Aleksy succeeded in having them returned.

But the memory of St. Seraphim had not died in the popular consciousness. Famine struck. Secular historians see the Volga Famine, estimated to have cost ten million lives between 1920 and 1923, as a direct result of the dislocations in the food supply resulting from the Russian Civil War, which broke out immediately after World War I. The struggle between the Red and White armies, with bands of armed partisans sweeping back and forth across the breadbasket of the country, disrupted everything—planting, harvesting, reaping, storing, and transporting grain. Russian peasants had their own explanation. As the *Journal of the Moscow Patriarchate* recalled in 1991, "It is specifically with the desecration of the holy relics of St. Serafim of Sarov that people's Orthodox consciousness connects the famine in the Volga Region."[30]

Aleksy knew that Seraphim's mysterious predictions on the future of Russia had been seared into the Orthodox popular memory. The hermit had predicted that the country would pass through a time of great torment, but would find once again the path of "great glory." Gorbachev had unwittingly unleashed long suppressed spiritual longing and hopes, which had percolated beneath the surface of Soviet power. The rediscovery of the bones of St. Seraphim became the catalyst for consequences that the KGB, Mikhail Gorbachev, and perhaps even Aleksy himself did not foresee.

The deacon of the Cathedral of the Dormition of the Mother of God and All Saints in London assessed the impact of their "wondrous" recovery. This is the most important Russian Orthodox shrine in England, part of the Sourozh diocese, the country's sole ROC diocese recognizing the authority of the Moscow Patriarchate.[31] Its deacon explained the explosion in the cult: "St. Seraphim is associated with the recovery and resurrection of Orthodoxy itself in Russia. This results from how and when his relics were rediscovered." He gave a succinct description from the Russian Orthodox perspective:

> In 1933, when Stalin ordered the closing of the Seraphim-Diveyevo Nunnery [in Sarov] and all the women banished, the holy relics disappeared as well. They were found concealed in a suitcase in a dusty closet in the basement of what had been the Kazan Cathedral [in Leningrad] and had been named by the unbelievers, the "Museum of Atheism." They were found in December 1990.[32]

The London Cathedral of the Dormition has an exceptionally close relationship with Aleksy himself. It is worth noting that Aleksy's first trip abroad, two months after the defeat of the August 19–21, 1991, coup, was to England. He had been invited by the archbishop of Canterbury. There he honored the London Cathedral by laying the cornerstone of its new religious education building adjacent to the sanctuary.

At that ceremony, he presented the cathedral with a precious gift: an exquisite icon of St. Seraphim, on which was applied a beautiful enamel badge within which a crystal displayed a tiny relic of the saint himself. The painted panel of the icon was covered with a gold *oklad* (a decorative border) studded with jewels and outlined in rows of pearls. Small apertures cut in the gold sheet allow the viewer to see the face of the saint. At the 2003 service for St. Olga (grandmother of St. Vladimir and the first member of the Slavic nobility to accept Christianity), Orthodox worshipers reverently venerated and kissed it. The fact that Aleksy brought this church a true relic of St. Seraphim on the occasion of laying the cornerstone of the cathedral's modern addition shows his ability to operate simultaneously in two time frames. With equal ease he could reach back into the deep Orthodox memory, while at the same moment, he could look forward. And all the while, he was improving the international ties between the Moscow Patriarchate and the Anglican community (not to mention the émigré Russian Orthodox community in London). Aleksy had spent years honing his diplomatic skills on the global front on behalf of the KGB. Now he was putting those skills to use for his church.

The donation to a London cathedral of an icon containing a minuscule bone of St. Seraphim caused a dynamic upsurge in that congregation's numbers and energy; the finding of the entire skeleton caused a sensation in Russia itself. The leading Soviet newspaper, *Izvestia*, covered it as important news, itself a sign that change was in the air. The actual handing over of the relics to the patriarch took place on January 11, 1991, in the same basement of the former Kazan Cathedral where just eighteen months earlier as metropolitan he had recovered the bones of St. Prince Alexander Nevsky.[33] The ensuing year and a half had seen the first swells of a sea change: the "Museum of Atheism" had changed its name to the "Museum of the History of Religion," a telling indication of the new dispensation. As with Nevsky's bones, the handover of Seraphim's relics was carried live on radio and television and also covered in the press.[34] These again were significant privileges; until the 1987–88 millennial celebrations, the Soviet authorities had maintained an extremely strict control over the media. But Aleksy now had powerful friends in Soviet television and radio, as well as the press, and they were pushing the glasnost boundaries.

From the moment Aleksy received the relics in his own hands, he began to make them a magnet for the sense that the Russian nation itself was reviving—breaking out of the Soviet straightjacket that had restricted it for seventy years. Inextricably, this energy entwined with the thrill of rediscovering the bones of a hermit. Only a day after getting them back, Aleksy received permission to televise his celebration of the Divine Liturgy in Leningrad's Trinity Cathedral of St. Aleksander Nevsky's Lavra. Just as they had done eighteen months earlier for the relics of St. Prince Alexander Nevsky, the faithful and the merely curious squeezed into the packed basilica.

Afterward, at a reception for the archpastors and clergy of the city, Aleksy described how the miracle had come into being:

> At our very first meeting with the director of the Museum of the History of Religion we came to an agreement that, being holy treasures, the relics should be returned to the Church. The first such treasures to have

been returned to the Church were the relics of the Orthodox Prince St. Aleksander Nevsky. Soon after, relics of Sts. Zosima, Savvaty and Gherman of Solovki were handed over to the Church. It was believed that there were no other relics in the museum. But in connection with a planned removal of the museum from the Cathedral of the Kazan Icon of the Mother of God, its workers inspected anew the museum's stocks and in the room where tapestries were stored they discovered relics sewed in bast matting [coarse, woven cloth similar to a feed sack, used for peasant shoes]. When these were opened, they saw an inscription on the glove which read, "Saintly father Seraphim, pray to God for us!" ... The relics were not totally incorrupted.[35]

This description includes a brief and modest recapitulation of Aleksy's other triumphs in relic recovery. It also illustrates his diplomacy. He begins by acknowledging the museum staff as church allies, not adversaries, in the recovery of church property.

Aleksy mentions almost in passing a "planned removal" *of the museum itself from the cathedral*. This deliberately casual allusion, buried in a dependent clause and thus easily missed, conceals an epic saga. Having turned the Kazan Cathedral into a "Museum of Atheism," Soviet planners installed dioramas of the torture chambers of the Catholic Inquisition and leg irons worn by recalcitrant monks of Russian Orthodox monasteries. As part of its virulent antireligion campaign, official Intourist guides and state "atheist workers" (i.e., paid teachers of Marxism-Leninism) led tourists and schoolchildren past these lurid chambers, which had all the ghoulish appeal of a high-octane Madame Tussaud's in London. In 1955, soon after Stalin's death, Truman Capote toured these exhibits when he accompanied the first Western troupe staging *Porgy and Bess* in the Soviet Union. He noted in his witty memoir, *The Muses are Heard*, that Soviet children were wide-eyed at the torture exhibits, finding them exciting and alluring.

Now the dioramas of the faggots and stake, the iron instruments of pain, the gleeful tormentors and their hapless victims were swept away, flotsam and jetsam of the Orthodox hurricane. The museum staff would have to set up shop elsewhere, and the "Cathedral of the Kazan Icon of the Mother of God" would be reconsecrated as a jewel of the Russian Orthodox Church. Aleksy was too smart to brag openly, but clergy and believers understood his seemingly offhand allusion to the "planned removal of the museum from the cathedral" to signal an important victory. Aleksy had ended his remarks by noticing that the bones "were not totally incorrupted." This alluded to the obvious fact that the skeleton had somewhat decayed, which is not supposed to happen to saints' remains, according to church dogma. But clearly this would not be permitted to delay Aleksy's plans. He organized and personally led a pilgrimage as the bones were "translated" to the Diveyevo Convent in faraway Sarov.

Here recourse to a medieval lexicon and mind-set is necessary. "Translation" means moving a saint's skeleton from one place to another. Given how highly the bodies of saints were valued, the bones were occasionally bought and sold. Sometimes entire skeletons would be shifted around, carried shoulder-high in a solemn procession to a prepared site. Or only a sliver of bone in a reliquary would be put on a litter. So valuable were saint's bones that they were sometimes stolen—in the ninth century the Venetians stole the entire body of St. Mark from Alexandria in Egypt and installed it in a chapel built for that purpose. The result was vastly increased prosperity for the city.[36] The possession of holy relics lent prestige to a church and made it a center of pilgrimage. All this contributed mightily to the economy of the surrounding town.

Relics were the engines of economic growth in the Middle Ages.[37] Pilgrims bought souvenirs of their journey, and these mementos were manufactured not only by enterprising monks but by townspeople. To take but one case in England, at the time of Henry VIII's dissolution of the monasteries (1536–40), the monks of Canterbury Cathedral were still selling vials containing what they claimed was the "blood of St. Thomas-à-Becket," martyred in 1170. The townspeople made their own modest fortunes out of selling small tin-lead pilgrim badges, often shaped like the sword that had cut off the saint's head, proclaiming in Latin *Optimvs egrorvm medicvs fit thoma Bonorum*, that is, "St. Thomas is the best doctor of the worthy sick."[38] Even King Henry II (the man responsible for his murder) made money out of Thomas's corpse. He controlled the Limoges factories in France where the beautiful deep blue enamel reliquaries that housed these bone fragments were created. Every monastery in England wanted its own St. Thomas relic, and more than seventy of these twelfth-century caskets still exist. The great majority of the population believed implicitly in the cures attributed to the healing properties of relics. And those who did *not* experience a miracle cure for whatever ailed them usually kept that information to themselves. Lack of success was deemed a sign that the pilgrim was lacking sufficient belief and piety to benefit from the saint's powers. However, there is no mistaking the sincerity of these beliefs, no matter how unscientific the claims. They testify to an enduring longing for visible signs of divine intervention.

In the Soviet Union in 1991, even after more than seventy years of officially proclaimed "scientific atheism," the translation of the bones of Seraphim became the focus for eight months of ecstatic ceremonies blending nationalism with spiritual hunger. Seraphim was a native-born Russian saint. He had been the peasants' saint long before Tsar Nicholas II and his tsarina had taken notice of him. Now Russian pride bubbled up at each step, becoming a communal experience of profound joy. It was exciting, and totally unexpected; the formerly impossible was happening, and the Soviet version of CNN was covering it every day. Perhaps it all had something to do with the lure of forbidden fruit. The body of St. Seraphim had disappeared into a Soviet oubliette. Why had the Soviet state, the believers reasoned, gone to all that trouble, unless the body was truly powerful? The sensational finding of the relics had aroused expectations of further startling, very un-Soviet events. What would happen next?

First, the bones made a circuit within Leningrad itself. On February 6, 1991, the patriarch celebrated the Divine Liturgy in the Church of the Smolensk Icon of the Mother of God. Canon Michael Bourdeaux, president of Keston Institute, has personally heard Aleksy celebrate the liturgy and testifies that he is possessed of a melodious, powerful bass-baritone with a sympathetic ring to it. This makes his celebration of the Orthodox liturgy, which uses only the human voice as its instrument of praise, particularly beautiful and moving.[39] Aleksy repeated singing the liturgy as the relics were again transferred back to the St. Aleksander Nevsky Lavra. Just as on January 12, 1991, thousands of worshipers again packed the huge cathedral. Then the procession with St. Seraphim's relics moved from the cathedral to the railroad station. At its head were "crosses and banners ... then clerics went in festal vestments, and behind them the Icon of the Saint was carried. Following it were bishops carrying the steel reliquary of St. Seraphim. Behind the reliquary surrounded by deacons His Holiness the Patriarch walked leaning on his staff, and then—a continuous flow of believers with candles."[40] Traffic stopped; the believers in their thousands sang prayers, and then moved on to the railway station where a special car was waiting to take the clergy and the precious cargo to Moscow.

The "Red Arrow" train (pride of the Soviet railroad system) carried the reliquary to Moscow, while along the tracks believers bowed and prayed. At the Moscow station waited more bishops and monks, more banners, and more thousands of believers. Once again Aleksy headed the procession. Traffic came to a standstill, and then "hierarchs in turn" hoisted the reliquary on their shoulders. At the Patriarchal Cathedral of the Epiphany, yet another "festal prayer service" (moleben) was conducted, capped by a patriarchal oration to the faithful and the distribution to all of a St. Seraphim postcard. The relics rested in Moscow until July, a magnet not just for believers. Soldiers just mustered out, World War II veterans, and young families joined the priests and babushki.

Meanwhile, feverish preparations were being conducted in faraway Sarov at the Diveyevo Convent to restore the cathedral and make all ready once again to receive the saint. At the beginning of July 1991, the relics set off on their long journey from Moscow to their original home—a journey of more than six hundred miles. The procession of patriarch and clergy, with its beautiful banners and icons carried before the steel reliquary, gathered new energy every step of the way. The original solid silver coffin had disappeared, probably melted down by the rapacious state. The *Journal of the Moscow Patriarchate* reported that everyone on the pilgrimage believed that they were witnessing unprecedented events, in which "miracles and signs are given to us by God to see." After decades of carefully planned and controlled Soviet demonstrations and marches, people rushed about following their own desires. It was intoxicating to have this amount of freedom.

It is clear that people were *expecting* things—they were conditioned by the ecstatic services and the heightened emotions of the vast pilgrimage escorting the relics to look for signs and portents.[41] At each stage of the journey, at each Divine Liturgy, the faithful were coming out in thousands. Indeed, people who did not consider themselves to be believers were lining the highways as well. The patriarch would stop and mingle with crowds, praying with people who perhaps had come first out of curiosity. The translation tapped into a changing mood inside the Soviet Union that few westerners appreciated. Hardly any noticed the pilgrimage leaving for Sarov.[42]

The KGB was equally careless. The Soviet Union, like all totalitarian governments, had monitored and controlled public demonstrations. Its officials organized and choreographed the threatening *parady* of the latest rockets and other weaponry, and jolly *demonstratsii* of gymnasts, workers, and floats. Perhaps they were so inured to the "forc'd hossanahs" that Milton's Satan gripes about in *Paradise Lost* that they failed to recognize the genuine article. At any rate, no official attempts were made to halt the translation during the critical month of July 1991. From Moscow through Noginsk, Orekhovo-Zuyevo, Vladimir, Bogolyubovo, Vyazniky, Nizhny Novgorod, on it went, a land cruise picking up more pilgrims in its wake. As the procession crossed the vast landscape, more and more "miracles" happened. During this month, Aleksy gave some fourteen speeches about the recovery of the relics of St. Seraphim. As subsequent events proved, he believed them.

Leading this enormous procession placed him at the center of a popular groundswell of emotion. Sarov itself was a restricted city. Originally, the patriarch believed that they would not be allowed to enter where the saint's hut had actually stood. A nuclear research institute, the forbidding Arzamas 16, surrounded the sacred spot. Arzamas 16 (even the name sent chills, implying it had at least fifteen clones) was one of the most secret locations of the Soviet Union. In 1949 Soviet scientists built their first atomic bomb there. Entry was strictly controlled. Arzamas was staffed by scientists who put their faith in the state's official ideology of "scientific atheism." Yet somehow, somewhere, someone opened a door and the patriarch led the procession into the forbidden zone.

And here, as if by magic, at atheism's "ground zero," the believers witnessed another miracle. On July 30, 1991, the patriarch was presented with an icon of St. Seraphim that had been saved and hidden by an elderly believer.[43] As he received it from the wrinkled hands of the old woman, the patriarch commented on how much of the church's property was being restored: "Monasteries are being returned, churches are being returned, holy relics are being returned, and also holy icons. Here today we witness the return of the holy icon of St. Seraphim of Sarov, which the cleaning woman, Maria Fedorovna Savvanina, preserved for 41 years."

He went on to say that she was nearly eighty years old and that "she had decided to donate the holy icon to the Diveyevo Convent. This icon, which was the work of the sisters of Diveyevo, is being returned to the place where it was created." The connotations of the return of the icon reinforced the general sense that time was turning around, and a new age was beginning.

As the relics were deposited in the Diveyevo Convent the next day, the patriarch reinforced those expectations. He made a statement that caused a stir in the audience. Because the event was carried live on Soviet television, his words spread throughout the Soviet Union: "The last page of the Diveyevo chronicle has been turned and the time has come for prophecies to come true." Had anyone paid attention in Western academe, the patriarch's words would have been as opaque as the moving finger's "MENE, MENE, TEKEL, UPHARSIN" at Belshazzar's feast (Daniel 5:25). But Orthodox believers understood his meaning and were uplifted by his promise. The "Diveyevo chronicle" is an actual document—it was assembled by Leonid Chichagov, an officer in Tsar Nicholas I's artillery who became a parish priest and then entered the monastic clergy to become Archimandrite Seraphim. He took the name Seraphim because of his utter devotion to the hermit. Even before Seraphim died in 1833, Archimandrite Seraphim had begun collecting every scrap of testimony related to Seraphim's healings and recorded it all in some forty notebooks. Given that the archimandrite recorded the peasants' comments verbatim, these notebooks are unique data of the actual speech patterns of a group normally voiceless in the record.

But the notebooks have more than a linguistic significance. Compiled as the Diveyevo Chronicle, they were printed in 1898 and then reprinted in 1903 by the Holy Synod as part of the canonization ceremonies. There were many reprints until the Bolshevik coup of 1917, at which time the Diveyevo Chronicle was officially forgotten. The memory had been driven underground, kept alive by oral transmission, and thus had taken on the connotations of hidden treasure. In alluding to the Diveyevo Chronicle, Aleksy was focusing the attention of his audience upon a part of its history that had been once erased—in effect, letting it in on a secret, long buried, and eagerly awaited. It was as if Pope John Paul II were using the occasion to reveal the "Third Secret of Fatima."

Having thus set up his audience's expectations, Aleksy promised that the time had come "for prophecies to come true." These words, uttered at this precise moment and at this location had a special resonance for Russian Orthodox believers. Believers immediately understood that he was alluding to Seraphim's "Letter to the Future" (about which more later), in which he had promised: "The Lord will have mercy on Russia and lead it along the path of suffering to great glory."[44] Though this prophecy had not been reprinted since 1903, the Russian Orthodox community still cherished it. This was confirmed years later, when in an important article issued on the centenary of the canonization (2003) an Orthodox prelate reiterated that this, the last of Seraphim's prophecies, was clung to as a subterranean hope during the seven decades of church persecution: "During the tragic years of our history [i.e., the entire Soviet period] believers recalled the saint's prophecy."[45] In July 1991 that hope was surfacing. Many Russians believed that the modest hermit Seraphim was a Russian Nostradamus, the voice who could "explain" all the heartbreak of the twentieth century and point the way to a glorious future. Aleksy's deliberate allusion to Seraphim's prophecies resonated. His words raised people's longing that life would change for the better.

It is crucial to remember the context in which the translation of Seraphim's relics occurred. The Soviet Union had emphasized to its citizens that their country was a superpower. It controlled Eastern Europe, and simultaneously it was leading the world toward global Communism. Two pillars held up this myth: The Warsaw Pact and COMECON, the economic treaty that required Warsaw Pact countries to accept Soviet rubles as if they were real money. Just thirty days before the relics were to arrive at Diveyevo Convent, however, both crashed. On July 1, 1991, the Warsaw Pact dissolved. This "Treaty of Friendship, Cooperation and Mutual Assistance" had been signed on May 14, 1955, in the capital of Poland to create the Soviet Union's counterweight to the West's North Atlantic Treaty Organization (NATO). Seven Eastern European states signed, along with the Soviet Union: Albania, Bulgaria, Czechoslovakia, East Germany, Hungary,

Poland, and Romania. The key provision of the pact allowed the USSR the right to continue stationing its troops in those countries, thus ensuring obedience to Soviet power. In 1956 the government of Hungary expressed the determination to withdraw from the pact, but the pact had given the USSR the legal cover it needed to intervene. Its tanks suppressed the revolt, killing a number of unarmed civilians in Budapest. The Soviet Union again invoked the Warsaw Pact in 1968 when it moved troops from Poland, East Germany, Hungary, and Bulgaria into Czechoslovakia to smash a rebellion of its satellite regime in Prague. The Warsaw Pact was renewed in 1975 and again in 1985, and Soviet citizens regarded it as the visible proof of their country's status as the sole equal to the United States. It disbanded, ironically, and from the Soviet perspective, humiliatingly, in Prague, Czechoslovakia, the very location where the "Prague spring" had been crushed by Red Army tank treads in 1968. Now the bonds that had held Eastern Europe in Soviet captivity snapped.

On the very same July 1, 1991, COMECON, the economic pact that had bound all Warsaw Pact countries together and allowed Soviets to use rubles to purchase goods from Eastern Europe, also dissolved. Based upon anecdotal evidence, probably 85 percent of the purchasing power of the ruble also disappeared that same day. Ironically, Gorbachev's perestroika campaign stigmatized as "the time of stagnation" the very years when COMECON was most favorable to Russians—the eighteen years under Leonid Brezhnev. Muscovites still recalled with nostalgia those halcyon days when they could buy from shelves stocked with East European foodstuffs. Now COMECON was gone, and with it Eastern European consumer products. Russians lamented that they would no longer be able to buy Hungarian shoes, Polish office equipment (including computers), Yugoslav pharmaceuticals, or Bulgarian jam and leather jackets. The net effect of losing both the Warsaw Pact and COMECON was disastrous to Soviet power and the Soviet standard of living. The strutting Socialist Realist statues of the New Soviet Man now seemed a sick joke.

The Soviet Union's facade as a superpower on the world stage was cracking. As the Red Army left its comfortable billets in Eastern Europe and headed back to the USSR, East European citizens made known their ingratitude for having been "liberated" from Nazi tyranny by the Red Army 1944–45. Russians, who remembered the huge numbers of casualties suffered by their soldiers on the march to Berlin, were surprised to see how much their former satellites hated them. The prophecies of Communism—its predictions that eventually the whole world would turn to its revolution under the leadership of the USSR—lay in tatters.

This rapid fall in international prestige and domestic purchasing power was the context for the general sense of fear and disillusion. Little wonder that increasing numbers of Russians were seeking another set of prophecies, ones that held out hope, however amorphous, of better things to come, that promised that all the death and destruction had not been in vain. New and exhilarating feelings were emerging. The festal procession carrying the relics of St. Seraphim revived old dreams. Because few believed anymore in the utopia promised through "building Communism," Russians recalled the words of a beloved hermit. The patriarch had publicly referenced St. Seraphim's prediction that Russians would overcome their humiliations and rise to greatness once again. This was an exhilarating message, not from a political leader but a holy man, and Aleksy delivered it at just the right moment.

The church did its best to fulfill Seraphim's prophecies. The saint said his body would lie in Diveyevo and arrive there by air; so the church had flown the reliquary part of the way on an airplane. Seraphim declared that his bones would lie at Diveyevo at a time when Easter would be celebrated in summer—a calendrical impossibility. Modern technology allowed Seraphim's "by air" prediction to come true. The patriarch made Seraphim's "summer Easter" prediction come true, mystically. Throughout the festal translation of the relics, he greeted believers with the traditional Easter greeting, "Christ is risen!" At his sermon given in the Dormition Cathedral in the ancient town of Vladimir (July 24, 1991), the patriarch explained the anomaly: "St. Seraphim ... was the bearer of special Easter joy—the joy of the Resurrected Lord the Saviour. He welcomed those who came to see him with the words 'Christ is risen, my joy!' He prophesied the time when Easter is glorified in mid-summer. So today we sing Easter hymns, for his prophecy has come true."[46] On July 31 Aleksy lay the relics to rest; the next day, the Russian Orthodox Calendar added August 1 as the "Feast of St. Seraphim, the Miracle Worker of Sarov and All Russia" to its calendar. The KGB, if it noticed at all, apparently considered this a minor addition to the stream of glittering processions the church performed to occupy its time and display its vestments.

The KGB ignored the penultimate stop on the pilgrimage, at which a curious and surprising event had taken place. On July 28, 1991, the patriarch and his motorcade of church dignitaries and bishops paid a visit to the 31st Vistula Armored Division in Nizhny Novgorod. The patriarch listened attentively while new recruits took their oath. After his address, as the *Journal of the Moscow Patriarchate* relates, "faithful soldiers approached His Holiness the Patriarch for his blessing and he presented them with small icons of St. Seraphim." The next lines of the account are worth quoting in full:

> Then Major-General Yefremov, the commander of the Nizhny Novgorod garrison, spoke about his troops taking part in the translation of the relics. In two weeks time they had built two tent camps around Diveyevo Convent for 20 thousand pilgrims. Major-General Yefremov reported to the Patriarch that 10 tons of nails and 1,500 cubic meters of timber were spent to make tent foundations.... Many soldiers put questions to the clergy about the basic precepts of faith while some prayed during a *moleben*; for some of them this day could become the starting point on their way to the Church.[47]

Of course, this enthusiastic description was published in the official organ of the Moscow Patriarchate. But the general was not exaggerating. Actually, Yefremov was being rather modest about his division's contribution: the correspondent for *Izvestia* revealed in his article printed three days later, July 31, 1991, that, in addition to setting up the tent cities, the army had arranged a "field kitchen, lighting, a medical station and sanitary facilities" for the thousands of pilgrims who had made the long journey, some by walking, to Diveyevo.[48]

From the KGB's perspective, fissures in its hegemony were opening. It was bad enough that someone allowed the patriarch and the reliquary into Arzamas 16. But Major General Yefremov commanded an important armored division in an important city, and for two weeks his men had used their time and the Red Army's nails and lumber to build tents for pilgrims. As in all armies, the rumor mill is frequently the fastest form of communication. What happened at the 31st Vistula Armored Division likely got back to other tank divisions. In the battle for hearts and minds, the patriarch had made a successful sortie. One would have assumed that top officials in the KGB and the party were paying attention to this completely illegal use of state funds and personnel and that heads would roll forthwith. Instead, they were on vacation in the Crimea— just like Mikhail Gorbachev, president of the USSR. They had reached their positions of power by demonstrating skill at intrigue. Yet, like the Philistines mocking Samson in the Hall of Dagon, they failed to see that the roof was about to cave in and were stunned to discover that the former Aleksey Ridiger, recipient of an award for thirty years of devoted service, was no longer their creature. Indeed, as Aleksy II, patriarch of Moscow and All Russia, he would help pull down the pillars.

On Friday, August 30, 1991, only a week after the crucial events themselves, James Billington published a prescient op-ed piece in the *New York Times*.

There he spoke of the people's search for a "new Russian identity that seeks to move forward to a Western-type democracy and backward to the moral roots of their own religious and cultural tradition."[49] Billington showed remarkable foresight in defining the two issues facing Russians in the post-Soviet era. "Western-type" democracy still remains beyond the horizon, particularly under President Putin, Yeltsin's handpicked successor, who took power in 2000. But more than two-thirds of Russians consider themselves Orthodox, at least on questionnaires. The Russian Orthodox Church has expanded its impact throughout Russian society; it has recovered and restored much of its property. Freedom of conscience and religious belief is enshrined in Russian laws, even if those laws are not always applied fairly. The party is indeed over, and the patriarchate has triumphed in the war of state symbols.

But, however elating were the winds of change after August 1991, all was not well with the Russian Orthodox Church. Both within and without its monasteries, a series of crises loomed. One of the most obvious was that the ROC had been bankrupted by the Soviet state, which had plundered its artistic masterpieces and sold many of them off to the West. In an attempt to curry favor with Joseph Davies, the U.S. ambassador to the Soviet Union, secret police officers (then the NKVD) allowed his wife, the former Marjorie Meriwether Post, to buy for virtually nothing beautiful vestments and church vessels of gold and silver. All this may be admired by tourists at Hillwood House, her estate in northern Washington, D.C. Some of Russia's crown jewels were sold to her during this fire sale, including the small crown entirely of diamonds made especially for Alexandra to wear at Nicholas II's coronation. But the bulk of her purchases came from NKVD warehouses of Orthodox treasure. Hillwood guides tell visitors that gorgeous repoussé and chased Orthodox silver was sold to her at five cents a pound.[50] To her credit, she also saved a huge number of icons; some she ordered literally snatched from bonfires in the streets.

Stolen Orthodox masterpieces decorate other Western capitals as well. In London, Somerset House acquired a set of "royal doors" standing seven feet tall and made of solid silver. The British Museum bought—for the laughable pittance of $250,000, given its true value—the Codex Sinaiticus, the sole copy of the entire New Testament in uncial Greek. The monks of St. Catherine's Monastery in the Sinai Peninsula gave this irreplaceable treasure to Russia in tsarist times. The NKVD treated it as it did all Orthodox loot: to be warehoused, sold, or stored, at the state's pleasure. Once stripped to the bones, even the carcasses of churches were desecrated. Some were dynamited, but others were occupied and renovated for secular purposes. A favorite remodeling technique was to place toilets where once the altars had stood.

As devastating as was this litany of material problems, even more threatening were spiritual cancers. The church was riven by warring factions. There were official disagreements with the Ukrainian "Uniates," who claim to be Orthodox but, because they acknowledge the primacy of the Catholic pope, are considered "Greek Catholics" by the ROC itself. Khrushchev had banned them, his sole act remembered with Orthodox gratitude. Now newly relegalized after forty years, the Uniates were reasserting their property rights and taking back hundreds of churches from the Moscow Patriarchate. The Ukrainian Autocephalous Church (i.e., the church not acknowledging the authority of the Moscow Patriarchate) and the Russian Orthodox Church Abroad had seceded in early Soviet times. Seventy years of rancor was breaking out anew. And the KGB had struck another blow at the Moscow Patriarchate. It had placed its own agents within the ranks of its clergy. During the Brezhnev era, this strategy, code-named "Z," had been the party's chief tool to control and ultimately discredit the church. If freedom of information took hold, then some of this collaboration would become public.

Furthermore, glasnost handed Aleksy an alarming problem. The new freedom of the press allowed the ROC to reprint for the first time since tsarist days Seraphim's prophecies and the Diveyevo Chronicle.[51] But it also opened up the press to anti-Semites who had an explanation for all the depredations visited upon the Russian people during the Soviet period: it was the Jews' fault. Many of these people were also fervent Orthodox believers who wished for a return of a new "autocratic tsar"; it was no coincidence that the last two, Nicholas and his father Alexander III, had made Jews their favorite scapegoat. Now anti-Semites wished to co-opt the hermit's mysterious predictions and link them to *The Protocols of the Elders of Zion*, one of the most important and fateful forgeries in modern history. It was bad enough that *The Protocols* had been disseminated with the collusion of the tsarist church. What made it far worse was that the contemporary ROC had collaborators who sought to perpetuate that forgery. Aleksy wanted to use the veneration for St. Seraphim as positive energy to restore and rebuild, as he had on the translation pilgrimage of July 1991. He did not want it colluding in the disinformation campaign already taking shape–namely, that the saint's words forecast that the Jews had destroyed Orthodoxy and the Orthodox tsar. Here was a cancer that threatened disaster if it metastasized and took over the body and spirit of the whole church.

And if all this were not enough, the 1990 law on Freedom of Conscience had unexpected and most unwelcome consequences: it opened the borders of the USSR to foreign missionaries. Now legally free to proselytize, armed with the Bible in the Russian vernacular, and supplied by plenty of capitalist lucre, missionaries from the Assembly of God, Campus Crusade for Christ, Child Evangelism Fellowship, Christian and Missionary Alliance, Church of Christ, Church of the Nazarene, Greater Europe Mission, Salvation Army, Seventh-Day Adventists, Southern Baptist Convention, United World Mission, Wesleyan World Mission, Youth with a Mission—the list went on and on—were deplaning and trying to poach on Russia's patch. Even the Hare Khrishna monks and the Moonies were making converts by taking advantage of the same law as the ROC had done itself.

Plundered relics, destroyed churches, believers waxing nostalgic for a return to an "Orthodox tsar," "agents in cassocks," Orthodox fanatics baying for Jewish blood, professional missionaries from Western faiths and Eastern cults proselytizing the flock—how was Aleksy going to address this complicated list of issues? As the years since the August 1991 turning point have demonstrated, he does have an agenda. Of course, many of his decisions occurred ad hoc as one crisis after another loomed. But in retrospect, he seems to have anticipated most of those challenges. He has conducted two campaigns simultaneously. One is the internal battle. He had to neutralize that faction within his own ranks consisting of virulent anti-Semites and/or ardent monarchists. (The two groups overlap, though it is possible to be one without the other.) While that has been largely an in-house struggle, on the world's stage he has also led the drive to recover church property and prestige. Sometimes the internal battles have been in the forefront; sometimes the consecration of new or restored Orthodox churches or the return of holy icons or relics grabbed the headlines.

His underlying premise is that the Marxist-Leninist label of *Novy chelovek* (New Soviet Man or Woman) was an alien and false identity imposed on Russians. Ridding them of it would require the application of three ancient Russian Orthodox concepts: *ochishchenie* (cleansing) with the connotations of spiritual cleansing; *primirenie* (conciliation), itself a startling 180 degree turn from the Communist Party's favorite word, *beskompromissny"* (uncompromising); and *sobornost*, literally, "togetherness" but with the connotations of "spiritual unity."[52] Thus decontaminated, Russians were to emerge from the Soviet shell reborn as *pravoslavnye*—"true believers" and inhabitants of Holy Rus once again.

THREE

Rebuilding Holy Moscow

We shape our buildings, and afterwards
our buildings shape us.
—*Winston Churchill, May 10, 1941, after bombs struck the House of Commons*

THE SOVIET UNION DID MORE than ignore the warning, "The fool hath said in his heart, 'there is no God'" (Psalms 14:1). From the perspective of the Orthodox believer, it committed idolatry by substituting its symbols and ethos for those of the faith. Instead of "Christ is risen," it proclaimed that "Lenin lives!" "Scientific atheism" was state ideology. Heaven was brought down to earth in the form of the "workers' paradise." Christianity's First Parents gardened in the nude; the Bolshevik Adam and Eve "built Communism" wearing industrial overalls. An early cover of the magazine *Bezbozhnik* (*The Atheist*) portrays a muscled "New Soviet Man" mounting a ladder and carrying a huge hammer. Caricatures of Christ, Jehovah, Yahweh, Allah, and the Devil cower above the clouds. The caption reads: "We've settled accounts with the tsars on earth; now we'll deal with the tsars in heaven" (*S zemnymi tsaryami razdelalis, prinimaemsya za nebesnykh*). At the bottom, smokestacks of the coming utopia thrust up above the smashed cupolas and crosses of the tsarist "opiate of the masses"[1] (figure 3.1). After the Soviet Tower of Babel crashed, an enormous campaign to rebuild destroyed or derelict churches exploded. Much more than real estate was at stake. The ROC saw immediately that each rebuilt church would demonstrate the victory of Orthodoxy over godlessness. And in the process, the volunteers who provided much of the labor would change from *Tovarishchi* (Comrades) back into *Khristiane* (Christians).

The church began to recover its property tentatively in the mid-1980s on a case-by-case basis. Church restoration accelerated in 1987 and 1988, concurrent with the celebrations of the Millennium of the Baptism of Rus. One example can illustrate the changing landscape. Father Sergy Romanov had fallen afoul of the KGB early on in the 1980s: he was a priest without an approved "prayer building," and that meant in Soviet terms, he literally had nothing to do, because celebrating the liturgy in such a structure was the

Figure 3.1 The 1924 cover to *Bezbozhnik* (*The Atheist*) exemplifies early Soviet antireligious propaganda for the masses. A muscled "New Soviet Man" mounts a ladder, carrying a hammer to finish the "tsars of heaven" because the "tsars on earth" have been destroyed. (Photo credit: Archive of Keston Institute)

sole legal activity of a priest. But he took his calling seriously, so he secretly taught children the catechism and held services in private apartments. He had children prepare reports on religious themes. He celebrated holidays in the Orthodox calendar and organized children preparing plays to reenact the appropriate Bible story. This included writing a script, making scenery and costumes, learning lines, having dress rehearsals, and finally performing in a cramped Moscow apartment in front of proud parents. Then, as one parishioner reminisced, "After the play, we enjoyed a feast of all the special foods that are traditional for these holidays."

Until the 1990 Law on Freedom of Conscience, all these activities were strictly illegal. Everyone in the congregation knew they were risking unpleasant encounters with Soviet authorities. At any minute there could be a ring at the door and people could burst in and disrupt their activities. The great majority of the believers were prepared morally for whatever would take place: "Thanks be to the Lord that we did not suffer, although Father Sergy himself did undergo persecution." The state summoned him on a number of occasions and warned him that he should cease. Letters denouncing him were written. (No one in the congregation would ever address the subject of who wrote these letters.) These epistles accused him of holding evening services in private apartments and of having connections with dissidents. As punishment, the compliant church authorities rusticated him to the provinces. The believers explained with resignation: "It was done so that we would be deprived of his leadership. These were very difficult years. Nevertheless, though we had to travel a long distance to get to the church to which Father Sergy had been transferred, and though the church was very tiny and we were very cramped, we went."

Liberal trends initiated by Gorbachev eased the situation, and in 1988 the celebration of the Baptism of Rus allowed Father Sergy's return to Moscow. With the church authorities now on his side, he petitioned the Moscow City Council to get a "prayer building" returned, specifically the Church of St. Vladimir, a beautiful eighteenth-century structure close to the heart of the city (figure 3.2). The skirmish was won easily, but the war was not over, as Father Sergy admitted: "It took more than a year to get the official transfer of the church on paper and then physically to occupy the church building. The church was being used as a book depository by the state historical library. There was nowhere to move the books, so the people who worked there refused to leave."

As for the provenance of the mysterious books, Father Sergy noted that they "belonged to the Third Reich, and perhaps some of them came from Hitler's Chancellery. Our army brought them back from Berlin after the

Figure 3.2 Once a depository for a trophy library of books brought back to Moscow by the Red Army from Germany, now St. Vladimir's Russian Orthodox Church has been returned to the church and restored by an army of volunteers. (Photo credit: St. Vladimir's Russian Orthodox Church)

Nazis surrendered." St. Vladimir's housed one of the "trophy libraries" that remain to this day part of the legacy of the eastern front.[2]

The presence of one of these trophy libraries in what was now legally an ROC building initially handed Father Sergy a conundrum. The captured books were "state property." The library workers had to answer to their own superiors, and they had no place to take the books. The standoff seemed permanent. Then help, in the form of the head of the local unit of Moscow Power and Light, arrived. The man told Father Sergy that he himself was a believer and would see what he could do. He was as good as his word: he simply cut off both power and light to the book depository. After just one week of a Moscow winter, the staff, freezing in the dark, negotiated. The church had already been divided into two halves. Therefore, the state bureaucrats vacated the half with the cupola, pushing and shoving the books into the other half. They shelved whatever cataloging system had been used prior to the forced commingling as well. With books wedged floor to ceiling, the staff could not curate them. In fact, several began spending their work hours helping restore the church. Eventually they were baptized and became ardent converts. The state still continues to pay their salaries. As for the eventual fate of the books, the Russian Federation declared in 2005 that it will not return further war booty.[3]

But while rats scurried up and down stacked columns of leather bindings, pausing thoughtfully to chew on vellum and parchment, the restoration of St. Vladimir's proceeded apace. Though paid professional workers did technical repairs and installed heating and water pipes, "sweat equity" mobilized all ages (see figure 3.3). Even children shifted rubbish. The children were soon rewarded, for St. Vladimir's established a beautifully clean primary school, serving wholesome meals and offering beds for afternoon naps or overnight stays. Harried parents lined up to get their offspring admitted within its pristine and peaceful walls.

St. Vladimir's is located near a number of mathematical institutes, and many students came over to watch the restoration. After sitting on the sidelines, quite a few asked Father Sergy if they might help. One elegant young man introduced himself to the priest, beginning the conversation by referring to the beauty of the seventeenth-century "Naryshkin baroque" derelict church that stood next to the institute. From this elevated language of history and archaeology, he abruptly dropped his bag and grabbed Father Sergy's hand, kissing it passionately. The priest put his stole over the young man's shoulders in a moment of intense privacy. The elegant young man reappeared the next day at the site, prepared to face the priest's invariable test of sincerity: digging out old sewer lines. Those who persevere through the

Figure 3.3 Father Sergy Romanov, priest of St. Vladimir, a volunteer, and a paid workers take a break from restoring their church. (Photo credit: John Garrard)

muck are accepted as veterans. Thus, a tea break for the volunteers illustrates a cross section of Moscow society. A woman mathematics professor from one of the nearby institutes arrives with two steaming kettles. Other ladies, paid book curators, will follow with buns, sugar, and Russian tea glasses. Seated next to *babushki*, students in Western-style knit caps sip tea. Backpacks from Gap jostle the *avoski*. Far more people participate in the physical restoration of the building than actually attend the services—a characteristic that holds true for the larger movement as well.

It can take time to move toward spiritual commitment. Perhaps some of the volunteers will never take the final step of baptism. But participating in church restoration transforms people in subtle but profound ways. Curiosity can segue into passionate engagement. Volunteers become discoverers, explorers, archaeologists. Teenagers find icons once sawn in half in moldy storerooms—that was how the bifurcated icon of St. Vladimir, which adorns the iconostasis of the church, was located. It still had its silver *oklad*. An old man digging out sewer lines pulls a cracked icon lamp from the mud. The art forms of fresco painting and mosaic are reborn. A young nun paints icons in her new cell (see figure 3.4). A whole ancient

Figure 3.4 A young nun's cell displays the damaged icons she repairs and the new ones she paints to aid St. Vladimir's Russian Orthodox Church. (Photo credit: John Garrard)

music is relearned and appreciated. Sacred embroidery, at which Orthodox women excelled, revives. Novices sew gifts of pearls onto gorgeous banners and altar cloths. Enormous changes take place in society as well. The compact between rulers and ruled is redrawn. An educational system, once eradicated, begins anew. The population's view of what is lawful changes. Church revival is a "package deal" that gives Russians bearings in a rapidly changing and somewhat chaotic present. On the national scale, it is led by the Moscow Patriarchate.

From practically the first moment of his June 10, 1990, enthronement, Aleksy energetically plunged into building new churches and reconsecrating old ones. Sir Rodric Braithwaite, British ambassador from 1988 to 1992, gives a fascinating glimpse of the man. He visited him May 5, 1992, at his official residence, Chisty Pereulok.[4] Aleksy entered the room "still glowing from having celebrated his first Easter in a non-Communist Russia." Aleksy then gave his schedule for the coming next few days; he would be off to St. Petersburg to consecrate four new churches. One in particular was very precious to him as it was a prison church. Ministering to prisoners once had been forbidden to the ROC, as had been all social service and charity. But with the changes heralded by the millennial celebrations, the authorities slackened their ban. Aleksy had seized this opportunity even before becoming patriarch. In 1990, while metropolitan for Leningrad, he visited a "corrective labor camp" attached to an engineering works on the outskirts of the city. There were 2,500 inmates in the camp, all recidivists, many of them professional people—lawyers, engineers, doctors. The convicts asked him to consecrate the church, which they were building inside the camp. The prisoners had put up their own money and painted the icons. Aleksy gave the copper for the roof. He would now return to the camp to fulfill his promise, and he was assigning a priest to it. Aleksy emphasized he wanted to develop pastoral work in prisons, hospitals, and the army.[5]

The story of this nameless church, built by volunteer convict labor in one of the anonymous backwaters of the immense Russian penal system, illustrates the revolution in the penal code. The very first time a Russian Orthodox priest was permitted to even step inside a "strict regime" camp during Soviet times—that is, without being sent there as an inmate—occurred in July 1989. That favored prelate had been Metropolitan Filaret, a permanent member of the Holy Synod who would be unmasked in January 1992 by three Orthodox priests as a KGB informant. The KGB sent any inmate wearing a cross to solitary confinement.[6] Yet a few years later the turnaround was such that the convicts were able to use some of their precious free hours during the day to build a church. Russian prisoners normally perform "corrective labor." This makes their effort all the more impressive.

Building this church testifies to the profound Russian longing to spiritualize one's surroundings. The harshness of ordinary life is such that Russians passionately desire some fragment of beauty. Traditionally, the best and most important place in the home was the *krasny ugol* ("beautiful corner"), where the icons hung (see figure 3.5). KGB officers with dead gray eyes commanded labor camps whose barracks had no *krasny ugol*. But now there would be an Orthodox sanctuary—the traditional image of heaven—in the

Figure 3.5 Every Russian Orthodox home contains a "beautiful corner" (*krasny ugol*) wherein hung the family's icons and lamp (*lampada*). (Photo credit: Olga Lugovaya)

middle of one of these frozen pits of hell. One wonders if the experience of building a church rehabilitated any of these recidivists. The whole episode calls out for Hollywood treatment, a Russian version of *Lilies of the Field*, Sidney Poitier's Oscar-winning performance as an itinerant builder who helps a group of German nuns build a chapel in the Arizona desert. Aleksy's personal intervention as far back as 1990 evidences his sincerity, but he did not promise "happy endings."

The ROC's restoration campaign covers a vast territory. But the centerpiece is Moscow, where the USSR itself died in the embers of the failed coup. And there is a deeper reason as well. Moscow was the ancient capital of the faith. When Lenin moved the capital of the infant Bolshevik state from St. Petersburg (renamed Petrograd at the time) back to Moscow, he immediately ordered its sacred identity obliterated. The Bolsheviks regarded Moscow's skyline of 1,600 golden cupolas and crosses as a block of heads to decapitate. They set to work with a vengeance, tearing up the basic fabric of the city, for from its earliest existence Moscow's architecture deliberately imitated both the historical Jerusalem and the numinous Jerusalem seen by St. John descending from the heavens at the end of the book of Revelation.

The imposition of mystical features upon the kremlin, wooden huts, and small churches of early Moscow has largely escaped the attention of Western historians (with the important exception of William Brumfield). But it did not escape the attention of the ROC, though it had to keep very quiet throughout the Soviet period. This approach to city planning derives from Scripture itself, where monks found four meanings in biblical passages: historical or literal, allegorical, moral, and anagogical. To what extent medieval Muscovite city planners intended all four meanings is unclear, but they did recall both the literal and the heavenly Jerusalem in naming and arranging the city's parts. In 1987 an article by Archpriest Lev Lebedev entitled innocuously "Veneration of St. Nicholas in Russia" appeared in the *Journal of the Moscow Patriarchate*, listed under the heading "Theology" in the table of contents. But in its footnotes occurs a statement whose relationship to St. Nicholas is tenuous at best: "architecture historians have discovered in a wide body of literature comprehensively studying early Russian cities patent images of the *new Jerusalem* [Lebedev's emphasis] of the Revelation of St. John the Divine in each of them."[7] What could only be whispered in 1987 (the editor-in-chief of the journal then was Metropolitan Pitirim, one of those "agents in cassocks" tasked with controlling the church) was rolled out after August 1991. Moscow would be rebranded as the holy city of the Orthodox: the city itself was a text, and the population would relearn how to interpret it.

Even after seventy years of Soviet destruction, the original traces of Moscow as New Jerusalem could still be seen, quite literally, in the walls of the Kremlin itself. All ancient Russian towns needed defensive walls, because warfare, whether between the princes or against outside invaders, was virtually incessant. First, the gates of its fortress walls were numbered. Whether of wood or stone, Moscow's walls contained twelve gates (cf. the New Jerusalem in Revelation 21:12–13: "descending out of heaven from God," as a walled city, with "twelve gates, and at the gates twelve angels, and names written thereon. . . . On the east three gates; on the north three gates; on the south three gates; and on the west three gates"). Monks regularly consecrated the city's walls, suspending religious processions around them only in 1765, when the walls themselves began to collapse.[8] For centuries the church overlaid the configuration of the city's walls, gates, and towers with sacred meanings. Gates were not just a way in; they represented the mysterious entrance of Christ into the town.

The arcane symbolism of the gates is developed at great length in a Russian version of a coffee table book, *Moscow: 850th Anniversary*, vol. 1.[9] This volume, published in both Russian and English, was heavily subsidized by Mayor Luzhkov as part of the city's celebrations of its first mention in the Chronicles in 1147. The subvention translated into silk paper and four-color illustrations demonstrating that ancient Moscow was deliberately built to resemble the historical Jerusalem of first-century Palestine as well as the mystical New Jerusalem from St. John's Revelation.[10] The English version states the "Gates (sometimes towers too) had holy icons outside and [inside] in front of which icon-lamps were often burning," testifying that the "Orthodox town's people hoped not so much for the strength of material town's walls, but for God's power and prayers of saints," which invisibly protect it.[11] The entire population witnessed the priest's consecration of the gates. Living inside walls whose very gates were consecrated must have itself forged a sense of "us" versus a "them" outside the sanctified border. In a sense, the city itself became a church.

Moscow was built as an Orthodox city. Occupiers—Muslim Turks, the Catholic Poles, the godless French—would come and go. The city was burned to the ground twice, first through an accidental spark in 1547, and second, when the Crimean Tatars sacked it for the last time in 1571. But each rebuilding became the occasion to make its links with Jerusalem more elaborate. The classic case is the city's "Golden Gates." Jesus had entered the historical city of Jerusalem circa A.D. 33 through its "Golden Gates." He was riding on a donkey and acclaimed as "king of kings" by followers waving palm fronds. Constantinople's gates deliberately recalled this episode. The emperor himself started a ritual whereby on Palm Sunday he held the bridle of the donkey upon which sat the patriarch as they both entered the city through its "Golden Gates." When the Turks took Constantinople in 1453, they walled these gates up. On one day of the year, they allowed them opened for the patriarch alone to reenact the ritual in front of a dwindling congregation of Orthodox. Muslims occupied the historical Jerusalem and walled up its Golden Gates, too. Even today, in the capital of the Jewish state they remain closed. The Israelis promise to open them on the day *their* Messiah arrives.

Grand Prince Vladimir built Golden Gates in Kiev; the Mongols destroyed them when they sacked the city in 1240. But Moscow's Golden Gates were rebuilt time and again; that is why the Soviets were so eager to blow them up permanently. In the thirteenth century, Metropolitan Kirill met Grand Prince Alexander Nevsky at the Golden Gates when he returned from paying the tribute to the Golden Horde. Those were destroyed in the next round of sacking and burning.[12] Then their location was made more secure by putting them in the Cathedral of the Assumption inside the Kremlin. In 1432 Grand Prince Vasily won from the Horde the right to collect the tribute paid by all Russians principalities. This meant that hereafter no rural princes had the opportunity to become grand princes; it was a significant step in the "rise" of Moscow. Vasily took the tax in the Cathedral of the Assumption "near the Golden Gates."[13] The pageant showed a canny medieval mind manipulating the symbolism for all it was worth.

Under the Romanovs, the architectural features of Moscow, especially the Kremlin cathedrals and Red Square, were manipulated as a vast stage upon which the various processions and rites performed by tsar and patriarch took on the overtones of religious drama. With the Golden Gates relocated inside the Kremlin's Cathedral of the Assumption, the fortress itself needed a magnificent entryway. The Savior Tower (Spasskaya Bashnya) became the formal entrance to the inner Kremlin. Originally completed as a squat gate tower in 1491 by the Italian architect Pietro Solario, it became the main entrance through which the tsars entered through the Kremlin on their coronation day—the point was to have their entrance resonate allegorically with the original entry of Jesus into Jerusalem.[14] In the early seventeenth century, Tsar Michael Romanov commissioned an English clockmaker, Christopher Halloway, to add a Gothic superstructure to the tower. Halloway supplied a ten-story steeple containing clock, chimes, and secret passageways.[15] Stalin and subsequent party leaders co-opted the gates' odor of sanctity and power by entering the Kremlin through this gate tower in their black limousines. The religious frescoes that had decorated the walls and ceiling of its central arch and its magnificent icons were covered up.

As with so many other megalomaniacs from imperial Rome to the present, Stalin's vision of what "his" capital should be meant destruction on a vast scale. In 1930, to commemorate the sixth anniversary of the death of Lenin, the city's workers were ordered to turn out on Saturday to "voluntarily" pull down the Simonov Monastery.[16] Then in 1935, on the eve of the Great Terror,

Stalin put his henchman Lazar Kaganovich in charge of a general plan for the reconstruction of the city. In brief, "reconstruction" meant obliterating as many churches as possible. What could not be renamed and renovated for secular purposes (the Savior Tower simply had its cross exchanged for a red star) was blown up. Thus perished the Krasnye (Beautiful) Gates, built in the reign of Elizabeth Petrovna—gates replete with sacred meaning to the Orthodox believer. The Spas na Boru (Savior in the Woods) Church in the Kremlin, dating back to 1328–33 to the reign of Ivan I, was dynamited, though its wooden frame was preserved as a historical artifact in the inner court of the Grand Kremlin Palace. Also destroyed were the Chudov (Miraculous) and Voskresensky (Resurrection) Monasteries of the Kremlin, and the Strastnoy (Passion) Monastery on Pushkin Square. The diminutive Kazan Cathedral on Red Square, a confection of pastel ogee arches and gilded cupolas built in 1636, also came down. A block north, the enormous red-brick Resurrection Gates crashed in rubble. Moscow was to be reconstructed as the product of a grand, utopian scheme.

The classic case of Stalin's determination to impose a static, end-state vision upon his capital is his destruction of the Cathedral of Christ the Savior. In 1931, the same year he ordered the seizure of Leningrad's Kazan Cathedral and its occupation by the "Museum of Atheism," Stalin had Moscow's biggest cathedral blasted to smithereens. The rebuilding of this enormous cathedral would become the outstanding example of the church's campaign to rebrand Russia by remaking its skyline.

In his campaign to rebuild Christ the Savior, Aleksy demonstrated all his diplomatic and organizational skills in gaining local and state approval, mobilizing manpower, and generating funds. The list of allies he gathered to his cause, as well as the resulting payoff within the structure of the rebuilt cathedral itself, is a concentrated projection of his entire program as patriarch. First, link the church with the Russian military. Next, enlist as partners the emerging democratic machinery of the new Russian state, such as the mayors of cities. Then get the newly privatized industries—particularly oil, gas, and banking—on board. Finally, secure the support of private donors from the newly rich strata of Russian capitalists. At the completion of the project, he declared, "The miracle of the resurrection of the Cathedral required several years of concentrated, selfless and loving labor. The Cathedral now glorifies Christ and helps our long-suffering people return to their spiritual roots—the Holy Faith of their ancestors."[17] As even a cursory reading of the story indicates, he did much to enable the marvel. We can safely predict that Aleksy will earn the title *chudotvorets* (wonder-worker).

To evaluate the significance of rebuilding Christ the Savior at such speed, we must understand what it meant originally to the Russian people. On December 25, 1812, Alexander I issued the original decree authorizing construction. This day signifies a military triumph: it is the day the last soldiers of Napoleon's invading "Grande armée" of 600,000 men were driven from Russian soil. Russians call their victory over the French emperor, whose troops had looted and occupied Moscow in 1812, the "Patriotic War." They reserve the name "Great Patriotic War" for the even more desperate victory over Hitler and his Nazis.

Alexander's proclamation read in part: "To signify Our gratitude to Divine Providence for saving Russia from the doom that overshadowed Her and to preserve the memory of the unheard-of efforts, loyalty and love for our Faith and Homeland displayed during these difficult days by the Russian people, We hereby intend to build a Cathedral in honor of Christ the Savior in our capital city of Moscow." Alexander's characterization of Moscow as "our capital city" represents an anachronistic use of the term. St. Petersburg was the ostensible capital of the empire, but the tsar was using the phrase in its older sense: Moscow as capital of the Orthodox faith. Americans are familiar with Tchaikovsky's tribute to their victory, *The 1812 Overture*, whose cannons, rockets, and fireworks have made it a staple of Fourth of July concerts. The cathedral aimed to create the same sense of patriotic excitement using stone and space. In the perceptive words of William Brumfield, it was designed to be "expressive of official ideology"—that is, to glorify the Russian state by restoring "the purity and orthodoxy of Russian church architecture."[18]

The architect chosen was Konstantin Ton; he received a prime site near Prechistenka Quay, not far from the Kremlin. Ton took as his inspiration a Russo-Byzantine medieval form but expanded the scale to proportions that are reminiscent of Franco-Italian grandeur. When Ton designed the cathedral, he was no longer imitating the pure medieval church form but was boosting its skeleton—the cathedral represents medieval architecture blown up to massive scale. Here, the proportions suggest, is a building that is worthy of an empire and will last forever. Work began in 1839 under Alexander's successor, his brother Nicholas I. When workers dug out the original foundation, they unearthed the bones of a prehistoric mammoth. The discovery was decoded as meaning that the cathedral would stand for all time. Finally finished in 1883 under Alexander III, it lasted only forty-eight years. But during those forty-eight years it was a favorite landmark for Muscovites, a compass needle to orient oneself when out walking—just as pedestrians look for the obelisk of the Washington monument in the United States' capital.

Alexander Solzhenitsyn gives a poignant example of how the cathedral resonated in his novel *The First Circle*, set in a Moscow *sharashka*, a secret prison research center. It is headed by a Colonel Yakonov, who in December 1949 revisits a spot he had been taken to twenty years before. Then he was only a young officer, and his fiancée Agniya promised to show him "one of the most beautiful places in Moscow." She took him to a small red and white brick church, the Church of St. John the Baptist. (The Russian reader recognizes that the church itself is "Naryshkin baroque"—a late seventeenth-century style popularized by the important eponymous boyar family.) Agniya drew him to the parapet, and he suddenly saw a marvelous panorama: "Yakonov drew in his breath. It was as if they had suddenly emerged from the crowded city onto a height with a broad, open view into the distance. A long, white stone stairway fell away from the portico in many flights and landings, down the hill to the Moscow River. The river burned in the sunset.... Into the Moscow River flowed the gleaming Yauza; behind it to the right stretched the Foundling Hospital; and behind rose the sharp contours of the Kremlin. Still farther off the five gilded cupolas of the Cathedral of Christ the Savior flamed in the sun."[19]

Solzhenitsyn knew what works in creating a vibrant metropolis: Agniya observes, "How well our old city planners laid out things!" In 1928 the cathedral beat as the heart of the city. Twenty years later, in December 1949 when Yakonov makes his next visit, it is gone. The small Church of St. John the Baptist is wrecked; its shell reeks of mold, crumbling bricks, and rotting trash. Yakonov broke with his fiancée and achieved success, importance, and status. Yet, as he peers inside the ruined church, he feels such despair that he, a paragon of the New Soviet Man, loses his will to live. Solzhenitsyn makes his point with remarkable subtlety: hope—the structure of human existence—is being deadened by destruction of the physical environment.

Perhaps it was the cathedral's quality of dominating space and viewer that led Stalin to make it one of his especial targets. Perhaps it was because it was very close to Red Square and he could see it from his Kremlin office. Or maybe it was just that, like all tyrants, he loved to erect his own monuments. At any rate, its systematic destruction began.[20] Given that forty-three years had been spent constructing the edifice to the highest technical standards of tsarist engineering, this was no small feat. The cathedral was no delicate medieval church. Beneath its outer skin stood good nineteenth-century steel, and bringing it down required weeks of dynamiting.

Other than those who watched it live during the 1930s, the first time the Soviet public was treated to a view of this expert demolition was in 1988, the millennial year. Television broadcast *Khram* (*The Church*), which showed

Orthodox believers in a sympathetic light. For the first time, the enormous amount of destruction wreaked upon church property was highlighted. The film showed the cathedral's huge dome imploding and the massive walls crashing down into dust and chunks of granite. Eventually a huge hole was all that was left. What the film did not show, and what was made public only in 1994, was that throughout the demolition of the building, the construction site became the scene of thousands of minor pilferings. Russian believers surreptitiously carted off bits and pieces of it, including chunks of concrete and pipe. It was as if they wished to hang on to some remnant of its existence. Iraq's Muslim Shia believers did exactly the same thing when the beautiful Golden Mosque of Samarra was dynamited by rival Sunnis in February 2006.

Having created a void, Stalin now planned to replace it with a gargantuan structure in a style of architecture that still defies description. "Socialist realist" was the official nomenclature. Western observers have used terms such as "Soviet brutal," referencing Le Corbusier's naming of buildings that shaped concrete into bold, sculptural forms as "brutalist" (*beton brut* is French for raw concrete).[21] He decreed that a Palace of Soviets be erected. The dimensions of this grand design approached, as William Brumfield noted, "the realm of fantasy." It would house halls with a seating capacity of 21,000 and 6,000, and its tiered columnar structure formed of massive pylons was intended "to rise to a height of 315 meters."[22] Topping the whole monstrosity would be a 100-meter statue of Lenin, the new godhead of the secular faith of Communism.[23] Quite deliberately, the plans disconnected the potential Russian viewer from the time frame he had known for centuries—the comforting continuum of past, present, and future, beheld simultaneously in the codified architecture of the Russian Orthodox Church. The iconostasis, carefully arranged to carry the believer safely through eternity, explained God's plan for His creation in a specific order: from the Old Testament through the Annunciation, Nativity, Crucifixion, Resurrection, Ascension, and final Second Coming of his son. Thus the Russian Orthodox believer knew where he stood in relation to the future. The final "end of days" to which this old, corrupt world was surely and swiftly heading, was traced by the icons all the way up to the cupola where Christ Pantocrator sat in judgment in the blue heaven of the ceiling.

Now, in place of an image of the Savior with a serious and intent expression gazing at the viewer while his hand made the sign of the cross, the Palace of Soviets would substitute Lenin with his jutting chin and index finger pointing to the glorious day when Communism would rule the earth. The form itself would reorient people toward the utopia promised—and prophesied—by

Marxism-Leninism. Had it been built, the architecture would have shifted the ground upon which the Russian viewer stood both psychologically and literally. Thus inflated to the gigantic scale of *Gulliver's Travels'* Brobdindnag, the building would have been the most perfect realization of megalomania since the reign of Nero. Stalin's architect was Boris Iofan, another non-Jewish Jew (like Kaganovich) willing to serve as the unholy Master's tool.

But as it became clear that the project was unbuildable, Russian Orthodox believers covertly glowed with *Schadenfreude*. Jackhammers excavated the foundation down to the bedrock, more than twenty yards beneath the nearby Moscow River. Trucks hauled away its pillars to decorate the office of the rector of Moscow State University. Stones from its walls appeared in the Kropotkinskaya Metro station. Just as the pyramids had been stripped of their white marble to face the city of Cairo, the cathedral's stones faced modern Soviet buildings on Tverskaya Street. These materials did not lose their efficacy when transferred to other building sites. But plagued by accidents and mishaps, whatever was constructed of the "Palace of Soviets" crumbled.

In 1958–60 Khrushchev ordered the foundation filled in, and a huge outdoor heated swimming pool constructed in its place. It was delightful to paddle contentedly in this heated, man-made lake. But even this far more modest Soviet attempt to master the elements failed. The heater did not work all the time, and outdoor swimming in a Moscow winter became hit and miss. If the would-be bather were lucky, one could break icicles off the handrails before diving into warm chlorinated water. But diving into a polar lagoon was not "according to plan," as the Soviets might say. The Orthodox view subtly suggested that the heating malfunction was attributable to divine displeasure. Swimmers could not use the pool during summer, for, with irreproachable Soviet logic, the pool closed then for cleaning.

Even before the defeat of the failed KGB coup, in the heady days of "openness and reorganization," on February 1990 the Holy Synod blessed the idea of reconstructing the cathedral and appealed to the Russian government for permission. It is another of the "what ifs" of history as to whether this would have been granted had not Aleksey Ridiger, metropolitan of Leningrad and Novgorod, been elected patriarch of Moscow and All Russia just three months later, June 6–7. No sooner had he taken off his robes for the enthroning ceremony than he announced he wished to reconstruct the cathedral. With Aleksy at the helm, things began to happen rapidly.

For the church not only to revive but to establish itself as a permanent force in society, Aleksy sensed that it had to link with the military and patriotism. The Cathedral of Christ the Savior, because it had been decreed on the very day Napoleon's troops were driven out, had always symbolized

Russians' willingness to die for their country. Six months after his enthronement, displaying the same rapid-fire energy he had used to earlier restore the Danilov Monastery, Aleksy secured the necessary permits from the authorities. On December 5, 1990, a slab of granite, installed on the original site of the cathedral, read, "This is the cornerstone of the Church of the Derzhavnaya [Sovereign] Icon of the Theotokos, which shall be the predecessor of the Cathedral of Christ the Savior, that will be reconstructed on this spot." Orthodox believers immediately began wearing a special *znachok*, a badge showing the outline of the cathedral. It was a signal that, though the Moscow pool still intermittently sent up clouds of steam over the pale green water, already plans to rebuild it were taking shape in the hearts of the believers.

Again, the timing could not have been more favorable. Throughout the entire postwar period, Soviet ideologues had attempted to co-opt the memory of the victory in the "Patriotic War" by linking it with the Red Army's victory in the "Great Patriotic War"—their term for World War II. This was a war that in 1990 still resonated in every Russian's memory. It was on the eastern front, on Soviet soil, where 75 to 80 percent of all German losses in men and matériel in all theaters occurred. Though arriving at an estimate for Soviet military and civilian casualties will bedevil historians and demographers well into the twenty-first century, it is clear that more of their country's citizens died than all other combatants combined. But while virtually every city, town, and village inside the USSR had its monument to the victory, Moscow alone had none. In the 1980s, the party decided to remedy that situation.

The party intended the Moscow monument to be bigger and more grandiose than any other. Further, it would be constructed on Poklonnaya Hill to link the Soviet triumph to 1812. Napoleon had camped on that hill waiting for Alexander I's ambassadors to arrive and supplicate for surrender. They never came. Napoleon occupied Moscow and quartered his cavalry and soldiers in cathedrals and palaces. But the population fled, and a suspicious fire burned food supplies. Soon the invaders were forced to withdraw as the early winter became particularly fierce, and they had no food. Napoleon abandoned his men and took a fast coach home. His columns, continually assaulted by guerrilla attacks from Kutuzov's cavalry, melted away in the snow. Fewer than 5 percent of the original invading force (half of whom were not French) reached home. It was a fatal blow for the emperor, although Waterloo was three years away.

The party's plans were proceeding smoothly—Poklonnaya Hill was virtually leveled—until Gorbachev came along. Now there would have to be a concession as to what the "people" themselves wanted. Nina Tumarkin's fascinating article "Story of a War Memorial" told what happened next.[24] In September 1986 the newspapers announced an open competition for the "Memorial to the Victory of the Soviet People in the Great Patriotic War." The party ideologues thought that because they ran the jury, they could control the "people's" competition. Those same ideologues were disconcerted to find that of the 377 entries, the most popular was entry No. 206, a model in the basic form of a Russian Orthodox Church. On February 21, 1987, the craven jury members, petrified at the wrath of the CPSU if they awarded the prize to this entry, announced they could not decide. So a new round of competition was opened. On April 15, 1988, a total of 477 models were put on display in the Manezh (a huge building just off Red Square, given the French name, *manège*, because it had been a riding school in tsarist times). Design No. 342 was "a skeletal structure of brass in the shape of the Cathedral of Christ the Savior. . . . A rival entry, No. 267, simply projected an accurate and total reconstruction of the same cathedral." Neither of these made the list of finalists. Ten of the party's picks submitted revisions of their designs for the next level.

By now an entire organization entitled Khram (The Church) showed up at the competition display every day, arguing that the Cathedral of Christ the Savior should be reconstructed first; the heroes of 1812 deserved to be commemorated properly before the victors of 1945. Indeed, as the population filed past the table of entries and was encouraged to make comments on which one the selection committee should pick, the overwhelming majority of Moscow citizens voted to put up a version of Entry No. 206 from the earlier competition—the outline of a Russian Orthodox Church. The party's attempt to subsume the 1945 victory under the hammer and sickle was being hijacked by the memory of patriotism united to Orthodoxy. After further study, the thoroughly petrified jury decided on December 25, 1989, to terminate the competition without giving any award.

While party ideologues ground their teeth at yet another of the pitfalls of glasnost, the patriarch saw opportunity. He knew there was no hope of rebuilding Christ the Savior on Poklonnaya Hill. He would deal with Poklonnaya Hill later. Instead, he pressed full steam ahead with rebuilding the cathedral *on its original site.* Any American who has ever been on a fundraising committee might inwardly groan, thinking of the endless meetings, targets, goals, bake sales, telethons, and pledge drives. But Aleksy knew where to go for allies. The first person within the Russian government he enlisted was the president of the Russian Federation, Boris Yeltsin. Perhaps Aleksy reminded him that back on August 20, 1991, Yeltsin was holed up in the Russian White House, surrounded by tanks. Yeltsin had publicly appealed to him for help, and Aleksy had answered with the two crucial public statements of August 20 and August 21. Now was the time for Yeltsin to return the favor. On July 16, 1992, he signed a decree, "The Establishment of a Fund for the Re-creation of Moscow." It was left unstated, but what was being "re-created" this time would be Moscow as the Holy City. And topping the list of buildings was the Cathedral of Christ the Savior.[25]

That rebuilding Christ the Savior topped the list suggests that Aleksy had also sold the project to the power structure of Moscow politics. The mayor, Yury Luzhkov, was looking to host a grand celebration in 1997, in honor of the 850th anniversary of the founding of Moscow. According to the Chronicles, in 1147 Yury Dolgoruky (George of the Long Arm), prince of Suzdal, invited his ally, Prince Svyatoslav of Novgorod-Seversk, to come to Moscow for a "mighty dinner." The Moskva River is small, but it connects with the Oka and the Volga and thus begins a waterway to the Caspian and the East. The river gave its name to Dolgoruky's mead hall and collection of small huts clustering around a wooden kremlin with a tiny church, "Our Savior in the Wood" (the original of the Spas na boru Church the Soviets had blown up), in their midst. From this first mention in the Chronicles, Moskva as obscure trading post evolved into enormous metropolis. Aleksy hitched the Christ the Savior bandwagon to Luzhkov's star, a calculation that paid off handsomely when the mayor announced that the 1997 celebrations to mark the 850th year of Moscow's existence would climax in a rebuilt Cathedral of Christ the Savior.

Thus, the goals of the patriarch and the mayor synchronized, with the convergence of two axes of power strengthening both. This made fundraising a great deal easier. A number of the newly rich oligarchs wanted to be associated with the coming celebrations. Though not articulated by the Orthodox Church as such, there is a general feeling among Russians involved in the new business of philanthropic fundraising that the powerful can donate as a form of repentance for having become wealthy.[26] Luzhkov adopted strong-arm tactics that a ghetto lender might well envy. According to Inga Pagava, the director of the Open Russia Foundation, once funded by Mikhail Khodorkovsky, Luzhkov would simply call *biznismeny*, order them to a *miting*, and demand a million or two in rubles, or an equivalent amount in *dollary*.[27] No one was immune to his pressure. Aleksy turned a blind eye to the arm twisting. In the heady but unstable days of post-Soviet Russia, rebuilding an immense cathedral from scratch required an enormous amount of money. The patriarch was a practical man with a sophisticated understanding of the art of compromise. Back in the bad old days under Andropov, Aleksey Ridiger, when chancellor of the Moscow diocese, had gotten the church a "foreign currency" account at a Vneshtorgbank to fund renovating the Danilov

Monastery. Though the *Journal of the Moscow Patriarate* has maintained a pristine silence on the subject, it is a safe bet that the original dollar account has not been shut down. Now he blessed Mayor Luzhkov's robust application of fundraising techniques for the cathedral.

Once underway, Aleksy demonstrated consummate skill in the art of publicly thanking his allies. His timing was exquisite. Because the original decree had been issued around Christmas, it became the main feast day of the year when all Moscow commemorated the victory over Napoleon. Therefore on January 7, 1995 (Orthodox Christmas Day), Aleksy conducted a festal prayer service and blessed the cornerstone in the foundation of the cathedral: Yury Luzhkov was the honored guest. On August 20, 1995, Victor Chernomyrdin, the prime minister of Russia, and Aleksy lay the first stone. On January 7, 1996, again Orthodox Christmas, he celebrated a service at the site by unveiling the first two memorial plaques listing donors. The patriarch, President Yeltsin, and Mayor Luzhkov—a trinity of the power brokers of modern Russia—lay the last three bricks in the wall of the main entrance. The ROC thus co-opted the celebrations for the victory over Napoleon, which had gone on even in Soviet times. After a seventy-year interregnum, their seamless blend with Orthodox ritual was restored. Now, to Aleksy's satisfaction, it was impossible to see where patriotism left off and faith began.

In 1997 Luzhkov hosted a summer extravaganza for the 850th anniversary of Moscow. This "People's Holiday" (the slogan was Luzhkov's) was secular. There was a parade down Tverskaya Street, complete with elaborate floats. The U.S. Embassy's float showed U.S. Marines and the diplomatic staff decked out as cowboys and Wild West bandits. Overhead, Russian fighter planes buzzed in V formations, trailing plumes of red, blue, and white smoke, the tsarist colors of Russia's post-Communist flag. A multimillion-dollar laser light show (put on by a French company at the impressive cost of $5 million) began at dusk. Millions of awed tourists from the outlying regions jammed the city. The huge party duly impressed westerners, too. Composed of equal amounts of civic pride, chamber-of-commerce boosterism, and rapacious capitalism, the mayor's carnival hailed Moscow as "The New York of the East."[28] Now would come the veneration of the city in its more ancient identity, queen of Orthodoxy.

On September 7, 1997, the focus of the celebration turned to the cathedral itself. Aleksy blessed the completed walls and presided over a festal prayer service in the square. Only the lower crypt was finished, but it was enough to satisfy Luzhkov. There was a four-hour liturgy, then a great procession outside the cathedral, witnessed by hundreds of thousands of people lining the streets and sidewalks. Instead of jets overhead and a laser light show, every church and monastery in Moscow rang its bells. The patriarch stopped at each side of the cathedral, prayed, and blessed the wall with holy water. At the end of the circumambulation, an eyewitness hosannahed:

> All the bishops ascended the steps of the cathedral with the Patriarch and the mayor. The Patriarch then read a proclamation about the 850th anniversary of Moscow and presented the mayor of Moscow with an icon of the Mother of God. The mayor made the sign of the cross, got on his knees, and venerated the icon. He then spoke and said, among other things, that the Russian Orthodox Church *is* the presiding religion in Russia. It was truly a moving moment.[29]

It was indeed a "moving moment" for Aleksy, what with the mayor at his feet and thousands of Muscovites weeping, praying, and crossing themselves.

Luzhkov had been the master of ceremonies during the summer party, but Aleksy was in charge here. Even his gift to Luzhkov resonated on several levels. It recalled the December 5, 1990, granite slab installed on the original site of the cathedral, promising that it was the cornerstone of the "Church of the Sovereign Icon of the God-Bearer," which would be the predecessor of the Cathedral of Christ the Savior, "that will be reconstructed on this spot." Erected in the days of Soviet power, the slab's proud promise had come true. It could only have come true, Aleksy was hinting, because he had called upon the Theotokos, the "Protector of Moscow" in his August 21, 1991, *obrashchenie* against the coup. Aleksy has always publicly attributed the miraculous failure of the coup to Mary. He was thanking Luzhkov, but he was simultaneously reminding the mayor and all the other Muscovites that the Mother of God was *his* ally. That he could convey all this through the gift of an icon of Mary and Jesus testifies to Aleksy's masterful manipulation of both public spectacle and the power of Orthodox icons.

The type of icon Aleksy gave Mayor Luzhkov was called a Hodegetria (Guide). The Virgin holds the Christ Child and gestures to him with her free hand as the way to salvation. The original Hodegetria icon, which the ROC claims was painted by the Apostle Luke from life, served as the protector of the city of Constantinople. The Ottomans smashed it the very day—May 29, 1453—that the city fell to them. But Sophia Palaiologina (who married Ivan III) had brought an icon of the Hodegetria's type to Moscow and its connotations were transferred to Russia. Copied many times, a Hodegetria icon had been paraded before the troops at the Battle of Borodino on August 25–26, 1812 o.s. (old style).[30] The same icon was paraded before Tsar Nicholas II at the grand ceremony commemorating the centenary of the battle. On August 25–26, 1912, the anniversary was marked by a massive parade, a requiem, and a solemn *Te Deum* in the Cathedral of Christ the Savior. Now, although only the outer walls of the lower crypt were available for blessing by Aleksy, the September 7, 1997, date deliberately recalled the Battle of Borodino. The thirteen-day disjunction between the old style (Julian) calendar used in 1912 and the new style (Gregorian) calendar used in 1997 meant that August 26 o.s. became September 7 n.s. With his gift to Luzhkov of the Hodegetria icon, the patriarch was connecting 850 years of history: the Theotokos was again protecting her city, as she had August 25–26, 1812 o.s. and 1:42 a.m. August 21, 1991 n.s.

The cathedral's physical layout underscored the union between faith and patriotism. Because the cathedral was commissioned to commemorate the victory over Napoleon, one of its two chapels is dedicated to St. Prince Alexander Nevsky, whose stature as the greatest military hero in Russian history is secure. (The other chapel was dedicated to St. Nicholas, one of the patron saints of Russia.) The Nevsky chapel visibly reaches out to the army: victory over foreign invaders is achieved under the Orthodox banner.

The cathedral earlier played a critical role in reviving the office of patriarch itself, a nice corollary to the Russian faith and patriotism nexus. Peter the Great abolished the office of patriarch. He substituted a Holy Governing Synod. It functioned as a department of state, headed by his own appointee as procurator. During the summer of 1917, the Local Council of 1917–18 reinstated the office of patriarch in the church. The first patriarch in two centuries was Tikhon. When the church began to suffer Bolshevik persecution in 1918, Tikhon founded the Brotherhood of the Cathedral of Christ the Savior in order to prevent it from being closed. The brotherhood had been successful until Stalin's iron hand ordered the building smashed to pieces. Now Stalin himself was dust and Tikhon was a saint. Aleksy had recovered his relics and reinterred them in the Monastery of Our Lady of the Don just one day before the August 19, 1991, coup attempt. Though the painstaking work of finishing mosaics and icons would go on into the twenty-first century, the cathedral was back, a visible symbol for the believer and nonbeliever alike that the Russian Orthodox faith was eternal.

Only a few years later, on January 29, 2000, Aleksy performed the Lesser Consecration of the upper church in the main part of the cathedral. The celebration in 1988 of the thousand-year anniversary of the Baptism of Rus had altered the topography of the USSR. Now a Russian Orthodox triumph capstoned the celebration of the secular millennium. In November 2001 Aleksy acknowledged the enormous contributions made by Lukoil, Russia's biggest oil producer, to the rebuilding of the cathedral. He appeared in a Lukoil television commercial, an interesting example of harnessing capitalist marketing to Orthodoxy's rebuilding campaign.[31] The camera zooms on him, in full regalia and miter, surrounded by Lukoil officials. He thanks Lukoil for "its support of many Russian Orthodox Church projects aimed at the restoration and revival of what was destroyed in the past years." As the lens pulled back, the slogan appears: "Ten years of Lukoil. For the good of Russia." Lukoil, the first Russian firm to complete a takeover of an American rival when it acquired Getty Petroleum, continues to donate to other Orthodox causes as well.

Of course, Aleksy could have achieved these successes only in the new atmosphere begun by Gorbachev's reforms. Aleksy's enthronement came at just the right time, not only the high point of glasnost but also the moment when Russians' disgust at the denigration of their churches as important historical and cultural monuments was reaching high tide.

In fact, there already existed a nongovernmental organization, The All-Russian Society for the Preservation of Monuments of History and Culture (Vserossiiskoe obshchestvo okhrany pamyatnikov istorii i kultury), better known by its acronym, VOOPIK (pronounced "Va-ah-peek," with stress on the last syllable). It had already put into place much of the infrastructure needed to mobilize the ROC's restoration campaign. Notably, its title makes no mention of churches or faith. But the date of its founding, 1965, is significant. Khrushchev had fallen from power in October 1964, outmaneuvered by fellow members of the Politburo. By then his campaign of church seizure and destruction had swallowed so many churches that it seemed as if the entire thousand-year history of the faith might be submerged under a Soviet flood. Khrushchev ordered two of the loveliest parts of old Moscow, replete with beautiful churches, blasted into rubble. Showpieces of Soviet architecture, Moscow's Kalinin Prospect and the monstrous Rossiya Hotel, were erected in the ruins. Even after he fell, his myrmidons were still in power on the Moscow City Council. Their dedication to the wrecking ball in the name of progress was unslaked. VOOPIK's founding as a Moscow-based "nongovernmental organization" got immediate support from Russians understandably frightened at the systematic destruction of their history.

Under Khrushchev's successor, Leonid Brezhnev, VOOPIK set about frustrating the city planners. It made no mention of the Russian Orthodox faith but tried to outmaneuver Soviet ideologues by marketing themselves as patriots who valued the country's heritage for purely historical reasons. In this VOOPIK was greatly aided by the fact that Russian nationalism (*narodnost*), always an uneasy integer in the Soviet trinity alongside *ideynost* and *partynost*, survived. It went underground and flowed into the catacombs of the Russian

Orthodox Church. VOOPIK's marketing campaign successfully appealed to the sense of wounded pride felt by patriotic Russians. The strategy was brilliant: because the Russian state had been coterminous with the Orthodox Church for almost a thousand years, saving one meant cherishing the other.

By 1974, only nine years after its founding, VOOPIK had more than nine million members.[32] One example will suffice to illustrate its entire approach. That year, the *Christian Science Monitor* reported that VOOPIK volunteers had spotted from a helicopter an intact seventeenth-century wooden church still standing amid the ruins of an abandoned village in Siberia. VOOPIK argued that it should be preserved as a folk museum. On that note, the entire church was dismantled, like so many enormous Lincoln logs, then helicoptered down to Novosibirsk, where volunteers reconstituted it, log by log.[33] Quite a bit is left unsaid in this brief article. Novosibirsk was the Siberian branch of the Soviet Academy of Sciences, an august and highly privileged body of elite academicians in both arts and sciences. The academy organized and ran research in the country and headed the institutes dotted from Moscow and Leningrad to Vladivostok. It may have had access to a military helicopter—there were no private helicopters inside the USSR. Or the initial spotting of the church could have been done by a member of the Soviet armed forces. The transportation of the structure by helicopter could well cover a loan of Red Army aircraft. That VOOPIK mustered support from within both the Novosibirsk Academy of Science and the military illustrates how powerful its message had become.

In the next six years, under the radar of Western Sovietologists, VOOPIK quietly grew. In 1980 its national headquarters fit comfortably and snugly within the walls of a charming seventeenth-century monastery close to Moscow's center. While the streets were disfigured with examples of modern architecture being maintained to Soviet standards of slovenliness, VOOPIK's cloister sparkled inside and out. By now VOOPIK had thirteen million members nationwide.[34]

Further, at some point in the 1970s, VOOPIK could pay salaries to several thousand employees. Significantly, this money did not come from the state. Members paid dues of thirty kopecks a year. Thirty kopecks a year, even when multiplied by thirteen million, did not go very far. But VOOPIK also owned twelve souvenir factories, and it was one of the very few Soviet organizations not obliged to plow its profits back to the rapacious Soviet state. In 1974 the assistant director of VOOPIK reported that its profits were about $11 million for its conservation work. In addition to its nominal subscriptions and souvenir profits, VOOPIK successfully marshaled volunteers, who came in droves. By 1974 thousands of students and workers spent their holidays in places like the Solovetsky Monastery in the Arctic Circle, once a Stalinist labor camp. VOOPIK volunteers replastered, repainted, repaired, and restored the lovely Orthodox complex. Because VOOPIK could not turn these buildings over to the ROC, they did the next best thing: they made them tourist attractions. To the Western eye, VOOPIK was evolving into a hybrid, combining features of the British Heritage Foundation and the United States' charity Habitat for Humanity. It uniquely combined tax subsidies from the state, volunteer labor, and nascent capitalism.

During the Brezhnev years of the 1970s, VOOPIK's covert but substantial support testified to a hidden debate within the Communist Party itself. Even *Pravda* began reporting favorably on church restoration, though it was always careful to package it as "architectural and historical" heritage. The state controlled all publications, and each had its own party committee. The party organized journalists in the Union of Journalists.[35] *Pravda* itself had the status of Holy Writ. (What secular newspaper in the West would ever call itself "Truth"?) In 1974 a short article on the 950th anniversary of the town of Suzdal reported that the "Presidium of the Supreme Soviet of the USSR" had issued a decree awarding Suzdal a "badge of honor." The article goes on to note almost in passing that "to mark this jubilee, the reconstruction of the Red Square in Suzdal and the Spas-yevfimiesky [Savior-Yevfim] and other architectural monuments" was approved.[36]

The casual, low-key sentence conceals a struggle over the country's history. Suzdal was the holding (or appanage) of the same Yury Dolgoruky who had invited his ally Prince Svyatoslav of Novgorod-Seversk to "Moskva" for that mighty dinner. Thus Suzdal was even older than Moscow. Rebuilding the church and the square enabled Russians to access lost events, the underbrush of the eventual establishment of Moscow as Russia's most important city. The rebuilt church constituted a portal into a past otherwise impossibly distant. That such a link was acknowledged in 1974 during Brezhnev's years of "stagnation" indicates that turbulence bubbled beneath the surface.

VOOPIK now began openly challenging Soviet planners by turning the legal code against them. Soviet law required city and region soviets ("soviet" in the generic sense of "council") to consult with the local population before redevelopment, but this law had been more honored in the breach than in the observance. VOOPIK learned to manipulate statutes; Russian lawyers too opposed the senseless destruction of the country's history. By 1974 VOOPIK succeeded in forcing city councils to submit redevelopment plans for review. Although it could not veto blueprints outright, VOOPIK could insist on alterations. That year its assistant director, Vladimir Ivanov, told the correspondent for the *Christian Science Monitor* (one of the few Western papers paying attention) that VOOPIK was generally able to negotiate some kind of compromise with the local city council: "After all, we can't demand that nothing be built, however much some of our members might like to. That would be too much like Don Quixote tilting at his windmills."[37]

Director Ivanov was being too modest. VOOPIK scored a number of successes that environmental groups in the United States might envy. One of its most noteworthy was its version of the "sit down." Taking a page from the handbook of techniques of the American civil rights movement (with which the Russians were, of course, familiar, as Soviet television had broadcast the struggle live throughout the 1960s), it literally stopped the wrecking ball in its tracks from destroying an eighteenth-century merchant's house on Moscow's Kropotkin Square. Members of VOOPIK plunked themselves down in front of the bulldozers night and day—Russians are masters at organizing a twenty-four-hour queue. The city soviet backed down.[38] VOOPIK chose this dramatic technique to save a secular, not a spiritual prize, an indicator of its care in marketing its raison d'être as saving "architectural and historical monuments." And individual members literally put their life on the line to save historic churches: an architect, one L. Antropov, saved the Church of Simeon the Stylite from destruction by crawling into the bucket of the excavator of the huge crane. He sat there until the Moscow soviet caved in,[39] a quixotic personal victory indeed.

Although Orthodoxy was not part of VOOPIK's overt agenda, party hacks knew very well what was going on. They struck back in print, arguing that the worth of "artistic and cultural monuments" (i.e., Orthodox churches and monasteries) must be assessed from the class-conscious party perspective. The bitter controversy, all couched in the Soviet lexicon of Marxism-Leninism neologisms, ran throughout the 1970s. One example will serve as a microcosm of both sides' positions. In 1973 a special correspondent for *Nauka i religiya* (*Science and Religion*), Alexander Shamaro, entered the fray. *Science and Religion* was not a publication about religion per se, but an avowedly atheist publication, campaigning *against* religion. Shamaro forthrightly stated that any evaluation of these old buildings should be done from the party's viewpoint: "The majority of monuments of ancient history and antique culture perpetuate, indeed, the memory of negative aspects of prerevolutionary history—of religious stupor and ecclesiastical domination, and of a class social system based on the exploitation of the toiling masses."[40] The party had been using these clichés in its anti-Orthodox propaganda for more than fifty years. Only the preferred medium had changed from visual aids (cartoons, posters) to the written word. For example, a 1924 propaganda comic book depicted the "light of the church" as carried, Atlas-like, on the backs of toiling serfs (figure 3.6). Shamaro lip-synched the party line, but that was not the end of the story.

Mirabile dictu, a public debate ensued. The historian S. Semanov, called on society to "rebuff decisively all frivolous or false tendencies concerned with the historical memory of our people." This sounds sufficiently opaque that Western readers may be mystified. The point came in the form of a clever question: what is to become of the Troitse-Sergiev (e.g., Trinity–St. Sergius) Monastery in Zagorsk (the Soviet name for Sergiev Posad)? Here Semanov alludes to a famous episode from medieval times, familiar to every Russian schoolchild, when the Poles besieged the monastery (1608–10) and the monks and their walls withstood the onslaught. Semanov pinioned the party's hack on the horns of a dilemma. If Shamaro says let the monastery deteriorate, he is unpatriotic. If he agrees that it must be preserved, then he acknowledges a fact that the party preferred to ignore: the fate of the state was entwined with the Russian Orthodox Church at that critical moment. A seemingly academic argument is of enormous significance—the battle for the historical memory is over the country's future.

With this exchange as the context, the reader will appreciate VOOPIK's creative legerdemain in justifying saving churches. Thus, for example, on October 2, 1975, *Sovietskaya Rossiya* reported that a museum was being created in the village where the famous poet Sergei Yesenin was born. As an afterthought, the newspaper slips in, "in order to recreate the atmosphere where Yesenin passed his childhood, the village church has been restored."[41] *Sovietskaya Rossiya* was a publication of what was then the Russian Republic, another sign that Russian nationalism was covertly linking with Orthodoxy. Yesenin was known for his poetry about village life. His simple, elegiac lines about rural Russia made him a hero to Russian nationalists. Believers read his 1925 suicide as a protest against the depredation visited upon the peasantry by the Bolsheviks.

But there was a limit to the number of new museums that could be opened and supported. As more churches were restored, existing Soviet art galleries and museums began to acquire them as annexes. In 1966 the Tretyakov Art Gallery, which houses Russia's principal collection of nineteenth-century paintings, lobbied to have the restored Church of the Resurrection at Kadashi attached to it. The Soviet state had restored the outer shell of the buildings, including the five green "onion" domes. In its wisdom, the state proposed using the structure for a metal pipe extrusion factory.[42] The Church of the Resurrection eventually was assigned to the Grabar All-Russian Artistic Scientific Restoration Center (VKhNRTs).[43]

Once Gorbachev showed his support for the millennial celebrations of the Baptism of Rus, VOOPIK no longer needed to emphasize the historical and

Figure 3.6 Early Soviet antireligious propaganda appealed to the peasants' land
hunger. This cartoon from *Bezbozhnik* (*The Atheist*) satirizes the "Candle of Faith"
by depicting the Volokolamsk Monastery, which owned an enormous amount of
land, as breaking the backs of serfs. (Photo credit: Archive of Keston Institute)

architectural importance of its mission to the authorities. History speeded up. Within days of the August 1991 coup's failure, VOOPIK became overtly what it was covertly all along—an organization to save Orthodox churches. Moscow newspapers now openly printed the name and address of churches in need of restoration, helpfully listing bus numbers and routes to the sites. "By Bus to Ancient Rus" was the slogan in 1979 when a VOOPIK army of volunteers restored the Church of the Epiphany (Bogoyavlenie), at Istra outside Moscow, beside the New Jerusalem Monastery. VOOPIK had promoted the project to the state planners for the 1980 Moscow Olympics, arguing that competitors and visitors would enjoy a "new open air museum of old Russian buildings."[44] VOOPIK needed to change only one word to spread the campaign nationwide: "By Bus to Holy Rus."

Since 1991 VOOPIK's army of volunteers has grown by leaps and bounds. It also began making sophisticated use of Western-style advertising techniques. Its current Web site (http:/voopik.ru/), lists seven principal sections: What is VOOPIK? Presidium, Products, Documents, Articles, SMI on VOOPIK, and Contacts. There are active branches in every region. VOOPIK sponsors conferences, roundtables, essay competitions on "Best Presentation of the Need to Preserve the National Heritage," and a plethora of other worthy activities. In one conference, "Volunteers of the Twentieth Century," members of a military historical club, met. Since its founding in 1965, VOOPIK has penetrated every corner of the vast Russian Federation. It appeals, as Rotary does in the United States, to patriotic and energetic people who want to do good. The Orthodox context adds a sacred overlay.

Church restoration for Russians does not mean creating a new country but restoring their old one. In this sense, the remains of Orthodox churches are not only spiritual centers but archaeological sites telling the ancestral nation's tale. This gives urgency to the campaign, for they are physical evidence affirming the perennial existence of the faith, the state, and the people. As the ROC formulates it, Moscow as the New Jerusalem of Orthodoxy lies beneath the skin of the contemporary city. The Soviet epidermis need only be peeled away. Participating in church reconstruction thus offers the volunteer the comfort that he or she is partaking of the divine plan.

In the midst of all this praiseworthy activity, it would only be human to find some potential for evil. Sadly, it is the old tsarist cancer of anti-Semitism. By 1989 an explanation for the church destruction had sprung into print: it had all been a sinister plan of the Zionists to destroy Holy Russia. A certain Vladimir Zamansky used the pages of *Literaturnaya Rossiya* to make this charge, giving as evidence the Jewish ethnicity of both of Stalin's satraps, Boris Iofan and Lev Kaganovich.[45] Aleksy wanted to focus on church recovery

without pausing for scapegoats. While leading the charge to restore Orthodox churches, he thus simultaneously fought a rearguard action against a
faction of his own flock. These people were frequently members of the same
VOOPIK who did so much to preserve churches during the post-Khrushchev
period.[46] Aleksy needed their energy and commitment; he did not want their
desire for revenge. The two major fronts upon which this mobile war of
maneuver clashed would be the cult of St. Seraphim and the memory of the
last imperial family, the Romanovs.

FOUR

Accursed Questions: Who Is to Blame?

We must realize that a good and clear future
for ourselves depends upon to what extent we
ourselves can become good and clear.

—*Patriarch Aleksy II at the "All Russian Scientific & Theological Conference on
St. Seraphim and the Destiny of Russia," October 4, 2004*

THE 1988 CELEBRATIONS of the Millennium of the Baptism of Rus permitted the church new and exhilarating privileges. But glasnost had other,
less praiseworthy consequences. It opened the media to right-wing nationalist
organizations known collectively as Pamyat (Memory). Each of the factions
that emerged by 1990 shared one core belief: Jews were the source of Russia's
problems. Skinheads adorned with swastika armbands goose-stepped on the
fringes of society in outright imitation of Hitler's SS. But the most dangerous of the splinter groups, the National Orthodox Movement, was embedded within the Russian Orthodox Church itself and appropriated Orthodox
symbols and traditions. Many of its members had participated in VOOPIK
and helped repair Russian Orthodox churches and monasteries across the
length and breadth of the country. But they were not content to renovate
and rebuild; they wanted vengeance. They presented a hideous dilemma
for the patriarch. These were some of the church's most ardent believers
and experienced volunteers—they even had supporters within the hierarchy
itself. How could their toxic message be neutralized? And at the moment
when Aleksy became patriarch, they had a head start in the race to shape
the church's revival.

On March 21, 1990, three months before Aleksy's enthronement, they
spewed Jew-hating on the public stage. Leaders of five Pamyat groups organized a national news conference; under the guise of attacking Zionism, they
brayed hatred of Jews and Judaism. The most outspoken of the cabal and a
leader of the National Orthodox Movement, Alexander Kulakov, asserted:

Russia has always stood on three principles—Orthodoxy, Autocracy and
Nationality. Revival of this tradition is the basis of our movement....

The destruction of the Russian Orthodox faith, the Aryan genotype, and the disintegration of Russia are the fundamental credo of Zionism.... We demand a stop to the emigration of Soviet Jews until we can carry out an investigation into the part they have played in destroying our country.[1]

Kulakov starts from the premise, first articulated 147 years earlier under Tsar Nicholas I (1825–55), that "Orthodoxy, Autocracy and Nationalism" formed the basis of Russian morality, education, and intellectual life. Count S. S. Uvarov, minister of education from 1833 to 1849, officially formulated this trinity in a sycophantic letter to the "iron tsar" in 1843. Thus forewarned, Nicholas I avoided the revolutions and public demonstrations that arose in Western Europe in 1848. Government documents, newspapers, and schoolbooks taught "Official Nationality" for generations. But what worked in the mid-nineteenth century (Nicholas I offered Russian troops to other monarchs to stamp out reform) became outmoded within a generation. Upholding "Official Nationality" alienated the government from the intelligentsia, the professional classes, and progressives within its own bureaucracy.

By 1917 the Autocracy could not even guarantee the people bread. After their takeover, the Bolsheviks interrogated General Sergey Khabalov, the commander of the military district of St. Petersburg. He testified he received a report on February 25, 1917, that, "as a consequence of a lack of bread, strikes have broken out in many works [factories]." Nicholas II, imperturbable as ever, sent him a telegram from army headquarters: "I command you to stop tomorrow the disorders in the capital, which are intolerable in the difficult time of war with Germany and Austria. [signed] Nicholas." The general was "thunderstruck" at the message's complete ignorance of reality: "How was I to stop the people? When they said 'Give us bread'—we gave bread and it was over. But now they write on their flags 'Down with autocracy'; what bread is going to calm that down?"[2]

Kulakov, leader of the National Orthodox Movement, began his platform in 1990 by repeating slogans that the Russian people had rejected in 1917. In a single diatribe, he melded the worst language of Hitler's fascism—ranting about the "Aryan genotype"—with the tsarist canard straight out of *The Protocols of the Elders of Zion* that the "disintegration of Russia" was the "credo of Zionism." Substitute "Judaism" for "Zionism" and he would be parroting anti-Semitic propaganda from the presses of 1906–7. Kulakov led an openly and avowedly Russian Orthodox pressure group that linked its appeal to a revival of tsarism. Its yellow and black banner was emblazoned with the badge of St. George, the same emblem added to the tsarist double eagle to form the state insignia in 1672.

On May 7, 1990, another feature of the group's platform surfaced in the Western press. *Newsweek*'s cover story was entitled "The Long Shadow: New Fears of Anti-Semitism in Eastern Europe and the Soviet Union." Sitting in his dingy Moscow apartment, Kulakov told the *Newsweek* reporter "the liberation of mankind will start in Russia. It was prophesied that Russia would be the one to eliminate world evil."[3] The comment is simply left there on the page. The journalist missed the unspoken context: Kulakov was referencing the prophecies of St. Seraphim of Sarov.

That elliptical allusion is key to what made the National Orthodox Movement so dangerous. By 1990 it had infiltrated two cults with many Orthodox supporters: the veneration for St. Seraphim and nostalgia for the Romanovs. This mix presented Aleksy, destined to become patriarch just weeks later, with a subtle problem. He planned to recover the saint's relics in December 1990 (he knew where they were because of his KGB connections), and he intended to use the St. Seraphim magic for his theme of spiritual renewal. He needed the Seraphim-inspired energy to generate a long-term campaign to restore church property. He did not want this energy diverted into scapegoating Jews. Aleksy had to pry the beloved hermit of Sarov from the grasp of anti-Semites and monarchists who claimed to represent the church.

Aleksy expended a great deal of ingenuity during the 1990s doing just that. He could not move simultaneously against both anti-Semites and monarchists (they overlap considerably). Like a skilled chess player, he did not take the gambit and pander to Russia's monarchists by immediately canonizing the imperial family. That would have resolved one issue the ROC faced internationally, because the Russian Orthodox Church Abroad (ROCA), which opposed Soviet rule from the outset, made the royal family's canonization a prerequisite for any "ecumenical" negotiations with the Moscow Patriarchate. Here Aleksy played for time. To canonize the Romanovs in the early 1990s would have split the church domestically. The Church Abroad had flooded Russia with émigré brochures and books, and the right-wing press eagerly popularized them.

Lenin issued secret orders to murder the royal family on the night of July 16–17, 1918 o.s. (the new style date would be July 30–31). Their bones were discovered in 1978 in Yekaterinburg, but this was kept very quiet. Under Gorbachev, facts about the horrific manner of their death dribbled out, reigniting passions. Aleksy accepted that the canonization would come, but only when he could set the agenda—just as he would co-opt the St. Seraphim magic in July 1991 by personally leading the translation pilgrimage of the saint's relics.

While Aleksy kept the canonization of the Romanovs on the back burner, he fought on a second front against the anti-Semites entrenched within his church. This was a hearts-and-minds struggle with enormous stakes. The Russian Orthodox Movement published on a hand press in Moscow in 1989 its Manifesto consisting of sixty-one demands. John Garrard obtained a copy during a 1990 research trip and published its translation and analysis in the fall of 1991.[4] He noted that a full thirteen of its sixty-one demands are drawn from a specifically Russian Orthodox perspective:

6. We demand the complete implementation of constitutional provisions guaranteeing freedom of belief for all religions, and in the first instance for Orthodox Christianity, which has been subjected to the greatest and harshest persecution.

7. We demand the publication of the names and the eternal memorialization of murdered Orthodox priests.

8. We demand that the names of their murderers be made public, and that the guilty should be brought to trial.

9. We demand a published list of ALL destroyed Religious Shrines [Khramy].

10. We demand that the names of those who destroyed these Religious Shrines be made public, and that the guilty should be brought to trial.

11. We demand that the whole truth be revealed concerning religious persecution and other outrages against the people.

12. We demand that the defilement of all Religious Shrines be halted.

13. We demand that all damaged and destroyed Religious Shrines be restored at the state's expense, and that the entire patrimony of the Orthodox Church, stolen at various times in the past, should be returned to it in perpetuity as its inalienable property.

14. We demand the right to construct new Religious Shrines throughout our Land without interference.

15. We demand that Holy Ritual be resumed in all Religious Shrines, and first of all at the Uspensky [Assumption] Cathedral in the Moscow Kremlin. The Kremlin must become not simply the political but also the spiritual center of the Nation.

16. We demand the separation of atheism [i.e., the state ideology called "Marxism-Leninism" and taught in every school by paid "atheist workers"] and the state.

35. Who thought up the abominable notion of preventing people from discussing God with children? We demand that a series of courses on the Holy Scriptures should be introduced into the school curriculum.

Aleksy wanted some of those demands met too, but by no means all.

Aleksy's adoption of demand 15—that the liturgy be celebrated once again in the Kremlin cathedrals, beginning with the Assumption—illustrates his principle of selection and the power of the forces arrayed against him. Aleksy was celebrating the Feast of the Transfiguration in this very cathedral when the KGB and party hard-liners ordered tanks and armor into Red Square on August 19, 1991. At that time, his service was a special privilege, for the building was not then a working cathedral. Like all the other Kremlin cathedrals, it was under the jurisdiction of a state agency, which regarded it as a museum through which tourists—both domestic and international—could be shepherded. Indeed, the first time since the Bolshevik takeover that a full-scale liturgy was celebrated at the Cathedral of the Assumption occurred on Sunday, September 23, 1990. That was not on a liturgical feast day but the secular calendar's holiday "Moscow Day"—a telling reminder of how grudgingly the CPSU doled out its favors. The Soviet Union still existed, and the cathedral was a state museum. Among the curators guarding it was no less a figure than the daughter of General Alexander Rodimtsev, one of the heroes of Stalingrad.

It took Aleksy several years to get the Kremlin cathedrals restored to the church. (This "war to the knife" replicates on a grand scale the skirmish between the book depository staff and Father Sergy Romanov over the building of St. Vladimir's Church.) Peter the Great transferred their ownership to the government when he abolished the patriarchate and established the Synod to run day-to-day ROC affairs. In the early 1990s Rodimtseva and the other curators were still fighting to keep the cathedrals under their control and just "lend" them out for specific occasions. Even after the official dissolution of the USSR on December 25, 1991, this remained state policy. On May 6, 1992, Aleksy celebrated the Feast of St. George's Day in the Assumption Cathedral. Rodimtseva and other staffers milled about outside lamenting the damage being done to "their" precious frescoes and icons.[5]

But the challenge from secular bureaucrats was not Aleksy's only headache that day. Because the National Orthodox Movement used the emblem of St. George, Aleksy did not want the celebration of St. George's feast day in the same Cathedral of the Assumption—demand 15 from its Manifesto—to be seen as a Movement victory. Immediately after the service, he led a procession through the streets of Moscow to the Church of the Ascension by the Nikitsky Gates. The BBC noted that many in the group held aloft portraits of Nicholas II, but the procession was orderly and Aleksy's authority stopped it segueing into a demonstration against the Jews, whom the monarchists blamed for the murder of the imperial family. This episode illustrates the soap opera quality of the early 1990s, so laden with subplots were the times. In the furor over the Assumption Cathedral, Aleksy outmaneuvered the old Soviet elite, many of whom still held their powerful positions, and simultaneously outfoxed a dangerous faction of his own church.

The National Orthodox Movement's pathological hatred of Jews is laid out in the Manifesto's preface: "Our aim is the spiritual revival and unification of the People of our Fatherland which has been tortured and plundered by aggressive Zionism, Talmudic atheism, and cosmopolitan usury." At the same time, several demands deliberately echo the tsarist trinity of "Autocracy, Orthodoxy and Nationalism":

1. We demand the rescue of our Great Power [Derzhava] from its position as a colony, a mere supplier of raw materials for the worldwide Zionist oligarchy, and its return to the status of spiritual, political and economic independence, which was bequeathed to it by our ancestors, and which it enjoyed for centuries.

3. We demand the whole truth be told about those responsible for the genocide of the Russian people and other peoples of our country.

4. We demand that the whole truth be revealed about the ritualistic, fanatical murder of the Russian Tsar.

40. Honorable people cannot countenance any compromise whatsoever with the Zionist state, which was established and continues to exist on the basis of the doctrine of Jewish Fascism. We categorically protest against the diplomatic relations that have been established with Israel.

50. We consider all incidents of separatism and ethnic hostility in our country to be vile Zionist-Masonic provocations, and demand the true names of those behind these incidents, and their punishment.

56. We demand an end to the brutal raping of our mineral resources, forests, and reservoirs by international usurious Zionist capitalists.

60. We demand the opening of archives and the uncovering of the secret levers of power that mutilated our people during the "red terror" and "war communism," and the "cult of personality," "reckless adventurism," and "stagnation." We demand also the names of those who gave over our country to wholesale rapine and pillage and who condemned all the peoples of our Great Power, chiefly the Russian people, to spiritual impoverishment and genocide. During the Zionist genocide that took place in our country, more people were killed than in all the wars ever fought in human history.

This grab bag of charges coheres neither logically nor historically. Demand 56 accuses the Jews, whom it earlier blamed for the depredations of

Communism, with spearheading the "usurious" capitalism "raping" Russia in the immediate present. Demand 60 gunnysacks over seventy years of Soviet history: "red terror" and "war communism" are synonyms for Lenin's tenure; the "cult of personality" is a code word for Stalin's rule; "reckless adventurism" means Khrushchev's time; and "stagnation" refers to Brezhnev. According to the National Orthodox Movement then, the Jews were behind every single zig and zag of Soviet policy, and every past, present, and any possible future evil visited upon Russia, the Russians, and the Russian Orthodox Church. Indeed, zigzagging becomes a new criminal charge, for somehow the Jews morph into shape-shifters like Satan himself. The Movement, looking for scapegoats for all its present humiliations, returned to medieval notions to find them.

It was as if a passion play from the Middle Ages had been running continuously in the minds of Kulakov and his fanatics. The Manifesto posits the Jews of 1990 reenacting the mob in the Gospel of Matthew, screaming to Pontius Pilate, "His blood be on us and on our children" (Matthew 27:25). No less a figure than Valentin Rasputin, a Russian intellectual, a respected writer, and fervent Orthodox believer who had been appointed to Gorbachev's Presidential Council, made a statement that exemplified the anti-Semites' ability to merge events separated by millennia. He asserted that the Jews "killed God" and were responsible for the October Revolution and the mass terror that followed it.[6] The Russian Orthodox Movement's Demand 4 called for the "truth [to] be revealed about the ritualistic, fanatical murder of the Russian Tsar." This demand, premised upon the fantasy that Jews murdered Christian children for blood to make *matzohs* for the Passover meal, had connotations that were truly feudal. The jumble of atavistic charges should have been dismissed out of hand, but the times were so tumultuous. The National Orthodox Movement paraded behind banners of St. George, carried portraits of Nicholas II and icons of the Theotokos, and sang "God Save the Tsar." Would they too, like the Nazis in Germany, infect society with mass hysteria?

The Pamyat Manifesto wraps its core of anti-Semitic rant with several layers of soothing and quite praiseworthy appeals. In addition to the demands for the revival of Russian Orthodoxy, there are points expressing support for the army, the family, concern for the environment and natural resources, a call for land to be given back to the peasantry, condemnation of officious bureaucrats, and a demand for greater decorum in the theater and the arts. These innocuous-sounding appeals are eerily similar to the original Nazi Party Manifesto. When it was issued in 1920, the Nazi Party had but sixty members. Only two of its twenty-five points were overtly anti-Semitic. However, it was Adolph Hitler who wrote those two points. In 1935, after he became chancellor, the Nuremberg Laws made them the law of the land.[7]

With the state's hegemony so weakened, in May 1990 the Russian Republic of the USSR paralleled Weimar Germany: once again a weak democracy went through hyperinflation and threatened the citizenry with economic ruin. The center was not holding. Yet another "blood-dimmed tide," to borrow W. B. Yeats's phrase from "The Second Coming," was gathering strength, this time to unleash its fury on Soviet Jewry. When Aleksy was enthroned as patriarch June 10, there was a very real possibility of a "Weimar Russia," a comparison first made in the authors' long cautionary letter to the *New York Times* dated May 27, 1990 (see appendix B).

To appreciate the full significance of the dilemma confronting Aleksy, the publishing history of *The Protocols of the Elders of Zion*, a "warrant for genocide" (to use the apt phraseology of Norman Cohn), and how it came to be entangled with the St. Seraphim and Romanov cults must be understood. In 1901 a strange figure, Sergey Nilus, published a pamphlet, *The Great in the Small; or, The Advent of the Antichrist and the Approaching Rule of the Devil on Earth*. This appears to have been an abbreviated form of what would become a larger book.[8] It propounded a weird and apocalyptic view of history—not surprising, because Nilus himself was so extravagant in his behavior that the ROC refused to accept him as a candidate for the priesthood, although he claimed to be a priest. Nilus believed that the Antichrist stood before the gates of St. Petersburg. The end of the world was at hand. The Antichrist had already overpowered the rest of Europe, "introducing liberal institutions such as constitutions, parliaments, universal suffrage, compulsory education, trial by jury, and so forth." Only the holy Autocracy of Russia, protected by its tsar, stood as a bulwark against the devil's power. Nilus then posed an explosive question. Who is this Antichrist? He had been vouchsafed the answer. The Antichrist was an ordinary mortal Jew:

> Before the return of the Lord and the Last Judgment will come the other in His name, the Antichrist, who springing from Jewish blood, will be tsar and master of the whole earth, a messiah out of the House of David, that is, Israel, which bears the guilt for the blood of the true messiah and whose destinies even today are government by Pharisees and scribes.

Nilus could not disregard that the Jews were dispersed around the world and seemed rather persecuted. He wrestled with the conundrum as to how such a small number of people were to bring about world domination. Then Nilus was granted an epiphany: "The advent of the Antichrist, the Second Coming of the Lord, and the end of the world shall not and must not be effected until the Holy Spirit prepares mankind in appropriate ways."[9] In spite of all the scholarship about *The Protocols*, the importance of Nilus's reference to "the Holy Spirit" is underestimated. Yet it was the crucial cog in the coming disinformation campaign. In 1903, the Seraphim canonization year, Nilus went to Diveyevo Convent. There he had a vision, which would have far-reaching consequences.

The modest hermit Seraphim never wrote anything down. But he had a disciple who did at great length. Nicholas Alexandrovich Motovilov was a young nobleman who claimed Seraphim healed him of his ailments in 1831. After his miraculous cure, Motovilov lived at the Diveyevo Convent. One day, he wrote, Seraphim summoned him to his forest hut. During a long conversation Motovilov saw Seraphim illuminated by a white incandescent light; he discovered that he too was enveloped by the same light. (The link with the Transfiguration luminescence is clear.) Motovilov wrote down the ensuing conversation in one of some twenty notebooks in which he recorded everything he witnessed of the hermit. He died in 1879, but his widow kept the notebooks in an attic. Motovilov wrote both illegibly and in code. For twenty-four years they reposed undeciphered.

And there it all might have stayed, except that Nilus examined their hundred-plus pounds of crumbling paper with bird droppings scattered throughout. He spent hours fruitlessly trying to understand Motovilov's handwriting, which he termed "ciphers." In despair, he finally called out: "Father Seraphim, why have you given me the opportunity to receive the manuscript of your 'servant' in so distant a place as Diveyevo if, undecipherable, it will return again to oblivion?" Miraculously, the very next day, he understood what had once been "gibberish" and "unsolved hieroglyphics"![10] Thus empowered, Nilus "transcribed" the key encounter between the disciple and the saint, entitling it: "The Holy Spirit Clearly Resting on Fr. Seraphim of Sarov in his Conversation on the Aim of the Christian Life with the Simbirsk Landowner and Judicial Counselor Nicholas Alexandrovich Motovilov." This conversation is described as a "classic of Russian spirituality and the theology of contemporary Orthodoxy," and a "precious pearl of Russian spirituality."[11] Here Seraphim declares that the aim of the Christian life is "the acquisition of the Holy Spirit."[12]

This did not remain in the arcane realm of Russian Orthodox patristics. Nilus immediately expanded his earlier pamphlet *The Great in the Small* and he appended to it his transcription of "The Conversation." In 1901 Nilus promised that the Antichrist would not come until "the Holy Spirit prepares mankind in appropriate ways." The 1903 edition of *The Great in the Small* explains how the Holy Spirit would be acquired—and the mouthpiece was the beloved hermit of Sarov, Seraphim.

The next link in the chain occurred when the tsar and the imperial family attended the canonization ceremony. Here Nicholas was informed of St. Seraphim's mysterious "prophecies" and the claim that one must be meant specifically for him. The Diveyevo Convent had a tradition of prophetic women identified as "holy fools" (*yurodivye*). One of these elderly nuns lived on from Seraphim's death in 1833 to 1903. She informed Nicholas that Seraphim directly confided information to her that she was to pass on to a tsar, and undoubtedly he was that tsar. These warnings paralleled those Motovilov swore Seraphim had dictated to him in a "Letter to the Future," instructing the young nobleman to take them to the then emperor, Nicholas I. The key prophecy relating to the tsar was:

> They will wait for a time of great hardship to afflict the Russian land, and on an agreed day, at the agreed hour, they will raise up a general rebellion all over the Russian land, and, since many soldiers will join in their evildoing, there will be no one to stop them, and at first much innocent blood will be spilt, it will run in rivers over the Russian land, and they will kill many of your brother nobles and priests as well as merchants who support the emperor.[13]

Seraphim had wanted his "Letter to the Future" to be delivered to Tsar Nicholas I, "his most Devout Consort Alexandra Feodorovna and his mother, the Dowager Empress Maria Feodorovna." Recalling the Sovereign Nicholas I, the hermit had said, "He is in soul a Christian."[14] This was all communicated verbally to Nicholas II at one of the most emotional moments of his life. He apparently regarded this prophecy as if written for him and his family. After all, the imperial couple reasoned, this prophecy had not been fulfilled during the reign of Nicholas I. But now, seventy years after the death of Seraphim, was he not the tsar named Nicholas with a consort named Alexandra Feodorovna and a mother, the dowager empress, named Maria Feodorovna?

The fallout from Nicholas and Alexandra's learning of the prophecies of Seraphim was enormous. In 1905 Alexandra ordered that copies "be made for her."[15] Seraphim himself never identifies the mysterious "they" who will wreak havoc on Russia.[16] Nicholas filled in the pronoun referent: the Jews. And the "Jews as agents of the apocalypse" canard did not stay just as chat between the imperial couple. In the last month of the revolutionary year of 1905, with the headlines dominated by strikes, protests, and the near fall of autocracy, Nilus was again allowed to reprint *The Great in the Small*. And this time he added to its appendix new material: *The Protocols of the Elders of Zion*.[17] When Nilus appended *The Protocols* to the 1905 edition of *The Great in the Small*, the book's subtitle functioned as an explanation for them: *The Advance of the Antichrist and the Kingdom of the Devil on Earth*.

In the subsequent editions of *The Great and the Small* that the ROC presses brought out between 1905 and 1917 both *The Protocols* and "The Conversation" were printed. As cataclysms began to overtake Russia, a kind of collective hysteria grew in the peasant mind-set: "Seraphim knew it would all come out," and "Seraphim knew it was all done by the Jews." Thus, through the convoluted publishing history of an obscure book, replete with fantastic and ludicrous warnings of a giant conspiracy akin to Dan Brown's *The Da Vinci Code*, a fatal and false linkage between *The Protocols* and the saint's cult was embedded in the Orthodox popular imagination. And no one in the tsar's administration would cut the Gordian knot by acknowledging that *The Protocols* was known to be a fabrication.

Where did Nilus get them?

Nilus thought he was the conduit to bring the insights of a saintly hermit to believers. Whether he realized it or not, he was actually carrying out a "false flag" intelligence operation. The work he attributed to Russia's Jews was disinformation concocted by the tsar's own intelligence service, the Okhrana, in Paris.[18] *The Protocols of the Elders of Zion* was part of its tactics to quell the revolutionary movement. The technique might be described as "backfire burning." The metaphor comes from firefighting, where in order to tamp down a blaze, a swathe of adjacent ground is purposely burned to the ground so that the fire cannot jump to fresh fuel. In practical terms, this meant that the Okhrana deliberately added to revolutionary violence through inserting *agents provocateurs*. By setting off controlled violence, the police could then extinguish the ensuing turmoil to the applause of the population and the gratitude of the dynasty. Because the police organized the carnage, they could contain it, or so went the theory. The general public was supposed to be frightened by the uproar, and thus turn away from the activists to passively obey the autocratic tsar.

To this end the Okhrana saturated revolutionary councils with men who directed and organized assassinations, strikes, and illegal presses. Ethnic Jews (nonpracticing) were their favorite double agents. The secret police positioned them in a wide variety of activist groups. Those Jews were hired outside the tsar's own regulations, which prohibited Jews from joining the Okhrana, or any other official agency for that matter, because a new recruit or employee had to swear allegiance on the Orthodox Bible to the Orthodox tsar. (Poles, as Catholics, were also automatically excluded from official work in the Okhrana as members of the hated "Latinizers" of Western Christianity.)

Because Jews who converted to Orthodoxy *were* eligible to join the Okhrana, some did. One Harting did so in 1890; the Okhrana Archive contains his letter making the request. Harting, code-named ARTAK, later served as chief of section in Berlin from 1901 to 1902. In 1904 he moved to Paris, where he was chief of the entire international wing of the Okhrana from 1905 until his retirement in 1909.[19] The record Harting left behind of the "backfire burning" policy is devastating. He forwarded to St. Petersburg from Paris reports on funds for arms purchases being funneled to the Jewish Bund, an early workers' union. He maps out the current methods and routes used by revolutionaries for smuggling arms and propaganda back into Russia. He is monitoring a plot to assassinate the tsar organized in Geneva by a man named Afanasiev. As his dispatches make clear, Harting successfully placed agents posing as radicals in the revolutionary movement's councils, committees, conferences, and congresses.[20] Backfire burning gave the Okhrana ready-made plots to foil at will; unwitting perpetrators, such as the luckless Afanasiev, to ensnare; and eager stool pigeons to testify against their duped confederates.

Sometime prior to 1903—the actual date is still uncertain—the Okhrana took yet another step in the dangerous double game it was playing. No longer content to place its agent, then watch and arrest, the secret police now decided to manufacture evidence and then use its own product to justify *pre-emptive* repression. The end result was their fabrication of *The Protocols of the Elders of Zion*.[21] The head of the Russian secret police abroad was at this time was Pyotr Ivanovich Rachkovsky, a sinister figure whose agent Azef would later throw the bomb that killed the tsar's uncle, Grand Duke Sergey Alexandrovich in 1905.

On its face *The Protocols* pretended to be the verbatim report of a meeting of Jewish leaders discussing a massive conspiracy to overthrow Nicholas's rule and then dominate the world. In fact, it was an adaptation of a French work written and published a generation earlier by Maurice Joly entitled *Dialogue aux enfers entre Machiavel et Montesquieu ou la politique au XIXe siècle (Dialogue between Machiavelli and Montesquieu in Hell; or, Politics in the Nineteenth Century)*. Joly intended his work to be a critique of French political figures, notably Napoleon III. He put it in the form of a genre well known among French intellectuals, the *dialogue des morts*, a fictional "dialogue of the dead" in which a writer invents exchanges between famous historical figures to satirize contemporary events.[22] An unknown agent in the Paris Okhrana did some judicious cutting and pasting, gave the work a new title and setting, and inserted new speakers for the same dialogue.[23] Thus transformed, Joly's sophisticated attack on Napoleon III read as a verbatim transcript of a meeting of Jewish leaders plotting world domination. *The Protocols of the Elders of Zion* is in essence a hate crime committed by the tsarist state against a segment of its own population.

In August and September 1903 a serialized version of *The Protocols* appeared in *Znamya (The Banner)*, a St. Petersburg newspaper whose editor was the infamous Pavolachi Krushevan, active in the pogrom that had decimated the Kishinyov ghetto during the preceding Easter.[24] In an eerie prelude to the Nazi Kristallnacht of November 1938, Russian anti-Semites plundered Jewish stores, smashing their windows, and attacked and murdered any Jews they came across.[25] The tsarist police stood aside. It signaled that Nicholas's government encouraged aggression against the empire's Jews and supported using them as scapegoats for the empire's problems. Like waves in phase, these two events of 1903 set the stage for even greater violence. The tsar's refusal to punish those responsible for the Kishinyov pogrom gave Russia's anti-Semites the license they wanted. It was not necessary for the tsarist police to organize these riots; they could just watch.

Meanwhile, the Okhrana waited for a "useful idiot" (to borrow Lenin's colorful phrase) to disseminate *The Protocols* in a form that would blend its anti-Semitism with religious fervor. The newspaper version was too easily traced to the openly anti-Semitic Krushevan. Nilus fit the bill perfectly. The tsar and tsarina themselves were completely devoted to the St. Seraphim cult. This imperial support ipso facto increased anti-Semitism's scope and fury. In 1905, the first time Nilus's *The Great in the Small* appeared with *The Protocols* attached, pogroms tore apart the Pale of Settlement. Concocted by the Paris Okhrana, disseminated inside a Russian Orthodox book, and embedded in the cult of St. Seraphim, *The Protocols* was accepted as forensic proof that the Jews were conspiring treason and murder. The Okhrana had the perfect frame. And Nilus helpfully swept the whole operation clean of its fingerprints.

Tsar Nicholas II continued blaming the Jews even after Pyotr Stolypin showed him that *The Protocols* was a forgery. At some point it ceased to matter to him that the work was a concoction. He wanted it to be true so fervently he made judgments as if it were. Nicholas-style obscurantism had not died out after 1917. Such is the schizophrenic quality of the human mind that even after the Joly source was revealed, many anti-Semites refused to accept that *The Protocols* was not the transcript of a Jewish cabal trying to destroy Russia.

Given this background, the situation in the 1990s was particularly dangerous. Kulakov and his myrmidons had a powerful ally within the hierarchy of the ROC itself. Ironically, the very man who succeeded Aleksy as metropolitan of Leningrad (St. Petersburg), Metropolitan Ioann, became their rallying point. Metropolitan Ioann was born in 1927 as Ivan Snychev in southwest Ukraine, the precise region that experienced the horrors of Stalin's terror famine. Until 1990, when he was named to Aleksy's former post, he spent his entire career in the provincial backwater of Kuybyshev. There he was known as an activist, popular priest. Scarcely had the tanks turned around following the collapse of the August 1991 coup, however, than he came out as a rabid anti-Semite. He threw the weight of his office and his prestige behind justifying *The Protocols of the Elders of Zion* as a true, verbatim transcript of a conspiracy by Jewish leaders to extirpate Orthodox Russia and the Orthodox tsar. He reasoned the entire Soviet period was Jewry's fault.

Father Ioann handed Aleksy a monstrous problem on his own doorstep.

Though it was ninety years since the meretricious merging of an ascetic hermit's cult with the Okhrana's concoction of *The Protocols*, and almost the same amount of time since it was revealed to be a forgery, Nilus still had supporters and admirers within the ROC hierarchy. Having declared that *The Protocols of the Elders of Zion* was authentic, Father Ioann then claimed in the press that the recent events in Russia bore out its assertions.[26] Pamyat was delighted and eagerly distributed copies on city streets.

But this time something new happened in Russia. Jewish groups took those who had published *The Protocols* to court. The trial continued on and off for eleven months. Finally, in December 1993, the judge of the Moscow District Court, Lyudmila Belikova, handed down a courageous ruling: she labeled *The Protocols of the Elders of Zion* a forgery. She was the first Russian official to declare publicly the obvious truth. Judge Belikova also declared that Pamyat's publication of the tract constituted an anti-Semitic act.[27] The Jewish press in the West paid special attention to this trial, which indeed was a salutary sign of progress.

But while the judicial process demonstrated integrity, the outcome of the subterranean battle within the ROC was uncertain. In 1993 and 1994, undeterred by the evidence presented at the Moscow trial, Father Ioann's diocese helped publish new multivolume editions of *both* Seraphim's prophecies and *The Protocols of the Elders of Zion*. Here was a charismatic ROC prelate lending authority to the charge that the Jews bore collective guilt for crimes committed in both the primordial past and the immediate present. Given that Aleksy had taken the official position that the predictions of St. Seraphim were true visions, he had to sever Father Ioann's linkage of them to *The Protocols*. This involved a rejection of the ROC's own history, but the patriarch determined to break with that past.

Occasionally, the ripples from the resulting vicious intramural struggle surfaced in the Russian press. Aleksy was legally powerless to stop Ioann—there were no judicial proscriptions against anti-Semitism, and there were no ecclesiastical courts or ecclesiastical censorship as there had been under the tsars. What he could do was issue instructions to the head of the Moscow Patriarchate's publishing department that Ioann's articles should not appear in official publications because they had "elicited an ambiguous reaction in public opinion."[28] Undeterred, Father Ioann published a series of anti-Semitic articles in a right-wing nationalistic newspaper, *Den* (*Day*). Consequently, Aleksy now forbade him from making any more contributions to the press in general.[29]

Father Ioann's supporters struck back. Aleksy's clandestine efforts to silence Father Ioann were revealed in an open letter to the patriarch, published in *Sovietskaya Rossiya*, a pro-Communist newspaper on February 18, 1993.[30] It criticized Aleksy for restricting the metropolitan's authority. And Ioann had admirers even on the staff of the *Journal of the Moscow Patriarchate*, who sidestepped Aleksy's ban and published one of his articles in 1993.[31] Completely unrepentant, Ioann himself simply ignored Aleksy's direct orders. In 1993 and 1994 he brought out more anti-Jewish rant in nationalist newspapers.

Aleksy had to speak out because his silence would have been taken as consent. In April 1994 he gave an interview to *Moscow News* (*Moskovskie novosti*), disassociating himself and the Orthodox Church from Ioann's views: "You must remember that whatever high position His Grace Ioann occupies in the church hierarchy, he cannot speak on behalf of the church. That right belongs to the Local and Archbishops' Councils.... The Russian Orthodox Church is free of racial prejudice.... And I repeat: the opinion of one hierarch is still not the opinion of the church."[32] Aleksy was trying to lead by example, but the Father Ioann saga shows the toxicity plaguing the church hierarchy. While Aleksy had his attention focused on his recalcitrant prelate in St. Petersburg, out in the hinterlands of Novosibirsk in Siberia, Blagovest (Good News) Press published another edition of *The Great in the Small* in 1994. This was "a reprint of the 3rd edition" with "corrections and additions" of the Sergiev Posad 1911 edition,[33] which had contained both the "Conversation" and *The Protocols of the Elders of Zion*. The editors say: "This is the first postrevolutionary edition to include the prophetic essay 'The end is nigh [i.e., the advent of] the Antichrist and the Kingdom of the Devil on Earth!"' They then go on to argue that reading this prophetic essay will help the reader "understand more deeply and recognize everything that is happening in the world and Russia." It slipped under Aleksy's radar through a clever publishing trick: its table of contents *omits* listing *The Protocols of the Elders of Zion*—but unannounced, there it is in the appendix. Thus, while Aleksy had his hands full with Father Ioann on his own doorstep, out in the provinces Orthodox hierarchs covertly approved another round of the Okhrana's forgery. And with ROC editors arguing that they would help the reader understand what was happening in contemporary Russia, the stage was set for pogroms.

The denouement for the whole ugly Father Ioann saga came suddenly and most strangely. Shortly after the patriarch's interview with *Moscow News*, Metropolitan Ioann attended a reception held at a bank in St. Petersburg. There, Anatoly Sobchak, who was then St. Petersburg's mayor, and his wife approached him to be blessed. When Ioann stretched out his hand, "he suffered a heart attack and died shortly afterwards."[34] Father Ioann's demise cost Orthodox anti-Semites their most vocal and charismatic leader. His death certainly came most conveniently for Aleksy, who immediately appointed a metropolitan more to his liking.[35] With Father Ioann dead, Aleksy no longer had a traitor in the heart of the church hierarchy willing to subsidize printing of *The Protocols of the Elders of Zion*. That was a huge step in neutralizing the anti-Semites within the ROC.

All this while, Aleksy delayed resolving the other explosive problem located within the bosom of the church: the demands of monarchists to canonize the Romanovs. Here too the ROC was riddled with sympathizers for a path Aleksy was reluctant to take. He must come up with a solution that would neither split the church at home, nor offend the Church Abroad, nor reward the anti-Semites who blamed the Jews for the family's murder. Aleksy had discarded the medieval "blood libel" charge; now he updated a medieval idea to solve a contemporary problem. The Romanovs would be saints, yes, but not martyrs. The distinction is crucial.

Aleksy began this decade of maneuver and delay in a defensive position. The Russian Orthodox Church Abroad (ROCA), which separated from the Moscow Patriarchate in 1927, canonized in 1981 at a church council in New York all the Romanovs as "royal martyrs." ROCA made canonizing the Romanovs a condition of reentering into communion with the Moscow Patriarchate. Much as that consummation was devoutly to be wished, Aleksy did not want a martyr's crown for the Romanovs. That would place the imperial family at the forefront of the huge category of people who were indeed murdered within the USSR because of their Orthodox faith. These were the "new martyrs" (*novomucheniki*) and Aleksy had special plans for them, plans that did not include the ghosts of the imperial family.

On July 5, 1990, barely one month after his enthronement, he announced that he planned to canonize a number of Christians persecuted in the Soviet Union since 1917. The ROC asked Soviet authorities to release all papers documenting the executions of church members in these years.[36] Thus, one part of Pamyat's own demands—the "names and eternal memorializations of all murdered Orthodox priests"—was requested, however polite the ROC's language. Missing from Aleksy's petition, however, was any information about naming the perpetrators.

At the same time, the church refused to deal separately with canonization proceedings for the Romanovs. Aleksy had been patriarch for only thirty days, but he already went public with the statement that the case of the murdered family must be seen as "part of a much larger and wider process of canonizing of the countless Russian martyrs of modern times that has presently begun in the Soviet Union." Thus, from the outset, Aleksy set forth an agenda: the family could not be martyrs, for that would make them the most famous exemplars of the thousands of Orthodox Christians who suffered "for their faithfulness to Christ." Another way would have to be found. It took him ten years to get the church machinery to grind out his solution. Throughout those years he fought a determined though largely submerged battle against those prelates and believers who opposed him.

Occasionally, ripples surfaced in the press. In 1992, while the Congress of Russian Orthodox Bishops discussed the issue, editors weighed in with their opinions. The same influential newspaper *Moscow News*, which later published Aleksy's interview vis-à-vis Father Ioann in April 1994, printed an extremely critical article by Yakov Krotov, "Russian Tsar and Thy Kingdom Come," which laid out the church's dilemma from a secular perspective. As Krotov saw it, "canonization of Nicholas II would mean the canonization of a certain policy. The Church would be hard put to express its opinion about the essence of the Russian revolution, about Russia's past and future, and more specifically about the political rather than spiritual aspect of those phenomena. The canonization of Nicholas II will inevitably amount to the glorification of his policy."[37] The language may be clumsy, but the meaning is clear. Krotov is warning the church not to saint a man whose policies had caused endless suffering.

Other Russians more openly opposed to the monarchist movement weighed in. Shortly after the *Moscow News* article, the magazine *Ogonyok* published an open letter to the Congress of Russian Orthodox Bishops entitled

"Is Nicholas II a Saint?" In it, Mikhail Krivov, a doctoral candidate in history at Solnechnogorsk in the province of Moscow, recalled "Bloody Sunday," when tsarist troops fired upon unarmed demonstrators carrying banners of Nicholas while attempting to bring the tsar a petition. The petitioners were totally loyal, begging him to "break down the wall between Yourself and your people and grant our request." Krivov reminds his readers that the tsar's Cossacks killed more than one thousand people and wounded another two thousand. Monarchists might wish to draw a halo around the tsar's head, but Krotov and Krivov spoke for many Russians who still regarded him as "Bloody Nicholas," the ruler whose feckless decisions led not only to Bloody Sunday and the loss of the Russo-Japanese War but also to the disasters of World War I and the 1917 revolution.

The solution to the dilemma floated in a short response to Krivov printed in the same pages of *Ogonyok*. The liberal commentator Alexander Nezhny began by admitting that what Krivov had stated was historical fact. But "[if] Nicholas II is to be canonized, he would not be grouped with such great political leaders and defenders of Russian sovereignty as Alexander Nevsky and Dmitry Donskoy, but with the first saints canonized by the Russian Church, the 'passion-bearing princes,' Boris and Gleb." The "passion bearer" category (*strastoterptsy*) is the ROC's lowest level of sainthood. It was originally used in the eleventh century to canonize the first native Eastern Slav saints, the princes Boris and Gleb, the sons of St. Grand Prince Vladimir. This type of sainthood is virtually unique to Orthodoxy. Boris and Gleb were not killed because of their faith; they were ordered murdered by their brother Sviatopolk to eliminate them as claimants to the throne. It was their nonresistance to their deaths that earned them holy rank.

Nezhny then did something extraordinary. To buttress his argument, he quoted an émigré theologian Georgy Fedotov, whose seminal work, *The Russian Religious Mind: Kievan Christianity from the 10th to the 13th Century*, was published abroad. Nezhny drew attention to Fedotov's statement that saints Boris and Gleb were canonized as *strastoterpsty* because their nonresistance to evil constituted an imitation of Christ's willingness to undergo crucifixion. Nezhny quotes Fedotov further as saying that such nonresistance "cleanses the murdered victim" [i.e., from the sins they had committed in their lives]. Fedotov perceptively noted that in the "passion-bearers category of sainthood ... we are in the very core of the Russian religious world. Many a Russian saint was canonized for the only obvious reason: his violent death."[38] It was a straw in the wind. The ROC had not made a habit of reaching out to émigré theologians to justify its decisions. It signaled that the church was already (in 1992) floating the category of *strastoterpsty* as the appropriate level of sainthood for the Romanovs.

This being Russia, there was a hidden agenda. What was going on beneath the surface was an argument about restoring the monarchy. Aleksy and more progressive elements within the ROC fervently wanted to separate the canonization issue from any movement to bring back an autocracy. Thus Nezhny castigates the church monarchists who opposed them for trying to "manipulate the canonization" issue by parading with huge portraits of the tsar, "above their unthinking heads"[39] (*nad svoimi nerazmyshlyiayushchimi golovami*). Nezhny's use of the word *nerazmyshlyayushchimi* is particularly derogatory; based upon the word "unreasoning," the term "boneheaded" conveys the connotations. Nicholas did not deserve canonization for the way he ruled Russia, but for how he and his family faced their deaths. This alone would qualify them as *strastoterptsy*.

Aleksy's subtle game with the monarchists saw both sides maneuvering to win battles fought over the treatment of anniversaries. In 1997 the monarchists presented the ROC with a crisis made doubly serious because it resurrected an explosive charge made by the anti-Semites of the National Orthodox Movement—that the murder of the tsar and his family was a "ritual murder." The Holy Synod was scheduled to create an ecclesiastical award to mark 1997's "Year of the Child." The monarchists and reactionaries already had their candidate: the last tsarevich, Aleksey Nikolayevich (1904–18). Their choice of Aleksey was psychologically acute. It would be much easier to mobilize a mob by concentrating on this pathetic teenager, so debilitated by hemophilia he could no longer stand. His father carried him down to the basement where the family was butchered.

Had the patriarch agreed, he would have been setting the stage for a terrifying medieval narrative to play out in modern Russia. Creating the award in the name of Aleksey could have turned 1997 into yet another repetition of the ancient canard that Jews kidnapped Christian children and drained their bodies of blood to be stirred into Passover *matzohs*. This charge (which ignored that the Jews were the first of all ancient peoples to give up human sacrifice) played a role in early European history. In 1295 Edward I expelled the Jews from England. The precipitant cause was the murder of a little boy, Hugh of Lincoln, which was laid at their door. In Chaucer's *Canterbury Tales* the Prioress recounts a miracle of the Virgin whose plot turns on this accusation. She tells how the "accursed Jews" killed a small boy, but their crime was uncovered thanks to the miracle that the boy's corpse sat up on a dung heap and sang "O Alma Redemptoris." Thus alerted, the townsfolk massacre the local Jewish community to the hearty approval of the listening pilgrims, including Chaucer himself.[40]

Chaucer wrote *Canterbury Tales* circa 1390, and the "blood libel" had fallen into disuse in Western Europe by the twentieth century. Not so in Russia. In 1903 just such a rumor sparked the Kishinyov pogrom. Then in 1911, Kiev, the crown jewel of Russian Orthodoxy since it was the capital of Vladimir I, saw it resurrected. A gang of thieves murdered a Christian boy; when his body was found in the River Dnieper, members of the press, probably Okhrana agents tasked with lending credence to *The Protocols of the Elders of Zion*, claimed he had been ritually murdered for his blood. The 1911 trial is known as the "Beilis affair," after Menahem Mendel Beilis, the poor factory clerk arrested and tried on these trumped-up charges.

The sensational trial riveted Russia. The Beilis case saw 355 witnesses called to the stand. Public officials colluded with the police to fabricate a case. The prosecutor offered testimony from "expert" witnesses that the Jews used Christian blood to mix with unleavened bread at Passover and that the Christian boy-victim had been drained of blood for this purpose. A Russian Orthodox priest, Father Pranaitis, claimed that the evidence of wounds on the boy's body showed that it was a ritual murder as laid down in the *Zohar*, the cabalistic book of the Hasidim. Another expert, a Professor Sikorsky of the University of St. Vladimir, also testified for the prosecution. To the immense credit of the jury, Beilis was found "not guilty."[41] But the charges themselves were not thrown out. Until the outbreak of World War I, the tsarist government tried to revive the case. There was no concept of "double jeopardy" in the judicial system. Beilis prudently emigrated to America, but the affair soaked into the popular Orthodox memory. Contemporary newspapers reported as if Beilis were guilty; what was printed acquired its own veracity.

By 1997 the details of the Romanov family's murders—the bayoneting, stripping, dismemberment, burning, and soaking in acid of the corpses— leaked out. If the natural reaction to this horror were concentrated on the figure of the fourteen-year old tsarevich, the way would be paved for a new "Beilis affair"—at least in the imagination of the Orthodox believer. The Pamyat Manifesto's use of the word "ritualistic" to describe the murder of the tsar cleverly taps into this anachronistic belief.

In a brilliant stroke, the patriarch outmaneuvered his monarchist opponents. Instead of selecting the twentieth-century heir to be honored with the "Year of the Child" award, he honored a sixteenth-century tsarevich, Prince Dmitry (1582–91), a son of Ivan IV, better known as Grozny, "Awe-inspiring" or "Terrible." Dmitry was born to Ivan's seventh wife, Maria Nagaya. Because the church permitted a man only three marriages (Ivan had already been granted one dispensation to take a fourth), Dmitry was canonically ineligible to become tsar. Dmitry and his mother were exiled to Uglich in the north; there the nine-year-old boy, who was an epileptic, died mysteriously of knife wounds. The boyars had acclaimed Boris Godunov tsar at a national assembly (*zemsky sobor*) in 1598 following the death of Ivan and subsequently his second son, the mentally defective Fyodor, who reigned 1584–98. Godunov's sister had married Fyodor, which meant he was brother-in-law to the feeble tsar. Godunov became the most powerful man at court; he even conducted correspondence with foreign governments. But as ruler in his own right, Godunov became hated by the boyars. They now put out the rumor that he had engineered the death of young Dmitry.

At this distance, the truth surrounding this detective story is impossible to recover. What is clear, however, is that Aleksy's selection of Ivan IV's young son rather than Nicholas II's boy was a superb solution to a 1997 problem. By creating an ecclesiastical award in the name of a prince killed at the end of the sixteenth century, Aleksy reached back into the deep memory of Russia and updated events to solve a modern dilemma. The Uglich church where Dmitry was supposedly murdered had already been restored as one of the jewels of the "Golden Ring of Russia," that circuit of beautiful churches serving as tourist attractions on Volga River cruises.[42] Now Uglich would attract more pilgrims and more donations.

But beyond such considerations, Aleksy was making a vital point. Ivan IV had put the state at risk. In 1581 he precipitated the succession crisis by killing with his own hand his adult and much beloved tsarevich. He launched foreign wars and lost them. Foreign invasions followed his death; a "False Dmitry" and other claimants bedeviled the country in a horrific period known as the Time of Troubles (Smutnoye vremya). Aleksy did not wish to invite a new Smuta by canonizing the Tsarevich Aleksey Nikolayevich. The twentieth century saw a *furore* about the "False Anastasia," the pathetic Anna Anderson who claimed to be the youngest grand duchess but turned out to be a Polish displaced person.[43] The patriarch did not want any "False Alekseys." To downplay the issue, the church even raised doubt that the bones recovered at Yekaterinburg were in fact those of the imperial family. That Dmitry was already canonized among the *strastoterpsty* fit nicely into the patriarch's plans to saint Tsarevich Aleksey and his family at the same level.

Aside from such crises, Aleksy kept the canonization question tabled. He created a "Commission on Canonization" headed by one Metropolitan Yuvenaly. Yuvenaly came up with a delaying tactic that worked beautifully. He invited those with opinions on the matter to send in their letters. For five years, letters flowed, which he carefully tabulated. He said in an interview that they were "of an extremely conflicting nature."[44] Some writers maintained that the tsar's relationship with Rasputin was an insurmountable obstacle to canonization. Other equally emotional letters demanded that Rasputin too be canonized. Fairness demanded that all should be read, so the careful charting of this mountain of correspondence went on at a snail's pace.

Having sidestepped the Romanov issue during the "Year of the Child," Aleksy threw the monarchists a bone. In February 1997 the Holy Synod opened deliberations in Moscow to put the canonization issue on its agenda. It would take three more years of meetings and tabulating letters before this item would be resolved.

In retrospect, the canonization could not be solved as long as Boris Yeltsin was still president of Russia. Aleksy had thrown the weight of his prestige against the KGB's attempted coup to bring Yeltsin down. And Yeltsin had played a role in the Romanov saga. The family's last prison was the Ipatiev House in Yekaterinburg. Yeltsin was regional Communist chief there in 1977, and he ordered the house demolished (the corpses had been removed and hidden in a nearby forest). In his memoirs, he excused himself by saying that "he was acting on secret orders from the Politburo in Moscow to bulldoze the building, because of fears that it could become a destination for monarchist pilgrims." He exculpated himself by saying he had no choice but to carry out "this senseless decision."[45] But the odor of regicide tainted him. Even though the family had been long dead and their bodies removed from the house when he sent in the bulldozers, Orthodox believers deeply resented the decision. That the CPSU renamed the area outside the Ipatiev House the "Square of Popular Vengeance" was another insult laid at his door.

The patriarch needed Yeltsin, who was his ally in the reconstruction of the Cathedral of Christ the Savior. Furthermore, 1997 would be the year Aleksy consecrated the cathedral walls as the high point of the "850th Anniversary of Moscow" celebrations. Neither Aleksy nor Mayor Luzhkov wanted anything to dim the joy of that moment. In 1998 Yeltsin ordered the reinterment of the bones of the imperial family (which had been exhumed from a forest near Yekaterinburg) in the Cathedral of Saints Peter and Paul in St. Petersburg. It signaled his public repentance, not that the monarchists were prepared to forgive. When Yeltsin left the presidency and his handpicked successor Vladimir Putin was elected in 2000, the canonization issue could be resolved expeditiously. August 2000 saw the church saint the entire family as "passion bearers."

Now the faithful needed to learn an important distinction. In the May 31, 2000, issue of the religious supplement to the *Nezavisimaya Gazeta* (*Independent Newspaper*), an interview with Father Georgy Mitrofanov, a member of the Moscow Patriarchate's Synodal Commission on the Canonization, laid out all the issues. The patriarch's fingerprints are all over this document. The interviewer had been primed. First he asked: "Why did the Commission on Canonization consider it necessary to canonize Nicholas II and the members of his family specifically as passion bearers and not as martyrs?" Father Mitrofanov's answer is instructive:

A martyr's death is for a person who accepts it when there is the possibility to save one's life through renunciation. And the main reason for the death of this Christian is one's faith. The sovereign family died precisely as the sovereign family. Renunciation of the faith was not demanded of them. Moreover, even if we can imagine such an impious picture as that they could renounce the faith, that would not have altered their fate at all. So their death cannot be called a martyr's death. Moreover the people who killed them were rather secularized in their worldview and they viewed them primarily as a symbol of imperial Russia which they hated. For them there was no problem of the faith of the sovereign family.[46]

There is quite a bit bubbling beneath the surface here. By canonizing the *entire* imperial family, the patriarch thinned out the emotion and reduced the focus on the tsarevich. By selecting the special category of "passion bearer," Father Mitrofanov links the Romanovs with medieval examples:

In our land there really has been a whole multitude of murdered rulers who were passion-bearing princes, for example, Mikhail of Chernigov and Mikhail of Tver. Last there even was Tsarevich Dmitry [the same Dmitry-the-Tsarevich to whom 1997's ecclesiastical award for the "Year of the Child" was given]. The sovereign's sanctity in our land seemed to have ceased with the canonization of the passion-bearing Tsarevich Dmitry at the end of the sixteenth century. And it turns out that the last Orthodox sovereign to rule in Russia also was murdered in the way that many rulers perished as passion bearers.

By putting this frame around the Romanov story, the ROC made it "turn out" that the last Orthodox tsar was to be ranked in this category of sainthood. (While much of Fedotov's language is copied here, the church no longer needs to reference an émigré theological volume to explain the *strastoterptsy* category. That had been useful in the 1992 *Ogonyok* article but was now old news.)

If it is possible to look at such an explosive issue calmly, Nicholas II's fatal passivity does echo Boris and Gleb's acceptance of death at the hands of their assassins. The imperial court knew his character well. Grand Duke Alexander Mikhailovich said:

> Nicholas II, Tsar of All Rus, supreme commander of fifteen million Russian soldiers, with all the zeal of a supine peasant, chose as his motto "God's Will be Done." [I responded] "Nicky, who taught you to yield to God's will in this way? You call it Christianity, but it sounds more like Mohammedan fatalism."
>
> "Everything is willed by God," replied Nicky deliberately. "I was born on 6 May, the day dedicated to Job the Long-Suffering. I am ready to accept my fate." These were his final words. Words of warning had no effect on him whatsoever. He went to his death believing that it was God's will.[47]

In a time of war, passivity in an autocrat is a disaster. That same passivity, once the individual is pinioned in a helpless position, can look like heroic fortitude. Father Mitrofanov, who is a troubleshooter for the patriarch, emphasized to *Nezavisimaya Gazeta* that the commission believed that it was solely the behavior of the imperial family during its last months that merited this honor: "Here was their spiritual transformation in expectation of death, a reliance on God's help, a rejection of any kind of human resistance, the strength to forgive their future murderers and those who held them in confinement which reflected that marvelous similarity to the life of the passion bearers of earlier centuries."

To justify Nicholas's canonization, the ROC emphasized a letter sent from Tobolsk by his oldest daughter, Grand Duchess Olga, in the spring of 1918: "Father asks you to tell all those who remain loyal to Him and those with whom they might have influence, not to take revenge for Him, because He has forgiven everyone and prays for everyone, and to remember that the evil that is now in the world will be stronger yet, but that it is not evil which overcomes evil, but only love."[48] When he was a prisoner, Nicholas's faith seems to have shed its anti-Semitism and become noble. Sadly, it was then too late.

Anyone who doubts the importance of getting the canonization issue resolved in this manner should recall the National Orthodox Movement's Manifesto, which demanded that the truth be revealed about the "ritual" murder of Nicholas. This played to the darkest, most atavistic prejudices of Russian anti-Semites. The interviewer put the question starkly to Mitrofanov: "Did the commission finally reject the idea that the murder of the tsarist family was a ritual murder?" He replied: "On this question the commission turned directly to the Moscow Ecclesiastical Academy. There an expert investigation was conducted into this circumstance. Representatives of the academy came to the conclusion that there are no bases for seeing in the death of the tsarist family elements of ritual murder." Ten years earlier, the National Orthodox Movement "demanded" an answer to this question, but now it was neither what it sought nor what it expected. That the commission turned to the Moscow Ecclesiastical Academy for an "expert investigation" shows just how far the Russian Orthodox Church had come. Once before, in 1911, one of its priests testified at the Beilis trial that the boy victim died from ritual murder. At the dawn of a new century, it solicited the judgment of experts who put paid to that same canard with respect to the Romanovs. This was a signal triumph for Aleksy. He took over a fractious hierarchy and a divided laity. The machinery of the ROC finally, after almost ten years, worked smoothly.

In an adroit move, the church presented the canonization as further evidence confirming the prophecies of St. Seraphim. Seraphim had predicted that the first half of the reign of the tsar in question would witness great sorrow and upheaval, but the second half would be a time of great joy and peace. The ROC now explained that Seraphim's description of the "first half" of the putative tsar's reign referred to *all* the earthly years (1894–1917) of Nicholas II's rule. The saint's description of the second half of the reign as bright and glorious referred to his glorification in heaven.

Whatever the contortions in logic, the outcome has given Russian Orthodox believers a positive outlet for their devotion. Walk into an Orthodox church, and worshipers can be seen kissing the icon of the murdered family, all in their halos. Sometimes they are in medieval dress, sometimes in tsarist costume. But whatever the clothing style, their arms and hands are the same: held upward from the elbow, with the palms facing out. Their soft hands and relaxed bodies display the classic pose of submission. The collapse of the dynasty as due to the disastrous decisions of Nicholas II seems irretrievably lost to secular dispassionate analysis: hence the powerful appeal of legend and myth. The church's new myth has not led to bloodshed but to thousands and thousands of new icons painted and sold in its kiosks (see figure 4.1).

By 2000 Aleksy had successfully subsumed the question of the Romanovs within the larger issue of honoring *novomucheniki*, those Orthodox Christians who suffered death at the hands of the Soviet state because of their faith. At the same August 2000 bishops' council that canonized the Romanov family as *strastoterptsy*, almost five hundred people, both clergy (bishops, priests, monks) and laity, were canonized as "new martyrs." Aleksy brought them to the foreground. He personally celebrated a Divine Liturgy at a place near Moscow called the Butovo Range Proving Ground—a former facility of

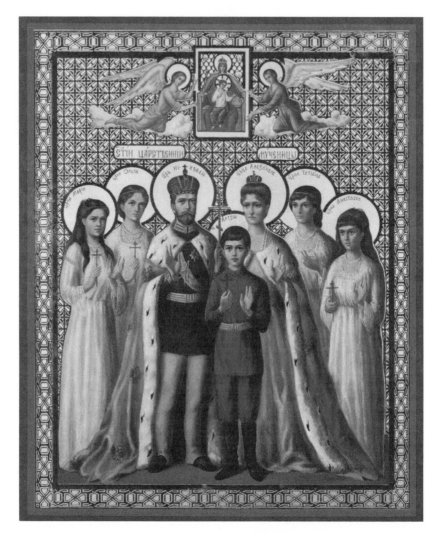

Figure 4.1 In 2000 the canonization of the Russian imperial family as "passion bearers" led to thousands of icons of the Romanovs being sold in Russian Orthodox Church kiosks. (Photo credit: Sofrino, the publication arm of the Moscow Patriarchate)

the Red Army artillery—where thousands of just such people were executed from 1937 to 1953 (i.e., the days of Stalinist Terror). A beautiful new icon commemorated their suffering. It was displayed in the Cathedral of Christ the Savior (2000) and entitled "The Gathering of New Russian Martyrs and Confessors." There the Romanovs almost disappear in the vast crowd.[49]

ACCURSED QUESTIONS

Since the failure of the KGB coup in August 1991, while busy rebuilding and reconsecrating churches, Aleksy fought to gain control of both the
St. Seraphim and Romanov cults. In the early 1990s it was questionable
whether the negative energy (i.e., the anti-Semitism) latent in both could
be recharged into something positive. But in 2003 Aleksy achieved triumphs
in both efforts. The year 2003 was always going to be critical. This would
be the centenary of the original canonization ceremony. The year 2003 was
also the tercentenary of the founding of St. Petersburg by Peter the Great.
Many Western diplomats and politicians attended its lavish ceremonies and
stayed in luxurious cruise ships docked in the port. But while the West was
fascinated with the secular celebrations in Russia's most Western city, *Sankt-
Peterburg*, within the country itself as much attention was paid to the "The
Year of St. Seraphim."

The church heralded 2003 by having the Synod reprint all the documents
relating to his canonization. These had been published in 1903 at the behest
of the tsarina. Now a lavish new edition, in two volumes, was available to the
public. In February the prime minister, Mikhail Kasyanov, signed an order of
the government of Russia for the "Creation of the Organizational Committee for Cooperating in Conducting Publicly Significant Cultural and Educational Events in Connection with the Celebration by the Russian Orthodox
Church of the Centennial of the Canonization of St. Seraphim of Sarov."
Chairing this august body was Sergey Kirienko, the presidential envoy for the
Volga federal district. With the government on board, leading companies of
the New Russia—Rosenergoat, Sarovbiznesbank, Mezhprombank—rushed
to help the reconstruction of the grounds and the Diveyevo buildings.

On August 1, the saint's day in the ecclesiastical calendar, both the patriarch and the president of Russia attended the ceremonies. A procession
of the Cross that originated more than six hundred miles away in Kursk
arrived at the convent. As it left the city, the mayor announced that when
a new submarine would be built to replace the doomed Kursk, he would
ask the navy to christen it the "St. Seraphim." Once again, as at the original canonization and the 1991 translation of the relics, people streamed
into Diveyevo from all over Russia. Although Sarov itself remains a "closed
city," on August 1, 2003, the sun rose at Diveyevo Convent over a scene
that looked virtually unchanged since 1903. A hundred years earlier, tsar
and metropolitan were present with the thousands of believers. Now it was
a president and patriarch. But the crowds seem identical. Again the reliquary
was shouldered, and circumambulations of the convent traced. Again pilgrims
pressed forward, their arms stretched upward and wide-eyed adoration on
their faces (see figure 4.2).

127

Figure 4.2 *Orthodox Moscow* marks the centenary of the St. Seraphim canonization with the headline, "And Again They Celebrated Easter in the Summer." (Photo credit: *Orthodox Moscow*)

President Putin spoke. Some hoped Putin would acknowledge Russia as a country of one faith—Orthodoxy—but instead he spoke of Russia as a country of "various faiths." He then raced off to speak to the scientists in Arzamas, the still secret nuclear research laboratory housed in Sarov. He returned in time for an evening champagne reception with the patriarch (figure 4.3). Article 14 of the Russian constitution specifies that the country is a secular nation

Figure 4.3 *Orthodox Moscow's* account of the 2003 centenary celebration of the canonization of St. Seraphim at Sarov shows President Putin and Patriarch Aleksy II sipping champagne together after the ceremonies. (Photo credit: *Orthodox Moscow*)

and that separation of church and state is enshrined therein. According to the constitution, the government may not show any special attention to one confession. The canonization ceremonies illustrate a creative interpretation of these statutes.

Aleksy himself was serene. In terms of deeds, the "Year of St. Seraphim" was a resounding success. Indeed, earlier in the summer of 2003 he consecrated a new church built over the murder site at Yekaterinburg. It was called the Tserkov na krovi, the "Church-on-the-Blood," a deliberate echo of the church in St. Petersburg that marks the spot where the Romanov tsar Alexander II was murdered by terrorists in 1881. That assassination sparked pogroms wherein many Jews had died. Now Aleksy could consecrate a new Tserkov na krovi, commemorating yet another assassination of a Romanov tsar and his entire family, and neither pogroms nor bloodshed marred the festivities. The year 2003 was also the centenary of the infamous pogrom at Kishinyov. There was no repeat at the Easter festivities of 2003. In Russian terms, this marks significant progress.

Finally, Aleksy held a well-behaved, seated press conference with members of the British media at his residence. He mentioned that the archbishop of Canterbury, Rowan Williams, had made the pilgrimage to Sarov and the Diveyevo Convent for the "specific purpose of taking part in the celebrations to mark the 100th anniversary of the canonization of St. Seraphim of Sarov and venerated this glorified man of God in places where he used to work."[50] After the ceremonies, national radio had held a marathon talk show, in which listeners called in with their questions about Seraphim and his prophecies. (Archbishop Williams was surprised to see that ordinary Russians believed in Seraphim as a sort of Russian Nostradamus.) Aleksy ignored the telethon but took the question of the Romanov canonization head on:

> In the act of canonization the Church does not bear witness to the holiness of a particular state order, or a particular social, professional, ethnic or any other background of a person, but to his or her exploit in life and death in Jesus Christ. Czar Nicholas II and his family are glorified by the Church as holy passion bearers. The act of their canonization was unanimously approved by the Bishops' Jubilee Council of our Church in 2000, but several years before their approval the episcopate was not so unanimous. I believe that what played a decisive role in this case was the popular veneration of the Imperial passion bearers, and this is one of the prerequisites for canonization.

After dealing with the Romanovs, Aleksy immediately went on to speak of the category much dearer to his heart, the "new martyrs" of the faith:

> In the 20th century, Russian Orthodoxy suffered the severest persecution in Christian history. It is impossible for people in the West to imagine what a crucible our Church went through. An enormous number of bishops, priest and lay people make up a great community of Russia's new martyrs and confessors who suffered for their faithfulness to Christ.

Without saying so, the patriarch contrasted the imperial family—who suffered because they were the imperial family—to the thousands of ordinary Russian people executed for their faith at any one of the Soviet Golgothas. The patriarch called their martyrdom "prepared by haters of Christ for the servants of Christ and faithful children of our Church." A different situation would have obtained had the patriarch put forth the line that the *Romanovs* were killed "by the haters of Christ." Orthodox anti-Semites would have taken it as a clear signal that their Manifesto's naming of the Jews as responsible for the imperial family's murders and every other crime of Soviet power had his support.

130

Change in the life of ordinary Russians takes place outside the headlines. Aleksy's masterful manipulation of the cult of St. Seraphim is microcosmed in the saga of the Cathedral of St. John Baptist, located within the high walls of the Ivanovsky Monastery, just a few miles from the Moscow Kremlin. In March 1993, the Ministry of Internal Affairs (MVD) occupied the entire complex down to the last outbuilding. Its location within the heart of the city and its large grounds shielded from popular gaze by a wall almost twenty feet high made it an ideal spot for its national training academy. The MVD was a pillar of the party, and admittance to its ranks signified that the recruit was on the fast track to success in the Soviet elite. Its "red arrow" members were intimately connected to the KGB. Its former head, Boris Pugo, was among the inner circle of the junta who attempted the August 1991 coup. Pugo shot himself hours after the tanks turned around, but his protégés in the MVD remained in power.

A stone's throw from this huge complex stood the same Russian Orthodox Church of St. Vladimir led by its dynamic priest, Father Sergy Romanov, discussed earlier. Such was the pace of the transformation of Russian society, that within a year of the coup's failure the congregation of St. Vladimir's began to extend its focus to the Cathedral of St. John the Baptist. Getting it back seemed impossible. However, friendly relations with the MVD academy's new commanding general were established immediately in the post-coup atmosphere. He invited Father Sergy over to his office for a talk. Glancing at the obligatory portrait of Vladimir Lenin on his wall, he joked that the priest had a portrait of a Vladimir, too — the first one. This comment was a giveaway that the commandant had been inside the church and seen its icon of St. Vladimir on the iconostasis.

Early in 1992 Father Sergy petitioned the Moscow City Council for permission to hold a religious procession around the cathedral on August 1, the liturgical calendar's feast day of St. John the Baptist. Permission was granted, but only to circumambulate the outer walls. He dressed in his robes and led a procession of singing and chanting children around the ramparts. Then, as he swung the censer and sprinkled the holy water, the gates to the massive parapets of the complex unexpectedly opened. Seizing the moment, he led his tiny pilgrimage inside.

Father Sergy next began to circumnavigate the cathedral itself. After having traced a concentric circle around its vast bulk, the procession prepared to exit. Suddenly the doors to the cathedral itself opened wide. Father Sergy had demonstrated courage and decisiveness throughout his career; he marched in, still followed closely by his small band of surprised and thrilled children and deacons. His procession wound through the enormous building, now converted into a cafeteria, printing shop, offices, firing range, and classrooms. Some of the uniformed MVD officers watching this completely unexpected spectacle jeered and laughed. But others did not. An eyewitness recounted: "Suddenly some of the men rushed over to Father Sergy. They threw themselves at his feet, and tears streamed down their faces. They held up their hands, and beseeched him, saying 'Sprinkle me with the Holy water too, Father. Bless me too.'"[51] Given that these men were uniformed MVD, this astonishing scene was a harbinger. By the end of 1993, the MVD began paying rent to Father Sergy for the entire monastery complex—a de facto acknowledgment that the property had been illegally seized from the Orthodox Church.

Ten years later came the great day. As part of the 2003 celebrations of "The Year of St. Seraphim," the MVD exited a large chapel of the Cathedral of St. John the Baptist and returned it to the ROC. For the first time since its seizure by the state, once again the beautiful Orthodox liturgy was heard within its walls. The congregation of St. Vladimir's—and its vast army of volunteers—had been feverishly repairing the monastery walls and restoring the beauty of the chapel. On August 1 (surely, the believers reasoned, it was "no accident" that both John the Baptist and Seraphim occupied the same day on the ecclesiastical calendar!), led by a bishop, they held a procession of the Cross around the walls of the monastery, tracing the same footsteps Father Sergy and the children had traveled in 1992 (figure 4.4). Once the ramparts had been a decrepit gray. Now their crenellations gleamed a pearly white. The climax came in the chapel, which the bishop solemnly reconsecrated (figure 4.5). The joy at having wrought a miracle was palpable. There was no hint of pain for all the lost years—only joy in the present, as the past folded into the future and the future looked bright indeed. Some of the same MVD officers who once jeered Father Sergy were now bowing and crossing themselves among the congregation.

By the end of 2003 Aleksy had shepherded his flock through the "Year of St. Seraphim" without allowing its fervor to be deflected into violence against supposed "enemies of Orthodoxy and Autocracy"—that is, the old code phrase for Russia's Jews. The year 2003 was a catalyst for yet more church recovery and restoration.

In 2004 he threw the full weight of his position against the fundamental credo of Russia's anti-Semites that the Jews were behind all the depredations and suffering of the Soviet period. He called the Russian Academy of Sciences to an "All Russian Scientific and Theological Conference" on "The Heritage of St. Seraphim of Sarov and the Destiny of Russia." In a canny move, this was *not* held in 2003. Making the conference part of the centenary canonization ceremonies would have connected the saint too much

Figure 4.4 A procession of the Cross winds around the Ivanovsky Monastery, prior to the consecration of one of its chapels to highlight the 2003 "Year of St. Seraphim." (Photo credit: Olga Lugovaya)

with the potentially explosive emotions surrounding the imperial family, because it was at the insistence of the tsar and tsarina that Seraphim had been sainted in the first place. Aleksy did not want his conference hijacked by Romanov sympathizers. It was far better to have the conference hosted by the Academy of Sciences. To the Western scientific community, it seems an odd coupling, a contradiction in terms, as if the prayers of St. Francis of Assisi were to be the agenda for a conference on bringing peace to the Balkans. But the patriarch spent years fine-tuning conferences through his work in the European Council of Churches. He gave the keynote address and set the agenda for the entire event.

Aleksy begins by folding the scientific community into those patriots who love Russia: "Today after decades of atheistic forgetfulness, our society learns anew to consider Russian saints as contributors to [our] history and culture

Figure 4.5 The "Year of St. Seraphim" (2003) saw the Ministry of Internal Affairs exit a large chapel of the Ivanovsky Monastery and return it to the Russian Orthodox Church. A bishop reconsecrates the space, which the volunteers of St. Vladimir's Church had restored. Father Sergy Romanov holds a small child in the audience. (Photo credit: Olga Lugovaya)

at the national scale, as those are significant not only to the Orthodox faithful, but to all who sincerely love Russia and connect the future of their children with her."[52] Aleksy next uses one of his standard techniques—inserting important information in a low-key, casual aside. He slips in the fact that the first St. Seraphim Church consecrated at Sarov back in 1903 had been restored "by the efforts of state and local authorities, *nuclear scientists who are now working in Sarov*, Russian entrepreneurs, [and] the broad Orthodox public" (emphasis added). This list of contributors begins with the innocuous "state and local authorities" and ends with the "broad Orthodox public," both phrases so common in Russian boilerplate that they scarcely register with the listener. But buried in the middle is the explosive nugget that "nuclear scientists" working at Sarov—that is, within the walls of Arzamas 16 itself, the most secret facility inside the Russian Federation—helped with the church restoration.[53]

The most subtle feature of this address is Aleksy's gloss of Seraphim's prophecies to "explain" all the horrors of the Soviet past. Kulakov, a leader of the National Orthodox Movement, at his infamous news conference held in Moscow March 21, 1990, had laid all of Russia's troubles at the door of the old scapegoat: "The Jews bear collective responsibility for the 73-year-old diabolical bacchanalia" of Soviet power. Fourteen years later, Aleksy spun the hermit's predictions into a different answer to the accursed question of who is to blame. He begins by alluding to the "destiny" of Russia. This opens up the entire question about St. Seraphim's ability to see the future. Aleksy reminds his listeners that the church teaches that humanity's eyes are blinded by sin and therefore cannot foresee the future, which is known only to God. There is a single exception: "Only such God-pleasing men as St. Seraphim of Sarov from time to time can penetrate through this curtain of time, and God grants them the gift of spiritual prophesy." Then Aleksy quotes Patriarch Tikhon—a martyr to Soviet power and canonized by the ROC—who said in his appeal to "all faithful of the Russian Orthodox Church" on July 26, 1918 o.s. (August 8, 1918 N.S.) concerning the reasons of the troubles in our Motherland:

> Ask your Orthodox conscience, and you will find the answer to this painful question. Sin which is within is the very root and reason of our illness, the source of all our troubles and unhappiness. Sin corrupted our earth, paralyzed [the] spiritual and bodily power of the Russian people. Sin darkened people's mind, and now *we grope in the dark without light: like a drunken man* (Job 2:25).

Aleksy called his audience to face a profoundly disquieting truth: the troubles of the motherland, which Seraphim foretold, are visited upon Russia because of the sin located within each believer's heart and soul. He urged the audience to accept personal responsibility for the past and for the future by invoking the saint's name:

> We must realize that a good and clear future for us depends upon to what extent we ourselves can become good and clear, to what extent we can follow our predecessors, and first and foremost our saints, in their love and sacrifice, to what extent we can get rid of paralyzing sin by the hard work of penitence and fulfill the commandment of St. Seraphim about acquiring a peaceful spirit.

Here is the keystone of Aleksy's "platform" for the future of Russia. Without ever uttering the word "Jew," he directs his audience away from the dead end of scapegoating imperial Russia's favorite victim. It is one of the most important moves Aleksy has ever made.

This speech contains a penetrating analysis of the entire Soviet period as "unlimited schemes of the authorities concerning the coming 'paradise on earth' [which] gave rise to natural skepticism and apathy." The heart of the Soviet experiment was its utopian belief that the party's leader could be trusted with godlike power. Indeed, in *We*, the powerful science fiction novel by Yevgeny Zamyatin written in 1921, and published in the USSR only in

1987, Zamyatin forecast Soviet quasi-religious worship of Lenin and Stalin. His novel projected the USSR as evolving into a "One State" where the population will venerate the leader as a surrogate deity. Zamyatin's protagonist enthusiastically compares the perfection of the One State to a prelapsarian world: "We have paradise again."[54] Aleksy may have read Zamyatin during his trips abroad at those meetings of the European Council of Churches, though he comes at the question of human nature from the perspective of faith. In place of utopian dreams, he asks the academicians to accept that the future will be hard, and trials—both internal and external—are inevitable. But the responsibility for both trials and solutions lies with the Russian people themselves.[55]

Insofar as this is meant to combat Russian Orthodox anti-Semitism, it has been rather too subtle for Western religious leaders to appreciate. They would like to see Aleksy cloak himself in all the authority of his office and unambiguously condemn it.[56] However, the Orthodox Church has no tradition of the patriarch speaking *ex cathedra* and writing encyclicals that carry the new dispensation to the faithful. Anti-Semitism is part of Russia's history; Aleksy's contribution to fighting it has been to silence it from ROC ranks or publications.[57] The capstone of his approach is this keynote address.

He has said nothing, however, about the case of Mikhail Khodorkovsky, former head of Yukos, the oil conglomerate, and once one of the richest men in the world. Alexander Kulakov demanded at his press conference on March 27, 1990, "a stop to emigration of Soviet Jews until we can carry out an investigation into the part they have played in destroying the country." Had this line been followed, the new Russia would have applied the Soviet method of stigmatizing "enemies of the people"—show trials—to the tsarist technique of blaming the Jews. Instead, the new Russia witnessed only one show trial: Khodorkovsky's. He challenged Putin politically and paid the price. He was sentenced to nine years for tax fraud and sent to Siberia, where in 2007 he is intermittently consigned to a punishment cell. The patriarch has kept silent. It seems that he and Putin agreed that there must be one scapegoat to pay for all those who got rich during privatization; who better than a Jew who did not contribute to the rebuilding of Christ the Savior? Khodorkovsky's grim fate represents a "what-might-have-been" future for Russian Jewry if the National Orthodox Movement had its way.[58]

A parallel case against which to measure Aleksy's achievement is the contrasting example of Yugoslavia. Here too was a multinational state with a large population of Orthodox Christians, the Serbs. It too broke up into constituent parts at approximately the same time. But there a vicious war of neighbor-on-neighbor violence broke out. Ethnically, the people of Yugoslavia

are virtually identical: overwhelmingly, they are all Southern Slavs and belong to the same linguistic family. When Christianity split in half in 1054,
the cleavage ran through what became modern Yugoslavia. The Serbs found
themselves on the Orthodox side; the Croats on the Catholic. The 1990s saw
a religious war break out as Serbs and Croats "ethnically cleansed" each other's
enclaves. They found common ground in a shared willingness to murder
their Muslim neighbors. Muslims in the former Yugoslavia are Southern
Slavs too; their ancestors had converted to Islam (and thus avoided paying
taxes) under the five-hundred-year rule of the Ottoman Empire. Tragically,
the hierarchy of the Serbian Orthodox Church colluded in murder.

The involvement of Serbian Orthodox priests and bishops in the massacres that bled Bosnia white has been confirmed by the most comprehensive
study of the war written to date, *Balkan Idols: Religion and Nationalism in
Yugoslav States.* The author is Vjekoslav Perica, himself a Croat. Perica acknowledges that all three of the religions had prelates who "were among the
principal engineers of the crisis and conflict." But Perica's conclusion is devastating: "radical faction tendencies were found in Croatian Catholicism and
in the Islamic Community as well. . . . The Serbian Orthodox Church is held
the most directly responsible for the advocacy of ethnic cleansing." Perica
evidences this charge from the lips of Serbian Orthodox prelates themselves:
"The Serbs did not deny that they struck first in Kosovo, in Croatia, and in
Bosnia-Herzegovina," but they explain their action as preemptive self-defense:
"A group of Serbian Orthodox Church leaders and Serb intellectuals defined
the war as a spontaneous civil war in which the Serbs, by striking first were trying to avoid the genocide that happened to them in 1941." Pantelic Lukijan,
bishop of Slavonia, published in March 1991 in the patriarchate's newspaper
an article entitled "Anti-Serbian March of the Ustaša State." The bishop described armed attacks by Croatian police on the city of Pakrac, assaults on
Serbs, and desecration of Orthodox churches.[59] Then he wrote:

> This conflict is a warning and reminder of the Croatian crimes of 1941
> when Ustašas attacked and massacred the unarmed Serbian people. But
> this time, we Serbs will not repeat the mistake of '41. We shall remain
> Christians, but for now, let us disregard the Gospel of Christ and turn to
> the Old Testament, which reads: *An eye for an eye, a tooth for a tooth!*
> After justice has been done, we will return to the New Testament, which
> says: *To him who strikes you on the cheek, offer the other also.*[60]

Bishop Lukijan's "justice" paved the way for a bleak repeat of history. At the
postwar trial of the Einsatzgruppe, the SS killing squads who targeted Jewish

civilians in the occupied USSR, a Lutheran clergyman, Ernst Biberstein, excused his rising to the rank of lieutenant colonel by citing the anti-Semitic remarks of Martin Luther. The Bosnian conflict witnessed yet again a cleric rationalizing an attack on human beings of another faith. While it is true that the Ustaša collaborated with the Nazis and murdered thousands of Serbs at a concentration camp, Jasenovac, the vast majority of Croats living in Yugoslavia in 1991 were not even born in 1941–45.

Once unleashed, the Serbians' bloodlust turned on their Muslim neighbors in Bosnia. Serbian Orthodox collusion was illustrated vividly on June 1, 2005, when Serbian state television broadcast a twelve-minute video taken almost ten years earlier in July 1995 when Serb troops overran the supposedly "safe" area of Srebrenica in eastern Bosnia. Seven thousand young Muslim men disappeared, though the area had been declared a safe haven guaranteed by United Nation's troops. What happened to them? For a decade the Serbian population denied guilt. The video—taken by a Serb himself—gave an answer that no one could deny. A Serbian Orthodox priest blesses a group of paramilitary uniformed Serb soldiers. The camera follows them as they next shot dead six unarmed and terrified teenage Muslim prisoners.[61] The video gave sickening confirmation to the contemporary relevance of Blaise Pascal's seventeenth-century conclusion: "Mankind never do evil so completely and cheerfully as when they do it from religious conviction."

It is worth taking a deeper look at the massacres at Srebrenica because they represent a "road not taken" by Russian Orthodoxy under approximately similar circumstances. In 1988, just as Kreshchenie Rusi was being celebrated in the USSR, an event took place in Serbia that unleashed powerful feelings. The relics of Lazar, the Serbian king defeated at the Battle of Kosovo, began a translation from site to site in greater Serbia. In his superb book, *In God's Name: Genocide and Religion in the Twentieth Century*, Michael Sells states that the translation pilgrimage of the Lazar bones "engendered ritual celebrations that were politicized and used by religious nationalism to stir up calls for revenge against the eternal persecutors of Lazar and of Serbs."[62] This defeat, when Lazar lost in 1389 to an Ottoman army under Murad I on the field of Gazimestan in Kosovo, is very much alive in Serbian memory. Sells argues that the components of the battle were manipulated by Serb nationalists to support "ethnic cleansing": Lazar is the Christ figure; the Turks are the Christ-killers; and Vuk Brankovic, who allegedly gave Lazar's battle plans to the Turks, is Judas. Thus a fourteenth-century turncoat becomes the "ancestral curse" of all Slavic Muslims, including living ones.[63] Serbs were being encouraged to read a fourteenth-century defeat as betrayal and to apply its events to their own times.

The translation ceremonies culminated on the 600th anniversary of the Battle of Kosovo, June 28, 1989. This is the day of Vidovdan, or St. Vitus Day, and it is the gloomiest day in the calendar for Serbs. It is normally marked with parades, Orthodox Church bells, and unhappy speeches. On that particular Vidovdan, the then Serbian president, Slobodan Milosevic, mounted a platform, and before a crowd estimated at one to two million people—almost a tenth of the population of Serbia—proclaimed the Serbs the defender of Christian Europe against Muslims and infidel "Turks." His use of the word "Turks" did not mean the citizens of Turkey, that sovereign country and member of NATO. "Turks" is a Serbian code word referring contemptuously to those Southern Slavs who had converted to Islam and lived next door to his Orthodox audience. In short, Milosevic encouraged his followers to regard themselves as victims of their neighbors.

Milosevic's speech tapped into Serbian feelings of imminent danger at the hands of those neighbors, both Catholic Croats and Bosnian Muslims. He rode the ensuing wave of fear to the presidency. Sells argued that:

> From 1987 to 1989, the Milosevic regime, with the help of the leadership of the Serbian Orthodox Church, manipulated the Kosovo [i.e., the Serb defeat in 1389] myth to secure its own power. For a time there was indeed a strong dissident movement. Within a few years, however, Milosevic was no longer directing Serb nationalism, he was following it. He had used the Kosovo mythology to crush the dissent, but in doing so, he had created something that was no longer in his control: an ideology of genocide that had gained its own critical mass of economic, religious, political, and social motivations and had taken on a life of its own.[64]

That "critical mass" went nuclear in Milosevic's speech at the 600th anniversary of the Battle of Kosovo. He kneaded the sacred time (the 1389 defeat), the sacred place (the battlefield and the monastery holding the relics of St. Prince Lazar), and the historical memory (newly lacerated by the disinterring of the corpses from World War II atrocities at the hands of Croatian fascists) into motivation for the ethnic cleansing in Bosnia.

Aleksy too resurrected a version of history by leading an emotionally charged translation of sacred relics that attracted thousands of believers along a pilgrimage route. He too spoke at a sacred space (the Diveyevo Convent) at a sacred time (July 31, 1991, the 87th anniversary of Seraphim's canonization and the original deposition of his relics.) He too resurrected a sacred memory, though he did not mention the Romanovs by name. But because the tsar and tsarina had ordered the canonization, the cult of St. Seraphim is intimately bound up in the Orthodox mind with their deaths. The imperial family was murdered the night of July 16–17, 1918 o.s. (July 30–31 n.s.), a near coincidence of dates with explosive connotations. But Aleksy would not speak as had the Serbian bishop of Slavonia, Lukijan in April 1991, who called upon his flock to resort to *"An eye for an eye and a tooth for a tooth."* Had he done so, had he manipulated the heightened emotions at Diveyevo to blame Jews as the perpetrators of the killing of the imperial family, the same kind of neighbor-on-neighbor violence that bloodied Bosnia in the 1990s could easily have occurred in Russia In its case, NATO would not have intervened. The world may be grateful that Russian Orthodoxy did not go the way of Serbian Orthodoxy.

That does not mean, however, that the time has come when "the wolf also shall dwell with the lamb ... and the calf and the young lion ... together" (Isaiah, 11:6). The Russian Orthodox Church can "share the Old Testament and its prophets with the Jews," as Aleksy described it to the British ambassador in his meeting with him April 12, 1992.[65] But it cannot share the New. For Orthodox Russians believe that they are the people of the Second Jerusalem, the chosen of Jesus himself, and thus their faith represents the true, unbroken descendant of the Church of Christ and the Apostles. This means their quarrel with Western Christianity is far more profound, for Catholicism claims to be the church of the "Apostolic Succession" as well.

Thus, from the point of view of the patriarch and many other Orthodox Russians, the real enemies of their faith were not the Jews—who were leaving in droves anyway—but the hordes of Western missionaries deplaning at the same airports. Popes had once blessed the warriors and monks who repeatedly crossed into the land of Rus to put its believers to the sword and send its priests to the stake. Now it was proselytizers from Catholicism and its offshoot "Catholicism Lite" (i.e., Protestantism), who crisscrossed Russia armed with Bibles, laden with capitalist lucre, and convinced they were bringing the Gospel to the godless. To the Orthodox, they resembled nothing so much as another wave of invaders out to liquidate them. Ironically, the same 1990 law on "Freedom of Conscience and Religion" that had helped the ROC revive now allowed these modern crusaders to roam the counry at will.

FIVE

Irreconcilable Differences: Orthodoxy and the West

We received our Christian faith from the early Church at the
time when Andrew, the brother of the Apostle Peter, visited
these lands on his way to Rome. . . . We received the
Christian faith here in Muscovy at the same time you
received it in Italy and we have preserved it intact.
— *Ivan Grozny's response to the emissary of Pope Gregory XIII in 1582*

THAT CATHOLICISM AND ORTHODOXY both claim to be the Church
of the Apostolic Succession meant religious war, as "peaceful coexistence"
was not part of medieval thinking. The Russians possess long memories; they
have not forgotten that with the Mongols attacking them in their rear, Catholics simultaneously attacked them from Europe. From their perspective, the
most dangerous adversary has always been the West—or, to put the conflict in
the lexicon of faith, they fear the heretic more than the infidel. The Mongols
would invade, plunder, rape, pillage, and murder. They did not proselytize.
The "Latinizers," the Orthodox way of referring to Catholicism, aimed to convert by exterminating their faith. The ROC maintains that the preservation
of both its faith and its people in spite of this assault can be attributed only to
God's intervention.

The dispute over the Apostolic Succession in Christianity can no more be
resolved than can the conflict in Islam between the Shiites and the Sunni,
who disagree as to the successor to Mohammed. Mohammed died leaving a
daughter but not a son. The Shia ("helpers of Ali") believe his blood relative
Ali ibn Abi Talib, a cousin and his son-in-law, should have been chosen. The
Sunni ("followers of the prophet's customs") believe that his father-in-law,
Abu Bakr, was the correct heir to the Prophet's authority and that the leader
of Islam should be named on merit and the consensus of the community.
Though both profess "There is no God but Allah and Mohammed is His
prophet," recite from the same Koran, and follow the same "five pillars of
Islam," they have never been able to agree on the succession.

Just so, Catholicism and Orthodoxy acknowledge one God, agree that Jesus of Nazareth is the "anointed one" ("Christ" in Greek, "Messiah" in Hebrew), and acknowledge one baptism for the remission of sins. But each claims that its church is the true descendant of Christ and the Apostles. The merits of the case do not relate to inheritance by blood (as in Islam), but which disciple was the first to be called by Jesus and which disciple was the first to acknowledge Jesus as the Christ. The Orthodox—from medieval Constantinople to contemporary Moscow—marshal evidence from the New Testament demonstrating that the Roman Catholic Church makes false allegations of superiority. The Catholic Church points to equally persuasive scriptural substantiation that the Orthodox challenge to its authority contravenes the word of Jesus Christ himself. On these two questions, the Gospels simply differ. The synoptic Gospels (the "one-eye" of Matthew, Mark, and Luke) say that Peter was the first disciple to be called by Jesus and the first to acknowledge Jesus as the Christ. But the fourth Gospel of John says the same of Andrew, Peter's older brother. Catholicism claims descent from Peter, the first pope. Russian Orthodoxy claims descent from Andrew (see figure 5.1), one of its two patron saints. This is a divorce based on irreconcilable differences.

Because the split in the Gospels is the crux of the matter, it is worth reviewing in some detail. Jesus' calling of the disciples is related roughly the same in Matthew, Mark, and Luke. (See Luke 5:3–10 and Mark 1:16–18 for slight variations of the "fishers of men" story, with Luke's involving only Peter.) Matthew 4:18–19 is the most succinct: "And Jesus, walking by the sea of Galilee, saw two brethren, Simon called Peter, and Andrew his brother, casting a net into the sea: for they were fishers. And he saith unto them, Follow me, and I will make you fishers of men."[1] While the two brothers act simultaneously, the order in which they are named, "Simon called Peter, and Andrew his brother," is regarded as significant.

But far more important is who first acknowledges Jesus as the Christ. Matthew, Mark, and Luke again answer "Peter." Popes particularly cherish Matthew's account. (See Mark 8:27–29 and Luke 9:18–20 for a briefer version of Christ asking the disciples "Whom say ye that I am?" and Peter answering "The Christ.") In Matthew 16:13–19 Jesus asks: "Whom do men say that I the Son of Man am?" The disciples first weasel out by responding with hearsay: "Some say thou art John the Baptist: some Elias; and others Jeremias, or one of the prophets." Jesus probes further: "But whom say ye that I am?" Simon Peter answers with the dramatic assertion: "Thou art the Christ, the Son of the living God." Instead of charging the disciples to say nothing of this revelation as he does in Mark and Luke, here Jesus blesses Peter and

Figure 5.1 The Church of St. Andrew "The First Called" in St. Petersburg proclaims the Russian Orthodox Church's claim to be the Church of the Apostolic Succession through Andrew, the older brother of Peter. (Photo credit: Liudmila Kiselyova)

declares: "thou art Peter, and upon this rock I will build my church.... And I will give unto thee the keys of the kingdom of heaven: and whatsoever thou shalt bind on this earth shall be bound in heaven: and whatsoever thou shalt loose on earth shall be loosed in heaven" (Matthew 16:19). This verse is simultaneously the "rock" upon which Catholic popes have built their claim to primacy in Christendom. The centrality accorded this passage by Catholic doctrine cannot be overstated. Because Peter was the first pope, ergo his successors still hold the keys to the kingdom of heaven. Until time itself dissolves, the pontiff holds sway over the whole world for as he binds and looses here on earth, so is it done in heaven. Only the Second Coming can displace the pope as the "vicar of Christ."

The corollaries to this premise are immense. Rome, the site of Peter's martyrdom, is a holy city, a destination for pilgrimage, because it is claimed that St. Peter's Cathedral was built over the very bones of the Chief Apostle. "Peter's Pence," an annual tax—formerly a penny—could be legitimately assessed on Christians everywhere for the maintenance of the papal see. The Vatican still uses the phrase today to indicate voluntary donations in its annual financial reports. Papal supremacy, according to the Gospel of Matthew, comes from Jesus Christ himself. The Renaissance popes so loved this verse that Pietro Perugino was hired to paint in 1485–86 on an immense canvas, measuring eleven by eighteen feet, "Christ handing the Keys of the Kingdom to Peter" inside the Sistine Chapel.

However, the Gospel of John tells a different story. The calling does not happen on the shores of the Sea of Galilee while Andrew and Peter are fishing. No, Andrew, already a disciple of John the Baptist (1:36), is "in Bethabara [Bethany] beyond Jordan where John was baptizing." The "whom do men say I am?" question and answer dialogue is transferred to the Pharisees and the Baptist (John 1:19–24). To their repeated queries, John answers: "I am not the Christ." The next day John sees Jesus walk by and declares, "Behold the Lamb of God." After hearing the Baptist say this, the text reports that two disciples (i.e., of John) "followed Jesus":

> Then Jesus turned, and saw them following, and saith unto them, What seek ye? They said unto him, Rabbi (which is to say, being interpreted, Master) where dwellest thou?
>
> He saith unto them, Come and see [*poidite i uvidite*, in the modern Russian translation of the Bible]. They came and saw where he dwelt, and abode with him that day: for it was about the tenth hour.
>
> One of the two, which heard John speak, and followed him, was Andrew, Simon Peter's brother.

He first findeth his own brother Simon, and saith unto him, We have found the Messias, which is, being interpreted, the Christ.

And he brought him [Peter] to Jesus. (John 1:38–41)

The Gospel of John, in just three verses, dissolves the rock-solid claim of the pope that he is the successor to the first disciple to be called by Jesus; instead Peter is "brought" by Andrew to Him. And Peter is not even the first to acknowledge Jesus as the Christ, but has to cede this honor to his brother as well, for Andrew says, "We have found the Messias ... the Christ." In John, even Jesus' thrilling statement found in Matthew—"Thou art Peter and upon this rock I will build my church"—dwindles into a rather mundane renaming procedure: "Thou art Simon the son of Jona: thou shalt be called Cephas, which is by interpretation, a stone" (John 1:42). There is nothing about Peter being the "rock" upon which the church will be built, and nothing about Peter binding and loosing here on earth as it shall be done in heaven. Popes had based their claim to absolute authority in the secular and political sphere precisely on Matthew 16:19. They asserted a right to make and depose emperors based upon it. However, if the Gospel account in John is followed, papal claims to keys and kingdoms disappear. The ROC regards the Gospel of John as the work of the Apostle John, eyewitness and participant in the events described. They believe him to be the unnamed disciple of John the Baptist who along with Andrew "follows" Jesus and whom Jesus invites to "Come and see."

To emphasize the momentous importance of these verses, Orthodoxy titles Andrew "The First Called" (Pervozvanny). Even the cross that is used by the ROC refers to Andrew. The upper bar represents the inscription over Jesus' head, "The King of the Jews." The slanted bar at the bottom recalls the X-shaped cross upon which the saint was crucified. He had asked that his cross be made differently than Jesus', for he was unworthy to die as had the Messiah. The Order of St. Andrew Pervozvanny, established by Peter the Great in 1699, was the first and highest award of the state. The tsars went on eventually to create twenty-two awards; the church had no ecclesiastical awards itself. Empress Catherine the Great ordered from the Lomonosov Factory an enormous set of china for the order's annual dinner. Each dinner plate replicates the gorgeous ribbon from which hung the deep red enamel medallion of the cross of St. Andrew.[2] Thus, however "Western" the tsar, the memory of Russian Orthodoxy was anchored in an event that happened circa A.D. 30. The cross is the universal symbol of Christianity; Catholics and the Orthodox do not agree upon how to depict it.

The Order of St. Andrew Pervozvanny became extinct when Autocracy died. In the Soviet period, paradoxically, the state permitted the church to create its own orders; they were considered politically innocuous. Until 1988 the highest church award was the Order of St. Sergius of Radonezh. (Pimen conferred it upon the patriarch of Constantinople in August 1987 after their co-celebration of the Feast of the Transfiguration.) Then, in the millennial year of 1988, the church received permission to create three new orders. The highest award of the church now became the Order of St. Andrew Pervozvanny. Neither the cross nor the ribbon itself changed, only the uniform of the man hanging it around the recipient's neck.

The final link in the chain by which the Russian Orthodox claim to be the Church of the Apostolic Succession is found in its medieval Chronicles. Seen as written by divinely inspired monks, here the Savior's plan for Rus (the proto-Eastern Slavic state) is brought into being, as foretold in the Gospels. Orthodoxy accords sacred weight to its Chronicles, just as Catholicism accords sacred weight—equal to that of Scripture—to its traditions. Russians believe the medieval Chronicle of St. Nestor picks up their story where the Gospel of John left off; it tells that Andrew Pervozvanny traveled up the Dnieper to the site of the future city of Kiev. There he erected a cross and prophesied to the assembled people, "Do you see these hills? On these hills divine grace will shine, there will be a great city, and God will erect many churches."[3]

The Chronicle of Nestor continues the story of Andrew Pervozvanny right into Russia's medieval history. It recounts that Andrew journeyed on from the hills of future Kiev to the Slav settlements located on the spot where Novgorod, an early progenitor of the future state of Russia, would be built. There, near the village of Gruzino, he planted a cross.[4] Every Russian child knows that it was the merchants of Novgorod who appealed to Prince Rurik in 862 to "come rule over us" because they quarreled among themselves. Grand Prince Vladimir originally came from Novgorod; he had been thrown out prior to becoming prince of Kiev. The Chronicle of Nestor is among the Russians' oldest documents. The contemporary ROC has skillfully updated its version of history.

Tsar Alexander II had done the same in the nineteenth century. In 1862 he commissioned the sculptor Mikhail Mikeshin to created a "Monument to the Millennium of Russia," erected in front of St. Sophia's Cathedral in Novgorod. It was cast in the shape of a giant bell.[5] The iconography of bells, "singing icons," is part and parcel of Orthodoxy's mythos. In 1852 Archimandrite Leonid made this comparison:

In Russia our motherland ... the variety of our calls to church, at first with wooden, and then with cast iron beams and finally with the ringing of bells, has its own significance and deep meaning, even an acoustical one between our time and that more distant—the past and future.... The weak sounds of the wood and iron remind us of the prophets' vague, cryptic language, but the clamor and harmonious ringing of bells is a proclamation of the Gospel, its exultation to the ends of the universe, and reminds us of the angel's trumpet on the final day."[6]

In the Orthodox mind, the sound of the bells connects the believer to the time of the prophets and to the equally distant future—the Apocalypse, when linear time shall dissolve. Their peal "makes present" both the Old Testament *shofar* and the trumpet that the angel will blow on the Last Day. The tocsin carries the believer through the Last Days to bliss. It reassures the listener who he is, where he has come from, and where his pilgrimage here on earth is going. Mikeshin's giant bell reifies this collapse of time. At the top, the Archangel Michael embraces the cross Andrew planted while the saint kneels at his feet. In the middle register, oversize statues of individual tsars act out specific incidents of Russia's history. The bottom frieze runs the entire circumference of the bell and brings the story up to date—tsars are now depicted in breeches and waistcoats. In 1862, counting back a thousand years brought Mikeshin to a time when Novgorod was still officially pagan. Yet Orthodoxy was somehow mystically present. The message is that the Christianity Andrew Pervozvanny planted with his cross near Novgorod was the true Church of the Apostolic Succession, unchanged sacramentally, doctrinally, or liturgically.[7]

By tracing the Apostolic Succession from Christ to Andrew and then his journeys to Kiev and the future Novgorod, the church sets forth a special connection between God and the destiny of the Russian *nation.* In 1049, just a generation after the death of Vladimir himself, Hilarion, Kiev's first metropolitan of Slavic as opposed to Byzantine Greek origin, wrote a prayer emphasizing the bond between the Savior and the Eastern Slavs: "We are Thy people and the sheep of Thy flock. Our souls are in Thy hands, and our breath is in Thy will."[8] This was not a private meditation but became for centuries the national prayer of the church recited on the first day of the New Year. It brilliantly evoked the key verse in the prologue to the Gospel of John, which bonds the New Testament to the Old: "In the beginning was the Word." This echoes Genesis 1:1–2, "In the beginning ... the spirit of God moved over the face of the waters." The Greek *logos* used for "Word" links a concept from the Old Testament, the idea of God's creative breath (*ruah*) from which creation comes, to Jesus of Nazareth who is Jesus the Incarnate Word of God. The Gospel of John states that Christ came into the world as a human being but is

God Himself. The Logos worked alongside God in creation.[9] Thus, from 1049 the prayer of the Slavs traced their spiritual journey through John 1:1–2 back to Creation itself.

A great deal of history and cartography has happened, however, since Grand Prince Vladimir Christianized the Eastern Slavs in A.D. 988. From the ROC's perspective, Kievan Rus is now quite inconveniently located in a different and sovereign country, Ukraine. The church however, "reads" the events of 988 the same way it interprets the events of the Old Testament: they prefigure the New. The classic case is the Orthodox interpretation of the episode in Genesis where Abraham entertains three angels unaware. The famous "Holy Trinity" icon painted by Andrey Rublyov gives no hint that what comes out of Abraham's alfresco picnic is an Isaac who begat a Jacob who will be renamed Israel by an angel with whom he will wrestle. Rublyov's angels prefigure the triune God—the Father, Son, and Holy Spirit of the *New* Testament.[10] Indeed, the Rublyov icon eliminates Sarah altogether and shows Abraham's dwelling place at Mamre very much in the background.

The same principle operates here: Grand Prince Vladimir was the mystical progenitor of Holy Rus. Makary Bulgakov, the metropolitan of Moscow and a widely respected church historian, gives the official church view in 1994: the Baptism of Rus "is without a doubt, the most important event in the history of all Russian lands. In several ways, it decided the eternal fate of all future generations of Russia and ... began a new period of our existence in every respect: our enlightenment, customs, judiciary, and building of our nation, our religious faith, and our morality."[11] Notably there is no mention of "Ukraine." That Kiev became capital of an independent and sovereign country begotten in August 1991 is ignored. The redoubtable Elizabeth Koutaissoff, a descendant of the same Marshal Kutuzov who defeated Napoleon, remarked that in her opinion the Ukrainians were really borderline Russians, because, after all, "Ukraina" itself meant "borderland." She spoke for many nationalists. While it is true that ethnically Ukrainians are Eastern Slavs like the Russians, their contemporary self-image is most certainly not that they are "borderline Russians."[12]

The ROC simply eliminates details like borders between Russia and Ukraine. It begins teaching this version of history to Russian children before they can read and write. The class for five- and six-year-olds at St. Vladimir's Russian Orthodox Church elementary school in Moscow in March 1992 absorbed the essence of the story from lesson plans taken from pages of a coloring book entitled *Kreshchenie Rusi*, that is, *The Baptism of Rus*. Its twenty-five pages, each page with one or two sentences of text, traces the church's view of Vladimir and his role in the history of the Eastern Slavs.[13]

The coloring book was printed March 1, 1992—that is, not long after the December 25, 1991, disbanding of the USSR. The Soviet Union had strictly forbidden any religious publications directed at children. Yet no sooner had the country dissolved than the machinery of the ROC was able to churn out a print run of 300,000 copies of this booklet. It failed to seek permission from the original publisher, however. This copy of *Kreshchenie Rusi* came from a "rogue" reprint, one of several that came out in Russia in the early 1990s in many thousands of copies. The provenance of *Kreshchenie Rusi* itself is a window not only into the complete collapse of Soviet control but also into the ROC's cavalier attitude toward international copyright law. Its publication passed totally unnoticed in the West. Within Moscow itself, every copy was snapped up immediately.

Already the energetic Russian Orthodox Church of St. Vladimir's had opened a primary school, and Moscow parents—some of them believers and some of them not—were vying to get their children into its sparkling clean rooms and peaceful and happy atmosphere. For Orthodox families, the school was a "miracle":

> Now our children can study God's word, and they can pray together, both before and after meals, before their classes, and can sing hymns.... two years ago [1990] when we prayed together, or sang hymns, or studied the Bible, it was all done in secret. Even just two years ago, our children had to be careful about wearing a cross around their neck. They were studying in Soviet schools and were subject to attacks by aggressively atheist students, and worst of all—teachers.[14]

But nonreligious parents were eager to enroll their children too. (The same phenomenon obtains in cities in the United States and Great Britain.)[15] St. Vladimir's serves as a support system for families, some single parent, many of whom are under stress. It manages both an after-school and preschool program for children whose parents have to work and commute long hours (figure 5.2). When a child needs to stay overnight, there are thirty small, immaculate beds in a large, light-filled dormitory (figure 5.3). This tender and gentle twenty-four-hour care induces a harried working mother and father to send their child to St. Vladimir's. Some of the parents confided that before the opening of this school, they had had to board their children from Monday to Friday at state-run crèches just so they could work.[16] In Russia, enrolling a child in an Orthodox school embeds the entire family in its ethos. Many of the "volunteers" helping with the church restoration were motivated by the desire to get their child accepted at its school.

Figure 5.2 Preschoolers enjoy a peaceful and nutritious lunch at St. Vladimir's Russian Orthodox Church's primary school. (Photo credit: John Garrard)

What made *Kreschchenie Rusi*'s story so dangerous to the Soviet Union that it could not be printed in a format for small children as long as the country itself existed? The cover shows Grand Prince Vladimir and a beautiful lady overlooking the Dnieper while priests carrying icons lead masses of huddled Slavs down to the river. Page one plunges into the pagan world of Kievan Rus showing an exciting drinking party. But Prince Vladimir quickly sends out embassies to find out about other faiths, and lo, as the caption says underneath a drawing of a wedding, "Prince Vladimir accepted baptism and married the Byzantine Princess Anna" (figure 5.4). This became the jumping off point for the teacher to teach that bit of history from the church perspective. As part of each lesson, the children were given crayons and pencils and told they could illustrate the page in their own way because the book itself was too precious for an individual child to be allowed to color. Several quite lovely drawings resulted. A little girl rendered the "wedding page" of Vladimir and Princess Anna by concentrating on what was important to her: the bride. The

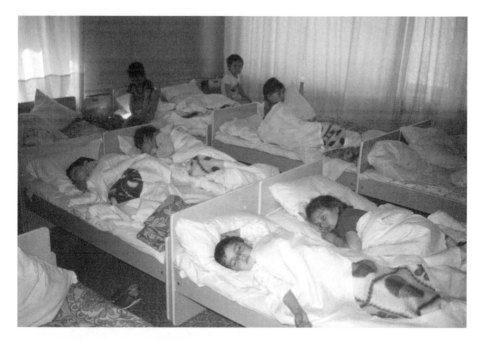

Figure 5.3 The preschool run by St. Vladimir's Russian Orthodox Church contains thirty small beds in a large, light-filled dormitory. Children take afternoon naps there and can stay overnight if need be. (Photo credit: John Garrard)

Byzantine Princess Anna is transformed into a "Russian beauty" *sans* either groom, guests, or church (figure 5.5).

The charm and naiveté of these drawings should not blind us to the importance of what is going on here. Children are learning to view history with Orthodox eyes. The church regards the history of the faith and its flock as both *sui generis* and miraculous. Its version alone furnishes the key to both the past and the future. Events partake of human endeavor, but the secular does not furnish the plot. Anyone who has been to Sunday school in the United States' Bible Belt will recognize this perspective; it is how fundamentalist Protestants approach Scripture. This is history discontinuous with the rational, which indeed is suspect, because analysis can never comprehend the divine. Its timeline is also discontinuous, because those periods when God is not active in man's affairs—such as the space between the Old and New Testaments—is not significant. (In the West we know this period as overlapping classical Greek antiquity.) The Soviet coloring books about

Figure 5.4 A page from *Kreshchenie Rusi* (*The Baptism of Rus*) depicts the wedding of Grand Prince Vladimir of Kiev and the Byzantine princess, Anna. (Photo credit: *Kreshchenie Rusi*, Serge A. Sauer, Publisher.)

Figure 5.5 The class of five-year-olds at the primary school run by St. Vladimir's interpreted the story of *The Baptism of Rus* with individual drawings. A little girl rendered the "wedding page" from the coloring book by concentrating on what was important to her: Princess Anna as the bride. (Photo credit: John Garrard)

Lenin and the benign Communist Party that once swamped children have been pulped. A medieval historian, fluent in the internecine warfare, rapine, and pillage of Vladimir's Rurikid dynasty, might argue that history has been pulped from *Kreshchenie Rusi* as well.

But what is being absorbed here is the myth, the pseudohistory, and drop by drop, a page a day, it is sinking in. The cover had depicted the mass baptism; the same illustration is repeated on page 20. The caption reads "The inhabitants of Kiev were baptized in the Dnieper River in 988 and then the whole of Kievan Rus was baptized, followed by other Slavic tribes" (figure 5.6). This phrase neatly erases any actual borders on current maps. Ukraine and Russia are simply blended together under an umbrella phrase. In another illustration, weeping Slavs kneel by the river as the waterlogged totems of their pagan gods float away—a man on horseback whips the pleading crowd back from trying to wade in and "save" them. This actually occurred at Novgorod where the populace rioted at seeing their idols toppled into the water. The caption explains that the people had to be taught the truth by their "Good and Just prince [who] defended the weak, helped the poor, and built many churches."

The last page has an elaborate border by the celebrated artist Bilibin framing a huge bell ringing over a stylized landscape of "Rus." The caption declares, "They [the people] loved their prince, and nicknamed him 'Beautiful Sun' [Krasnoe Solnyshko]. Our holy church canonized Prince Vladimir as a Saint, and called him 'Equal to the Apostles' [Ravnoapostolny]." The children of the preschool were now told that they would be taking a "field trip" over to the church next door. And there on its iconostasis they would see a beautiful icon of the same Grand Prince Vladimir that they would be allowed to copy and color. To say the five- and six-year-olds were excited is an understatement. Western parents—veterans of being conscripted to chaperone school field trips—will know the denouement. The class would need several stalwarts to come along and help. Thus the way is paved for a modern version of the Gospel's promise that "a little child shall lead them." A children's coloring book segues into a salutary lesson in child evangelism.

The caption of this last page slipped in a word that had not been heard in a Soviet school—Ravnoapostolny. Russian children will now learn how to pronounce, define, and spell a word that signifies one of the irreconcilable differences with the West. Ravnoapostolny is a status unique to the lexicon of Orthodoxy. It is given to those people regarded as "Apostles to the Slavs"[17] (*vide* Paul's status as "Apostle to the Gentiles"). By canonizing Vladimir as "equal to the apostles" in the thirteenth century, the church linked the Gospel of John and the Chronicle of Nestor. Thus, much as Acts is seen as

Figure 5.6 Grand Prince Vladimir of Kiev and his wife Anna oversee the mass baptism of huddled Slavs in the Dnieper River in A.D. 988. (Photo credit: *Kreshchenie Rusi*, Serge A. Sauer)

the continuation of the Gospel of Luke, the Chronicle of Nestor functions as an "Acts of the *Ravnoapostolnye*."

The first of the Ravnoapostolny pantheon is Constantine, the Roman general whose vision of a cross in the heavens before the critical Battle of the Milvian Bridge in A.D. 312 paved the way for him to become sole Roman emperor and to make Christianity the religion of the empire.[18] This turning point in history has always been part of the deep memory of Orthodoxy, as attested by the actions of the Moscow crowd on August 21, 1991, who replaced the forbidding bronze statue of Feliks Dzerzhinsky with an Orthodox cross and "By this sign, conquer" painted on the black granite. While Western Christianity sainted Constantine, he is not titled "Equal to the Apostles." In fact, because he moved the capital of the Roman Empire from Rome to his new city of Constantinople, Catholicism prefers to play down his role.

Not so the Russian Orthodox. From the outset, his conversion has been deliberately paralleled with that of Grand Prince Vladimir. Metropolitan Hilarion of Kiev made the point in 1049, with Vladimir dead only since 1015 and his son Yaroslav the Wise (Premudry) on the throne: "He [Constantine] with his mother St. Helen brought the Cross of Jerusalem, glorified it widely and consolidated the belief. And you [the dead Grand Prince Vladimir] with your grandmother St. Olga brought the Cross from *the new Jerusalem-Constantinople*, installed it all over the country and consolidated the belief."[19] The real life Vladimir was a ruthless and wily Viking who had blinded his brother (thus making him ineligible to rule), raped his brother's fiancée, Rogneda, and had to give up about 1,000 concubines (according to the horrified monastery scribe) to marry the Princess Anna, a lady so reluctant to accept the match that she initially declared that she would rather die. None of that will be mentioned in the classroom. Anyway, it all happened before he saw the light. As St. Vladimir, he fulfills the divine prophecy of St. Andrew Pervozvanny and deserves to be named Ravnoapostolny.

What was taught in an Orthodox primary school classroom in 1992, using a coloring book's pages for lesson plans, were the first gentle shoots of an entire rewriting of history that has been propagated ever since. The plot and characters of *Kreshchenie Rusi*, first portrayed by monks illuminating manuscripts in the eleventh century, is drawn a thousand years later by childish hands. The point is the same: God marked out the Russians for a special destiny. Whether or not this story will be taught in *state* schools remains an issue; but because the ROC can now open its own schools, it already has a channel to inculcate its curriculum. In 2006 a high-budget, lavishly marketed animated film, *Prince Vladimir*, came out in Russian theaters. The story line weaves in and out of the pages of *Kreshchenie Rusi* and takes the plot further.

After having Christianized the Slavs, Vladimir Fair Sun has to battle "against the enemies of the ancient land of the Eastern Slavs" by uniting the nobles and the simple folk. Now one of the pagan idols burned at Novgorod uncannily resembles the Statue of Liberty. The leaders of the enemy tribes look like clones of Mikhail Khodorkovsky. Here in glorious color is a world where the heroes and villains are black and white. *Prince Vladimir* was made with backing from the Ministry of Culture who cited its "patriotic" as well as "historic" value.[20] When it was released on the eve of the "Defenders of the Fatherland Day," Aleksy publicly blessed it.[21] The Chronicle, the coloring book, and the cartoon propound a view first articulated by Hilarion in 1049: the Rus are the Chosen People of the New Testament. In later grades the students will read the Chronicle of Nestor itself.

Of course, being the chosen means that others who have not been so selected are banished outside the blessed circle. This can elicit envy and outright rejection by the nonselected. It is hard to know how fast news traveled between Kiev and Rome in 1049, but if the "Bishop of Rome" did learn of Hilarion's prayer, it could not have made him happy. Resentment came to a head in 1054, when Cardinal Humbert laid a Papal Bull of Excommunication of Patriarch Michael Cerularius on the Altar of St. Sophia: "Whoever shall contradict obstinately the faith of the Holy Roman and Apostolic See and its Host, let him be anathematized and not be held a catholic Christian, but a heretical prozymite! [i.e., an advocate of leavened communion bread]."[22] Though the professed reasons for the split concern whether the priesthood should be celibate or married, whether the Eucharist should use unleavened bread versus leavened bread, and how the Holy Spirit "proceeds," the language of the papal bull itself indicates the decisive conflict: which church, east or west, had the right to be called the Church of the Apostolic Succession.

From the Orthodox viewpoint, the Western churches got it wrong on the key questions of who was the first disciple to be called by Jesus and who was the first to acknowledge Jesus as Christ. Now the Western churches went further astray by introducing new and dangerous ideas into the nature of the Holy Spirit, the third part of the Trinity. The issue occurs in a key clause in the Nicene Creed, which was agreed upon by the Council of Nicaea in A.D. 325. Emperor Constantine himself, saint and Ravnoapostolny, gave it his stamp of approval. This is the only creed that Orthodox believers recognize because they do not acknowledge the Apostle's Creed. In the original form of the Nicene Creed, the speaker declares "I believe ... in the Holy Spirit, the Lord, the Giver of the Life, Who proceeds from the Father, Who with the Father and the Son is equally worshipped and glorified." The Western "Latinizers" wished to adopt a version that added "and the Son" (*filioque*), thus turning the phrase into "Who proceeds from the Father *and the Son*, Who with the Father and the Son is equally worshipped and glorified." The Roman popes adopted this version. Eastern Christianity refused, and the *filioque* clause became the ostensible theological reason for the Great Schism of 1054.[23]

But if the Orthodox-Catholic schism were just about the Procession of the Holy Spirit, then the breach could have been healed in recent memory. Pope John Paul II offered what he regarded as an important concession: Catholicism would agree that when the Nicene Creed is recited *in Greek*, the "and the Son" clause would be omitted.[24] The Orthodox rejected this, believing that it was yet another attempt to assert papal supremacy. The clash over which church "owns" the right to be called the Church of the Apostolic Succession is the issue upon which neither the irresistible force of Roman Catholicism nor the immovable object of Russian Orthodoxy can budge. When the mutual anathemas of 1054 were "banished to oblivion" in 1965, a year after the pope and the patriarch of Constantinople held a meeting in Istanbul, it is noteworthy that the patriarch of Russia was not there. The divisions between the ROC and Roman Catholicism continue at a fundamental level to this day.

From A.D. 1054 on, the Rus found themselves hemmed in by the barriers of faith. Given that the Gospels themselves disagree, the clash of evidence can be "resolved" only by choosing either John or Matthew. Having each made their selection, Orthodoxy and Catholicism insist that theirs was the only right, the only "true" decision. In an age of faith, this meant that those who disagreed were not only wrong but also heretic and apostate. Once a faith chooses one Gospel to follow on these questions, its believers cannot compromise. The Orthodox do not acknowledge that the pope has authority over them, although they do accept him as the head of the Western church. Their view of Peter is that yes, he was the "supreme" apostle, but, in the words of the Orthodox theologian Alexander Schmemann, "this primacy has been understood as a gift of grace to be the voice of apostolic unanimity—not in terms of any special power over the apostles or the Church."[25] In return, Catholicism does not regard the Chronicle of St. Nestor as a sacred text.

Seen through the ROC's angle of vision, the Schism is entirely Catholicism's fault. In 1987 the *Journal of the Moscow Patriarchate* put the case starkly: "Let us not forget that in the Russian Orthodox consciousness the Roman Church's break with the family of Eastern Churches has always been viewed as a step away from Christ Himself."[26] And indeed the ROC has not forgotten. While the 950th anniversary of the 1054 split passed virtually without comment in the West, the ROC commemorated the date with a major theological conference. The Orthodox still hold that the faith accepted by

Vladimir was complete—no further modifications to Creed, language, or liturgy were required.

Since Western Christendom took its fateful "step away from Christ Himself," the religion naturally continued to splinter. As a contemporary Orthodox Catechism pamphlet describes it, after the Schism the West experienced little else but turmoil and corruption:

> The Crusades began, and included an attack on the Church in the East [e.g., the capture of Constantinople by the Fourth Crusade, sponsored by Venice, in 1204]. The Renaissance revived pagan ideals and mixed them with Christianity, the Inquisition brought death and destruction, and finally the Protestant Reformation divided Western Christianity and led to civil strife and endless wars. The Middle Ages marked the gradual transition between the ancient Christian world-view and the modern godless one. The East experienced no such Middle Ages, since there the Orthodox Church preserved the true Christian faith.[27]

That encapsulates the Orthodox view of the Crusades, the Reformation, the Renaissance, and the Counter-Reformation.

Each of those events left a very different footprint in Western consciousness. The average westerner thinks of the Crusades as that foreign trip which took Richard the Lion Hearted away from England, leaving it in the hands of Prince John and Robin Hood. Historically, Richard's was the Third Crusade, which ended with the Kurdish general Saladin marching triumphant into the City of Jerusalem in the fall of 1187. In marked contrast to the way Western crusaders had behaved almost a century earlier when they took the city, Saladin forbade his troops from taking vengeance on the population. Saladin assessed a token ransom (some of which he himself paid for those too poor) and the Christian refugees were sent back with his own soldiers for guards. However chivalrously Saladin had behaved, the crusaders' defeat meant that Jerusalem was once again in the hands of the infidel. The West could not accept that this was "God's will" but must try again to retake Jerusalem. The next "crusade" would be the Fourth, which did indeed become "an attack on the Church in the East"—Constantinople.

In October 1202 Pope Innocent III blessed crusaders sailing from Venice. They were supposed to retake Jerusalem from Islam. Instead they landed at Christian Constantinople on June 23, 1203. On April 9, 1204, they assaulted it, and in three days captured it. With the same zeal with which in 1099 crusaders had stabled their horses in Jerusalem's al-Aqsa mosque and desecrated the Dome of the Rock (believed by Muslims to be the site from which Mohammed had ascended to heaven with the angel Gabriel on his mystical night-journey to Jerusalem), they now looted St. Sophia. *Deus vult!* (God wills it!) knights shouted when Pope Urban had called upon them in 1095 to retake Jerusalem; *Deus vult!* they cried as they murdered the population of the historical Jerusalem. *Deus vult!* they howled 105 years later as they killed the Christian inhabitants of the "new Jerusalem," Constantinople.

Pope Innocent was euphoric at the city's fall. (He apparently regarded its taking as a way to fund the real goal of going on to Jerusalem. The Venetians refused.) In a letter addressed to the monks and priests who had accompanied the crusaders (November 13, 1204), he praised the city's capture, because it meant that the Byzantine Empire would be transferred from "the proud to the humble, from the disobedient to the obedient, from schismatics to Catholics." He concluded that it was "done by the Lord and is wondrous in our eyes."[28] With Pope Innocent so disposed, the knights of the Fourth Crusade cheerfully carted, boxed, and shipped back to Venice its priceless treasures. Western tourists much admire these spoils, particularly the horses that decorate St. Mark's Cathedral, without knowing their provenance. Baldwin of Flanders was installed as emperor of what was retitled the "Latin Empire." The pope placed it under his protection, and decreed that any crusader who would try to preserve these newly conquered lands for the true faith of Catholicism would be rewarded with the remission of sins. This was the same promise extended to crusaders who tried to retake Jerusalem and the Holy Land from Islam.[29] Now crusaders who killed Orthodox Christians were entitled to the same bonus as those who killed Muslims.

Pope Innocent III (1198–1216) turned religious animosity against the infidel to the heretic. He initiated crusades against the Cathars of Languedoc, an ascetic Christian sect whose main center was the city of Albi. French knights pillaged the heretical Cathars secure in the knowledge that they were doing God's work. (These atrocities originate the phrase: "Kill them all; let God sort them out.") Once having justified crusading against heresy rather than Islam, the same pope could justify crusaders sacking Constantinople. Innocent marketed as a "just war" what modern historians see as a fight over trade led by the Doge of Venice, John Dandelo, against a commercial rival. Because the Orthodox used the wrong bread during the Eucharist (leavened versus unleavened), misstated the procession of the Holy Spirit in the Trinity, and did not accede to papal supremacy over Christendom, the pope blessed their extermination. Innocent III had opened his papacy by answering Christ's question (Matthew 24:45) "Who then is a faithful and wise servant, whom his lord hath made ruler over his household, to give them meat in due season?" He simply gave his version of the papal job description: "Now you shall see what kind of servant he is who commands the Household, truly the vicar of Jesus Christ, the Successor of Peter, Anointed of the Lord, God of the Pharaohs, who is the mediator between God and man, placed below God but above men, who is less than God but greater than man."[30] In short, while Innocent III admitted he was the "Servant" of God, he regarded himself as Lord and Master of humanity.

The fifty-seven-year occupation of Constantinople by Western crusaders fatally weakened the Byzantine Empire and impoverished the city irretrievably. Michael VIII Palaiologus (r. 1259–82) finally retook the city on August 15, 1261, the feast day celebrating the Dormition (Koimesis in Greek) of the Virgin, by entering through the Golden Gates and proceeding to Hagia Sophia. The famous Hodegetria icon of the Theotokos was carried before him. (The same icon was smashed by the army of Mehmed the Conqueror on the day the city fell in 1453.) In an effort to secure the city protection from further attacks, the desperate emperor recognized papal claims of primacy and accepted the *filioque* clause at the Council of Lyons in 1274. But papal promises were not kept. The legacy of the Fourth Crusade remains a significant part of Russian Orthodox anger. The ROC's 2004 national conference to mark the 950th anniversary of the Great Schism simultaneously commemorated its 800th anniversary. Entwined caduceus-like, these two events still permeate the Orthodox memory.[31] They are key to why members of the ROC see themselves exclusively as victims at the hand of Western Christianity.

The sequel to the taking of Constantinople meant the next popes turned their attention to Russia, the last bastion of the heretical Orthodox. The modern Orthodox Catechism pamphlet states that "the Inquisition brought death and destruction." The successor to Pope Innocent III was Pope Gregory IX. In 1232–33 he founded the Inquisition, which continued the crusades against the Cathars of Languedoc.[32] Over the next several generations, popes blessed warrior monks and inquisitors who burned heretics at the stake in France. By 1300 that heresy was largely exterminated. But in the meantime, the church and its Inquisition turned their attention to other "heretics"—the Eastern Slavs.

Western knights could be dazzled with the hope of more rich pickings—the sacking of Constantinople had made many Venetian and Frankish knights wealthy beyond their wildest dreams. And the papal assurance that these were "just wars" applied to crusading against the Rus. Russia found itself in the unenviable position of being attacked from the East by the Mongols, while from the West it had to face a simultaneous invasion by Catholic Teutonic Knights. Accompanying these holy warriors were Inquisitors who intended to extirpate Orthodoxy and reintroduce Catholicism by fire and the sword. The Mongols first appeared in 1224 at the Battle of the Kalka River. It was a warning shot, and in 1237–40, a much larger force attacked and razed Kiev, leaving it a pyramid of skulls. At this moment, the pope decided to mount his new crusade against the most important remaining city-state of the Eastern Slavs, Novgorod. Independently, the Swedes sent a fleet along the Neva River.

It looked as if the Eastern Slavs and their faith (either the "true faith" or heresy, depending upon whether one was an Eastern or Western Christian) might indeed be liquidated. But Prince Alexander of Novgorod emerged to save the day. As mentioned earlier, his famous victory over the Swedes on the bank of the Neva River, near modern St. Petersburg, in 1240 earned him the honorific, Alexander Nevsky. Two years later, in 1242, the pope's Teutonic Knights sacked and burned Pskov. The Inquisitors sent all Orthodox priests and monks to the stake, a preview of what they planned for Novgorod. Eisenstein's film does not show Orthodox monks being roasted alive. Instead, the Inquisitors— in forbidding conical hoods having slits for eyes—drop naked blonde Russian babies and toddlers into flames. Nevsky annihilated the Teutonic Knights on Lake Peipus at the famous "battle on the ice." That the savior of Russia should come from Novgorod is read as part of the divine plan, for St. Andrew Pervozvanny had planted his cross nearby.

The 1242 papal army was destroyed, but papal dreams to exterminate the heretical Russians were not. With enemies hemming in the Orthodox Slavs on both sides, Nevsky decided Russia could not fight on two fronts simultaneously. The Mongols would have to be bought off. It would take many generations to defeat them. And so even after his victories over Western Christianity in 1240 and 1242, Nevsky himself traveled to the Golden Horde in 1252 to pay the tribute and was received back in Moscow by all the prelates of the church, who assembled at the city's Golden Gates to greet him. When Novgorod did not want to pay, Nevsky entered the city and forced it—his show of military strength was again blessed by the church. The recalcitrant merchants capitulated.

From the outset, the church threw its full weight behind Nevsky's decision: the Latin West must be defeated first. If the pope's warrior monks triumphed, the "wrong" Christianity would be spread over the land. The Mongols invaded, but they did not stay. The Latin Christians would. Had they not set up a Crusader kingdom in Jerusalem after their victory there in 1099 that lasted until Saladin retook the city in 1187? Were they not now (i.e., from 1204 to 1261) in Constantinople, looting it of its precious relics, even stealing from the Church of the Holy Apostles the bones of St. Andrew—Russian

Orthodoxy's own St. Andrew Pervozvanny—and sending them back to Italy?[33] Better tribute paid to the infidel than absorption by the heretic.

Historians have also noted a certain amount of canny self-interest behind this reasoning. The church prospered rather well under the Mongols. Its priests and monks were not subject to forced conscription by the Mongol army; even laymen associated with the church were exempt, a rather powerful inducement to nonsecular employment in those times. The Golden Horde exempted the church from taxation, so its coffers benefited financially. The church received a *yarlyk* (patent) confirming these privileges in 1267. In 1261 the Horde even allowed the church to open a diocese at the Tatar capital of Saray (near the place where the Volga flows into the Caspian Sea). And most important of all, while the Horde soon converted to Islam, it did not pressure the Rus to follow suit. So the Orthodox Church in exchange, prayed for the Tatars in its services, and served as their emissaries.[34] Some might call it collaboration or collusion, but it preserved the faith. Over in Constantinople the emperors of the Palaiologan dynasty were also buying off the Mongol khans of the Golden Horde and the Ilkhanids of Persia: they sent them their illegitimate daughters in marriage, laden down with enormous dowries.[35]

Because Alexander Nevsky saved his country twice on the battlefield, the church decided that he would also be the mouthpiece for rejecting "the Latinizers" on theological terms as well. According to the hagiography of his life, after the failure of the Teutonic Knights to fulfill the papal directive, the pope sent envoys to try argument and persuasion. With the same resolute defiance with which he slaughtered the Swedes on the banks of the Neva and sent the Teutonic Knights crashing through the ice in Estonia, Nevsky silenced them with the power of his rhetoric:

> From Adam up to the flood, and to the division of languages, and to the beginning of Abraham, from Abraham to the passage of Israel through the Red Sea ... to Augustus and the Nativity of Christ, the Passion and Resurrection, from Resurrection to the Ascension into heaven, and to the reign of Constantine, to the First Council and to the Seventh, I know well all this. Our doctrines are those preached by the apostles.... The tradition of the holy fathers of the seven councils we scrupulously keep. As to your words, we do not listen to them and we do not want your doctrine.[36]

Whether Nevsky ever said any such thing is lost in the mists of time. But here he speaks the Orthodox *credo*, rejecting the "words"—such as the *filioque*— that Western Christianity had added to the Nicene Creed. When Nevsky proudly spoke of "our" doctrines, which "are those preached by the apostles" and keeping "the tradition of the holy fathers of the seven councils," he was drawing a line under his faith as doctrinally complete. Orthodoxy calls itself the Church "of the Seven Councils." From the first council, which had met in Nicaea in A.D. 325 to the last, which met in A.D. 787, the dogma, phraseology, and liturgy of the faith were defined. Changes could be made only by another ecumenical council. No such council—a putative eighth—has ever met. Nevsky's words also show human history as taking place on a single plane. Persons such as Augustus Caesar and Emperor Constantine are mentioned in the same breath as Adam and Abraham, figures known only through the Old Testament.

By buying off the Mongols, though other nomads sacked and burned Moscow later, Russians could always rebuild their capital as an Orthodox city. Believers find divine purpose in this fact. The Teutonic Knights never occupied it; later invaders never stayed long enough to make it into a Muslim city. In stark contrast, Constantinople not only was defeated and occupied by Latin crusaders from 1204 to 1261 but also was finally taken and permanently occupied by Muslim Turks in 1453, who renamed it Istanbul. Whereas the Latin crusaders had looted St. Sophia, now the Turks desecrated it by turning it into a mosque and adding minarets.

According to the Orthodox perspective, Constantinople's fall was divine punishment for capitulating to the Latinizers. This betrayal of Orthodoxy occurred at the Council of Florence, the last occasion (1438–39) on which the Greek East and the Latin West met at the highest level in an attempt to heal the break.[37] The patriarch of Constantinople, Joseph II, attended with eighteen bishops of the Orthodox faith. The Russian delegation included one Isidore, then based in Kiev. The emperor of Constantinople, John Palaiologos [i.e., John VIII], was eager to have support from the West in his struggle against the Turks so his delegation came prepared to compromise. To encourage the Greeks, the pope offered to pay their expenses.

The council ended with the Greek-speaking East signing an Act of Union. The Decree from the Ecumenical Council at Florence (July 6, 1439) opened ecstatically:

> "Let the heavens be glad and let the earth rejoice" [cf. First Chronicles 16:31], for the wall that divided the western and the eastern church has been removed, peace and harmony have returned, since the cornerstone, Christ, who made both one, has joined both sides with a very strong bond of love and peace, uniting and holding them together in a covenant of everlasting unity. After a long haze of grief and a dark and

unlovely gloom of long-enduring strife, the radiance of hoped-for union has illuminated all.[38]

The decree made it clear that the reunion was achieved on papal terms:

> We also define that the holy apostolic see and the Roman pontiff holds the primacy over the whole world and the Roman pontiff is the successor of blessed Peter prince of the apostles, and that he is the true vicar of Christ, the head of the whole church and the father and teacher of all Christians, and to him was committed in blessed Peter the full power of tending, ruling and governing the whole church.[39]

Here was the crux of the matter: the decree confirms the powers the popes ascribe to themselves based upon the crucial verse of Matthew 16:19. In 1439, for one brief moment, it seemed the Muslim juggernaut heading toward the walls of Constantinople had finally cracked Orthodoxy's adamantine objection to the papal claim of supremacy through "blessed Peter."

Alas, the radiance faded quickly to gloom. Alone among the Eastern delegates, the Russian bishop Isidore did not sign the Act of Union. Prudently, he apparently said nothing on record for the entire two years and then left the council early. For all his pains, when he got back to Russia, the grand prince of Muscovy, Vasily II, threw him into prison. The outraged Russians responded to the news of the "Unity Accord" forthwith: "Today the Church of Tsargrad [i.e., Constantinople] wavered, renounced our orthodoxy."[40] From the Russian perspective, they, alone among the Orthodox, never capitulated to the heretic West. In signing on to the pope's terms, Constantinople showed itself a traitor to the true faith.

The Greeks themselves could not sell the Union agreement when they got back home. They got cold feet on the return journey and excused their signing by declaring that it had been done under duress. The emperor's reason for going—hope that the Western pope could get Western princes to send him military aid against the Turks—crashed in disappointment. The pope even reneged on paying their expenses. John VIII was succeeded by Constantine XI Palaiologus (r. 1449–53). Western Christianity sent him no help either, so he faced the young and dynamic Sultan Mehmed II alone. No amount of gold or treasure, no Byzantine princess, could divert the Ottoman. Constantine XI died fighting on the city's walls. Two centuries earlier, the Russian Orthodox Church had agreed with Alexander Nevsky to buy off the Mongols so they could throw all their resources against fighting invasion from the Catholic West. Now, they reasoned that it was better to let "Tsargrad" be occupied by another Muslim power than renounce "our orthodoxy."[41]

At the same time that disaster befell Constantinople things were going well for the Moscow Grand Princes. The "Rise of Muscovy" began in the momentous fourteenth century, when the Rus began to throw off the "Tatar yoke" by defeating Khan Mamay at Kulikovo in 1380. Dmitry Donskoy was grand prince of Moscow, and this too enacted the Savior's plan for His chosen people. Muscovy's Grand Princes would never accept reunion with the West.[42] In 1438, while Isidore was away in distant Italy twiddling his thumbs at the Council of Florence, Orthodox prelates based in Moscow had named the bishop of Riazan as their own metropolitan without bothering to get confirmation from the patriarch of Constantinople. Vasily II agreed to this show of independence. For these acts, a grateful church rewarded him with fulsome praise as "Protector of the Faith."

His son, the future Ivan III, born in 1440, assumed the throne in 1462. When Ivan III became grand prince of Muscovy at the age of twenty-two, he signaled immediately that he intended to rule absolutely and with a grand title. When the Holy Roman Emperor Frederick III offered him the title of "King of Russia," Ivan responded with contempt:

> We by the grace of God have been sovereigns over our dominions from the beginning, from our first forebears, and our right we hold from God, as did our forebears. We pray to God that it may be granted to us and our children for all time to continue as sovereigns as we are at present, and as in the past we have never needed appointment from anyone, so now we do not desire it.[43]

Ivan III then proceeded to finish the "gathering of the Russian lands" begun by Prince Daniel who founded the Danilov Monastery. Ivan absorbed the principality of Yaroslavl in 1463. In 1471 he stopped paying the tribute to the Golden Horde. Two years later, on November 12, 1472, he married the niece of the last emperor of Constantinople, Sophia Palaiologina, and received the Byzantine emblem—a double-headed eagle. Sophia also brought from Constantinople a copy of the famous Hodegetria icon that had been the Protector of the City of Constantinople before being smashed by the Turks on May 29, 1453, when they occupied the city. The copy that Sophia brought transferred its protective and miracle-working properties to Moscow.[44] Ivan absorbed Rostov in 1474 and Novgorod the Great in 1478. Thus, by 1480 Moscow could legitimately claim that it alone was the one Orthodox Church not under the thrall of Muslim Turks, a mark of God's favor to the Russians for having refused the Unity Accord with the heretic West.

Ivan was the first to call himself "Tsar and Autocrat of All the Russias." Looking at it from his perspective, the title "tsar"—which derives from Caesar—was justified. The last of the Constantinople emperors was dead. And "Caesar," of course, looks back to Constantine, saint and Ravnoapostolny. "Tsargrad" conflates linguistically all the history that links the Russians' preservation of the true faith to him, the most important Caesar of all. The nomenclature has powerful connotations—calling it the "tsar's city" sets off the hint that the "tsar" should have it. Nicholas II, the last of the tsars, told his general staff in 1915 to prepare plans to retake the city for Russia. (Needless to say, this scheme never got off the ground.) Ivan died in 1505.

This is the spiritual and temporal context out of which Abbot Filofey of Pskov would write (ca. 1520) his famous epistle to Ivan and Sophia's son, Tsar Vasily III. It is worth quoting in full:

> By the exalted and omnipotent and all-sustaining right hand of God, through whom monarchs reign and the great and mighty are magnified, righteousness is ascribed to you, most serene and most august Grand Prince Vasily Ivanovich of Moscow, Orthodox Christian tsar and lord of all and protector of the altars of God and of the holy ecumenical Catholic and Apostolic church of the holy and glorious Dormition of our Most Holy Lady the Mother of God, which has now shone forth instead of the churches of Rome and Constantinople. For the church of Old Rome fell through the Apollinarian heresy, and the Ishmaelites [i.e., the Muslims who claim descent through Ishmael, Abraham's first born son by the Egyptian concubine Hagar] have broken down the doors of the church of the New Rome, Constantinople, with pikes and axes.
>
> This then, is now the holy Catholic and Apostolic Church of the Third Rome, your sovereign realm, which shines brighter than the sun in its Orthodox Christian faith to the very ends of the universe.
>
> Let it be known to Your Majesty, O pious tsar, that all the realms of Orthodox Christendom have been reduced to your realm alone, and you alone on the earth bear the name of a Christian emperor.
>
> And you shall be called a citizen of the Heavenly Jerusalem for the justice of your rule; for to them that order earthly things well, heavenly things will be given.
>
> Observe then, and take heed, O pious tsar, for all Christian realms are reduced to your realm alone, and two Romes have fallen, the third stands, and a fourth there will not be.[45]

Filofey's "Third Rome" letter should be read as a refutation of the Unity Accord's claim that "the Roman pontiff holds the primacy over the whole world and ... is the true vicar of Christ, the head of the whole church." In contrast, Filofey claims Vasily's realm to be "the holy Catholic and Apostolic

Church," using the word "Catholic"—as does Western Christianity—in its original meaning from the Greek, *katholikos*, or universal (from *kata-* "according to" and *holos* "whole").

Filofey was looking back, but he had unintentionally given the tsars a weapon by which they would subjugate the Pravoslavie (i.e., the faith) in the future. The tsars loved his epistle just as much as the popes loved Matthew 16:19. The dynasty made it the "rock" upon which they built their own view of themselves as Lord and Master of all. The descendants of Vasily III saw themselves as combining the temporal powers of Caesar with the spiritual powers of the Vicar of Christ. Historians term this fusion "Caesaropapism." In the ROC view, the tsars would stray from the true path because they imported false ideas from the West and used them against the church.

No one exemplifies this better than does Vasily's son, Ivan IV, the "Awe-inspiring" or "Terrible." Ivan regarded himself as quite literally above the church. In 1547 Ivan had himself crowned as tsar in the Cathedral of the Assumption inside the Kremlin. Now things went radically wrong for the church. Innocent III had seen himself lord of the earth, but he had had to manipulate other leaders to have access to an army. Ivan controlled the entire machinery of the state. Ivan admired the dissolution of the monasteries by Henry VIII (1536–40). Henry liquidated more than eight hundred houses, bringing the crown enormous revenues. Ivan's version was on a much larger scale. In one of the bloodiest episodes of his long reign, he cordoned off Novgorod on January 2, 1570, and during the next six weeks pillaged it and massacred its monks, priests, and inhabitants. The orgy of rape and looting by his Praetorian Guard, the Oprichnina (special force), went on until February 13, when Ivan pardoned the few remaining alive. The Chronicles differ on the total number slain. The Russian historian Ruslan Skrynnikov estimates 27,000 ordinary folk and most of the elite. Famine followed the massacres, and the city, known as "Great Lord Novgorod" (Gospodin Veliky Novgorod) and former member of the Hanseatic League, was dead. Ivan seems to have moved in and out of clinical insanity—certainly the fact that his thugs were dressed like monks testifies to their master's schizophrenia.

Henry VIII and Ivan IV share many similarities in kind while differing in degree. The difference can be judged by how each dealt with his senior prelate. Henry VIII was furious with his archbishop, John Fisher, when he refused to sign the Supremacy Act (1534) that made the monarch the supreme governor of the Church of England. He put the hapless and brave archbishop through a Tudor version of a show trial, and the jury of obliging nobles ordered him beheaded. (One month later they did the same thing to Sir Thomas More.) Ivan got mad at his senior prelate too, an equally brave

Metropolitan Phillip. On November 8, 1568, he had him kidnapped by the *Oprichnina* as he conducted the festival of the Archangel Michael in the Cathedral of the Assumption. On December 23, 1569, one of his henchmen strangled Phillip in the Otroch Monastery in Tver.[46]

Like Henry VIII, Ivan the Terrible faced a succession crisis intimately bound up with religion. The ROC view of the ensuing Time of Troubles was that it was God's punishment for Ivan insisting on his primacy. He had broken the bond established between the Muscovy Grand Princes and the church. The one bright note in this time was that in 1598 the patriarch of Constantinople visited Moscow and created a patriarchate for Russia.

Ivan also engaged in disastrous military adventures, which had unpleasant consequences for the ROC. Visitors to Moscow will inevitably be struck by the multicolored onion domes of St. Basil's Cathedral on Red Square, built to commemorate Ivan's conquest of the capital of the Kazan Tatars in 1552. But they will be less likely to hear that in 1571 the Crimean Tatars exacted revenge by sacking Moscow. Similarly, Ivan launched a catastrophic "Livonian War" against the powerful Polish-Lithuanian Commonwealth to the west and south of Muscovy. Things went so badly that Ivan petitioned Pope Gregory XIII to mediate. The pope immediately saw dreams of luring Muscovy back into the Roman fold. In his letter to Ivan, dated March 15, 1580, he got down to business: "There is one Church, one Christian flock, one only after Christ is his vicar on earth and universal shepherd." He sent a Jesuit, Antonio Possevino, on a *Missio moscovitica* to negotiate terms—and get Ivan to sign on to papal supremacy.[47]

No matter how much Ivan needed papal help, he could not agree to that. The two debated before the whole court, with every word being taken down. Ivan propounded the crux of the matter, the ROC's descent from St. Andrew Pervozvanny:

> We received our Christian faith from the early Church at the time when Andrew, the brother of the Apostle Peter, visited these lands on his way to Rome. Vladimir was converted to the faith, and Christianity spread far and wide among us. We received the Christian faith here in Muscovy at the same time you received it in Italy and we have preserved it intact."[48]

In his response, the Jesuit ignored Ivan's claim, seeking no further elucidation. Instead, he simply harped on the primacy of Peter, quoting the key verse from Matthew (16:19):

> Christ sent all the Apostles forth into the world . . . with different degrees of power. But to Peter alone He entrusted the Keys of the Kingdom of

Heaven.... If we grant that the bishops who are descended from the other Apostles retain their authority, we must also agree that the See of Peter retains much greater authority.

Had Ivan agreed, he would have annulled the basis of the Russian Orthodox Church. Both tsar and Jesuit were left in mutual incomprehension. The Catholic priest did not even seem to realize that the Russians had never agreed to the Council of Florence's Decree of Union. Possevino entered Moscow on February 13, 1582, with high hopes of winning the schismatic Orthodox back to the true faith of Catholicism; he left the city on March 14 glad to be alive.

Ivan came out of his debate with Gregory XIII's emissary rather well, but the aftermath of the war was disastrous. The church now faced a new challenge from Catholic Poland: the Counter-Reformation. Ivan's enemies occupied Ukraine, which was thoroughly Polonized and hence became Catholic. So it was that the Russian Orthodox Church found itself challenged in Belorussia and Ukraine by Catholics who were more sophisticated and better educated. The Polish overlords, vanguard of the Counter- Reformation in Eastern Europe, established the Uniate Church in 1596 with the Union of Brest-Litovsk. Orthodox bishops, finding themselves occupied by the forces of a powerful Polish-Lithuanian state, accepted the primacy of the pope, while trying to maintain the Orthodox liturgy. According to the ROC, with the support of the Catholic Church, the Polish-Lithuanian state began imposing the Unia on the land of Ukraine and Belarus. Uniates claim to be Orthodox, but because they acknowledge the authority of the pope of Rome, not the patriarch in Moscow, the ROC terms them "Greek Catholics" and does not regard them as fellow Orthodox.

Although Left Bank Ukraine, that is, the land east of the Dnieper River, was later united with Russia through an alliance with the Cossacks, Catholic Uniate western Ukraine continued to spread disturbing "Latinizer" ideas into Muscovy. To meet the challenge of vigorous Catholic churchmen introducing their ideas into Russia, Patriarch Nikon in the middle of the seventeenth century decided to introduce reforms. This "reformation" caused a disaster. Of all the changes he desired to make in liturgy and practices, one—making the sign of the cross—became the symbol for all. Nikon sent round a pastoral letter in Lent of 1653 declaring that the sign of the cross should be made with three fingers extended, and the thumb and little finger curled in the palm. But only a hundred years before Nikon decided to change this—an act performed many times during the day by the Orthodox believer—a church council in Moscow had declared: "The sign of the cross must be made according to the rules, ... with the thumb and the two lower fingers joined together [in the palm] and the extended index finger joined to the middle finger ... [and] if anyone should fail to give his blessing with two fingers, as Christ did, or should fail to make the sign of the cross with two fingers, may he be accursed."[49] In short, Nikon now ordered the faithful to do what they had been taught would cause them to be "accursed." This caused a serious schism in the church, leading to the breakaway of the Staroobryadtsy (Old Believers). During the reign of Peter the Great, and often later, when Old Believers were on the point of being arrested, they would lock themselves into a wooden building and set themselves on fire. It is estimated that as many as twenty thousand perished this way in the fifty years after the Schism.[50]

The reforms of Nikon split the church, but worse followed. Peter set out to Europeanize Russia, and it was inevitable that he would turn his formidable energy against the church. Beginning in 1721, Peter introduced a Most Holy Synod to run the Orthodox Church like a department of state. The Most Holy Synod's name and duties were openly borrowed from the Lutheran Church in Scandinavia and the Netherlands. Peter encouraged Lutherans, Freemasons, and other heretics to settle in the lands of the Rus. At Peter's order, a cleric from Kiev, Feofan Prokopovich, drew up a new authoritative document, the Spiritual Regulation (Dukhovny reglament), to govern the church's affairs. One part of the Spiritual Regulation spelled out that priests were to report anything suspicious they had learned in the confessional:

> If someone in confession informs his spiritual father of some illegality that has not been committed, but that he yet intends to commit, especially treason or mutiny against the Sovereign or against the state, or evil designs upon the honor or well-being of the sovereign and upon His Majesty's family ... then the confessor must not only honor as valid the forgiveness and remission of the confessed sins, but he must expeditiously report concern then ... to whom it is appropriate.[51]

With the sanctity of the confessional destroyed, the emperor's bureaucracy enslaved the church. There was no longer a patriarch because Peter had declined to appoint a new one when the sitting Adrian died in 1700. Peter appropriated much of the role of patriarch himself.

Even his changing the calendar was seen as an act of tyranny. Prior to 1700, Russia used the Hebrew calendar, which was reckoned from the presumed date of the world's creation. Peter arrived in Moscow back home from his "Great Embassy" to the West on August 25 in the Hebrew year of 7206. The Julian calendar reckoned the date to be 1698. At that time, "New Year's

Day" was September 1. Peter had arrived one week before the New Year of 7207 as figured on the Hebrew calendar or 1699 by the Julian. Peter then simply decreed that the New Year would be celebrated on January 1, and that beginning with the new century the years would be counted from the presumed date of the birth of Jesus of Nazareth. Thus the next "New Year's Day" after September 1, 7207 (i.e., 1699) was celebrated on January 1, 1700.[52] The Julian calendar remains the ecclesiastical calendar of Russian Orthodoxy today.[53] But at the time, ordinary Russians were bewildered. Some considered his return to Russia as signifying the advent of the Antichrist, for the year 1699 had dark connotations.

Peter's faith defies description, but he was no atheist; he was a committed blasphemer.[54] With a gang of drinking buddies, he founded the All-Jocular Synod (Vseshuteyshy sobor) sometimes called the "All-Drunken Synod" (*vsepyaneyshy sobor*). This appropriated more than ecclesiastical language: their orgies parodied church rituals. The mocking of deeply held beliefs and a deeply loved liturgy left Orthodox churchmen shaken and fearful. His death in 1725 ended the *Vsepyaneyshy sobor* but the subordination of the Orthodox Church to the state continued to the end of the tsarist period in 1917. The last procurator of the Holy Synod, the obscurantist Konstantin Pobedonostsev, tutored both Alexander III and Nicholas II, and thus had a hand in forming their doctrinaire horizons.

Repression of the church under the tsars pales in the face of Soviet persecution. Sometimes the church describes the seventy years of Soviet power as a "Babylonian captivity." The villains were not foreign invaders but Russians, fellow countrymen, infected by Western notions. In their view, the fact that Marx was German is equally as significant as that he was Jewish. Marxism is yet another of the alien imports brought into the land of the Rus through the caged bacillus of Lenin and his sealed train.

Then, just as the church was slowly beginning to revive in the days of glasnost and perestroika, the 1990 law on Freedom of Conscience and Religious Organizations, passed October 1, landed the problem of Western Christianity on its doorstep in an entirely new and dangerous form. It made "all denominations and religions ... equal under the law" and guaranteed every citizen's right to "freedom of conscience." It declared Russia to be a secular state, prohibited the establishment of a state religion, and denied to the state any right of intervention in religion. Churches and religious organizations were permitted to freely engage in worship, proselytism, and school and seminary operation. They could also own property and publish religious literature, all without the requirement of registering with the government. The result was a classic case of unintended consequences. The law opened the country to a veritable religious crusade by Western Christian evangelists and missionaries.

Given the hostility between the ROC and Western Christianity ever since the great Schism of 1054, church leaders were offended. Since 1990, relations between the ROC and Roman Catholicism have ratcheted steadily downhill. In 1991 a Russian Orthodox priest made a statement which encapsulates the ROC's view: "Moscow isn't a Babylon for secondary cults, for Protestant congregations who resemble wild wolves rushing in here or for Catholics like thieves using their billions to try to occupy new territory."[55] Orthodoxy ceased evolving theologically in the eleventh century. It refused to compromise with those faiths—that is, Catholicism and its Protestant offshoots—who had.

The church spent years lobbying against the 1990 law and finally in 1997 the Duma (Russian Parliament) passed a new law "On Freedom of Conscience and Religious Associations," duly signed by Yeltsin. The 1997 law again declares that Russia is a secular state, but it gives a privileged place to Orthodoxy as coterminous with the state from its very beginnings. It also insists that "religious organizations" from all other confessions must prove they have been *legally registered* in Russia for at least fifteen years in order to acquire legal status. The law was designed to make it extremely difficult for foreign Christians to enter the country and proselytize. In effect, the 1997 law codified the idea that being Christian and being Orthodox are one and the same thing. At the same time, there was no effort to make Orthodoxy the state faith. This was tolerance Russian style: the "traditional faiths" of Judaism, Islam, and Buddhism were to be allowed to "own property, to have radio and television stations, and to disseminate religious literature." They would be exempt from taxes and able to conduct services—including in cemeteries and hospitals.

Pointedly absent from the list was any form of Western Christianity, whose evangelists had flooded the country under the provisions of the 1990 law. Orthodoxy saw them as religious carpetbaggers, but if they had registered after 1990, they would be offered a middle ground. They would be able to do charity and receive donations. But there were a number of activities latecomers would not be permitted: they could not run schools, distribute religious literature, or invite foreigners to work as clergy. And those who had not registered at all were severely restricted. Given that the rights of religious proselytism had been granted in 1990 without the proviso of state registration, the 1997 law acted as a classic "Catch 22" for Western missionaries. The 1997 law did not stop Western proselytizers from arriving but would circumscribe and hedge their efforts.

On an ad hoc basis, the authorities made it difficult for other Christian confessions to "register" legally. Sometimes visas would be denied to foreign prelates. At other times, more imaginative techniques could be employed. The classic example here is the application of Article 14 of the 1997 law, "The Liquidation of a Religious Organization and the Banning of a Religious Association's Activities in the Event of the Breaking of the Law." Among the actions that can prompt this "liquidation" is "the creation of armed units." On the grounds that it was a "quasi-military corps," this proviso was activated to suppress the Salvation Army.

The ROC's fingerprints are all over this episode, though Mayor Luzhkov of Moscow exercised the legal muscle.[56] Luzhkov endorsed the 2002 publication of a school textbook, *The Basics of Living Safely*, which characterized the Salvation Army thus: "Posing as an evangelical Protestant Church, the Salvation Army is in essence a militarized formation with a strictly hierarchical system, military ranks, uniforms and commands, as well as unflinching subordination of juniors to seniors." This description of their activities became the formal basis for the Army's complaint at the European Court of Human Rights (ECHR) in Strasbourg, France. The court, which must have read Shaw's *Major Barbara* and knew perfectly well that the corps are armed solely with trombones and tambourines, found for the Army. They awarded it a judgment of U.S.$12,557 (or the equivalent in rubles or Norwegian kroner.) The Russian government paid the Army the compensation but refused to resolve the legal situation.[57] By April 2007 the Moscow branch had still not been able to legally register. Aleksy did nothing to clear up this linguistic comedy of errors. Indeed, he is on record as believing that any form of Christianity other than Orthodoxy contains the seed for civil war. When the Duma passed the 1997 law, he said: "I am sure that the sects and pseudo-missionaries who have flooded Russia are motivated by the desire not to enlighten but to divide our people along religious, confessional lines. And this poses a danger not only for the church but also for the state. For the state, unity of the people is the guarantee of the future."[58] Here Aleksy returns to his critical concept of *sobornost* (togetherness).

If suppressing the Salvation Army in Moscow has been one of his concerns, imagine the patriarchal energy and time spent keeping Catholicism out of Holy Rus. Basking in the triumph of the 1997 law, Aleksy squelched Pope John Paul's long-cherished summit with the patriarch that had been set for Graz, Austria. The official reason for its cancellation was given in an interview with Father Igor Vyzhanov, "Secretary to the Patriarch for Inter-Christian Relations," broadcast in April 2005 as John Paul II lay dying. Vyzhanov spoke at great length with a journalist from Russia's government-owned RIA Novosti Agency. Vyzhanov began by reviewing the entire history with the Uniates of Ukraine, going back to 1596.[59] He stated the Catholic Church's "aggressive missionary activities" in Russia and countries of the Commonwealth of Independent States constituted behavior that the Orthodox Church could not help but see as unfriendly. Yes, he recalled, in 1992, there had been a meeting between the Vatican and the Moscow Patriarchate in Geneva. The pope's *Pro Russia* commission had published a document entitled "General principles and practical regulations to coordinate the evangelizing activities and ecumenical obligation of the Catholic Church in Russia and other countries of the CIS." But while *Pro Russia* obliged the Catholic clergy to refrain from proselytizing the Russian Orthodox, the ROC had seen precious little cooperation and a great deal of "missionary activities" in the ensuing decade. According to Vyzhanov, "since the paper was published, there wasn't a single case of Roman Catholics obeying its demands."

As for the cancellation of the 1997 meeting, Father Vyzhanov declared that the two churches prepared a "joint disclaimer" that the proposed meeting would not attempt to reunite the two halves of Christianity. Further, this joint communiqué would officially announce that Catholicism would reject proselytizing in Russia or any other countries of the Commonwealth of Independent States. At the last moment, the Catholic Church decided to "eliminate these two points from the document." Vyzhanov gave no further explanation, but what happened is obvious. Aleksy, with his long years of past experience at running meetings, conferences, and assemblies in the World Council of Churches, realized he could not set the agenda for this summit. So he called it off.

Vyzhanov resumed with other complaints. Only ten years after *Pro Russia*, the Catholic Church—without asking the patriarchate—established four "Catholic eparchies"—that is, four dioceses, the district under a bishop. Two were established in "the traditionally Orthodox lands of Ukraine South and East." In May 2003, two more were established in Kazakhstan. A westerner might note that Ukraine and Kazakhstan did not belong to the Russian Federation but were sovereign countries. Nevertheless, Father Vyzhanov spoke with genuine anger at the Catholic Church attempting to poach in lands Orthodox Russians regard as traditionally theirs: "Most Russian believers belong to the Orthodox Church. The new Catholic structures are clearly too big for the small number of Russian Catholics that is overestimated by their authorities." In short, the ROC saw this as proselytism by stealth conducted by the rival claimant to the title of the Church of the Apostolic Succession.

As John Paul breathed his last, Father Vyzhanov recounted with suspicion the Polish prelate's offer to personally return an icon of the Virgin of Kazan to Russia. This episode will be dealt with more fully in the next chapter, but what is relevant here is the ROC's skepticism toward every *papal* overture. The icon had hung in the papal study for centuries. The patriarchate responded that this was not the original but a copy, and actually the church was well supplied with copies of this particular icon. The Vatican was welcome to mail it back however. Vyzhanov does not quote the *Aeneid's "Timeo Danaos et dona ferentes"* (I fear the Greeks, even when they are bearing gifts), but the sentiment is the same; the icon would be a Trojan horse, a ploy to sneak the Latinizers' Christianity into Moscow the Holy City. Vyzhanov does not say so, but the fact that John Paul II had been born a Pole made any of his proposals doubly suspect, for Poland was the archenemy of the true believers of the Pravoslavnye.

John Paul II remained optimistic about his chances for reconciliation with the Orthodox for a very long time. He wrote *three* official addresses designed to heal the thousand-year rift. The first came out in 1980, *Slavonium Apostali,* an "apostolic letter" in which he named Cyril and Methodius as "co-patrons of Europe, along with St. Benedict." It was not quite acknowledging them as Ravnoapostolny—"Equal to the Apostles"—but it was a conciliatory step. In 1988 he brought out for the Millennium of the Baptism of Rus *Euntes in Mundium Universum (We Live in One Universal World).* The ROC read this title as yet another Catholic crusade, this time conducted through encyclical. It sounded just like the ominous opening of Pope Gregory XIII's 1580 letter to Ivan the Terrible, "There is one Church, one Christian flock." The ROC remembered that Gregory's next phrase made clear under whose authority this "oneness" was to be subsumed, the "one only after Christ is his vicar on earth and universal shepherd." The ROC had heard all this before, all the way back to Innocent III's self-description in 1198 as "truly the vicar of Jesus Christ, the Successor of Peter, Anointed of the Lord, God of the Pharaohs, who is the mediator between God and man." Given that the ROC had no desire to be part of any "oneness" with Catholicism, *Euntes in Mundium Universum* did not earn John Paul an invitation to the celebrations.

The 1992 *Pro Russia* Commission, which abjured Catholic proselytism, was supposed to open the door to cooperation between Catholic and Orthodox clergymen. When it failed, in 1995, still undeterred from the loud silence emanating from the Moscow Patriarchate, John Paul wrote *Ut Unum Sint (That They All May Be One).* In this he stated the "Catholic Church desires nothing less than full communion between East and West."

To this end, he tried visiting the former republics of the USSR. In 1992 he went to Rumania. In November 1999 he visited Georgia. In May 2001 he went to Greece. In June 2001 he went to sovereign Ukraine. (This outraged the patriarchate doubly.) In May 2002 he went to Orthodox Bulgaria. On June 5, 2000, he met President Vladimir Putin in the Vatican. It is considered standard diplomatic protocol to issue a return invitation when a head of state visits the pope. Apparently, Putin did so. When he returned to Moscow to be greeted by an incandescent Aleksy, he rescinded the invitation. The Orthodox interpreted all the pope's efforts "That they all may be One" to mean Orthodoxy would be forced to acknowledge Catholicism as the Church of the Apostolic Succession. What then about their descent from St. Andrew Pervozvanny? What about the Chronicle of St. Nestor? Cardinal Walter Casper, head of the papal Council on Christian Union Assistance, visited Moscow in February 2004 and declared that Catholicism saw the Orthodox Church as a "sister-Church" and sought brotherhood with it. His overture was met with deafening silence.

Pope John Paul II went to his grave stating that his inability to reunite the Eastern and Western churches was the great disappointment of his papacy. He could never set foot inside the borders of the Russian Federation. Had he been poorly briefed by Vatican advisers? It is hard to believe that he did not recall that the Gospels themselves do not agree as to the primacy of Peter and Andrew. Did he feel that the patriarch of Moscow and All Russia would set aside the basis of the Russian Orthodox Church to come to some ecumenical agreement? For that, in the view of Aleksy, would inevitably be the price for rapprochement with Catholicism. To avoid paying it, Aleksy and many of his clergy and flock would willingly lay down their lives.

In April 2005 Catholicism chose a new pope, Joseph Ratzinger, the future Benedict XVI. Because he came from Germany, the Orthodox, still smarting from the German invasions launched against them—1242, February 18, 1918, and June 22, 1941—were not disposed to see him as an improvement.[60] The West was inclined to overlook his participation as a teenager in the Hitler Youth, but the Russians were not. Then one of his first acts was to exacerbate an issue of the Catholic-Orthodox conflict, which John Paul had been careful to placate: the situation of "Greek Catholics" in western Ukraine. In his harsh words for the dying Pope John Paul, Father Vyzhanov brought up the subject, which is clearly a very sore point with the Russian Orthodox Church: "During World War II Ukrainian Greek Catholics cooperated with Nazi invaders. In 1946 the Soviet government prohibited Ukrainian Greek Catholic Church activity on the territory of the USSR." (This may be one of the very few actions of the Soviet state remembered with gratitude by the Moscow Patriarchate.) But in the final years of glasnost and perestroika, the Soviet state legalized Uniate churches. In 1990 a board was formed to decide how to divide church property. Representatives from Roman Catholicism, the Ukrainian Greek Catholics, the Russian Orthodox Church, and the Ukrainian Orthodox Church all came. Soon however, the representatives from the Greek Catholics pulled out, and physical battles between warring priests and congregations ensued in Lvov, the Ivano-Frank region, and Ternopol. The Greek Catholics had their headquarters in Lvov but wished to move to Kiev and achieve their own patriarchate. Under John Paul II, the Vatican resisted agreeing to this move.

Only a few months into Benedict XVI's papacy, on August 21, 2005, he agreed to the requested transfer. This confirmed the ROC's worst fears. The head of the Ukrainian "Greek Catholics," Cardinal Lubomyr Husar, held a Mass for one thousand believers to mark the occasion in a church still under construction. Bells rang in celebration, and prelates calling themselves the "Ukrainian Orthodox Church" of the "Kiev Patriarchate" officiated. The Russian Orthodox Church does not recognize this as a true patriarchate, any more than it recognizes Greek Catholics as Orthodox. More than three hundred Orthodox believers protested outside the mass. Aleksy termed the move an "unfriendly" act.

Pope Benedict visited the ecumenical patriarch of Constantinople, Bartholomew, in December 2006. Aleksy saw this as an unfriendly act on both their parts.[61] Aleksy's relationship with Bartholomew has degenerated into recrimination and name calling largely because he believes Constantinople will reunify with the "Latinizers."[62] Back in November 1979, the new Pope John Paul II made one of his first trips abroad to the ecumenical patriarch of Constantinople, then Demetrios I. On November 30, John Paul issued a cheerful statement: "This visit to the first see of the Orthodox Church shows clearly the will of the whole Christian Church to go forward . . . towards the unity of all, and also its conviction that the re-establishment of full communion with the Orthodox Church is a fundamental stage of the decisive progress of the whole ecumenical movement."[63] At the end of the visit, the two prelates issued a joint communiqué: they announced they had productively just completed "the first official deliberations of this type since the end of the Council of Florence." Perhaps only the most learned recalled that when the news that the Council of Florence agreed upon a Decree of Union reached Moscow in 1439, the reaction was "Today the Church of Constantinople wavered, [and] renounced our Orthodoxy." The Russians have never forgiven the Constantinople delegation for signing the Council of Florence Decree on papal terms. They were not going to "waver" or "relinquish our Orthodoxy" for John Paul II in the twentieth century any more than they had in 1439.

John Paul continued cultivating Demetrios's successor, Bartholomew, and invited him to the Vatican itself. On June 29, 2004, all had been cordiality at their joint press conference. John Paul was perfectly well aware that the

Russian Orthodox had just hosted a conference simultaneously "commemo-rating" the 950-year anniversary of the 1054 Great Schism and the 800th anniversary of the sack of Constantinople by the Fourth Crusade. He used the occasion of Bartholomew's visit to apologize for the 1204 sack of the city: "In particular, we cannot forget what happened in the month of April 1204. How can we not share, at a distance of eight centuries the pain and disgust."[64] The disgust Aleksy felt back in Moscow as he read the account of this news conference can be well imagined. Time will tell if Constantinople will, yet again, as it did at the Council of Lyons and the Council of Florence, come to some kind of ecumenical agreement with the pope, the rival claim-ant to the Apostolic Succession. What is certain, however, is that the Russian Orthodox Church will not sign on.

As for the question of the "Apostolic Succession" itself, that has been tabled for the foreseeable future. In *Introduction to Ecumenism,* a handbook written by a Catholic priest for laymen attempting reconciliation among the various Christian faiths in the United States, the author, Father Jeffrey Gros, FSC, takes up the thorny issue of the original church divide, the cleavage of West-ern and Christian Christianity into Catholic and Orthodox halves in 1054. He reviews the points they disagree on, and in general his tone here is concilia-tory and positive. Then he gets to the last issue on the agenda of differences: the Apostolic Succession. In 1988—the millennial year of the Baptism of Rus—Catholic and Russian Orthodox prelates met at Valaamo, Finland. The weighty title of this section of the meeting was "The Sacrament of Order in the Sacramental Structure of the Church, with Particular Reference to the Impor-tance of Apostolic Succession for the Sanctification and Unity of the People of God." A joint declaration resulted: "The question of primacy in the Church in general and in particular the primacy of the bishop of Rome, a question which constitutes a serious divergence among us . . . will be discussed in the future."[65] That "future" discussion was supposed to take place at a "Joint Commission" on the subject to be held in 1990 at Freising. At that time, however, this item did not even make it on the commission agenda.

In July 2007 Pope Benedict XVI made headlines on this issue yet again. He promulgated a document restating that Catholicism alone represents the true path to salvation. The basis of Benedict's claim was that it was the Church of the Apostolic Succession through "Blessed Peter" to whom Christ entrusted "the keys of the kingdom." Benedict defined a church as being traceable through its bishops to Christ's original apostles. He ac-knowledged that Orthodox Christians do make up a church because of shared history, though they "separated" from the "proper" Catholic tradi-tion. Protestants however are not really a church at all, because they split from Catholicism during the Reformation. Thus they are considered only "Christian communities."

Many newspapers noted that the document restated ideas from the earlier *Dominus Iesus*, issued in 2000 when Benedict was head of the Vatican's office on doctrine, the successor organization of the Inquisition. Back in Moscow, Russian prelates heard echoes from a much most distant past. It was déjà vu all the way back to 1582, when Gregory XIII sent the Jesuit Antonio Possevino to persuade Ivan the Terrible to return to the true Church of the Apostolic Succession. Ivan and the court rejected the papal claim then; Aleksy chose to ignore Benedict now. At this rate of reconciliation, it can be predicted that the question of the "Apostolic Succession" will be resolved at the Second Coming.

But while Aleksy and the prelates of the ROC have set that item aside to await the Parousia, the ROC has energetically sought reconciliation on another front: within the ranks of the Pravoslavnye themselves, that is between the ROC and the émigré churches, Russian Orthodox Church Outside Russia (ROCOR) and Russian Orthodox Church Abroad (ROCA). This schism did not date from 1054 but from the Bolshevik takeover. The diaspora children were fervent Orthodox, and they accused Aleksy and the church he represented of having betrayed the true faith. They had neither forgiven nor forgotten seventy years of cooperation between the ROC and the Soviet state, and they were ready to lay detailed and furious charges against a long list of both dead and living clergy, including the patriarch himself.

SIX

The Babylonian Legacy: Exiles, Martyrs, and Collaborators

Oh Mother of God, help us to reconcile ourselves to
one another, to the truth, and to God.
—*Patriarch Aleksy's address to the nation, 1:30 A.M., August 21, 1991*

IN 2006 ALEKSY COULD LOOK BACK upon a series of major accomplishments since becoming patriarch of Moscow and All Russia. He had restored the Russian Orthodox Church within the new Russian Federation, defending it against Western evangelists and domestic anti-Semites. But other obstacles loomed both within and beyond the borders of the Russian Federation. Some of the schisms date back centuries, to the time of Ivan the Terrible, who bequeathed the enduring conflict over the Uniates. Some, however, were the burden of the Soviet past. The ROC suffered seventy years of death and destruction at the hands of its government. Thousands of "new martyrs" testified to this. To survive and not be driven into the catacombs, the church cooperated with the Soviet authorities. Cooperation ranged from passive acquiescence in party decisions, to serving as a mouthpiece for KGB propaganda (*vide* the "peace" campaign), up to and including active collaboration by "false brothers" (Aleksy's description) who denounced their own flock. The end of Soviet power meant that some of this collusion would inevitably become public. Cleansing the church of its collaborators was the most painful of all the challenges the Moscow Patriarchate faced.

The patriarch knew how deeply the church had been penetrated—he had been a recruited agent himself for more than thirty years. *Keston News Service* evaluated his culpability after an extensive review of all the documents its researchers could unearth:

All senior clerical appointments in the Soviet era were made by the KGB and mediated through the government's Council for Religious Affairs (the public face of the 4th department of the KGB Fifth Directorate)—and many junior appointments besides. Aleksy's collaboration

was nothing exceptional. Almost all senior leaders of all officially recognized religious faiths—including the Catholics, Baptists, Adventists,
Muslims and Buddhists—were recruited KGB agents.[1]

No one could get clearances, move up in rank, receive visas, speak to foreigners, or manage church bank accounts unless the KGB had vetted and
approved him. Aleksey Ridiger had used the proprietary knowledge he had
gained from KGB tutelage to outmaneuver his former masters. But exposure
could tarnish the ROC with a very broad brush indeed.

Within days of the putsch's failure, Aleksy decided to speak to this delicate
subject. On August 30, 1991, he faxed an "Address [*Obrashchenie*] of the Holy
Synod of the Russian Orthodox Church" to "Archpastors, Pastors and All Its
Faithful Children." The connotations of its title communicate its *gravitas*.
Obrashchenie is the same word used to head his August 21, 1991, address issued at 1:30 A.M. at the crisis of the coup. The ROC's August 30 message identifies its key concern, which it calls the "bitter legacy left by former rulers":

> History is now pronouncing its judgment [*sud*]. And each of us might
> present his own claim to the former ruling party and state circles for
> those unexampled sufferings, which have fallen to our lot or to the lots
> of our neighbors for the last 73 years [i.e., the Soviet period]. But let this
> judgment not allow the diabolical seeds of malice and bitterness to settle
> in our hearts. Let our minds be transformed and freed from a totalitarian
> model of consciousness which made millions of people in our Father-
> land voluntary or involuntary participants in unlawful actions.

The phrase "voluntary or involuntary" hints at the either-or dilemma posed
by the Soviet state to the Orthodox Church: collaborate or die. Those who
emigrated would be cut off from the motherland, exiled from their roots. For
those who remained behind, there were no good choices. Many people tried
to practice "the genre of silence"—to borrow the words of doomed writer
Isaac Babel—to avoid saying or doing anything to compromise someone else.
But there was no way to live and be completely innocent.

From the outset the Soviet Union's existence was premised upon betrayal.
Everyone was encouraged to spy on friends, family, priests, teachers, fellow
students. Statues to Pavlik Morozov, a small boy who denounced his own
parents to the authorities and then was murdered by neighbors, sprouted like
weeds over the country. (We might think of him as a Soviet "martyr.") The
state welcomed anonymous denunciations and rewarded those who tattled.
Its thirty pieces of silver could be petty privileges, such as a few extra square
yards in the epic apartment battles, but greater prizes beckoned. Denouncing

a colleague could get you his job. This was how the "gang of '38," young men like Yury Andropov, made their careers.

The Soviet writer, Vasily Grossman, the great chronicler of the Battle of Stalingrad, inserted in his final work, *Forever Flowing . . .* (*Vse techyot*), a mini-play he called "The Four Judases," indicting all the traitors.[2] The "four Judases" are a quartet of defendants who each personify a variant of Soviet betrayal. Each articulates the excuses for his perfidy. Grossman accuses these Judases, but advises caution. Who, he asks, will serve as prosecutor? Who can be the judge? And who is the jury? Indeed, the author's voice says, "And I am guilty too, as I think about it." No one ever said it better: Soviet citizens were forced to be Judases, whether the betrayal was paltry or life and death.

The church knew it had given its kiss in the Soviet Gethsemane. The end of the August 30 address mixed both pride and humility:

> By the mercy of God and by the power of His grace, the Russian Ortho-
> dox Church has stood fast, kept the faith pure and attracted millions of
> representatives of new generations who now make up its flock and clergy.
> At the same time we recognize with humility that not all the servants of
> the Church were equal to the task of their vocation in the years of trials.
> Our Lord and Righteous Judge will reward everyone according to his
> deserts. We get down to the cleansing and restoration of our Church,
> and in doing this we should be guided by a conciliatory mind, canonical
> order and personal responsibility of everyone before God, one's own con-
> science and the people of God, eschewing temptation to act "according
> to the elemental spirits of the world" [*po stikhiyam mira sego*].[3]

This appeal still resonates, and not just within Russia itself. Has the Moscow Patriarchate truly repented of its collaboration?

Within months of this penitent address, Aleksy did not seem very eager for more glasnost on the subject. In April 1992 a journalist from *Moscow News* told the then British ambassador to Russia, Sir Rodric Braithwaite, that she had been investigating the patriarch's links with the KGB. Her editor refused to print it, terming the story "inopportune."[4] The ambassador noted in his diary that "the KGB have recovered their morale since the events of last August; they are no longer letting outsiders look at their files." The very next month, on May 5, 1992, Braithwaite met the patriarch at his private residence. The subject of collaboration came up:

> [Aleksy] is aware that the church's reputation is not impeccable. Many
> accusations of collaboration with the KGB have been made against

members of the clergy. Aleksy has set up a commission of seven recently consecrated bishops, who are too young to be suspected of KGB links, to investigate any cases brought before them. They will reject any for which there is no documentary evidence. The others will be pursued with determination. He agrees that this should help the relationship with the Church Abroad.

We need to decode Braithwaite's dry comment on Aleksy's disquisition: "He protests too much, but on the right lines." Aleksy knew that the ambassador, a diplomat with fluent Russian and a superb command of intelligence (he would go on to chair Britain's Joint Intelligence Committee), was perfectly aware of the church's collaboration.[5] Aleksy's announcement that the church had set up a commission whose seven bishops are "too young to be suspected" is disingenuous. No one was ever "too young" to be approached by the KGB. Aleksey Ridiger ~~himself~~ was recruited by the KGB within a month of his twenty-ninth birthday. The patriarch's further statement that any cases will be rejected if there is no "documentary evidence" is a masterpiece of *dez-informatsiya*, that is, text without the surrounding context—such as citing 1 Timothy 6:10: "Money is the root of all evil" without its preceding phrase, "the love of." Aleksy can outline his plans for reform secure in the knowledge that the KGB will control all data to be released. The patriarchate and the KGB—and its successor, the Federativnaya Sluzhba Bezopasnosti (Federal Security Service; FSB)—have likely done an invisible deal. Both get to vet what is released. In legal terms, because the "prosecutor" gets to select the facts, he subsumes the roles of judge and jury too. Aleksy's final comment that this course of action "should help the relationship with the Church Abroad" is the tip-off to his real focus. The seven bishops and their commission will persuade the émigré churches ROCOR and ROCA that a purge of the guilty is taking place back in the fatherland.

To understand the conflict between the Moscow Patriarchate and the Orthodox churches abroad, we need to learn a new vocabulary, for the debates use special words and phrases coined by both sides. The neologism for the furor is "Sergianism" (Sergiyanstvo—meaning a period of time under "Sergy," the ecclesiastical spelling of the name). Metropolitan Sergy's fate was to head the church during the period of its greatest trials. At the outbreak of the First World War, Sergy, born Ivan Nikolayevich Stragorodsky, had risen high in the ranks of the ROC. He became bishop of Finland and Vyborg in October 1905 and was appointed to the Holy Synod in 1911.[6] In 1912 he chaired the commission for the long-awaited Mestny Soviet, or "Local Council" (the name is misleading, for it actually denotes a national council of senior clerics). The church wanted two things: some modest reforms to lessen the church's dependency on the chief procurator of the Holy Synod, the reactionary Konstantin Pobedonostsev; and, the far more ardent wish, restoration of the office of patriarch, after its absence for two centuries. With regard to the latter, Sergy's chairmanship marked him out for promotion in the ranks of the ROC, just as Aleksey Ridiger's 1986 appointment as "chairman for the Preparatory Committee for the Celebration of the Baptism of Rus" singled him out for future preferment.

Defeat in the devastating war that began in August 1914 changed everything. The fall of the Romanov dynasty, the collapse of the Provisional Government, and the Bolshevik coup followed in rapid succession. But the Local Council courageously opened in December 1917. Reforms followed swiftly—including the election of bishops (rather than their appointment through the procurator's office). The Local Council also elected Tikhon as patriarch and Venyamin as metropolitan of Petrograd. Sergy himself settled for the lesser prize of archbishop of Vladimir, though he did become a member of the Holy Synod soon thereafter. Then in January 1918 the Bolsheviks closed the "Constituent Assembly" in which they got only 23 percent of the vote. Lenin's dismissal of the delegates shut down the Russians' one experience of self-government until their election of Boris Yeltsin as president of the Russian Federation in June 1991. Lenin sent Trotsky to negotiate a humiliating peace treaty with Germany in Brest-Litovsk in July 1918. To prevent the White Army from having a figurehead around which to rally, he ordered the murder of the imperial family on the night of July 30–31, 1918 N.S., in the basement of the Ipatiev House, code-named the "House of Special Purpose" in Yekaterinburg. The capstone of this *annus horribilis* came in September. The Bolsheviks forcibly closed the Local Council.

Lenin could now concentrate on suppressing dissent and winning the ensuing Civil War (1918–21). But he was desperately short of money. The Bolsheviks began funding the Red Army through seizing church plate and valuables. Sergy, archbishop of Vladimir, went along with this, urging a policy of nonresistance when bands of thugs showed up to strip sanctuaries. Tikhon too urged nonviolence, but in May 1922 Lenin ordered him placed in brutal confinement. Then Metropolitan Venyamin of Petrograd was arrested, put through a show trial, and executed in the summer of 1923. In the midst of this persecution, the church began splintering. A great many clergy and believers simply fled and set up Orthodox churches on foreign soil. Sergy remained and joined the offshoot created by the Bolsheviks: the "Renovationists." These clerics were willing to submit to Soviet power—in effect, acknowledging the atheist state as the church's supreme governor rather than the patriarch. Sergy's prestige provided a cover to recruit other bishops and priests.

But Sergy changed his mind about leading the "Renovationists." He sought to be reconciled with Patriarch Tikhon. When Tikhon was released from confinement at the end of 1923, Sergy appeared before him, penitent. An eyewitness describes the scene:

> Metropolitan Sergy of Vladimir and Shuysk, that brilliant theologian and Canon lawyer, following whose example hundreds of bishops and priests have become Renovationists, stands on the *amvon* [dais upon which the deacon reads the litanies and the priest pronounced the sermon during the liturgy], stripped of his archepiscopal cope, mitre, *panagia* [a bishop's medallion bearing an image of Christ and the Mother-of-God], and cross. He bows low to Patriarch Tikhon, acknowledging his submission and his guilt, and in a voice trembling with emotion he recites the confession. He prostrates himself on the floor.... Slowly the patriarch hands him back his *panagia* and the cross, his white mitre, his cope and his staff. The patriarch, who all this while has been looking at him sternly and sorrowfully, breaks into a smile, teasingly takes the penitent by his beard, and shaking his head says, "*I ty, stary, ot menya otkololsya.*" (You too, old friend, you too abandoned me.) Thereupon the two old men, no longer containing their emotion, weep and embrace each other.[7]

Whether or not Tikhon meant the echo deliberately, his "*I ty, stary*" recalls the "*Et tu, Brute!*" of Shakespeare's Julius Caesar dying at the foot of Pompey's statue in the Roman Forum.

Tikhon's forgiveness testifies to the true spiritual courage of a remarkable man. For the émigré churches, however, while they could not send Sergy to the stake, they stoked the fire for the reputation of the ROC itself. Aleksy knew that Tikhon's martyrdom was the best defense against the charge of "Sergianism." He had been reburying his relics on August 18, 1991, the day before the tanks moved stealthily into the square in front of the Russian Parliament Building. The August 30, 1991, address quotes Tikhon at length, calling him "the great confessor of the twentieth century." It emphasizes Tikhon's famous words addressed to the faithful in July 1919 as the Bolshevik campaign of church seizure and despoiling accelerated:

> We implore you, we entreat all our Orthodox children not to diverge from the only path of salvation for a Christian, not to abandon the way of the Cross passed down to us by God, through succumbing to earthly

power or to revenge. Do not blacken your Christian deeds by returning to defend your own well-being, which would humiliate the Church of Christ and would degrade you to the level of its abusers. Guard, O Lord, our Orthodox Russia from such horrors! [*Uberegi, Gospodi, nashu Pravoslavnuyu Rus ot takogo uzhasa!*]

Tikhon acknowledges that forgiveness and love are very hard, especially when "your enemy is overthrown." When the former victim finally has the opportunity, it is only human nature to want to "pronounce judgment (*sud*) over his recent oppressor and persecutor. The Providence of God is already calling some children of the Russian Orthodox Church to this trial. Feelings are running high. Revolts are breaking out. New camps are being formed. The fire of settling scores is flaring up." In 1919 the floodtide of the Russian Civil War, Tikhon pleaded with his Orthodox children not to let their hands "be stained with blood crying out to heaven. Do not let the Devil, the enemy of Christ, entice you with passions of vengeance." Fatally weakened by the vicious treatment he had endured during imprisonment, Tikhon died in March 1925. He never had the chance to see his enemies "overthrown."

By August 30, 1991, Soviet power was eroding. Aleksy opens his address by saying "History is now pronouncing its judgment." Finally, the church could do what Tikhon could only envision in 1919, "pronounce judgment on [the] recent oppressor." Repetition of the key word *sud* (judgment), deliberately recalls Tikhon's famous entreaty. But whereas Tikhon pleaded in 1919 for forgiveness for the Soviet state, the 1991 appeal is for forgiveness for the church itself. The church thus sought to draw a line under the entire subject of collaboration with the state not by denying it but by seeking forgiveness. This is another of Aleksy's decisions whose wisdom becomes obvious in hindsight. The address taps into one of Orthodoxy's most powerful tenets: as Christ forgave us (cf. "Father, forgive them," uttered from the cross), so we are called to forgive one another. The faith places an extraordinary emphasis upon God's forgiveness and the necessity for human beings to imitate it.

Over and over in the liturgy is heard "*Gospodi, Gospodi, Gospodi, pomiluy*" (Lord, have mercy [upon us]). Before a Russian Orthodox receives the "Holy Gifts" of the sacrament, he often turns to the person standing next to him and says "Forgive me." This is a crucial moment in the service. The Russian Orthodox liturgy does not "repeat" the death of Jesus on Golgotha. Theologically, the "Lamb of God" was sacrificed "once only, for all time." But the liturgy sacramentally "makes present again" that death. When Jesus was on the cross, the Good Thief said, "Lord, remember me when You come into your kingdom." These words are "happening" in the Great Entrance through the Royal Doors, when the priest carries the covered chalice and paten which contain the consecrated bread and wine out to the people, and prays, "Remember, O Lord each one of us when You come into Your kingdom." The Orthodox hold that after the consecration, performed at the altar behind the iconostasis, the covered chalice and paten contain the actual body and blood of Christ. This is a "real presence" which cannot be explained, as it is a mystery. But it can be felt and believed. Therefore the believer is sacramentally present at Golgotha when the thief appealed to Christ, who is also present in the here and now of liturgical time. The believer at this moment *is* the Good Thief who asks to be remembered. He or she is comforted by the same response from Jesus: "Today you will be with me in paradise" (Luke 23: 43). "Today" means this day, for the linear timeline collapses into the mystical moment. "Today" also emphasizes that the sanctuary is a symbol of Paradise. Indeed, sometimes an icon of the Good Thief replaces an archangel on the south door of the iconostasis.[8]

When Boris Yeltsin emerged victorious from the White House, he went immediately to the parents of the three young men killed by the tanks and said, "Forgive me, your president, that I was unable to defend and save your sons." There followed a brief moment of peace and harmony during the victims' funeral procession. The strains of the Orthodox funeral hymn "Eternal Memory" mingled with the sounds of the Kaddish, because one of the victims was Jewish.[9] The three young men died on the Garden Ring road that circles central Moscow. Flowers, icons, and crosses soon covered the ground. The ancient peasant belief that the soul is sustained by bread and vodka as it leaves the body reappeared at these makeshift shrines as well: loaves and bottles nestled among the crosses. People spoke of the young men's resemblance to the first Slavic saints, the Strastoterptsy Boris and Gleb, who accepted death at the hands of their brother Svyatopolk and thus prevented civil war over the succession.

As the exaltation of the post-coup atmosphere began to dissipate, human nature reasserted its messy self. Baptists had been in the crowd of human shields as was the leader of the Chechen separatists, Shamil Basayev, a startling fact revealed only in his obituary. But the Baptists, the Chechens, the Afghan veterans, and the Muscovites did not discover that they were now living in the New Jerusalem where there is neither death, nor sorrow, nor crying, nor pain (Revelation 21:4). A short time after the August 30 missive, a Russian Orthodox priest, Father Gleb Yakunin, took a very unforgiving step. He unmasked three of the ten signatories, all members of the Holy Synod, as serving officers of the KGB. The ROC retaliated by defrocking and excommunicating him in November 1993.[10]

Thus ended the official career of a charismatic and courageous cleric. Yakunin had appeared on the balcony of Yeltsin's stronghold, urging the crowd to "take courage and fulfill your duty as citizens." He promised: "God will help you and will help Russia."[11] The USSR had once sentenced him to five years in a strict regime camp for his activism. There he froze in minus 50 degrees Fahrenheit. He had been released only early in 1987 (another concession to Gorbachev's reforms). On June 5, 1987, the ROC readmitted him to the priesthood, and on August 11, 1987, it assigned him a parish near Moscow.[12] That brief period of rapprochement with the hierarchy now ended with a thump. Once thrown out of the ROC, he founded his own version of Orthodoxy with its own mini Synod. He had defied the Soviet government and paid a terrible price. With those who had cooperated, Yakunin refused to compromise or "get down to the cleansing of the Church" guided by "a conciliatory mind," as Aleksy urged in his address.

Perhaps Yakunin is entitled to his stance; for those who were never subject to the terrible pressures of the Soviet system, passing moral judgments is problematical. Many people were broken upon its wheel. An illustrative case of what its *strappado* tortures could do to individuals is the tragic fate of Father Dmitry Dudko. In 1948, as a twenty-six-year old seminary student, he was arrested and sentenced to ten years' imprisonment for "anti-Soviet agitation and propaganda." His crime was actually writing religious poetry. The government announced he had been sentenced as a collaborator with the Nazis. Stalin died in 1953; Dudko was released in 1956 and returned to the seminary, graduating in 1960. He became a widely respected priest, who gave inspiring sermons at the small parish churches he was assigned to in Moscow. Many intellectuals—including Alexander Solzhenitsyn—were impressed. He baptized thousands of adults and taught the catechism.

In December 1972 the church dismissed him from his parish as per the instructions from the KGB. Dudko refused to go quietly. He told his congregation of his sacking, and it rallied to defend him. The next year he started an open forum of questions and answers after evening vespers. In May 1974 Patriarch Pimen ordered a halt to the forum and removed him. He was exiled to a village church outside Moscow—the favorite technique of the supine patriarchate under Pimen to punish its most dynamic and committed priests. There he continued his question-and-answer sessions, which were tape-recorded and became the publication (in English) *Our Hope*. In January 1980, he was rearrested. This time, threatened with going back to the Gulag, the fifty-eight-year-old Dudko broke. In June 1980 he publicly recanted his "crimes" on Soviet television, saying: "I renounce what I have done, and I regard my so-called struggle with godlessness as a struggle with Soviet Power." Mollified, the KGB released him. The patriarchate immediately reappointed Dudko as a parish priest, but his confession left his spiritual followers stunned.

Dudko tried to overcome his guilt by later calling his confession a "fateful mistake." After the collapse of the USSR, he wrote regularly for the anti-Semitic newspaper *Zavtra* (Tomorrow), the same newspaper in which Father Ioann brought out his rant. Dudko appealed "for an alliance of communists with Orthodox Christians."[13] He declaimed against the "brutal democracy" of post-Soviet Russia, which he said made Stalin's repression a pale shadow. He praised Stalin as a "believer" who in 1939 had prevented the final destruction of the Russian Orthodox Church. Dudko died in Moscow June 28, 2004. Even those who were brave once can fail under repeated agony.

Father Dmitry Dudko's complex history of suffering and betrayal was a tiny part of the Soviet legacy. The émigrés dismissed all excuses as "Sergianism." Tikhon forgave Sergy but the émigré ROC would not follow his example of *imitatio Christi*. The exiles went first to a part of what would become Yugoslavia and then moved to New York. Here they took the name the Russian Orthodox Church Outside Russia (ROCOR) and Russian Orthodox Church Abroad (ROCA). They were furious at the "Declaration of Loyalty" signed in 1927 by Metropolitan Sergy, then acting as the canonical head of the ROC, and eight members of the "Temporary Patriarchal Holy Synod." Before Tikhon died, he had sensed correctly that the Soviet government would refuse to permit a Local Council to name his successor. He tried to prevent the office from being left vacant by naming three bishops as acting in his stead, until a new patriarch could be voted. However, by the end of 1925, two of the three had fled into exile, and the third, Metropolitan Pyotr (Polyansky) was arrested. Once Pyotr was imprisoned, his deputy Sergy stepped into his shoes. When Pyotr was shot in 1927, Sergy ipso facto became "acting patriarch." He would occupy this unenviable position for the next eighteen years.

Like the 1939 Nazi-Soviet Non-Aggression Pact, the Declaration of Loyalty had secret protocols. Significantly, the church agreed to allow the secret police to appoint its bishops. Sergy was sadly mistaken if he thought this concession, which allowed the police to control the church from within, would win any favors. In 1929 the church was forbidden to do anything except perform the liturgy and pray. It became a crime to do missionary work, to print the Bible, to hold catechism classes, to do charity work. It was not illegal per se to "be" a believer, just to behave like one. This is identical to the legal position of drug addicts in the United States: it is not illegal to "be" an addict, but to possess drugs or drug paraphernalia is a crime. The Soviet approach cleverly reified the metaphor that religion was the "opium" of the masses.

The Roman emperor Diocletian himself might have envied how thoroughly the Soviet state tormented its Christians. To be fair, the USSR was an "equal opportunity" persecutor of observant Jews, Moslems, Baptists, et alii. But Orthodoxy, as the former tsarist-established faith, was their special target. Lenin hated the church, despising its believers and its clergy with equal ferocity. In 1922, with famine in the Volga basin, he wrote a letter to the Politburo urging the crisis as an opportunity to crush it:

> Famine is the only occasion when we can beat the enemy [the Church] over the head.... Right now ... when people are being eaten in hunger-stricken areas, we can carry out the expropriation of Church valuables with the most furious and ruthless energy.... Now, victory over the reactionary clergy is assured.... We must crush their resistance with such cruelty that they will not forget it for decades.[14]

Lenin's death did not halt the persecution. By the time war broke out in 1941, there were only four bishops not under arrest. Sergy was forced to sign a public pronouncement that there was no religious persecution inside the USSR.

In a strange paradox, the German invasion "saved" the church. Sergy certainly kept his head, while Stalin froze into immobility and left it to Molotov to announce to the frightened public that the country had been invaded. The "Boss" would not emerge for two weeks. But on invasion day, Sergy sent a message to all parishes entitled "To the Leaders and Faithful of the Orthodox Church of Christ":

> The fascist brigands have fallen upon our native land. Trampling upon all pacts and pledges [i.e., violating the Nazi-Soviet Non-Aggression Pact signed in August 1939] they have suddenly descended upon us, and the blood of our peaceful citizens is already drenching our native earth. The times of Batu Khan, of the Teutonic Knights, of Charles of Sweden, of Napoleon, are being repeated. The miserable descendants of the enemies of Orthodox Christianity are once more striving to force our people onto their knees before unrighteousness, to compel them by naked violence to sacrifice the welfare and integrity of their native country and their blood-covenant of love for their Fatherland....
>
> Let us lay down our lives together with our flock. Innumerable thousands of our Orthodox warriors have followed the path of self-sacrifice and laid down their lives for their country and their faith at all times of enemy invasion of their Fatherland. They have died, not thinking of glory, but thinking only that their country was in need of sacrifice on their part and humbly sacrificed everything, even life itself.

The Church of Christ blesses all Orthodox believers for the defense
of the sacred frontiers of our native land.

The Lord will grant us victory.

Acting Patriarch, Humble Sergius,

Metropolitan of Moscow and Kolumna, Moscow, 22 June, 1941.[15]

During the war itself, the church donated enough rubles to fund the "Dmitry
Donskoy" armored division and the "St. Prince Alexander Nevsky" squadron.

Stalin, however, never practiced gratitude. He restored the patriarchate,
but only because the archbishop of York was due to land in Moscow at the
end of September 1943, and he wanted a Potemkin church to show his
much needed British ally. So Red Army planes plucked the blinking Sergy
and two other prelates from their evacuation hovels and flew them to the
Kremlin. There he told them they could elect a patriarch. He offered office premises—they could set up shop in the former German ambassador's
residence. He told them there would be a "Council for the Affairs of the
Russian Orthodox Church," which would be headed by Grigory Karpov, a
colonel of the NKVD (the current acronym of the secret police). The hierarchs said they would be pleased to accept Comrade Karpov in this post.
Then Stalin asked impishly, "Where are your personnel? Where have they
got to?" This alluded to an earlier statement by the bishops that they wished
to open a theological academy but they lacked the priests to do so. Given
that he knew perfectly well that all these missing "personnel" were either
in prison or dead, this was Stalin at his most roguish. Who was going to
acknowledge the gorilla in the corner and say: "Well, your security organs
have arrested and murdered the lot"? Most people would have been tongue-
tied, but Stalin met his match. Sergy responded, "We lack personnel for
several reasons, one of which is we train a man to be a priest, but he becomes a marshal of the Soviet Union."[16] The former seminarian Joseph Dju-
gashvili, who had trained at the Tiflis academy for years and never forgot
the treatment he had received there, always enjoyed tormenting the church.
But here he decided to be magnanimous. He helped Sergy down the stairs.
Younger men than Sergy often went weak in the knees or the bowels after a
meeting with Stalin.

On September 8, the remaining nineteen hierarchs of the ROC were pulled
from their confinements, put on planes, and flown to Moscow on Red Army
aircraft. These survivors formed a Holy Synod, and on September 12, Sergy
was duly "elected" patriarch of Moscow and All Rus. Stalin forgot most of his
promises, but the archbishop of York, Dr. Cyril Garbett, flew back to Great
Britain to tell all of the freedom of worship enjoyed by Soviet believers.

Before we judge Patriarch Sergy, we should listen to the eyewitness testimony of Hieromonk Trifon, who watched his "enthronement" in 1943. He described him as a very sick man, who looked as if he had just come out of a "Nazi concentration camp."[17] It is a salutary reminder that the worth of a man must be judged by his whole life, not by his failure at a particular trial.

Sergy died in 1945, and was succeeded by the metropolitan of Leningrad, the same Aleksy who had rallied the people of Moscow with a stirring oration August 10, 1941. But as Aleksy I he was no more fortunate than his predecessor at winning independence from the state. Postwar, Stalin clamped down even harder on the church just as he did on the whole of Soviet society. Yes, he supported the Theological Institute at Zagorsk (i.e., Sergiev Posad) with Kremlin funds. And the church prayed for Stalin as "the Leader Elected of God," just as it had prayed for the Golden Horde during the two hundred years of the "Tatar yoke." No matter how docile the church was, the secret police (now the KGB) made the decisions. Any concession granted by Stalin was given as a favor from an all-powerful emperor to beggars at his feet. Thus, the one Orthodox prelate he had the most reason to hate, the church inspector Abakadze who had expelled him from the seminary when he failed to take his final exams, had been left untouched on Stalin's orders.[18] It was more amusing to watch him worry himself to death than to arrest and execute him.

When Stalin died in March 1953, his eventual successor, Nikita Khrushchev, known to the West as the "great reformer" of the USSR, disassembled the apparatus of mass terror. But he hated the church, too, and continued targeted terror against its believers and priests. A new round of closures and arrests ensued. Patriarchs came and went—the repression of the church was a constant. Pimen, Aleksy's immediate predecessor, was an elderly man who was uneducated. He obediently read the statements the KGB wrote for him at Geneva (1973) and the United Nations (1982). These declared that there was neither injustice, nor want, nor religious persecution in the blessed USSR.

All this time, thousands of priests and believers continued to be arrested and die in the Gulag. A representative example, and one illustrating the collusion displayed by the ROC, is the fate of Boris Talantov. A devout believer, he was arrested and sentenced under Article 190, Section 1, that he had developed "anti-Soviet slanders." He had been a prominent writer, condemning Marxist-Leninist ideology as misguided *zabluzhdenie* (the verb form is *zabluzhdatsya*, "to lose one's way"). He sent more than a thousand letters protesting the destruction of churches to journals, papers, institutions (including Keston Institute), and Patriarch Aleksy I. He died in prison in 1971 without the official ROC ever lifting a finger on his behalf. The Russian Orthodox Church Abroad—not to be confused with the Russian Orthodox Church Outside Russia—sainted him in 1980. He was officially "rehabilitated" by the Soviet state in 1990. He has not yet been sainted by the ROC, however, and given that he accused the patriarchate of being traitors to the Church of Christ, his path to canonization may be rather rocky.[19]

The killing of Orthodox priests went on for a very long time, even during glasnost and perestroika. On September 9, 1990, the courageous and charismatic Father Alexander Men was axed to death on his way to perform the liturgy. His vicious murder has never been solved. Neither has he been sainted.

But the ROC has sainted plenty of other martyr-priests. It would use them as a counter to the émigré Orthodox churches' position that it had been the church of collaborators. In December 8–12, 2003, a historic "All Diaspora Pastoral Conference" was held in Nyack, New York, between representatives of the Moscow Patriarchate and priests and bishops of both the Russian Orthodox Church Abroad (ROCA) and the Russian Orthodox Churches Outside Russia. (ROCOR). Aleksy sent three crack operatives: first was Archpriest Georgy Mitrofanov. Mitrofanov was an expert on the Russian Orthodox Church in the pre-Stalin Soviet period, having written an authoritative study making use of the original documents: *Istoriya russkoi pravoslavnoi tserkvi 1900–1927 (History of the Russian Orthodox Church, 1900–1927)*.[20] Mitrofanov had been teaching since 1988 a course on the history of the Russian Orthodox Church in the twentieth century. He had immersed himself in the archive of the Synod of the Church Abroad in the State Archive of the Russian Federation. Mitrofanov knew more about the founding fathers of both ROCOR and ROCA than the émigrés themselves. Accompanying Mitrofanov was Archimandrite Tikhon Shevkunov, who had participated in two earlier conferences in 2001 and 2002 with the émigrés. According to the official explanation, Archpriest Maxim Kozlov was chosen to be the final member of the trio because, as a lecturer of comparative theology in the Moscow Theological Academy, he was an authority on the disputatious issue of "ecumenism."[21]

The Nyack Conference brought into an open arena the entire question of "Sergianism." ROCOR had said that the collapse of godless Communism would provide the first opportunity since 1918 to hold a Local Council. Its clergy would participate. Thus the "restoration of Church unity" would be underway immediately. By 2003 it had been twelve years since the dissolution of the USSR and still there was no restoration of communion between the

Russian Orthodox Church inside Russia and the Russian Orthodox Church outside its borders. Now, younger clergy of both ROCOR and ROCA accused Mitrofanov and the entire Moscow Patriarchate of "Sergianism" and the sin of "ecumenism." Things came to head on the second day of the conference. The Moscow delegation set forth its agenda vis-à-vis collaboration at the roundtable, "The Russian Orthodox Church (Moscow Patriarchate) during the Soviet Regime." Mitrofanov had come prepared: he pointed out that the ROC, ROCA, and ROCOR shared common saints among the "New Martyrs." He rattled off the names of the clerics who had been executed in the 1920s and reminded the roundtable that the GRU—forerunner of NKVD and KGB—had deliberately set out to split the church and set its hierarchs against one another. Were they now, in 2003, to continue those policies? No, the blood of *novomucheniki* bound together the church both inside and outside Russia. Though that evening the priests of the ROC could not commune with the priests of ROCA and ROCOR, there was a new spirit at the conference.

On the third day of the conference, Mitrofanov gave his report about the New Martyrs, and it was a revelation to the émigrés. Once "repressed clergymen" had been rehabilitated by the state, and the church had been able to get the transcripts of their interrogations. Mitrofanov had himself seen more than 1,000 of these transcripts (*vide* his deep knowledge of the archives). The ROC had canonized more than 1,500 of these priests and monks. All died under torture or were executed by "judicial" decree afterward. *Up to 90 percent of these men had admitted their "guilt" during interrogation.* Mitrofanov stated that ROC canonization was possible even for those who "slandered themselves—but only themselves." If they slandered others, and then perished, or if the individual was a secret agent of the NKVD and then was himself arrested, interrogated, and then shot, then he could not be glorified. (Sometimes the NKVD's own tools got caught up in the Terror. Such was the mincing machine's implacability that even spies died in its custody.) Because ROCOR and ROCA had canonized some of the 90 percent who admitted guilt, Mitrofanov gave some of the specifics of their "interrogation"—that is, the horrific, sustained, imaginative tortures visited upon them. These details were sickening; Mitrofanov's release of such vivid specifics reminded his listeners of what the clergy had suffered inside the USSR. Yet more than 1,500 of them, under hideous torture, had refused to name anyone *else* as "guilty."

Of course, there were diehards in Mitrofanov's audience whose self-righteousness was impregnable. Some of the sanctimonious declared that the sin of "Sergianism" was not redeemed even with a martyr's blood. Mitrofanov was prepared for that kind of intolerance: "At first, we were accused of not revering the new martyrs. After we glorified them, now [you] say that we had no right to do so.... It seemed we were bad just because we had survived, because not all the clergy had been murdered, and the only thing we can do now is to apologize that we were still alive and more over, we dared to glorify the martyrs."[22] Most of the audience collapsed into laughter and applause. Then, a young priest of the Diaspora, secure in his "holier-than-thou" stance, took the floor and said that the churches of the émigrés could restore the eucharistic communion and fully unite only if the ROC "anathematized" Metropolitan Sergy. He challenged Mitrofanov directly: "It will be the best rejection of 'Sergianism.' Are you ready to anathematize Metropolitan Sergius?" Mitrofanov again was primed: "I am just a normal priest and not a young *starets* (elder) who is ready to personally anathematize any bishop." Thus having put the young man into the same place as those Pharisees who banged on about their righteousness and sounded like "clanging cymbals," Mitrofanov carried the day. The point had been made: because the ROC shared many of the "new martyrs" with ROCOR and ROCA, their blood could unite them.

Within six months, all the work Mitrofanov and his colleagues had done paid off. On May 27, 2004, another historic meeting took place. Patriarch Aleksy II and the "First Hierarch of the Russian Church Outside of Russia (ROCOR) Metropolitan Laurus of Eastern America and New York" met inside Russia, as was reported on the Web site of the Moscow Patriarchate. The meeting took place at the residence for the president of the Russian Federation, Vladimir Putin. It was the first time that such a visit was paid officially, rather than incognito. Aleksy had not invited the Americans—Putin had. He had met a ROCOR delegation in New York during his state visit to the United States. But Aleksy had given his stamp of approval. He did not want the official visit, however, to take place in his private residence or the patriarchate's headquarters at the Danilov Monastery. That had been the setting for an informal meeting with them in their guise as pilgrims who had traced the St. Seraphim route: Yakaterinburg (site of the murder of the Romanovs), Sarov, Diveyevo, Nizhny Novgorod, St. Petersburg, and Kursk. He thanked them that they were "in bright spirits. The trip has not tired but rather inspired them. The participants in the trip were astounded and moved by the piety of the people and the general revival of the spiritual life." Aleksy had led the relic translation. There was plenty to reminisce about.

A short while later, everyone drove to Novo-Ogarevo, the presidential palace. Now was staged the first photo opportunity ever conducted between the ROC patriarch and the head of ROCOR. The president and the patriarch, two former KGB agents, worked brilliantly in tandem to handle the issue. All three power brokers showed themselves masters of diplomacy. President Putin stated that "under no circumstances did the state intend to intervene in any form into the affairs of the Church." (He didn't interject *Upasi Bog!* or "God save us from that!" at this point, but he might as well have.) He had nothing but praise:

> I am very glad the process of rapprochement of the two parts of the Russian Orthodox Church is going positively. I shall not talk about there being "two Churches," as the Russian Church is one in the consciousness of our people. I note with pleasure that after our meeting in New York [i.e., Putin's meeting with ROCOR], the clergymen who protect, defend, and propagate Orthodoxy beyond the frontiers of Russia visited the Russian Federation and saw with their own eyes the spiritual revival of our Fatherland.[23]

Metropolitan Laurus from ROCOR responded how positive the entire visit had been:

> We got very good impressions. The churches and monasteries are being revived, a lot of the restoration is being done, and the divine services are celebrated. It is not only that the external grandeur is being revived, but a spiritual wealth is also being built up.

Finally, Aleksy pronounced his own judgment:

> We thank Metropolitan Laurus and the members of the delegation for the spirit of openness, benevolence and mutual understanding in which the visit took place, as well as for the wish to bring our positions closer and find a way for the resolution of contradictions, which appeared as a result of the tragic events of the Revolution of 1917 and the Civil War, when a great number of our compatriots were forced to leave their Motherland and the Russian Church Outside of Russia took spiritual care of them. But the love to Russia has always been preserved and passed from generation to generation. I think that the first generation, which was forced to leave the Fatherland, would have been happy to see the present way to the reunion with the Motherland and with the Russian Orthodox Church.
>
> In the documents published on the results of [our] discussions, we underlined that the Russian Orthodox Church is one, and that only the circumstances divided us. Let us hope that we were divided only for the time being.

The two prelates agreed that they would undertake "happily" all possible measures to complete the reunion of the ROC and its émigré churches. The tone of the press conference signaled that peace was indeed breaking out between the ROC and its diaspora child.

Scarcely six weeks later, an olive branch arrived from across the Atlantic. ROCOR sent back to Russia the Virgin of Tikhvin, a miracle-working icon that the Orthodox believe St. Luke painted during Mary's lifetime.[24] They trace its ancestry from Jerusalem to Constantinople in the fifth century. It disappeared shortly before the Ottoman Turks took the city in 1453. Fortunately, however, in 1383, it had already been seen floating in the sky above Russia's Lake Ladoga (north of modern St. Petersburg.) Sometime after the fall of Constantinople, the icon "fulfilled its wishes" by descending into the hands of the faithful. In 1547 Ivan Grozny visited Tikhvin to pray before it, and in 1560 he decreed that a monastery be built there. The Swedes besieged the monastery in the Time of Troubles between 1611 and 1613 but could not take it. What the Swedes could not do, the Bolsheviks did. They closed the monastery and turned it into military barracks and museum. The Nazis seized the icon in 1944, only to have the bishop of Riga, Ioann Garklavs, snatch it back and spirit it away to America.

Now the rapprochement between ROCOR and the ROC meant it could come home. The icon, measuring thirty-four by forty-three inches, stood in the Cathedral of Christ the Savior while hundreds of thousands filed past. The Moscow tabloids reported it cured a young boy of his debilitating allergies, and its touch healed a *babushka's* headache. Then the icon went to St. Petersburg, where Aleksy celebrated the divine liturgy before it and announced, Tuesday, July 6, 2004, that he saw its return as "a historical landmark." The head of the Tikhvin monastery echoed: "to us its return is God's signal that we Russians are on the right path—the path towards brotherhood and faith."[25] An armored train then took it onboard for the last leg of its journey home.

At Tikhvin, on July 8, 2004, Orthodox prelates translated it on their shoulders to the same Cathedral of the Assumption ordered built by Ivan Grozny. President Putin and the patriarch were there, along with thousands of believers. Just as they had done for the pilgrim city at the St. Seraphim ceremonies in July 1991 at Diveyevo, the army put up hundreds of tents and installed the temporary field kitchens and sanitation infrastructure for the pilgrims' city. In a concession to the twenty-first century, ultralight airplanes and go-karts ferried the disabled around the festivities. An army of volunteers spruced up Tikhvin itself, demolishing shabby buildings and painting and restoring houses and shops. What could not be hidden or repaired they hid with huge decorative shields—thus continuing the honorable tradition of Prince Potemkin and his villages for the Empress Catherine. Saturation media coverage, tens of thousands of believers along the icon's path, tent cities for the pilgrims—it was the same formula of the 1991 "translation" of the bones of St. Seraphim. Again the old magic worked. Attendance spiked at Orthodox services; congregations once again experienced an uptick.

Scarcely had the Virgin of Tikhvin been put back in its chapel, indeed, in less than forty-eight hours, the Vatican deliberately leaked to the Western press that the pope too had an icon to return. On July 12, 2004, readers of the *International Herald Tribune* learned: "Pope Intends to Return Prized Icon to Russia," as bylined by Jason Horowitz, the paper's Rome correspondent. The icon in question was of the type entitled "The Mother of God of Kazan." Ever hopeful, Pope John Paul II announced that not only would he give it back but would graciously hand it over himself. (This episode has been touched upon in chapter 5.) Apparently, John Paul reasoned that if ROCOR and ROCA could wangle invitations to Russia after seventy years of bitterness, then surely his icon might serve as a visa, too? A year earlier he had proposed going to Mongolia (weren't there a few Catholics there?) and stopping off in Kazan, in Russia's autonomous republic of Tatarstan, because the icon was the Virgin of Kazan. Aleksy had squelched the papal trip to Mongolia and to Tatarstan, just as he had earlier vetoed Putin's invitation to the pope in 2000. He saw this latest ploy, four years later, as another machination on the part of the world's first Slavic pope to bring the wrong Christianity to Holy Rus. What if John Paul now approached Putin directly and asked for a visa to return "state property"? Unless scotched immediately, a papal visit would take on the coloring of a fait accompli. Aleksy thereupon issued an invitation to *Putin* to come visit him for the first time at his new residence in Peredelkino. It was time for a chat.

Scarcely a month after the Vatican's leak to the *International Herald Tribune,* on August 14, 2004, Putin showed up with flowers and planted three kisses on Aleksy's cheeks. After the tour, a "photo opportunity" was held, which meant that a decorous press conference would take place. Journalists asked about the Kazan Icon pretext for the pope's visit, and Putin let Aleksy take the first questions. He gave a diplomatic response, couched in his most exquisite language. It was still *nyet.* Then Putin got the last word. He announced that, actually, he and the patriarch were in agreement over this issue: "Well, here is that problem that you touched upon in conclusion and it is extremely important. I think that we, of course, will discuss all of our preliminary agreements. And it is pleasant for me to note that we have continued such a constructive dialogue with the Russian Orthodox

Church." After this definitive nonanswer, Aleksy gave Putin a little gift—a book about himself—and the visit ended cordially. The press conference put paid to John Paul's hopes. The Kazan icon did finally make it back to its homeland, but later. It was returned by lower-level Catholic prelates in very muted ceremonies.[26] When the pope died in April 2005, the Orthodox Church sent a delegation to the funeral, but neither the patriarch nor President Putin attended.

Simultaneously, things were moving along nicely vis-à-vis the ROC and its diaspora child, ROCOR. Scarcely a year after Aleksy had met Metropolitan Laurus in Putin's residence, in June 2005, the hopes expressed there took a giant step toward fruition. The ROC and ROCOR published a joint document, which was released to the press by the Department for External Church Relations, stating that the "1927 Declaration of Loyalty" by Metropolitan Sergy was "one of the most tragic phenomena of recent Church history" and "a morbid, tragic compromise." But the document also said that it "was written under unprecedented pressure from the militantly atheistic state which threatened to completely eliminate all legal forms of Church life." Moreover, "the policies of Metropolitan Sergius [sic] enabled the reestablishment of Church life during and after the Second World War."[27] Thus, there would be no "anathematization" of Sergy: the church had broken with his pact with the state but had forgiven him. The text of this resolution is a superb piece of international negotiation, a balance among competing voices that the Security Council of the United Nations might envy. It was a resolution that only a master diplomat, a man who had spent thirty years chairing conferences, roundtables, and retreats for the World Council of Churches, could have brought about.

The ROC, ROCOR, and ROCA were once again headed to being one. On June 27, 2006, delegates began their "Seventh Working Meeting" of their "Commission on Dialogue." The tipping point had been achieved. On September 8, 2006, Interfax reported that the Synod of ROCOR and the Moscow Patriarchate had approved an "Act on Canonical Dialogue." It was signed and put on the ROC Web site November 30, 2006. After an eighty-year schism, full communion between ROCOR and the Moscow Patriarchate was to be restored.[28] The "Act of Canonical Communion," ends with citing the Gospel of John, "but that also he should gather together in one the children of God that were scattered abroad" (John 11:52). The context of the passage, about which the document is silent, is also instructive: this is the prophesy of Caiaphas, the high priest, that Jesus should die not for the Jews only but that also "he should gather together in one the children of God that were scattered abroad." Thus does the Act, in reuniting the ROC and its "diaspora" of ROCOR, fulfill the purpose of Jesus' death. The same concept, applied to describe the Jewish dispersal that followed the A.D. 135 destruction of Jerusalem by Emperor Hadrian, is now applied to the scattering of the Orthodox by the atheist Soviet state.

The Act of Canonical Communion between the Moscow Patriarchate, ROCA, and ROCOR was signed on Thursday, May 17, 2007, in the Cathedral of Christ the Savior. Putin had earlier invited the delegation from ROCOR and hosted its press conference with Aleksy at his official residence. He had been working behind the scenes on his visits to the United States as well. As early as 2003 he had met in New York with ROCA leaders and assured them that the "godless regime is no longer there. You are sitting with a believing president."[29] When Aleksy and Putin met in the Kremlin on April 2, 2007, they exchanged mutual compliments on how hard each had labored to make this a reality; Aleksy seemed to speak for both when he said, "This is really not only a church event, but one which unites Russian people who by God's will were separated."[30] The festivities of May 17–21, 2007, illustrate just how closely Putin and Aleksy work together. May 17 was the Feast of the Ascension on the ecclesiastical calendar; Sergey Markov, a political analyst well connected in the Kremlin, suggested that it also be declared a national holiday.

Aleksy continued the theme of national reunion and reconciliation in a news broadcast. He was interviewed on Monday, May 14, 2007, on Vesti-24, a government-run news channel and said, "The Lord is helping us in this, this time of spiritual revival, to gather up the stones that were so thoughtlessly scattered in the past." Without citing it as such, he alludes to the famous chapter of Ecclesiastes, which states that "to every thing there is a season and a time to every purpose under the heaven." This moment, Aleksy underlines, is the "time to gather stones together" (Ecclesiastes 3:5). Similarly, the leaders of ROCA looked upon the reunion, in the words of the Reverend Alexander Lebedeff of Los Angeles, as "closing the book, or at least a chapter, of one of the most difficult times in Russian and Russian church history."

The signing of the act of reunion was followed by joint services held at Butovo, the former Red Army artillery proving ground outside Moscow, which had been a killing field for the secret police. At that site in August 2000, immediately after the canonization of five hundred people as "new martyrs," Aleksy had personally celebrated the divine liturgy in their memory. Mitrofanov had said that the "blood of new martyrs unifies us" at the Nyack conference. Now the first joint services between the ROC and its former diaspora children were held where so much of that blood had been spilled. By choosing this location, the patriarch made a vital point. It is the *novomucheniki*, those who died for their faith, whom he wishes to commemorate—not the imperial family, who died because they were the imperial family. Had Aleksy chosen to hold these first joint services at the "Church on the Blood" in Yekaterinburg where the Romanovs were killed, he would have been siding with the monarchists.

Success on the international front has been matched by internal resolution of the collaboration issue as well. The ROC has acknowledged that it collaborated, but it asserts that only by cooperating with the KGB, by taking that sin upon its head, could the church survive at all. And, church leaders claim, we had to allow the church to survive, for we knew one day that the USSR would fall. After all, its ultimate demise is predicted in the book of Revelation and confirmed by the prophecies of St. Seraphim. This argument first emerged from the pages of the 1994 publication of a lavish coffee-table book written by the architectural historian Mikhail P. Kudryavtsev, *Moskva, Trety Rim* (*Moscow, the Third Rome*).[31] It is stated in such convoluted terms that few in the West understood it, even those with near-native Russian. Kudryavtsev died before his life's work was published, though he did get to see the book in proofs. The *tirage* (number of copies in the print run) was only ten thousand. Inside the front cover appears the statement that the book has "the blessing of Aleksy II, Patriarch of Moscow and All Russia." The purpose of the book sounds innocuous:

> Ancient Moscow is generally held to be the greatest product of the Russian town builder's art, and was seen by the Church as the earthly embodiment of the Celestial City. This richly illustrated history of the city is the first title in a series commemorating the 850th Anniversary of Christian Moscow. A wealth of rare photographs, maps and diagrams, and historical town plans coupled with the author's imaginative reconstructions of XVII century townscapes, bring old Moscow truly to life.[32]

So far, this is straightforward. The book's publication is part of the hoopla surrounding the 850th anniversary of the founding of Moscow, just as was the publication of *Moscow: 850th Anniversary* and the rebuilding of the Cathedral of Christ the Savior were. Only in the afterword does the ROC's ingenious decoding of the book of Revelation enter. The afterword is entitled "The Orthodox View and Teaching about the Third Rome." Here the Protohierarch Alexander Saltykov explains that Filofey's sixteenth-century portrait of Moscow as the Third Rome actually predicts the fall of the USSR.

Saltykov's argument is worthy of the Jesuits at their most refined. Soviet ideologues had tried to remake Moscow into the capital of an international movement leading the entire planet to a heaven brought down to earth—in effect a "Fourth Rome," though Saltykov does not use that image. Instead, he argues, there could be no Communist holy city called Moscow: Scripture itself declares the Holy City can move "only three times, for it is done only in the name of the Father, the Son, and the Holy Ghost. And this Trinity is a sacred number."[33] The number three thus represents an eschatological barrier.

To the contemporary Western secular mind, such reasoning is reminiscent of Columbus's reluctance to admit he had discovered a new continent. Columbus believed, as did most Christians at the time, that there were only three continents—Africa, Asia, and Europe—because these are the only ones mentioned in the Bible. Columbus went to his grave trying to hang onto the idea that the islands he had discovered in the Gulf of Mexico were outer banks belonging to the Japanese archipelago.

Saltykov now turns to the book of Revelation, which provides the precise metaphors describing the entire Soviet period. These are the years when the faithful would be forced to "flee into the desert (or wilderness)." Saltykov alludes to verses 5–14 of chapter 12 of Revelation though he does not quote them. When mystified readers (such as the authors) turn to the text, these verses describe the war in heaven fought between Michael and his angels against the dragon and the rebel host. When the dragon is cast out of heaven into the earth (12:9) he "persecuted the woman which brought forth the man child" (12:13) The woman flees into the desert, "And to the woman were given two wings of a great eagle, that she might fly into the wilderness, into her place, where she is nourished for a time, and times, and half a time, from the face of the serpent." Saltykov claims the years of Soviet power literalize this metaphor, with the dragon standing for the atheist state, and the "remnant" of the woman's seed, "which keep the commandments of God and have the testimony of Jesus Christ" (Revelation 12:17) representing the Russian Orthodox. Though Saltykov does not come out and say so, every Russian could understand the unspoken reference to the two wings of Revelation's "eagle." This is the double eagle of the Romanov dynasty, revived post-coup as the symbol of Russia.

However convoluted, this interpretation represents a welcome break from the gloss the tsarist ROC applied to these verses. In 1905 the "Union of the Archangel Michael" justified its pogroms in Odessa and Kiev by referring to the war in heaven. The tsarist police had approvingly stood by and the ROC hierarchy had remained silent while Jews were murdered with impunity. The anti-Semites of Nicholas II's day saw themselves as the contemporary equivalent of Archangel Michael's army and happily identified their Jewish neighbors as the latter-day spawn of Satan and his rebels. Indeed, Nilus made the reference to the woman being nourished away from the "face of the serpent" into a little schematic drawing to illustrate *The Great in the*

Small. Who were the little snakes descended from the serpent? Why, of course, the Jews! And the complaisant tsarist ROC allowed the mishmash of metaphors found in Revelation 12:17 to be cited as scriptural rationale to kill them. Now the ROC wanted to interpret the verse differently. Construing it as predicting the fall of the Soviet Union kills two birds with one stone: it neutralizes both the tsarist reading and the church's collaboration during the Soviet past.

It is human nature to want to see pattern in the blizzard of chaos. During the twentieth century, Russians lived through the worst years of their thou-sand-year history. This has left many susceptible to the idea that prophecy can somehow *explain* all the bloodshed and destruction. And Saltykov is careful to link Filofey's prophecy that Moscow was the Third Rome and "a Fourth can never be" with St. Seraphim, calling the duo the two saints who "head the prophetic ranks of the Russian church."[34] It may sound ludicrous to the secular, but it is a comforting explanation for the Russians of seventy-three years of torment at the hands of their own government.

The basic theme of the ROC campaign to deal with collaboration during the Soviet period was laid out at the crisis of the coup when the outcome was still undecided. It was there in Aleksy's closing prayer-petition to Mater Bozhia, the Mother of God, for her help "to reconcile ourselves to one an-other, to the truth, and to God." Reconciliation would be premised upon setting a large chunk of the messy historical truth aside and adopting the church's "Truth"—as spelled with a capital "T." The distinction between what Western historians would call "the truth" and the church's definition of this term is stated by Vladimir Lossky, an important theologian, in his essay "Tradition and Traditions." He declares that the church's "Truth in the Light" belongs to it alone and is not perceived "according to the light of human reason. This is true gnosis owed to an action of the Divine Light (cf. 2 Corinthians 4:6).... This freedom from every condition of nature, every contingency of history, is the first characteristic of the vertical line of the Tradition."[35] It is a close question whether or not the ROC's version of the "Truth," detached as it is from notions of historicity, fact, and rational-ity, would be anything recognizable to the West. But this is language on another plane.

One week after the coup's defeat, the church's August 30, 1991 Appeal pleads penitence and seeks forgiveness. Here the ROC, in a brilliant stroke, pointed to the émigrés' own words as the path to follow. This is the "Prayer for the Salvation of Russia," which was established at the first Council of the Russian Church abroad in 1921, in Sremske Karlovce, Yugoslavia. It was then read at the Divine Liturgy in place of the prayer for the emperor. After that, it was so read, with slight changes, for seventy-seven years. The prayer is for forgiveness for the *tormentors*:

Accept from us, Thy unworthy servants,
this fervent supplication, and,
having forgiven us all our sins,
remember all our enemies
that hate and wrong us,
and render not unto them according to their deeds,
but according to Thy great mercy convert them:
the unbelieving to true faith and piety,
and the believing that they may turn away from evil and do good.[36]

Now the great enemy of Orthodox Christianity, the officially atheist USSR, is no more, the ROC argued. Were the émigrés to now refuse their own appeal?

Within Russia itself, the overwhelming majority of Orthodox believers are willing not only to forgive but to forget. That was the attitude of both the remarkable congregation and the priest of St. Vladimir's Russian Orthodox Church of Moscow. In the bad old days, the complaisant church authorities had exiled this courageous man to the interior. When he was allowed back to Moscow as part of the millennial celebrations, he was not only untainted by the whiff of collaboration but was still utterly devoted and loyal to the Moscow Patriarchate.

It is true that an exiguous band of dissidents do not adopt such a positive posture. For those who are interested in the dissenting views about Aleksy, there are critical articles about him that can be accessed on the Internet.[37] The story about Aleksy receiving his *gramota* from the KGB circulated in the press within Russia by the spring of 1992. The church, however, spun that information quite cleverly. It admitted what everyone knew: all bishops had to forward materials to the Council for Religious Affairs, which forwarded everything to the KGB. And, it went on, we are contrite; we have repented. The KGB had divided the church, using the old jailor's trick to set the inmates on each other. Now we are free of the KGB, argues the ROC. Why continue its technique of denouncing one another? In short, Aleksy managed what President Nixon never could about the Watergate scandal. He achieved a "limited hang-out," that is, releasing just enough of the facts to satisfy the believers.

The success of the ROC's carefully calibrated penitence may be instructively paralleled to the disastrous handling of the problem of church collusion in another country: Poland. The Soviet system was replicated all over the Warsaw Pact states. Polish Catholicism was subjected to exactly the same devil's bargain as was Russian Orthodoxy; the Vatican could have imitated the ROC's *Obrashchenie* of August 30, 1991, to get out in front of this issue. Instead, it remained silent for years, until the inevitable trickle of information from the Security Service files became public.

Beginning in January 2005, Poland suffered convulsions of finger-pointing and recriminations. A Catholic priest, Rev. Tadeusz Isakowicz-Zaleski of Krakow, began releasing evidence from the secret police files that possibly 10 to 15 percent of Polish priests and nuns had collaborated with the Communist government. The contemporary Polish secret police do not have the tight control over its files that the FSB does in Russia. Priests have been able to visit archives, find their own files, and read information about themselves that could have been supplied only by other priests. Informers had code names of course, but the details were so precise the victims in question could figure out who had betrayed them.

What has shocked and deeply troubled the Polish faithful the most is the gradually dawning realization that this collaboration was known by the Catholic Church for decades. It was kept quiet out of respect for, possibly at the behest of, Pope John Paul II. By January 2007, the Catholic Church was in turmoil when two senior prelates were forced to resign because of their ties to the Polish Security Service (Sluzba Bezpieczenstwa) during Communist times.[38] Then on January 16, 2007, the archbishop of Warsaw, Stanislaw Wielgus, had to step down, the latest in a string of revelations that forced the rector of Wawel Cathedral in Krakow, as well as the co-president of Poland's Council of Christians and Jews to resign their positions. As for the whistle-blower, Rev. Zaleski, the Catholic hierarchy of Poland first ignored his evidence, then suggested he burn the documents, and finally forbade him to publish any disclosures, because they would undermine "love for the church and Christ."[39] Rev. Zaleski, however, declared he will publish an entire book of the documents and name names. Polish Catholicism did not learn the lesson of Watergate: it is not the crime, but the cover-up that people cannot forgive.

Exactly how much *Schadenfreude* this spectacle has occasioned back in the patriarchal residence will never be known; the ROC has kept one of its pristine silences on the subject. It can be inferred that the ROC is paying close attention to these events if only to reject any sort of conciliation or reunion with the papacy now or in the future.

All the while that Aleksy has worked to heal the wounds of the Soviet past, he has simultaneously moved forward on the most important priority of his patriarchate: forging a close relationship with the military. He has sought no other ally more ardently or more successfully.

SEVEN

A Faith-Based Army

The Russian Orthodox Church has always come to the
assistance of the military in defending the Holy Borders
of our Fatherland.
— *Patriarch Aleksy II, at the official signing of the accord between
the ROC and the Russian military, March 2, 1994*

THE TOPPLING OF DZERZHINSKY'S STATUE on August 21, 1991, presaged the crash of many thousands of bronze and granite Lenins across the Soviet Union. The party's pantheon of heroes and catalog of villains went out with the garbage. Russians were left looking for a usable past, something immutably Russian that could forge a proud destiny for the future. No organization was in more need of support than the Russian military. Aleksy became metropolitan of Leningrad and Novgorod as the army was chased out of Afghanistan after losing at least 13,000 dead in a futile campaign. The formal dissolution of the Warsaw Pact in Prague, Czechoslovakia, on July 1, 1991, deepened the gloom. Once servile Eastern European satellites now evicted the army from comfortable billets. Hungary declared a national holiday on the day the last Red Army troops decamped, and cheering crowds saw off the final trains from Budapest. Soon, to add insult to injury, the breakup of the USSR on December 25, 1991, saw former Soviet republics become sovereign countries inheriting parts of the bases and arsenals of the 4-million-strong army. While the Russians retained the nuclear armaments, they lost a large share of their most advanced conventional weapons.[1] By the end of 2001, the Russian military had shrunk to 1.2 million military personnel. The downsizing meant misery for the conscripts, who were often starved and brutalized by their superiors. The officer corps, who remembered when it commanded a superpower whose global reach ranged from an electronic intelligence station in Cuba to a naval base in Vietnam, was no less depressed.

Many saw the post-Soviet Russian army as a slough of despond, riddled with fraud, beset by low morale, and leeched by draft-dodging and desertion. The ROC saw it as a target of opportunity. Together with the remaining patriots who commanded the mess, the church set out to restore the military as fully as it would rebuild Moscow's skyline of cupolas and crosses. In contrast to the downward spiral of the church's relationship with Western Christianity, here the ROC's operations have been largely successful, sometimes dazzlingly so. There have been setbacks, true, but at the organizational level, the ROC has successfully embedded its ethos and its symbols in both the high command and the men.

The Russian military's defeat in Afghanistan came as a shock to a country regarding itself as a superpower. In 1980 the Soviet Union glowed with prestige. It hosted the Olympics in its capital; its army reached the foothills of the Hindu Kush. Russian imperialism's long cherished goal of carving an opening to the Indian Ocean seemed achievable. During the nineteenth century the British Empire stymied this drive in what it called the "Great Game." Now Britain had given up its empire; all that stood between the soldiers of the Red Army and a march through landlocked Afghanistan to dip their boots in the Indian Ocean were ragtag auxiliaries calling themselves mujaheddin.

But all was not as it seemed. The party predicted easy victory, so the privileged sent off their sons to be officers, fully expecting a little combat experience would merit an Order of the Red Banner for service to the motherland.[2] Alas, history repeated itself. Alexander the Great had enjoyed rapid victories over the Persian Empire. But though he founded the city of Kandahar in one of the region's beautiful valleys, his soldiers bogged down in the mountains and caves of the Hindu Kush. Legend has it that his mother, Olympia, sent him a message from Greece—what is taking you so long? In return, Alexander sent back several prisoners, with instructions to pour a small leather bag of dust in front of the queen—this, they were to say, is what we fight over to the death. For more than two millennia, when not battling off invaders, Afghani tribesmen kept their appetite for carnage whetted by practicing blood feuds. Afghanistan's terrain is such that Russian helicopters found themselves being shot at *from above*. When the U.S. military armed the mujaheddin with shoulder-held Stinger missiles, the additional firepower greatly increased Soviet casualties.[3] Twice in the nineteenth century, at the height of its empire, the British lost two Afghan wars. The Red Army's last divisions left February 15, 1989, just as raddled and spent as Queen Victoria's soldiers.

After the coup's defeat, Aleksy told the British ambassador that one of his highest priorities would be to develop the church's links with the military.[4] Initially, priests began to make informal visits to units. Legally, these occurred outside regulations. Aleksy had made just such an ad hoc stop on the St. Seraphim translation pilgrimage in 1991, to the 31st Vistula Armored Division in Nizhny Novgorod. Retroactively, a deeper significance was read into it. Once the risen Christ walked three furlongs with two disciples to Emmaus and broke bread with them. They did not realize who the stranger was until he was gone.[5] Believers now drew a similar ex post facto inference from Aleksy's talk with soldiers that day. Surely it was "no accident" that some of the same "unbelieving" soldiers who had put questions to the patriarch on July 28, 1991, had since seen the truth. Aleksy's visit was possible because the center was not holding and an individual general had freedom to maneuver. Now, instead of taking advantage of wavering Soviet control, the patriarch committed to shoring up the authority and morale of the army of the Russian Federation.

The obvious path would pursue reinstituting a military clergy—that is, installing ROC priests as chaplains for every regiment. The history was there. Catherine the Great's son, Tsar Paul, who admired the Prussian army model, established military clergy in 1800. All were Orthodox priests. By 1900 they numbered more than six hundred. They administered several hundred regimental churches and eighteen cathedrals. They supervised military cemeteries, organized church libraries, oversaw philanthropy for the families, led educational "brotherhoods," and spoke frequently with the men in "extraliturgical religious and moral conversations." They also blessed the troops and performed liturgies on Sunday and Feast days.[6] A number won decorations for valor in World War I. In January 1918 the Bolsheviks simply liquidated the institution and many of the priests themselves. They substituted the *politruk*, the political commissar, charged with ensuring ideological correctness in the unit. Bringing back chaplains might seem a praiseworthy tradition whose revival could only help the army.

But the obvious path had obstacles. The patriarch first had to persuade the supreme command that he would not restore the tsarist model of church-state relations. The generals and admirals remembered all too well that Nicholas II, the most Orthodox tsar since the seventeenth century, practiced "faith-based" logistics as commander-in-chief. His belief that icons and prayers could substitute for ammunition and rations led to the deaths of hundreds of thousands, indeed millions, of Russian soldiers in two disastrous wars, the Russo-Japanese in 1904–5 and World War I in 1914–18. Russian commanders would not allow Orthodoxy back into the military if it led to a repeat of that fatuous behavior.

The case of St. Seraphim had left a particularly bitter memory in the high command. His canonization reverberated in global politics when the hermit's prophecies caught Nicholas's eye. He interpreted their mystical and elliptical phraseology to mean that Russia would soon go to war with Japan and that a victorious peace would be signed in Tokyo.[7] The canonization was July 19,

1903 o.s. Only eleven days later, July 30, 1903 o.s., his government suddenly announced the formation of a "Viceroyalty of the Far East," a territory that took in Port Arthur and northern Manchuria. This action took the power politics of Russia's expansion to the Pacific a step further. From the outset, old-fashioned imperialism had fueled it. Russia helped suppress the Boxer Rebellion in China in 1900 and then left its troops in Manchuria. Russia wanted to connect Vladivostok on the Pacific to the South China Railway in Manchuria, and that would mean building a railroad across Korea. Japan however, wished Korea to be under its thumb so it wanted Russian troops out of the entire region. Russia refused, and the stage was set for war.

Nicholas's reign added new ingredients to the mix. Personal prejudice played its part. Nicholas despised the Japanese ever since his tour of the islands while still tsarevich. A samurai tried to assassinate him; he carried the scar of this head wound to his death. Now he glossed Russia's occupation of Port Arthur with messianism. When it was first occupied in 1898, the admiral who commanded the Pacific Ocean naval squadron and directed the newly annexed Kwantung Peninsula built an Orthodox cathedral on the highest promontory of the city. No one could mistake the symbolism in this gesture. The admiral's wife designed the cathedral's iconostasis. Empress Alexandra became the project's patron. As a contemporary journal ecstatically hymned,

> Her August Majesty thus continues the custom coming down from our ancient tsaritsas and grand princesses. Russia's monasteries and cathedrals preserve in shrouds and icons numerous works by royal hands. The Christian devotion of wives and daughters of our sovereigns is incarnate in the holy succession from ancient days, and in the Far East appears one of the examples of this spiritual continuity.[8]

The covert message was that Russia would carry the true faith to the heathen. Given Nicholas II's uxorious devotion to his obsessively religious wife, it was the fanatic leading the intellectually challenged.

The tsar then proceeded—over the strenuous objections of Count Witte—to take precisely the worst possible attitude toward the proud and insular Japanese: arrogance. At the christening of a battleship in the fateful summer of 1903, Nicholas said, "the Lord put into my heart the thought that I must not delay that which I was already persuaded to do."[9] Witte summed up the whole situation in his memoirs. The tsar had caught "mystic diseases" from his spouse, which boiled down to an "abnormal mood of Orthodox paganism and searching for miracles."[10] Chapter 2 recounted how the royal couple, desperate for a son, had installed a French charlatan, Philippe, in a suite next to the royal bedroom so Alexandra could conceive a son. When that failed (her 1902 "pregnancy" turned out to be a phantom), they forced the canonization of St. Seraphim for the same objective.[11] Then Nicholas undertook a war with Japan for reasons he rationalized as evangelism. There was neither Parliament nor prime minister to check him. He then conducted his war through strategy premised upon divine intervention.

Nicholas II's rule bridged the nineteenth and twentieth centuries, yet his decisions are eerily reminiscent of Louis VII of France, who reigned in the twelfth. On June 11, 1144, Louis and Queen Eleanor traveled to Saint-Denis for the consecration of a new Abbey. Present were two giants of the Middle Ages, Bernard of Clairvaux and Abbot Suger. Louis personally took part in the ceremony. Hoisting on his shoulder "the new solid-silver reliquary containing the bones of the martyred St. Denis the Areopagite, patron saint of France, which had hitherto rested in the crypt of the old church, the king led the procession round the great edifice and placed the relics reverently in their new bejeweled shrine. Louis was greatly moved by the ceremony of dedication." Louis's wife had failed to provide the dynasty with a male heir. Two absolute rulers, separated by virtually 750 years, sought a son through identical means. After the ceremony, Eleanor appealed to the ascetic Bernard of Clairvaux for his help to "move Heaven to bestow on her the gift of motherhood."[12] Empress Alexandra bathed in the burning-cold springs of Sarov and prayed to St. Seraphim to intercede in heaven so that she might bear a boy.[13]

In yet another creepy parallel, both rulers left these consecration ceremonies to embark upon ruinous foreign adventures. In 1144 Louis VII quit the Abbey of St. Denis to undertake the disastrous Second Crusade. The narrative of that doomed expedition of arrogance fueled by religious delusion lies outside this book; suffice it to say that the Turks massacred thousands on the way. Though both Louis and Eleanor made it to Jerusalem and the Tomb of the Holy Sepulcher, the whole enterprise came to an ignominious end when Louis unsuccessfully assaulted the Turkish emirate of Damascus (a hitherto friendly neighbor) and his army disintegrated.[14] His soldiers, "impelled by want," deserted Jerusalem in 1149. When Louis and Eleanor finally returned to Paris more than two years later, the general judgment of Christendom was appalled surprise at the inscrutable ways of the Lord. A contemporary observer, William of Tyre, said: "No one may question the acts of God, for all His works are just and right, but it remains a mystery to the feeble judgment of mankind why Our Lord should suffer the French, who of all the people in the world have the deepest faith and most honour Him, to be destroyed by the enemies of religion."[15]

Tsar Nicholas put down the solid silver reliquary of Seraphim to set out upon an equally ludicrous quest. This time it was not a crusader city that must be taken back from the infidel (Edessa had fallen in 1144 to Zengi of Mosel), but heathen Japan, whose "impudence" must be taught a lesson. The outcome was as surprising to the faithful. History repeated itself in a darker context. Warfare had changed since 1144. Knights on armored horses carrying shields, halberds, and flails fought the Second Crusade; catapults and battering rams were the heavy artillery. In 1903 Russian officers still practiced mandatory fencing. Japan however, while also paying homage to an emperor, had successfully melded its medieval code of bushido to modern weaponry. Nicholas relied upon prayers and icons while his adversary had switched to long-range guns with heavy shells. This would multiply Russian casualties exponentially.

On January 26, 1904, the war officially began when the Japanese attacked and damaged three Russian ships lying at anchor at Port Arthur. One day later, the tsar mentioned the bombardment in his diary, then cheered himself up: "Casualties were not significant. At 4 o'clock I proceeded through the over-filled halls to a service in the cathedral. On the way back there were deafening hurrahs! In general on all sides touching signs of a rise of spirits and of indignation with the impudence of the Japanese."[16] Nicholas was certain that Russia could not be defeated by such "monkeys"—his favorite word for the Japanese. The Russian commander, General Stessel, shared his insouciance. He was hosting a ball and concerned about the caviar and the dancing on the precise night the Japanese fleet entered Port Arthur. The Japanese intelligence service had obtained the chart of the mines placed by the Russians. Negotiating their way through a swept channel, the Japanese opened fire with deadly effect.

Less than a year later, December 21, 1904 o.s., the siege of Port Arthur ended with the surrender of the garrison. (The new style date would be January 2, 1905.) Nicholas again recorded his diary:

> Received staggering news from Stessel in the night, about the surrender of Port Arthur to the Japanese in the light of immense losses and disease among the garrison and the complete lack of shells. It's hard and painful, although it had been foreseen, but one wanted to believe that the army would come to the assistance of the fortress. The defenders are all heroes and did more than could have been expected. It was God's Will then![17]

The day before, Nicholas read a cable from the hapless Stessel (all cables by this time had to be taken from Port Arthur to the Russian consul at Chefoo by smugglers' junks) detailing the situation: "Will be able to hold just for a few more days. Have almost no artillery shells. Will take measures to prevent slaughter on the streets. Scurvy is ruining the garrison; I have just 10,000 men capable of carrying rifles and all of them are sick."[18] Nicholas read it, yet the information failed to penetrate. Instead, sounding like William of Tyre surveying in 1151 the incomprehensible defeat of the French at the hand of the infidel Turks, he lays the entire disaster down to "God's Will."

Logistics—that is, ammunition and supplies—was the fatal flaw of his army. Icons and blessings proved a poor substitute for shells, guns, and rations. But the emperor would not admit this. In 1903 a Crimean War veteran saw the Mother of God "standing on the banks of a sea, holding a linen cloth with the image of Christ." As related by Vera Shevzov in *Russian Orthodoxy on the Eve of Revolution*:

> She [i.e., Mary] warned him that Russia would soon become involved in a difficult war on the shores of a distant sea and directed him to have an image of her depicted as he saw her in the dream. Many believers subsequently tied this icon, which came to be known as "The Victory of the Blessed Mother of God," to Russia's fate in the Russo-Japanese war. The icon started on a long odyssey to Port Arthur that involved members of the imperial family, statesmen, and church hierarchs along the way through Vladivostok. Many believers attributed Russia's defeat in that war to the fact that the icon never made it to Port Arthur.[19]

Nicholas and Alexandra liked this excuse very much.

Faith-based logistics left the Russian navy of the 1990s with especially bitter memories of St. Seraphim. It remembered that Nicholas dispatched the Baltic Fleet to relieve the siege at Port Arthur in September 1904. He personally visited twenty-two ships of this armada during that month. The mission of the squadron was officially "to reach Port Arthur and together with the 1st Squadron master the Sea of Japan."[20] The admiral, Zinovy Petrovich Rozhdestvensky, told the tsar bluntly that in all likelihood the Port Arthur squadron would cease to exist before the armada reached the Far East. To Rozhdestvensky's astonishment, the tsar cheerfully dismissed his concerns. Nicholas presented each ship with an icon[21] and each sailor with a *znachok* (medallion) of St. Seraphim (see figure 7.1). These gifts, he confidently predicted, would protect them. According to Witte, Nicholas cited the prophecy by St. Seraphim as "proof" for his optimism. With what bitterness may well be imagined, Witte recorded in his memoirs: "After all, Serafim of Sarov had prophesied that peace would be concluded in Tokyo, which means only Yids (*Zhidy*) and the intelligentsia might think differently."[22] One must feel some compassion for Witte, a man of rational intellect continually stymied by a commander-in-chief whose religious delusions could not be dislodged, no

Figure 7.1 The icon of St. Seraphim shows him before the Diveyevo Convent, where he was spiritual adviser to the nuns for years, and where his relics now repose. (Photo credit: Sofrino, the publication arm of the Moscow Patriarchate)

matter how many catastrophes they caused. When the armada left the last Russian port, the tsar recorded in his diary, "Bless its path, Lord, let it reach its destination whole to fulfill its hard mission for the good and benefit of Russia!" He then drew a cross.[23]

But as the fleet steamed on its long journey, the Russian garrison's surrender at Port Arthur profoundly altered the battlefield situation. As the admiral had predicted, the Port Arthur Squadron no longer existed. From January 2,

1905 N.s., the Japanese had complete control of the Sea of Japan, the very body of water Admiral Rozhdestvensky was ordered to "master." The armada's mission was now moot. Yet the tsar refused to call his fleet back. Meanwhile, the Japanese defeated the Russian army at Mukden in February 1905. There exists a photograph of Nicholas II on horseback holding an icon of St. Seraphim as he visits the 148th Caspian Regiment before its departure for the front in Manchuria in 1905.[24] Unaccountably, from Nicholas's perspective, Seraphim did not intervene to save his troops from disaster.

And still his armada chugged on, its engines coaled by Germany, for the Kaiser encouraged Nicholas to see himself as the "Admiral of the Pacific." ("Cousin Willy" sent Nicholas as a gift an enormous portrait of the tsar tricked out in a Roman emperor's breastplate gazing beatifically over the ocean. The kaiser had a companion portrait done of himself as "Admiral of the Atlantic.") For months the ships steamed halfway around the globe to fulfill a mission that surrender at Port Arthur had made impossible. In the Straits at Tsushima, May 14, 1905, the Japanese sank virtually the entire 2nd Pacific Squadron. The vessels Nicholas believed would be protected by icons went to the bottom. The sailors Nicholas believed would be protected by medallions of St. Seraphim were buried in unmarked mass graves.

When word trickled back of the catastrophe, the battleship *Potemkin* and other vessels in the Black Sea fleet mutinied in June 1905. The crew sailed the ship to Constanza, Rumania. On July 22, 1905, they scuttled it, and then surrendered to the authorities. Russia was forced to sign a humiliating treaty with Japan. Count Witte negotiated terms at the Treaty of Portsmouth (so called because the two parties met in Portsmouth, New Hampshire). Signed in September 1905, the treaty required both combatants to withdraw from Manchuria. Russia ceded its lease on the Liaodong Peninsula and Port Arthur, its coal mines, the South Manchurian Railroad, and the southern half of Sakhalin Island to Japan.[25] But Russia refused to pay an indemnity, in effect, refusing to admit defeat. It was an outward manifestation of the tsar's reliance upon language creating its own reality. Still, such proud intransigence was a poor return for a war that cost hundreds of thousands of lives. Japan, on the other hand, had made clear that it would be treated as an equal on the world stage.[26]

The reforms granted unwillingly by the tsar in 1905 eventually steadied the tottering empire, but within a decade Nicholas involved Russia in an even more disastrous foreign war. The tsar took the fateful step of mobilizing in August 1914, thus throwing his ill-prepared country against an even better equipped and modernized army than the Japanese. For all the scholarly work on the coming of the Great War, it bears mentioning that it was a Serb who assassinated Grand Duke Franz Ferdinand, the heir to the Austro-Hungarian Empire, in Sarajevo, capital of Bosnia. The Serbs were Orthodox, and Russia had fought a successful war against the Turks from 1876–78 to help its Orthodox "little brothers" against the infidel Ottomans. In the crisis of 1908, the tsar declared himself unable to prevent Bosnia from being absorbed by the Austro-Hungarian Empire. Now, only six years later, had Serbia crawled on its knees to Germany, Kaiser William would not let go of this pretext for a war that he had been craving. In spite of the fact that Russia was not bound by treaty to intervene, coming to the assistance of the Serbs, fellow Orthodox, led the tsar to call up his army. His "Manifesto on the Entry into the War" (July 20, 1914 O.S. and August 2, 1914 N.S.) declared:

> In accordance with her historical precepts, Russia, one in faith and blood with the Slav peoples, has never looked upon them with disinterest. With one accord and with particular force, the fraternal feelings of the Russian people towards the Slavs have made themselves manifest in recent days, when Austria-Hungary presented Serbia with demands obviously unacceptable to a sovereign state.[27]

In the end, the ties of "faith and blood" trumped rationality.

Nicholas had learned nothing from his defeat in 1905. He applied the same faith-based tactics, strategy, and logistics to this conflict: the outcome will be God's will; because our war is just, God will reward us with victory. Icons and prayers will defeat the kaiser's heavy artillery. Nicholas left St. Petersburg and personally went to headquarters at Baronovichi (in modern Belarus) to assume command. There he requested that the famous Vladimir icon of the Mother of God be "brought to the General Headquarters at the war front."[28] But once again, the same "complete lack of shells" that determined the fall of the Port Arthur garrison bedeviled Russian soldiers sent to face German machine guns. Nicholas was not clinically mad, but an operational definition of madness, "doing the same thing over and over again and expecting a different outcome," accurately describes his behavior. This time, literally millions of his subjects were sent to their deaths with no bullets in their guns. The exact number of Russian war dead will never be known, but by June 1915 the Russian Imperial Army had lost 3.8 million of its soldiers killed or missing in action. Grand Duke Nicholas Nikolayevich stated, as Warsaw and then Vilna fell to the Germans, "The army is drowning in its own blood." By March 2, 1917, so much ammunition had run out, and so many men had been ordered into suicidal human wave assaults, that mass desertions resulted.

The memories of the Straits of Tsushima and the horrific defeats of World War I were still very much alive in the Russian military during the 1990s. The patriarch's repeated assurances that he would not push for Orthodoxy to be a state church and would not interfere in modern logistics and tactics finally bore fruit in 1994. On March 3, 1994, *Segodnya* (*Today*) made a startling announcement on its front page: "The Church and Army Are Ready to Cooperate." The subtitle read, "Patriarch Aleksy II and General Grachev Sign a Cooperation Agreement." The church and the army adopted a five-point plan:

- To form a joint Coordinating Committee for Interaction between the Russian Federation Armed Forces and the Russian Orthodox Church" (cochairs, lieutenant-general and Defense Ministry chief directorate for personnel, and deputy head of the Moscow Patriarchate Department for External Church Relations for the ROC)
- To charge the Coordinating Committee with developing a long-term program of interaction between the church and the army in scientific, cultural, religious, and ethical fields and research into the religious situation in the Russian Armed Forces for preparation of proposals to their leaders
- To organize interaction in regeneration of Russian spirituality and tradition of faithful service to the Fatherland ... including the field of charity, ... social security for servicemen and their families, veterans of war, ... Russian civilian wounded ... and bereaved families who need assistance in grave tending ...
- To ... promote pastoral visits to Orthodox servicemen and their families in garrisons ... to ensure the opportunity for servicemen and their families to attend divine services and to provide them with requested services in their spare time on a voluntary basis
- To help provide army units with religious literature, periodicals, and other religious educational resources at the desire of the command and the personnel

The staffs of both the patriarch and the general assured the *Today* correspondent that "following the formation of [this] committee, representatives of all confessions will be attracted to participate. We consider that our army is multinational." After this nod to ecumenicalism, General Grachev continued that the army and the church "already share a common language and Orthodox clerics are permitted to visit various units. Now the cooperation will be legalized and centralized." General Grachev concluded that he would "instruct commanders of various military units to obtain and study religious literature."[29] This accord put the ROC on a new footing with the army.

Just a month prior to its announcement, using an old Soviet technique to test new policies, the supreme command floated this change abroad. The

Defense Ministry sent a delegation to the international conference of service chaplains held in Budapest, Hungary. One Lieutenant-Colonel Boris Lukichev, head of the government department which liaised between the state and religious organizations, headed it.[30] Chaplains from the West, especially the United States, the United Kingdom, and Germany, as well as chaplains from former Warsaw Pact countries such as Bulgaria, heard from Lukichev's lips that ties between the military and the church were being actively developed and strengthened. Indeed, he stated that the Ministry of Defense was now supplying religious literature for military libraries; sponsoring officers to participate in round table discussions and seminars with religious organizations; allowing clergy to visit bases, schools, and families; welcoming clergy to bless new recruits; permitting clergy to offer succor during basic training; and distributing pocket Bibles (thousands of which were supplied by North American Protestant congregations) to the troops. Lukichev expressed interest in learning from other countries how the church could also help tackle such problems as drug abuse, alcoholism, and brutality. Those with long memories in his audience gulped. At one fell swoop, a central plank of Soviet power crumbled. In Stalin's time, uttering such heresy would have meant a bullet in the back of the brain. Now the lieutenant-colonel clearly had the full approval of the supreme command.

Lukichev explained the rationale that had gone into this turnaround. The Ministry of Defense had begun to conduct biannually a poll to "evaluate servicemen's religiousness" based on a representative sample of one thousand servicemen who were asked to identify their level of belief. The results of the latest "sociological" study showed 25 percent as "believers" (5 percent of whom are "active believers"); 30 percent as "passive believers"; 35 percent as waverers between "belief" and "atheism"; and 10 percent as "convinced atheists." The conclusion to be drawn from these figures, he admitted, was that a quarter of Russian servicemen were "not free from religious conception."

For seventy years the state shoved "scientific atheism" down the population's throats. Endless Komsomol meetings, Young Pioneer summer camps, the "League of Militant Godless," ubiquitous antireligious propaganda, ideologues in the Union of Soviet Writers rooting out "god-making" in literature, the teaching of atheism in every Soviet school—all were tried. The rituals of birth, naming, marriage, and death were secularized. The political commissar had authority to ensure that the principles of *partinost* and *ideinost* were followed in every military unit. The result? Three years after closing down the most sustained state-sponsored assault on Christianity in human history, only 10 percent of the army's soldiers considered themselves "convinced" atheists. In 1938 Yury Andropov warned his Komsomol comrades they underestimated religion. From his grave he might well have muttered *Ya i vam skazal!* (I told you so).

The fact that a lieutenant colonel in the Russian military publicly admitted these statistics was a most startling example of glasnost indeed—though Gorbachev himself was now gone with the wind that had swept through Moscow. The timing of this admission is key. In a decade of fluctuating fortunes for the Russian military, 1994 was the nadir. Gorbachev called the Afghanistan war a bleeding wound, and it exsanguinated even after the army had left the Hindu Kush. The retreat was completed in February 1989. But 1994 witnessed the "unkindest cut of all." In August, the army was forced to leave East Germany.

What this meant to the Russian military must be looked at from its perspective. From 1943 to May 1945, the Red Army made a blood-soaked march from Stalingrad to Berlin. Along the way, it installed satraps in all the capitals of the Eastern European satellites. When the Warsaw Pact dissolved July 1, 1991, it was forced to evacuate them. The last country exited would be East Germany. The Red Army's fifty-year occupation had been the visible symbol of their triumph over the nation that had invaded and plundered them in June 1941. The horror of that conflict had been pounded into every senior commander of the Russian military, even those who were not born when it occurred. No country suffered more grievously than Russia; in July 2007 the latest casualty figures available are 8,860,400 for the number of Soviet troops killed.[31] And no country inflicted more damage on the Wehrmacht; Western historians calculate that at least 75–80 percent of all German casualties in all theaters were inflicted by the Red Army. Now the spoils of war, which had cost them so dearly, were gone. As the army pulled out of its barracks, hundreds of soldiers sold their equipment and went AWOL. These desertions troubled the high command greatly, but it was unable to prevent them.

No longer deployed in the capitals of the eastern bloc, the military faced a massive discipline problem on its own soil. The same General Grachev, the defense minister who signed the cooperation pact with the ROC, had earlier praised the army as "the only reliable force in society" but then admitted that "several thousand officers, including a number of generals" either had been disciplined or were facing prosecution for corruption. He also released the startling statistic that fully 60 percent of all young men conscripted that year had failed to report to their units.[32] Given that Russian law still mandates that all Russian men between eighteen and twenty-seven are required to serve two years in the military, this was a breakdown of catastrophic proportions. It is in the context of the military crisis of 1994 that the official "cooperation" agreement between the church and the army was signed. With this level of rot, the military was willing to veer around—with a lurch that must have induced nausea in some—to seek help from the foe they tried so long and so fruitlessly to exterminate: faith.

From the outset, the signing of the accord between the army and the ROC laid down what would be the perimeter of tolerance. Servicemen who were Buddhist, Jewish, or Muslim would be accorded equal opportunity to be observant. Pointedly absent from the list is any other confession of Christianity save Russian Orthodoxy. This omission must have been Aleksy's one "nonnegotiable" demand as the accord was being hammered out.

What did the army expect to get out of this agreement? The joint statement declares that the accord "will help solve many a burning problem faced by both the Russian Armed Forces and the Russian Orthodox Church." And what was the army's most "burning problem"? In the words of General Grachev to the patriarch, "the Russian Army needs the help of the church in order to educate [*vospitanie*—the word carries the connotations of "nurture"] young recruits." The elevated diction of the accord speaks of the church's role in "strengthening of spiritual-moral principles in the life of Russian soldiership [*sic*]." In short, the army needed the church to foster patriotism in the conscripts—and help stem the tide of desertion. A 60 percent AWOL rate constitutes a tipping point to disintegration.

The Defense Ministry accord was the first of what would be four key agreements of this kind. Over the next year, the ROC signed similar accords with the Interior Ministry, the Federal Border Guards Service, and the Emergencies Ministry. All four ministries have troops at their disposal. Each one of these cooperation agreements is designed and implemented virtually identically:

- First a "joint committee"—chaired at the highest level by both generals and ROC clerics—is created.
- The joint committee comes up with a five-point plan, designed to teach Russian soldiers how to serve "God and Fatherland."
- The generals are lavished with ecclesiastical awards.
- The patriarch and other bishops visit individual units on special occasions.
- At the close of the visit, the "Working Committee on Cooperation between the ROC and Ministry X" holds a secret meeting to evaluate what worked and what still needs improvement.

Sovietologists might suggest that these "Coordinating Committees for Cooperation" bear an uncanny resemblance to the "Party Committee," the method of control during the bad old days when the CPSU ran the government. Even the "five-point plan" emits a whiff of déjà vu reminiscent of the "Five

Year Plans" so dear to the party's heart. The country's elite were moving their chairs from the party's committee meetings to the patriarch's.

The agreement signed between Aleksy II and Colonel-General Andrew Nikolayev, head of the Russian Federation Federal Border Service (FBS), illustrates the process. (The FBS is not to be confused with the FSB, or "Federal Security Service," the acronym for the updated version of the KGB.) On April 12, 1995, Yury Golotyuk, correspondent of *Segodnya* (which announced the first accord), reported that the patriarch met with the head of the FBS. Aleksy declared the ROC "deeply respects military valor and especially the fighting men who protect the borders of our great homeland."[33] He went on: "the Church is prepared to revive what was once characteristic of Russia — close cooperation between the Orthodox clergy and the military." Colonel General Nikolayev responded: "The Orthodox Church and the border troops are two of the most important elements of our identity as a state." He added, "Faith and homeland are synonyms: without faith there cannot be a homeland, and without a homeland there cannot be faith." The specific areas for cooperation would be religious and moral education; training future officers; facilitating clergy visits to border garrisons, however remote; and providing ROC literature and videos to border units' libraries.

This agreement ended with a surprise. To continue the prerevolutionary "tradition of conscientious service to God and Fatherland," the Corps of Border Guards would revive the custom of having Orthodox churches perform a liturgy dedicated to the protectors of the fatherland's borders. The day selected would be the feast celebrating the "Presentation of the Mother of God." "Border Guard Day" was always celebrated in Soviet times. Now the holiday would be moved from the secular to the ecclesiastical calendar. That this was the feast commemorating the presentation of the Theotokos was seen as no accident. On August 10, 1941, with the Wehrmacht at the gates of Moscow, Metropolitan Aleksy of Leningrad had appealed to the Mother of God to spread her protecting veil. On August 21, 1991, at 1:30 A.M., Patriarch Aleksy II closed his address with a prayer-petition to her. Now the Border Guards, too, wished to link themselves with Mary, the most ancient weapon in Russia's arsenal.

The patriarch and the head of the Border Guards then graciously agreed to take questions. The correspondent for *Segodnya* asked a natural question: where would these services be held? Colonel General Nikolayev responded that although "at present" there were neither Orthodox churches nor chapels on the grounds of FBS units and installations, there were nearby churches that could serve the purpose. The general deliberately left unspoken the logical next step: if the Border Guards were to host their holiday on the Feast Day of the Presentation of the Theotokos, why not have an Orthodox chapel on the grounds of the unit? In this exchange was the first hint of the ROC's subsequent campaign to reinstall regimental chapels in every unit. But chapels were premature in 1994. There was no money to build or restore them. And a lot of spadework needed to be done before that seed—so delicately planted by General Nikolayev's offhand response—could grow and propagate.

The joint press conference closed with both Aleksy and Colonel General Nikolayev repeating the familiar mantra that Border Troops who profess Islam, Judaism, and Buddhism were to have rights equal to those of their Orthodox fellow servicemen. Once again, missing-in-action is Western Christianity. Nikolayev quite openly stated: "Because ethnic Russians currently account for 75–78 percent of the border troops personnel and as much as 85–90% of the officers' corps, Orthodoxy still plays a special role." The signing of the accord ended with an exchange of gifts. The Border Guards presented the patriarch with a book, *Russia's Devoted Christian Warriors* (*Khristolyubi-voye voinstvo russkoye*), a Border Guard watch, and a souvenir Border Guard banner. The patriarch gave the Border Guards in return an icon of the Savior, which Colonel General Nikolayev promised to hang in the *krasny ugol* ("red" or "beautiful" corner) of the House of the Border Guards. In prerevolutionary times, every regimental chapel had such a corner, loaded with icons. In Soviet times, it became a reading and recreation center strewn with Marxist-Leninist propaganda and hung with pictures of Lenin and Stalin. Now the commander of the Border Guards let the world know that the Soviet detritus had been swept away and the icon corner was back at headquarters.

The signing of the ROC accord with the Emergencies Ministry later in the year followed the same template. Again there were fulsome compliments exchanged by the parties. Sergey Shoigu, Russia's emergencies minister, complimented the patriarch by saying "We are colleagues—you save people's souls and our role is to save their lives."[34] The two would cooperate in joint humanitarian actions in the case of serious accidents; clergy would assist in the care of sick, wounded, and refugees; and priests would partner with the state to set up joint shelters for catastrophe victims. Patriarch Aleksy emphasized that the agreement was open "to having other traditional religions of Russia, such as Islam, Buddhism and Judaism, join and cooperate in rescue operations." A spokesman for the Roman Catholic Church in Moscow, Victor Barciewicz (almost certainly a Pole), plaintively expressed the hope that "signing a treaty with one religion does not mean closing the way for the others." Based on the evidence of the four accords, that is precisely what they meant for Catholicism.

Each agreement was at pains to state that Russia maintained separation of church and state and that any question of having Russian Orthodox priests serve as military chaplains was "premature." (This acknowledged that they were also against the law.) Aleksy's reply to a question about chaplains was a masterpiece, a testament to a man who knows what is possible and what must be put on hold: "I think it is time we considered a system of minister service in the forces until the establishment of a permanent institution of military chaplains. This could be done by assigning a clergyman from the nearest parish to every unit and naval base to minister to servicemen."[35] In short, while it was too soon to agitate for military chaplains, the ROC wished to barrel ahead with "minister service" at no cost to the Russian army.

The importance of the church's willingness to offer its services voluntarily should not be underestimated. In the mid-1990s, the Russian economy continued to decline; the state's hegemony was so shaky that few paid taxes. The Russian "mafia" controlled probably more than 50 percent of the economy. Within the Russian armed forces, the air force was so short of fuel (given Russia's billions of barrels of oil, this was doubly insulting) that it could fly only twenty-five hours a year on average, compared to the minimum of two hundred in the West; the military was even asking parents of conscripts to send their sons off with a civilian heavy topcoat for the colder climes of Chechnya.[36] Even in the worst days of World War II, the government had issued every Red Army private a greatcoat. In the midst of all this, the ROC did not simply bide its time. Priests made contact with far-flung units and succored the men, the officers, and their families. Prelates funneled a considerable amount of aid (including topcoats) to soldiers. Given how bad things were, the ROC stored up considerable capital in goodwill.

It simultaneously embarked on a sophisticated marketing campaign to publicize the pantheon of Russia's warrior saints. (The book given by the Border Guards to Aleksy at the signing of their August 12, 1995, accord, *Russia's Devoted Christian Warriors,* was itself an early manifestation of the promotion's success.) Saints Boris and Gleb moved to deep background. They passively accepted death at the hands of their evil brother. While this merited canonization as "passion bearers," nonresistance was not the response the Russian Federation wanted from its soldiers. Russia has no provision for "conscientious objection." Notably, the ROC has not supported any such movement. On the contrary, the ROC has a long and honorable history of soldier saints. Now it resurrected old names and highlighted new ones.

In retrospect, the ROC had been preparing to link with the military since at least the 1988 celebrations of the Millennium of the Baptism of Rus. During that June, the church canonized nine new saints, the first to be elevated since the Bolshevik takeover. Heading the list was none other than the victor of Kulikovo, Grand Prince Dmitry Donskoy.[37] This took place on the world's stage. But practically unnoticed by anyone who was not a regular reader of the *Journal of the Moscow Patriarchate*, an important meeting was held simultaneously at Sergiev Posad (June 6–9). There the ROC created three new ecclesiastical awards. The creation of the Order of St. Andrew "the First Called" has been detailed earlier. The second order was the Order of Grand Princess Olga "Equal to the Apostles," which would be given to women. But the most intriguing was created in the name of St. Prince Daniel. This was to be given to an individual who had distinguished himself in the "*defense* of the Fatherland." Daniel would be the focus of the coming marketing blitz. From the outset, the target audience for the Order of St. Prince Daniel was the officer corps of the Russian military, though it would take several years to get the corps to want it or accept it.[38]

Why should an obscure saint be sold as the ideal warrior-prince for the new Russia? A unique and unpublished typescript of the report submitted by a participant at the millennium conference gives a hint. This document is the closest we can ever get to the inner workings of the ROC, because its agendas for in-house meetings are secret. The report, entitled "The Canonization of Saints in the Russian Orthodox Church," was written by Metropolitan Yuvenaly of Kruytitsky and Kolomna. (Yuvenaly, however, did not pass the document to Keston.) It states that Daniel was canonized during the "synodal period"—that is, 1700 to 1917—but the exact date was unknown. He was canonized because he showed the following virtues in his life, "love of neighbors, service to the Fatherland, charity, and the building of churches."[39] Aleksey Ridiger, then metropolitan of Leningrad, was not at the June 1988 meeting. Yuvenaly has since helped the patriarch through many crises. When he presented the idea for the new order, we infer it had Ridiger's blessing.

There is no "executive summary" for this document, but its main thrust is clear: the millennium conference sought to link the church with the army, a path then illegal under the USSR constitution. It is highly likely that several members of this committee, in their other lives as KGB agents, had been through the secret police course studying Dale Carnegie's *How to Win Friends and Influence People*. In the early 1980s, the KGB began paying careful attention to the American guru. (Vladimir Putin himself took this course prior to his 1985 posting to Dresden, in East Germany.)[40] So the committee highlighted its veneration of Grand Prince Dmitry Donskoy, the victor at Kulikovo over the Horde and newly minted Orthodox saint.[41] The conference was held at the very place where Donskoy had approached Sergius for advice before the battle. These were subtle hints that the church had been the ally of the military in earlier, equally dire, times.

As saints and warriors, Prince Daniel and Grand Prince Dmitry Donskoy became the starting and ending points for the ROC's new (i.e., old) deep-roots myth for Russia. Fourteenth-century Rus provided the necessary ingredients of a sacred place, a sacred time, and native-born soldier heroes. Daniel died in 1303; Donskoy in 1389. Given that no one knows very much about what really happened then—the only sources are from monks writing from the perspective of faith—the church was free to shape a narrative of the times and the men as divinely inspired. Here was a model of church-state relations that leapfrogged not only the Soviet but also the entire tsarist period before and after Peter the Great. Selecting the rise of Muscovy as their golden age allows the church to grandly ignore a whole host of topics. The Muscovite period joined faith and patriotism under the Orthodox banner, and there was no Autocrat. The people were led by princes such as Daniel and Donskoy, who fought in partnership with the church to repel the invaders—Mongols, Tatars, and Catholic Teutonic Knights. Simultaneously, they laid down a sense of what it means to be "Russian." By acting in concert, they established a national identity that avoided being absorbed by either the Mongols from the East or the Catholics from the West.

The appeal of this story to Russians is multifaceted. Its methodology approaches history itself in a way that Russians find deeply satisfying. It is a "one truth." There are no ambiguities and no shades of gray. It avoids the dead hand of tsarist control while simultaneously hymning those martial virtues that the military needs in its recruits. It is not necessary to know the "facts" as a Western historian might define the word, because there is no common consensus about what such facts were in the fourteenth century. The question of what happened is subsumed under the larger question of "why" it happened.

Preparatory work to sell this story began immediately after the millennial celebrations were over. The church began presenting the fourteenth century as the golden age in 1989, the 600th anniversary of the "Blessed Demise" of St. Grand Prince Dmitry Donskoy. The *Journal of the Moscow Patriarchate* explained how what looked like a time of plague and invasion should be understood as an age of heroes inspired and led by the Theotokos:

> The 14th century was a time of profound change in the history of Russia, which affected the hidden depths of her spirit and every aspect of her life. The events of that century were marked by the imprint left by the preceding age of Tatar-Mongol domination, which had been a time

of social decay and despair. Divine Providence, however, guided Russia into a new period in her history, i.e., to the age of the Moscow State. The 14th century proved to be predominantly creative in its nature, one in which God's participation in earthly life revealed itself most visibly, and in which the course of history was greatly influence by people endowed with special Divine gifts.[42]

Thus it was God's plan that in the course of successfully fighting off the invaders, the Muscovy princes would come to dominate the land of Rus. The article buttresses this view by citing the words of the famous tsarist historian Klyuchevsky, who wrote in 1892 about "secret historical forces that were at work preparing the successes of the Moscow principality from the first minutes of its existence."[43] That the journal locates this "history" under the heading "Theology" is itself a microcosm of how the church views human events as taking place in liturgical time.

Prince Daniel, a hitherto quite obscure saint, now plays a key role. The bare facts of Prince Daniel's life are easy to manipulate, given that monks were his only biographers. His real character is lost in the mists; the very vagueness of the evidence makes the ideal substance out of which to construct a hero. What is known is that he established Moscow in desperate times. One measure of his achievement is that, under his rule, Moscow was sacked by the Tatar hordes only once—in 1293. Moscow was then part of the Kievan federation—when the Tatars attacked, they were usually content to sack outlying cities and then fall back, sated with spoils. Thus many refugees poured into Moscow. Indeed, as one historian notes, during this violent time, "no other city in northern Russia escaped enemy attack for as long a time."[44] Muscovy was still small and unimportant when Alexander Nevsky was alive. Daniel began the process of "gathering in the Russian lands," a centralization of power that the church had taught as divinely inspired for centuries. After the seventy-year interregnum of the atheist Soviet state, the ROC happily resurrected the "rise of Moscow as God's will" theme.

Aleksy highlighted Daniel's role as the first *Moscow* saint in an important speech, "The Role of Moscow in the Defense of the Fatherland," given March 22, 1995: "Daniel set the stage for peaceful cooperation and the beginning of the 'gathering in of the Russian lands' [*obyedinenie russkikh zemel*]. His reputation is as a peacemaker and wise leader, establishing a moral foundation for the future state policy of his descendants."[45] Aleksy's linkage of the "gathering in of the Russian lands" with Prince Daniel mines powerful emotional connotations. (In the nineteenth century, American politicians used "Manifest Destiny" to justify the United States' expansion from sea to shining sea.) Once

226

Aleksy had spearheaded the KGB *dezinformatsiya* campaign promulgated through the World Council of Churches that the USSR would lead the world to universal peace. Now he revealed different aspirations: the Russian Orthodox Church would help revive and defend the fatherland.

This particular speech merits close attention. The patriarch emphasizes that Daniel gathered in Russian lands

> not by wars with his neighbors but by mercy and brotherly love. He tried to avoid conflicts and quarrels using peaceful means. If he did draw his sword it was only to defend his own inheritance from God. He was, like his father, distinguished by his great personal bravery in battle. In 1300 he destroyed the forces of the prince of Ryazan, Constantine Romanovich, who was preparing to attack Moscow. The prince of Ryazan had Tatars as his allies. Notably, after their defeat, the losers did not seek vengeance against Daniel. Even more remarkable, Daniel himself did not carry out bloody reprisals, but preferred to stand as an example of peace and fraternal love [*nestyazhanie*]. In 1302 Daniel's nephew, Ivan Dmitrievich, died childless and bequeathed to Daniel Pereslavl Zalessky.[46]

In the church's hagiography of Prince Daniel's life, his rule of Moscow began its divinely ordained rise to power; ergo, Daniel was holy too. All the Chronicles agree that he was able and ambitious, though they differ on his methods.[47] By fair means or foul, Prince Daniel was enormously successful at enlarging his holdings by "gathering in" the lands of his neighbors. By the time he died, he controlled the mouth of the Moscow River, the most strategic waterway of Rus. The bulk of trade was carried on it, and the headwaters of four rivers—the Oka, Don, Volga, and Dnieper were close by. Moscow was thus astride the trade and commerce routes of the land, and its importance grew exponentially.

Aleksy laid out the Orthodox view of Daniel's importance in his introduction to *Moscow: 850th Anniversary*, the lavish book printed for Mayor Luzhkov's 1997 extravaganza. Here was the first opportunity on the national stage to hymn Daniel as the "new" soldier-saint. Luzhkov has been an ally of the patriarch since he denounced the coup on August 20, 1991, the same day as did Aleksy. The mayor was eager for a Moscow saint to feature in his celebrations. Aleksy provided just the hero: "The life history of Moscow, closely connected with the history of Russian holiness, began with his name [i.e., St. Prince Daniel], the name of the first Moscow Saint."

Aleksy continues his encomium by talking about Daniel's son, Prince Ivan Kalita, under whose rule the next momentous step in the rise of Moscow occurred. Metropolitan Peter then had his see, the seat of the principal

Orthodox jurisdiction of Rus, in Kiev. He "fell in love with the God-loving small town of Moscow, its pious and cordial Prince John, St. Daniel's son, who got the nickname Kalita due to his love of giving alms away, and the people of Moscow themselves."[48] The nickname "Kalita," translates as "moneybags." To the skeptical, this might indicate that the pious prince loved lucre itself, but Aleksy chooses to ignore any ambiguity.

Having laid out the background, Aleksy next cites Peter's famous prophecy identifying Moscow as the "Second Jerusalem," the Divine city of Revelation. As such, Moscow "will hold great power, and will be glorified not only in Russia, but in all Eastern, Southern and Northern countries; it will possess many hordes up to the warm sea and cold ocean; its power will be extolled by God from now till the end of the world."[49] Peter told John to build a cathedral to the "Most Holy Theotokos." He promised John that if he did so, "you will glorify both yourself with your dynasty more than other princes, and your city among other Russian towns, and hierarchs will live in it, and my bones will be buried here." John did as he was bid, beginning the first Cathedral of the Assumption in 1326, and Peter, canonized in 1339, did have his bones buried in the Cathedral of the Dormition, the first stone church built inside the Kremlin. Thus, the historical facts connecting Moscow to the fulfillment of a saint's prophecies and God's Divine Plan occurred in the first quarter of the 14th century. The ROC now resurrected the story, burnished it anew, and marketed it to modern Russia.

With that as the exegetical framework, Aleksy quotes approvingly the prayer of St. Hierarch Philaret. Though uttered 150 years ago, he terms it "of vital importance again":

> We glorify Your blissful choice and Providence concerning us, for You turned a small settlement into a city, and through Your hermit St. Hierarch Peter, You said beforehand, that this city would be glorified. It would conquer its enemies and glorify Your name. Then the throne of the Orthodox Church was made strong and the root of the Russian autocracy was implanted by You. You exalted the throne of the kingdom and from here You made the faded light of the tsar's family to shine even brighter; upon Your wish Your saint hermits lived and deceased in fragrance here; by their prayers, like by a diamond wall, You defended this city from troubles and disasters, and in our time You reconstructed it from ashes and ruins, adorned with new splendour and filled with abundance.[50]

It is disconcerting to hear Aleksy quote a prayer that hymns the Russian autocracy and the tsars so blatantly. But Philaret's prayer looks back to Metropolitan

Peter, the hierarch who moved the Orthodox Church's administration to Moscow only twenty-five years after the death of St. Prince Daniel.

Aleksy closes by describing the icon, "Implantation of the Tree of the Russian State," painted by Simon Ushakov in the seventeenth century. (Ushakov too is an Orthodox saint.) This shows an icon within-an-icon. The embedded icon is none other than the Vladimir icon, which has always been connected with the life and defense of the Rus:

> There is the Vladimir Icon of the Most Holy Mother of God, with John Kalita and St. Hierarch Peter depicted at the roots of the Tree on the background of the Cathedral of the Assumption.... Probably it contains the essence of the Russian history, the great importance of Orthodox Moscow, preserving in its sacred earth the roots of the tree of the Russian State System. Thus we bear responsibility for the moral and spiritual situation in Moscow and its flourishing before God and History![51]

It is interesting to juxtapose Aleksy's interpretation of this icon against a Western expert's decoding. Wil van den Bercken agrees that it shows the unity of church and state, with the Mother of God as the patroness of Muscovite power. He points out however, that Ushakov is doing something rather secular: "In 'The Tree of the Russian State' Mary does not represent [the] sacred; she sanctifies Russian state power."[52] Thus, the blending of Mary's power as the Mother of God with sanctification of the Russian state is potent.[53] All of this is part of a mosaic the patriarch has crafted since at least that crucial 1:30 A.M. address that went out over national radio and television on August 21, 1991, when he had prayed to Mater Bozhia to save Russia from civil war.

During the 1990s, the Daniel-to-Donskoy myth made a powerful emotional appeal to the sense Russians felt that they too were beset and besieged. In the year 2000, the sinking of the submarine Kursk in August, with 118 sailors onboard, revealed to Russians that their vaunted navy had mothballed all its rescue vessels and fired its deep sea divers. The exercise was supposed to be training for the navy's first major deployment to the Mediterranean since the dissolution of the USSR in December 1991. The disaster put paid to those plans. The navy complained that it could not even fight off poachers in Russia's territorial waters. By 2001 NATO was expanding eastward. President George W. Bush withdrew from the 1972 Anti-Ballistic Missile Treaty. The Kremlin was powerless to stop the newly sovereign countries of Central Asia from allowing U.S. troops to set up bases. What better way to rally Russians under the Orthodox banner than in this new time of near invasion, to look back with nostalgia at a period when Russians overcame similar challenges? The Russians were throwing off a Soviet identity they now discovered to be as alien as was the Tatar yoke. And the rise of Muscovy itself paralleled their own attempt to restore themselves as a *derzhava*, a "great power."

By 2002, Russia, newly flush with petrol-dollars, and its coffers enriched with vastly increased taxes wrung from the population, started paying off its debts to the World Bank. President Putin could now implement his plans to modernize the military. Putin announced he wanted to trim a full one-third off the 1.2 million military personnel he inherited, modernize the arsenals, abolish the draft, and turn the military into a fully professional force. The generals were not pleased, but Putin had an ally in the patriarch. The patriarch had a plan to mollify the generals and simultaneously implement the dream he had cherished for years: the restoration of regimental chapels. Putin and Aleksy both began with the most prestigious elements of the military: the air force, specifically the "Long Range Aviation" garrisons. The air force would get new planes courtesy of the newly swollen defense budget. It would also get a new chapel, and the commanding generals would be pleased to receive the Order of St. Prince Daniel from the patriarch's own hands. According to the Russians, theirs was the first heavy bomber unit in any air force of any country. This had been their own squadron of "Ilya of Murom" air ships, named after a Russian hero and saint. It had been created on December 23, 1914, in a decision by the Defense Council of the Russian Army and a royal decree. The year 2004 would mark the ninetieth anniversary of its founding. ("Ilya Muromets" would become the name of a modern four-engine bomber.) In 2000 the Russian air force and the patriarch began working together to make the celebration a memorable occasion.

Fresh from consecrating the upper portion of the Cathedral of Christ the Savior, the patriarch flew to bless the groundbreaking for a memorial chapel for the headquarters of Long Range Aviation. Two years later, on August 21, 2002, he was back to consecrate it.[54] It was dedicated to Elijah, the patron saint of pilots—a fitting honor for the prophet who was carried up to heaven in a golden-wheeled chariot. Two more years of feverish building ensued to construct a "memorial complex" around the chapel. On December 23, 2004, the 90th anniversary of Russian Long Range Aviation, Aleksy again flew to its headquarters. Lieutenant-General I. Khvorov, commander of the 37th Strategic Aviation Army of the Supreme Command and the other members of the military council greeted him as he deplaned. He performed a prayer service in the St. Elijah chapel and then presented Lieutenant-General Khvorov the Order of St. Prince Daniel of Moscow, 2nd degree, "for his activity in strengthening the liaisons between the Air Force and the Russian Orthodox Church." The patriarch next toured the complex's conference hall, cinema, museum, and housing for the families of the officers and men when they visit. In addition to regular lectures on Orthodox culture, the facility would host pilgrimages from Moscow. A regular rota of clergymen sent from the patriarchate was already in place. Aleksy watched a film on the history of long-range bombers before his next, momentous task. In Soviet times, anything about the military's strategic bombers was a state secret. However, the Web site of *The Orthodox Encyclopaedia* (Sedmitza.Ru) tells the reader that Aleksy (with the help of other priests) capped this visit to the headquarters of Long Range Aviation by consecrating all 160 of the new strategic bombers and their crews. He then presented the officers and men an icon of St. Prophet Elijah before flying back to Moscow.

Decoding this account tells volumes about the "corporate culture" emerging in the new Russian military. Russian strategic bombers of the Tu-160 class are named after people who served Russia selflessly. The inference is that the planes are again being named after saints. There are two words missing from this account: "rocket" and "missile." But the Long Range Aviation forces control both these key components of the modern Russian air force as well. The article mentions in passing that "Orthodox churches are being constructed in the Long Range Aviation garrisons." Thus, a regimental Orthodox chapel was in the pipeline for each and every base, however remote. It took less than ten years since the April 12, 1995, announcement by Colonel General Nikolayev that the Border Guards would be celebrating their holiday on the Day of the Presentation of the Mother of God for the head of the equally prestigious Long Range Aviation forces to announce that the necessary Orthodox chapels were being built. And this sea change occurred just a few years after the end of the 1990s, when "one survey revealed that some 39 percent of senior officers opposed the idea of military chaplains, and 41 percent opposed the creation of religious parishes within military bases."[55]

Only two weeks after the patriarch's triumphal consecration of the 160 new bombers, on January 5, 2005, Aleksy greeted on the doorstep of his private residence, the "Church of the Icon of the Mother of God the Swift Listener," none other than Sergey Ivanov, Russia's minister of defense. While ITAR-TASS reported this visit, *Red Star*, the legendary newspaper for the Russian military, gives a fuller account. Practically alone among the vast number of things renamed after the fall of the Soviet Union, the newspaper retains its Soviet name. *Red Star* never ceased publication during World War II—even *Pravda* went silent during a few horrific days in October 1941. A great many of its combat correspondents and photographers were killed on the eastern front. On January 12, exactly one week after the visit, the front page of *Red Star* showed Aleksy in his full regalia smiling at Ivanov, next to the headline "Together with the Army and the Nation" (*Vmeste s armiey i narodom*).

According to correspondent Aleksey Ventslovsky, "In his conversation with the patriarch, the minister of defense raised hopes about further development of relations between the church and the army." Minister Ivanov noted that these two "institutions" held strong ties even during times of trial. Because of this, they represent the people (*samye narodnye*). He looked forward to the coming year of 2005, when "the armed forces will develop further, and relations between the armed forces and the church will also develop strong ties." He stated that there were approximately two thousand priests "chaperoning" the constantly moving Russian army. "What is more important," noted the minister, "is that in some of the places where the army is stationed, there are special temples for prayer. In places where this is not possible, we are opening special rooms for prayer." In short, the patriarch's consecration of the new St. Elijah Chapel for the air force just weeks earlier was changing the vast, geodetic structure of the entire Russian military. "Special rooms for prayer" was Ivanov's characterization of what are essentially regimental chapels. Though in 1999 41 percent of serving military officers did not want a chapel on their base, in January of 2005 they learned they would be getting one.

How did this happen? The Russian military, like that of the United States, is under civilian control. Sergey Ivanov is a leader in the Donald Rumsfeld mold—that is, a man not known for collegial and consensual decision making. But he was gradually outmaneuvered by an unlikely coalition of forces. At the grass roots, his nemesis, the Union of the Committees of Soldiers' Mothers (UCSM) had done an invisible deal with the Moscow Patriarchate. The issue was the vicious hazing commonly practiced against conscripts.

Since its formation in 1989, the UCSM has tried to stop the maltreatment of the conscripts. All young men are eligible, but more than 90 percent, through a combination of bribes and deferments, get out of military service. This leaves the least privileged members of society to be the draftees. In 1994, in the Far East, four young soldiers died and thousands were hospitalized for serious medical problems, including malnutrition and beatings. The Web page of the UCSM reported this incident in June 1996: "The statistics are terrible. In times of peace, four to five thousand soldiers die every year, without counting those participating in military actions, through cold, hunger, and absence of medicine. Also, and what is most terrible, young recruits are subject to maltreatment and torture by older soldiers and officers." The UCSM was the first organization to report the casualties in Chechnya. It attempts to secure the pension rights for families of soldiers killed in action, as well as medical treatment for veterans. And most irritating of all, from the supreme command's perspective, they will not keep quiet.

In September 2002 they made national headlines. Fifty-four young service-men fled their unit near Volgograd to protest beatings. They marched thirty-five miles to the local UCSM office. The deserters were returned to military custody, but the widespread media attention gave the military a black-eye. September 2002 was the sixtieth anniversary of the start of the street fight-ing at the Battle of Stalingrad—that is, the same Volgograd from which the soldiers had deserted. The sixtieth anniversary of the German surrender at Stalingrad—January 30, 1943—was scheduled to be celebrated with great pomp and circumstance at the enormous memorial complex at Mamaev Kurgan. And now the hosannahs were being tarnished. Ivanov glowed with rage. He told the press that the "so-called" Committees of Soldiers' Mothers stood in the way of military justice. Soldiers, he declared, should take their complaints to their superiors instead of going on "marathon treks" to search for sympathy. At his urging, the chief procurator of the Ministry of Justice made several dark references to investigating UCSM funding.

But the women were hardened to such bullying. They went public, say-ing "They want soldiers to complain to their commander. But what if he was the one who beat them?" The army was forced to dismiss the "Volgo-grad 54"'s commander and to transfer several of the young recruits to differ-ent bases.[56] At this crucial moment—the defense minister furious, the Com-mittees of Soldiers' Mothers recalcitrant, and Russian and Western media all paying attention—the patriarch delicately stepped forward and proposed a solution. He knew perfectly well that the young privates could not complain to their superiors as per Ivanov's suggestion. Right now there was no one on the base to whom the conscripts could confide their troubles. Why not in-stall a chapel with an ROC priest? He would listen to individual complaints and, if necessary, mediate with officers who would listen. He could also be trusted to keep the situation "in house" and would not take the story to *Mos-cow News* or Reuters.

There is no published record of such a meeting between the patriarch, the Supreme Command, and the minister of defense. Such deliberations were highly unlikely to be committed to paper. When the *Red Star* account of the critical January 2005 meeting between the patriarch and Ivanov was published, Igor Glazin, the same member of the Estonian Parliament who had survived the August 19–21, 1991, coup inside the Russian Parliament Building with Yeltsin, explained its implications. He stated that the Com-mittees of Soldiers' Mothers had immediately supported the idea of chapels with an Orthodox priest. They saw right away it was a line of communica-tion *outside* the rigid military chain of command. It would yield another channel—another pair of eyes—to monitor the treatment of their sons.[57]

Both the patriarch and the mothers wanted the same thing: the hazing halted. Any mother—in Kirov or Chita—could go to her local Orthodox priest and tell him about the tearstained letters she was getting from her Volodya. He would contact Moscow, who would contact the priest at Volodya's base, who would call in the young man for a talk. Whether Ivanov liked it or not, the coalition of the Committees of Soldiers' Mothers and the patriarch were determined to get a "chapel on every base." The patriarch had pulled off a bloodless coup. While signing accords and distributing ecclesiastical awards to the top of the four ministries commanding troops, he simultaneously reached out to the grass roots, to the organization Ivanov heartily despised. It took more than ten years to position this patriarchal version of the "double envelopment"; Aleksy first called for priests at every garrison back in February 1994. Now, like Hannibal at Cannae, he had his opponent surrounded. Ivanov's smile in the *Red Star* photograph looks rather forced.

The final paragraph of this crucial front-page article states that the patriarch and the minister of defense agreed that the sixtieth anniversary celebrating the homeland's victory in "the Great Patriotic War of 1941–45" would be led by both the church and the Ministry of Defense: "The patriarch, in accordance with tradition, will conduct a religious service at the St. George temple on the Poklonnaya Hill, which is dedicated to the saint and was erected in the memory of all those who gave their lives to save the homeland from the fascists in the war." *Red Star* concluded that the minister and the patriarch "expressed hopes for the further strengthening of prosperous relations and collaboration of the two people's institutions—the church and the army (*narodnye instituty-armiya i tserkov*)—for the benefit of all Russia." This restates the central theme of "Together with the Army and the Nation": the church and the army are the only two *national* organizations for the new Russia.

With "Together with the Army and the Nation," the January 2005 issue of *Red Star* printed information once considered traitorous. While Stalin was alive, the propaganda was that the dictator—who never visited the front lines—was the architect of victory in the Great Patriotic War. After Stalin's death, the party claimed that honor. Both Khrushchev (a commissar at Stalingrad) and Brezhnev (a commissar in the Caucasus) made a concerted effort to co-opt the population's memories of the 1941–45 war under the flag of the hammer and sickle.[58] The lavish monument built on Mamaev Kurgan to honor the victory at Stalingrad opened in 1967—deliberately timed to coincide with the fiftieth anniversary of the Bolshevik Revolution. For thirty years, according to Lazar Lazarev, himself a decorated veteran of the Red Army, the party conducted a campaign, "Ring Out Victorious Thunder!" hymning its leadership.[59] This marketing blitz outlasted even the Soviet Union itself. And now, without uttering either the word "Stalin" or "CPSU," the identity of the grand marshal for the victory parade was changing. Finally, the ordinary Red Army soldier, the "Ivan" so disastrously underestimated by the Wehrmacht and so callously expended by the Soviet high command, would be given his due.

After surveying the entire layout of the Victory Memorial on Poklonnaya Hill, which covers an area of 40,663 square yards, it looks as if faith and patriotism have reconciled in a uniquely Russian form of compromise. There are three separate religious buildings in the memorial: the largest is the Church of the Great Martyr and Victory Bearer St. George, which Aleksy II consecrated May 6, 1995. But in 1997 a memorial mosque, built in memory of Muslim servicemen who perished, was added. And in 1998, a memorial synagogue to honor those Jews killed in action and a Holocaust Memorial Museum were opened.[60] An Orthodox cathedral, a synagogue, a mosque—this is Russia's version of tolerance.

For those "traditional faiths," the patriarch has tried to curb Orthodox proselytism. Aleksy is perfectly aware than in some subunits of the army 50–60 percent of the soldiers and sergeants are Muslim.[61] On October 24, 2005, BBC Monitoring reported from the Russian news agency Interfax in Moscow that the Russian Orthodox Church opposed any missionary activities in the armed forces. The deputy head of the external church relations department of the Moscow Patriarchate, Archpriest Vsevolod Chaplin, told Interfax: "All self-respecting countries have banned missionary activities in the army. Christian priests, mullahs, rabbis, and pastors should only go to the army to visit followers of their faith, proceeding from the wish of believers." However, what prompted this remark was the publishing and distribution to Russian servicemen of a "Bible in camouflage." According to Chaplin, "if you look underneath the cover, you will see not just the Bible itself, but also Protestant preaching texts." The organization distributing this dodgy text was the "Union of Russian Christian Servicemen," a group of Protestants Chaplin saw as hiding behind the name "Christian"—in short, yet another sneak attack by Western Christianity.

The war in Chechnya goes on, and Aleksy is keen to discourage the army and the civilian population from seeing it as a religious war. This can be judged by the kid-gloves manner with which he has treated the case of Yevgeny Rodionov, a nineteen-year-old conscript sent to Chechnya in 1996. Private Rodionov and three other soldiers were seized while manning a checkpoint. They were tortured and imprisoned in a cellar for one hundred days. Rodionov was offered his freedom if he would remove his baptismal cross and renounce his faith. When he refused, he was beheaded—his captors made a gruesome video of his murder. His mother paid a ransom for his corpse during a lull in the fighting, and she brought it back to Kurilovo, his hometown, northeast of Moscow. She claimed that when she exhumed his body, the cross was there among his bones, glinting in the flashlight, stained with his blood. As his story spread, pilgrims came to visit his grave, located on a hillside beside the church. An icon was painted of him, standing full length in his private's uniform. Pamphlets, songs, and poems, even Web sites, began to clamor for his canonization.[62] Aleksy has resisted such a step, but he blessed the popular accounts of his life published in the fifth edition of a booklet entitled *The New Martyr for Christ: The Soldier Yevgeny* (*Novy muchenik za Khrista voin Yevgeny*).[63] The patriarch is trying to strike a compromise: he does not want either to support a cult that could balloon into anti-Muslim rage, or to ignore a parable that blends devotion to Orthodoxy with the performance of a soldier's duty.

Here again Aleksy proves himself master of the art of public spectacle. In 1999 the church established yet another new award, Glory to Russia! (*Slava Rossii!*), for "conspicuous achievements in the field of culture, science, sport and economics." But its target audience, like the award of St. Prince Daniel, was the Russian army. By March 2007 ROC bishops gave it not only to famous artists but to Cosmonaut Nikolay Romanenko (who had twice been awarded "Hero of the Soviet Union") and to the "directors of major military, space, aviation, and industrial corporations." The roll call listed the elite of the Russian military-industrial complex. But special excitement was occasioned by the awarding of *Slava Rossii!* posthumously, to "soldier-martyr" Yevgeny Rodionov, who "refused to reject Christ or to take off his Orthodox cross while a prisoner of the Chechen militants." In accepting the award, Rodionov's mother, Lyubov Vasilievna, thanked those who "in spite of everything continue to serve the Motherland. I ask all present not to forget our soldiers, who carry this heavy burden in areas of military conflict."[64] Thus both the supreme command and the hierarchy of the ROC characterize the enemy as "Chechen militants" or terrorists rather than as Muslims.[65] And the Glory to Russia! award can be given to both the elite who run ministries and a nineteen-year-old cook who was beheaded. This absolute equality of candidates will probably make *Slava Rossii!* as desirable as once was "Hero of the Soviet Union." Rodionov is the newest model of the ideal Orthodox warrior personified by Prince Daniel and Grand Prince Dmitry Donskoy. His eventual canonization will happen as soon as the Chechnya situation is resolved.[66]

Within the military itself, Orthodoxy is well on its way to winning the culture war, even if it has not prevailed in every skirmish. The brutal hazing has not stopped, but changing an organization like the Russian army will take time. The September–October 2006 issue of *Russian Life* gives the startling statistic that 17 soldiers died and another 3,500 suffered injuries in hazing crimes between January and July of that year.[67] It took Aleksy ten years to get the agreement that chapels would be available on every garrison. The priest, backed by an organization the military desperately wants on their side, will have to change the facts on the ground. The Russian military is so aware of its negative image among young people that it is opening its own television channel to endorse itself. A youth organization, Nasha Strana (Our Country), has proposed launching a reality TV show on Channel One to promote army service. *Army Week* would follow thirty uniformed volunteers through the same training course for conscripts.[68] The ROC may well propose adding a priest to the cast, someone as affable and approachable as the Padre in the American movie and subsequent television series *MASH*.

But as the chapel saga plays out, Aleksy has already won over the minister of defense, the same Sergey Ivanov. An extraordinary Russian television program was broadcast on Channel One TV (like all media, controlled by the Russian state) on August 19, 2005. It covered the Feast of the Transfiguration as celebrated at Valaam, located in Lake Ladoga in the Far North. Westerners know it as part of the "Golden Ring of Russia" cruise ship tours that run through St. Petersburg and Moscow.[69] The presenter, Dmitry Vitov, opened with this voice-over:

> Today is an Orthodox festival, the Transfiguration.... The main ceremonies, with Patriarch Aleksy II taking part, took place at Valaam, where the upper church of the Valaam Monastery of the Holy Transfiguration of the Saviour, the symbol of the island, was reopened after 15 years of restoration.... After its restoration in time for the Transfiguration [Feast], the cathedral stands renewed and was sanctified today by Patriarch Aleksy II in the presence of the defense minister ...
>
> This prayer is seen by both monks and the military as a sign of conciliation and cleansing [*primirenie* and *ochishchenie*]. In recent years the army and church have been successfully working together. More than 1000 priests serve at various army units.
>
> There is a unique unit at Valaam. By agreement with the Ministry of Defense, since 1995 [i.e., after the signing of the first accord] the monastery has been sending its 18-year old novices here, to the other end of the island, where there is a unique and wholly Orthodox military subunit, the 66th Separate Radar Company. It is the only one of its type in the country. It has just 18 servicemen, comprising five officers and 13 novices from the monastery on conscript service.... Commanders

decided recently to build a chapel by the entrance to the barrack block, in honor of St. George the Triumphant, the patron saint of all warriors. The minister of defense invited the patriarch himself to lay the foundation stone. After prayers, Sergey Ivanov and Aleksy II inspected the company.

"Conditions of service here," said the minister of defense, "have been designed, firstly, not to detract from the purpose of this military unit. And, secondly, to combine it with spiritual needs. I think this is entirely proper and natural. And it brings the main result, in that all is in good order with both service and discipline and law and order. Splendid."

Correspondent Vitov concluded: "The Patriarch congratulated the soldiers on the Feast of the Transfiguration, blessed the officers' wives and children, and wished for clear skies to always be, like today, over the company as it defends our airspace." Without allowing for conscientious objectors, the army and the church have solved how a young man may simultaneously fulfill his duty as conscript and novice.

Sergey Ivanov seems to have undergone somewhat of a transfiguration himself. His compliment of "splendid" indicates a change of heart. He will someday accept from the patriarch's hand his own "St. Prince Daniel of Moscow" award for "services to the ROC and the Fatherland." In February 2007 Putin promoted him to first deputy prime minister. Though he gave up being minister of defense, he remains responsible for Russia's powerful military-industrial complex. Indeed, in 2007 he was a leading candidate to replace Putin as president in 2008. Ivanov now ostentatiously crosses himself in public.

For Aleksy, who was taken to Valaam as a child and is on record as having been impressed with its pristine beauty, this must have been a very special moment indeed. Perhaps he thought back to February 23, 1989, when on the occasion of his sixtieth birthday, while he was metropolitan of Leningrad and Novgorod, he had been treated to a lavish party at which Archpriest Igor Mazur, dean of the Holy Trinity Cathedral, had delivered a public encomium for his work on a project that no one outside the ROC knew anything about:

We also know well of your work for the future of the holy Valaam islands, which has recently won the approval of His Holiness the Patriarch and the Holy Synod. We prayerfully wish for your efforts to be crowned with success as soon as possible. May church singing ring out again on the beautiful Island of Valaam and the place become once again one of the beacons of Universal Orthodoxy.[70]

All this had come to pass. The project that he sold to Pimen and his syco-phants was now crowned with such success that the minister of defense blessed the effort.

The script for Channel One's coverage echoes patriarchal themes. The presenter's voice-over spoke of Aleksy's sanctification of the cathedral as seen "by both monks and the military as a sign of conciliation and cleansing." Aleksy had used cognates of just those two words in his August 30, 1991, address to all pastors and "faithful children" of the ROC, pledging that the church would get down to its "cleansing" guided by a "conciliatory mind." The repetition of *primirenie* and *ochishchenie* here indicates how the ROC has made its values resonate within the Russian military, even in shaping the narrative for the state-run media.

In April 2006 the Holy Synod openly called for the restoration of chaplains in the Russian army. The official statement noted Russia's glorious tradition of Orthodox chaplains, which the "Godless time" had interrupted. It contin-ued that in the West the institute of chaplains exists and is now being imple-mented in Baltic countries and Armenia, while Ukraine and Georgia have announced their willingness to introduce them. The Holy Synod concluded:

> At the same time the army units should not become a field for prosely-tism. Working in the army should be only those religious organizations whose members service it. We believe that active work of clergymen in the armed forces would help reduce cases of suicide and humiliation of dignity as well as other actions that violate the law. The Holy Synod of the Russian Orthodox Church calls upon the state, society and all tradi-tional religions of Russia to combine their efforts for the restoration of the institute of chaplains.[71]

While heading off proselytism by Western Christian sects, the statement also hints that the patriarch has done a quiet deal with Islam. Indeed, Rus-sian officers who wish to remain anonymous have stated that the patriarch has urged commanders on remote bases to allow Muslims to pray five times a day. However, the "call to prayer" from the *muezzin* would be silent. Orthodox priests have been told to leave Muslim soldiers—and Muslim prisoners—strictly alone. The hope is that in reciprocity, should Russian Orthodox soldiers be taken prisoner by Muslim fighters in Chechnya, there will be no other forced conversions or martyrdoms, as was the choice fac-ing Yevgeny Rodionov.

All the threads of the faith and patriotism quilt came together on the 625th anniversary of victory at Kulikovo. A lavish ceremony was held at the battle-field. (The battle took place September 8, 1380 o.s.; in 2005, the new style date is September 21.) The patriarch laid flowers at the monument to Dmitry Donskoy, then blessed the new bell tower of the Church of the Mother of God. Next he delivered the keynote address. His message harked back to the theme of Russian unity: "Separate forces from principalities northeast of Rus came to the Battlefield of Kulikovo, but they left a united Russian people [*yediny russky narod*]."[72] Aleksy declared passionately that the triumph was given to the Russian people because their wise grand prince, St. Dmitry Donskoy, sought the counsel of Sergius of Radonezh, who prayed to the Theotokos, and then urged the grand prince to go against the Horde. Aleksy warmed to the image of the single combat between the monk Peresvet, who put a helmet over his tonsure, and the Horde's own knight, Chelubey. Aleksy hymned this memory as "forever entered into [the] national memory as an example of bravery, courage, and selfless devotion to the Fatherland [*Otchizna*]." The once derelict churches dedicated to the two monks had been renovated posthaste following the defeat of the August 1991 coup. The patriarch recalled that the Russian army had carried banners depicting the Theotokos into battle. Indeed, the victory occurred on the very day in the Orthodox calendar that celebrates the Nativity of the Mother-of-God, one of the twelve great feasts of the year, and one of the five celebrating Mary. Thus the ecclesiastical and the secular calendars meshed: the Theotokos was born on the very day she would spread her protecting veil to help the Russians defeat the savage Mamay. (Aleksy made no reference to it, but the Border Guards had earlier moved "their" day to one of the great feasts in the ROC calendar celebrating the Theotokos, the Presentation of the Virgin, back in 1995.)

In Aleksy's speech, the entire ROC plan to re-create Russia in its own image circled back to Sergiev Posad. It was there that the "co-celebration" of the Feast of the Transfiguration was jointly celebrated by Patriarch Pimen and the patriarch of Constantinople, Demetrios, in August 1987. It was there that in 1988 the decision was made to create the Order of St. Prince Daniel of Moscow and to restore the Orthodox framework to Donskoy's victory at Kulikovo, which had saved Moscow.

Aleksy had earlier demonstrated a masterful manipulation of the Kulikovo story within days of the defeat of the August 19–21, 1991, coup. Back in 1380, Donskoy led a triumphant procession into the Kremlin's Cathedral of Archangel Michael to give thanks to God; he then marched to the Cathedral of the Assumption to repeat the whole display. The church decreed that the Saturday on or before October 26 (his name day according to the Orthodox calendar) was to be observed as a memorial day "as long as Russia exists."[73] Kulikovo was fought to forge a nation; the coup was defeated on August 21, 1991, to revive one. The story was right for the "new" Russia because it was old. Aleksy's Requiem liturgy in the Kremlin Cathedral of the Assumption immediately after the defeat of the coup recalled Donskoy's celebratory liturgy after the defeat of Khan Mamay. The parallel with the events of 1380 gave the patriarch's actions legitimacy.

On September 21, 2005, the color guard at the battlefield was from Tula. Tula itself was the site of an important engagement in the defense of Moscow. In the fall of 1941 Colonel General Heinz Guderian's 2nd Panzer Army raced toward the city. As he approached Tula, Guderian felt it would fall as had every other of his objectives. He was ordered to take it on October 10, 1941. He could not. He was stopped by Russians of the 4th Armored Brigade of Colonel Katukov using the famous T-34 tank, acknowledged as the best tank of the war. Katukov's was, at that stage of the battle for Moscow, the only independent tank force the Red Army had left to hold up Guderian's advance. Had Tula fallen, it is quite likely that Moscow itself would have fallen to the Wehrmacht by the end of October, with consequences that are simply incalculable for world history. The Wehrmacht would pay a heavy penalty for Guderian's failure to capture Tula. The Red Army launched its successful counterattack before Moscow on December 5, just two days before the Japanese attack on Pearl Harbor would lead Hitler to declare war on the United States, and on December 10, the United States to declare war on Germany. But America had no troops in the field yet, and the magnificent stand by the brigade of Colonel Katukov bought Marshall Zhukov time to organize a brilliant counteroffensive.[74] The Russians December 1941 offensive drove the Germans back forty miles at the approaches to Moscow, saving the city and possibly the war.

As the Tula color guard passed beneath the dais from which Aleksy spoke, it carried icons of the "Virgin of the Don." Grand Prince Dmitry Donskoy's troops had carried the original onto the field of Kulikovo. Though the original icon was lost, it had been copied many times. Indeed, one copy hung in the Monastery "Our Lady of the Don," the same monastery in which Aleksy had been reburying relics of Patriarch Tikhon on August 18, 1991, the day before the coup attempt. It was satisfying indeed to see her icon again on the field of Kulikovo, restating the constant theme of his patriarchate: "as long as Russia exists," faith and patriotism are united under the Orthodox banner.

Twenty Years After: From Party to Patriarch

The past is not dead; it is not even past.
—*William Faulkner*

THE USSR'S FATAL MISTAKE was to deny Russian patriotism and subsume it under the rubric of Soviet internationalism. The end result was that the once-despised and supine Russian Orthodox Church became the reliquary of pride in being Russian. Russians have always been ready to die for their country; they proved that again August 19–21, 1991. When the spell of Soviet hegemony broke that drizzling morning of August 21, the crowd did not hoist signs saying *Svoboda!* (Freedom!) or *Demokratiya!* (Democracy!) The multitude who streamed to the Lubyanka to topple Dzerzhinsky's statue did not replace it with a Statue of Liberty. The revival of Russian Orthodoxy had been a trend; it reached critical mass when the crowd erected an Orthodox cross on the empty pedestal and painted "by this sign, conquer" on the granite plinth. Though the police immediately removed the cross, the message left behind, highly charged and highly symbolic, has resonated throughout the Russian Federation ever since.

Guiding and shaping the resurgence of Russian Orthodoxy has been the ambiguous figure of Aleksy II, patriarch of Moscow and all the Russias. In 1986, as Aleksey Ridiger, chancellor of Moscow, he wrote to Mikhail Gorbachev, president of the USSR and chairman of the CPSU, urging that the church assist in spiritually reviving the motherland. That temerity got him removed from Moscow and transferred to Leningrad. Sixteen years later, Gorbachev, the Soviet Union, and the party were gone. On June 11, 2004, in the Yekaterinisky Hall of the Kremlin Palace, Vladimir Putin, in the presence of the Holy Synod and the cream of Russian bureaucracy, awarded him the Order for Services to the Fatherland, 1st degree. The decree (*ukaz*) declared it was given for his "outstanding contribution to the strengthening of peace and accord among nations [and] for the revival of [the] historical and cultural heritage of Russia." Putin repeated the "revival" concept when he singled out Aleksy's work for "the revival of spirituality and the strengthening of Russia."

In his acceptance speech, Aleksy modestly declared that the award did not belong to him alone. No, "the spiritual revival of the Fatherland" must be credited to the entire church. Considering that it was just such a suggestion that got him fired back in 1986, Aleksy might be forgiven had he invited Gorbachev to be his guest at the ceremony. But the patriarch was far too smart. Instead, he emphasized that

> during the one thousand years of its history the Russian Orthodox Church has always stayed with its people and actively participated both in the spiritual care for them and in the building up of the state. Today we take part in the building up of the Russian state by nonpolitical methods. We educate our believers in the spirit of respect to the authorities, love of the Motherland, and aspiration to peace and accord among people of different nationalities and religions.[1]

This statement adroitly touches upon a theme key to the church's resurgence: for a thousand years, the faith, the state, and the people have been one. The "thousand years" also subtly reminds the listener that the consequences of the 1988 millennial anniversary of Kreshchenie Rusi had momentous consequences for all three.[2] What then is the model of church-state relations the ROC envisions for the next millennium?

Aleksy has consistently said he does not want Orthodoxy established as the state faith, because "sooner or later the church would become a department of the State."[3] Instead, the church will partner with the state but stay within its spiritual sphere.[4] The ROC explained its mission in a long document, *Bases of the Social Concept of the Russian Orthodox Church*, issued in 2000. It believes it can cooperate on:

> a) peacemaking on international, inter-ethnic and civic levels and promoting mutual understanding and co-operation among people, nations and states;
> b) concern for the preservation of morality in society;
> c) spiritual, cultural, moral and patriotic education and formation;
> d) charity and the development of joint social programmes;
> e) preservation, restoration and development of the historical and cultural heritage, including concern for the preservation of historical and cultural monuments;

f) dialogue with governmental bodies of all branches and levels on issues important for the Church and society, including the development of appropriate laws, by-laws, instructions and decisions;

g) care of the military and law enforcement workers and their spiritual and moral education;

h) efforts to prevent crime and care of prisoners;

i) science and research;

j) healthcare;

k) culture and arts;

l) work of ecclesiastical and secular mass media;

m) preservation of the environment;

n) economic activity for the benefit of the Church, state and society;

o) support for the institution of the family, for motherhood and childhood;

p) opposition to the work of pseudo-religious structures presenting a threat to the individual and society.[5]

This expands exponentially the one activity the ROC was legally permitted prior to 1990: celebrating the liturgy in an approved "prayer-building."[6] Westerners may see some discordance between Aleksy's disclaimer that the church intends to use only "non-political methods" to build up the Russian state, when point f on the agenda speaks of "dialogue with governmental bodies ... including the development of appropriate laws, bylaws, instructions, and decisions." If carried out to their fullest extent, the ROC schema would displace the CPSU as playing the "leading role" in society.

It would do so, however, without being committed to paper or implemented by statute. Europe, with its state-established faiths—such as Lutheranism in Sweden, Norway, and Denmark, Catholicism in Italy, and Anglicanism in Great Britain—has the largest proportion of invincibly secular citizens of any continent on the planet. In Germany, the state collects church taxes; the result is empty churches. In Sweden, instruction in the Lutheran faith is part of the state curriculum. The result is empty churches. Aleksy became president of the European Council of Churches back in 1987; he saw their vacant pews. In contrast, the United States, Israel, and India, all of whose constitutions proclaim a secular state, are home to the most passionately religious citizenry on earth.

The Russian model then is not the "symphony of power" hymned by the Byzantine Empire. The original Byzantine Empire saw the state as protecting the church. This fatally compromised Jesus' admonition to "Render therefore unto Caesar the things which are Caesar's; and unto God the things that are God's" (Matthew 22:21; see also Mark 12:17 and Luke 20:25 for virtually identical formulations). By linking the things of Caesar with the things of God, the Byzantine tradition led to the fusion of state and church. But Jesus himself had disdained this alliance, declaring to Pilate at his trial, "My kingdom is not of this world." Translated to Russia, the tsar—even the name derives from Caesar—focused devotion upon himself as the earthly representation of the divine. No Innocent III sitting in the Vatican had greater self-love. The tsars progressively made the church servile to their whims.

By avoiding the pitfall of state establishment, the ROC has achieved a cultural dominance akin to Western Christianity's in the United States.[7] The difference is that there is no corresponding level of church attendance inside the Russian Federation. Whereas some 82 percent of all Russian respondents call themselves Orthodox, only 42 percent of Russians call themselves "believers." Indeed, 50 percent of nonbelievers call themselves Orthodox, as do 42 percent of atheists![8] In short, claiming to be "Orthodox" reasserts the speaker's pride in being Russian—much as Jews in the United States can say sincerely, "I am a proud Jew," though they might not attend synagogue.

Such successes result from Aleksy's mastery of the art of adaptation. He has switched the ROC's defensive stance to the more complex structure of an offensive pattern. The ROC counteroffensive, however, is based on "soft" rather than "hard" power, to borrow the perceptive terms of Joseph Nye of Harvard. To put the change in military terms, once the church survived because its tiny band of true believers was aided by the hierarchy's skill in camouflage. Volunteers marshaled to save derelict Orthodox churches under VOOPIK's banner of "saving the country's history." Urbane prelates ran a successful "false flag" operation in the World Council and European Council of Churches, enthusiastically lip-synching the KGB's peace campaign to justify the church's existence. Since the failure of the coup, the church has altered its tactics. Now initiative, tact, and diplomacy must carry the day.

An illustrative example of the ROC's skill at retaining the upper hand is its handling of Russia's remaining militant atheists. On December 25, 2004, the thirteenth anniversary of the dissolution of the USSR, the Atheist Society of Moscow held a conference on "The Protection of Secular Rights and the Rights of Conscience." The Moscow Academy of Agricultural Sciences supplied the venue. The Atheists hoped for 150 participants; 40 showed up. The plucky attendees adopted a "Declaration of Freedom of Choice" pleading that along with religious freedom, there should be government support for atheists. They protested the dramatic deterioration of secular principles and the abuse of power by radical Orthodox clergy. Their closing resolution warned: "Beware religion! You are destroying our country's reputation."[9] Then they packed their bags. Cannily, the ROC ignored the conference. It would deal with the Atheist Society in its own way.

Three months after having allowed them to meet within the halls of the Moscow Academy of Agricultural Sciences, on March 9, 2005, the chairman of the Parliamentary Committee for Agricultural Affairs accepted the Order of St. Prince Daniel, 2nd degree, from the hands of the patriarch himself. This swift action testifies to the church's conviction that however tiny the bridgehead of "scientific atheism" inside the state apparatus, it must be immediately eliminated. Thus, under the leadership of a savvy patriarch, by incremental, even imperceptible steps, the ROC's plan to recreate Russia in its own image has acquired its own momentum. In Moscow, hub of the state, the vogue for Orthodoxy has swept virtually the entire government apparatus, some protesting, some ecstatic, to a new dawn whose inevitability they have all come to recognize.

That this aurora has been largely free of casualties came as a huge surprise to Russians. Two years after the 1987 "Co-celebration" of the Feast of the Transfiguration in the Trinity Cathedral at Sergiev Posad, the abbot of its Theological Academy was asked, "What is going to happen to the country now?" He responded, with a smile, "Civil war.... It began with civil war and it will end with civil war: they lived by the sword and they will perish by the sword."[10] The allusion to both the Gospels and the concluding lines from the movie *Alexander Nevsky* summarized the pervasive feeling that the USSR's death certificate would be signed in a bloodbath. In a country where political change has traditionally been marked by thousands of corpses, the post-1991 absence of large-scale violence is an enormous achievement. The patriarch's trinity of ideas—conciliation, cleansing, and togetherness—have helped ensure that, in place of bodies, the casualties of Russia's culture war are symbols.

On the world's stage, the most obvious substitutions are the flag, the anthem, and public holidays. The "hammer and sickle" was pulled down over the Russian parliament immediately, and the tricolor stripes of independent, sovereign Russia—white, blue, and red—run up the flagpole. Peter the Great created this flag; he admired the Dutch one of red, white, and blue, from the top. He moved the red stripe to the bottom, ending up with red, blue, and white going upward. Next began the search for a new national anthem. First the Duma went back to the music by the nineteenth-century composer Mikhail Glinka, whose opera *A Life for the Tsar*, with lyrics by Alexander Serov, contributed the tsarist national anthem. But while the *music* to the tsarist anthem was used, the words were not. Glinka's "God save the Tsar!" would not do, so the first Russian post-1991 anthem had no words at all. On December 31, 2000, the Russian Parliament changed the music. Out went Glinka; back came the music from the old Soviet anthem. It needed new words because in Soviet times they praised Joseph Stalin. During the "de-Stalinization" of the country, the lyrics fell into disuse. Next, the Parliament commissioned Sergey Mikhalkov, the same man who coauthored the Stalin-era words, to write new ones. Mikhalkov had grown so rich that "as rich as Mikhalkov" became a byword for Midas-like wealth. At eighty-seven years old, he was still able to trim his talent to the prevailing wind. The new anthem begins praising "Russia, our holy country!" It goes on to proclaim that Russia is "protected by God."[11] There is, however, no tsar.

To reinforce the message of the new anthem, Russia needed a new holiday. November 7, the former "Day of the October Revolution," had once been the big holiday on the Soviet calendar. That merited military parades, the closure of business, and the granting of the day off to employees. Now it was obsolete. Its place on the secular calendar was simply renamed the "Day of Accord and Reconciliation." The parade is gone, but the day off allows the remaining Communists to march in cities to support their cause, and the Russian Orthodox to attend a beautiful liturgy emphasizing forgiveness in the remembrance of things past. The name of the holiday itself subliminally recalls the patriarch's prayer-petition to the Theotokos, for her help to reconcile (*primirit*) Russians to one another, to the Truth, and to God.

Then the government instituted yet another brand new holiday, the "Day of People's Unity," to occupy a spot on the calendar close to the former November 7. (The name links to the patriarch's idea of "togetherness.") Russians celebrated it for the first time November 4, 2005. It commemorates the popular uprising that ejected the Polish and Lithuanian occupying force from Moscow in November 1612. This ended the Time of Troubles, when the Muscovite state deteriorated into complete anarchy. By 1611 it looked as if a partition of Muscovy between the Lutheran Swedes to the North and the Catholic Poles to the West loomed. With the existence of the state and the faith hanging in the balance, a butcher in Nizhni Novgorod named Kuzma Minin formed a people's army. He enlisted Prince Dmitry Pozharsky to head it. Joined with a Cossack force, they advanced on the capital. After investing the city for three months, in October 1612 they attacked, carrying banners of saints and the Theotokos. The Poles surrendered. It was the last time the Muscovite state's existence was threatened by the Latin West.

The message of Minin and Pozharsky still resonates in the immediate present. The Russian people, united under the princes and led by the banners of Orthodoxy, needed no tsar to throw out the foreign invaders and restore stability. The situation today substitutes the oligarchs and elites for the princes; people and banner stay the same. (This spin quietly downplays the denouement to the Minin-Pozharsky victory—a *zemsky sobor* that picked young Mikhail Romanov to be tsar.) National Unity Day is an official holiday, when shops, government offices, and embassies are closed.[12] In 2007 the holiday will see the release of a lavishly budgeted film, *1612*.[13] While being advertised as a "patriotic" epic, it is a safe bet that the monks' heroic defense of the Trinity–St. Sergius Monastery in 1610 will figure prominently in the plot. The 1973 argument detailed in chapter 3 between the party hack Shamaro and the historian Semanov over the meaning of this episode has been decisively settled in the ROC's favor. It is also a safe bet that the ROC has graciously allowed the walls of the monastery used for filming.

While flag, anthem, and holidays are overt, much of the real revolution has taken place behind the scenes, an almost perfect parallel to Constantine's slow and careful substitution of the symbols of Christianity for those of pagan Rome. At the moment of Constantine's victory over Maxentius at the Battle of the Milvian Bridge, most of the Roman Senate, the bureaucracy, and the aristocracy were still erecting statues to emperors and pagan gods. Constantine moved carefully on his path to Christianizing the empire, so much so that Edward Gibbon has said, "the nicest accuracy is required in tracing the slow and almost imperceptible gradations by which the monarch declared himself the protector, and at length the proselyte, of the church."[14] In the Russian context, while it is obvious that the red star no longer glows atop government buildings, it is in the corridors of power, invisible to outside eyes, that the substitution of Orthodox for Soviet signs proceeds apace.

A single occasion exemplifies the change. On Monday, April 24, 2006, the day after Easter, the Foreign Ministry invited the patriarch to brunch. In addition to the standard fare of tea, vodka, and platters of fruit, the menu featured a *paskha*, a domed cheesecake made of sweetened pot cheese molded, drained, and then chilled; and *kulich*, a rich, eggy, yeasty bread baked in a high cylindrical mold. Both are pregnant with symbolic meaning: the shape of the *paskha* signifies the empty tomb; the leaven of the tall *kulich* literalizes that Christ has risen. Candied fruits on top of the iced *kulich* spelled out *X.B.*—the initials for *Khristos voskres!* (Christ is Risen!). In Savile row suits and silk ties, the best and the brightest of Russia's civil service mingled with ROC hierarchs, spreading slabs of the *paskha* onto thick slices of the *kulich*. Russia's diplomats responded to *Khristos voskres!* with the traditional answer, *Voistinu voskres!* (He is risen indeed). It was another quiet triumph for Orthodoxy's soft power.

The brunch simply reified a linkup which the patriarch had been working toward for several years. The ROC and the Foreign Ministry signed their accord in 2003. On March 6 of that year, the patriarch paid them a visit. There, a committee entitled "The Working Group for Cooperation between the ROC and the Foreign Ministry" was formed. Only two months later, May 8, 2003, the grand hall of the Moscow Patriarchate's Department for External Church Relations hosted a lavish ceremony to mark the 200th anniversary of the Russian Foreign Ministry. Hierarchs presented the Order of St. Prince Daniel, 3rd degree, to the consulate service director, the Middle East Department director, the foreign policy planning department director, the humanitarian cooperation and human rights department director, and the deputy financial director. Each gentleman was honored to "acknowledge their work for the benefit of the Russian Orthodox Church and the Foreign Ministry." The patriarch himself awarded the deputy foreign ministers their own Order of the Holy Prince Daniel of Moscow, 2nd degree. The Foreign Ministry contains Russia's most astute and westernized executives.[15] As a man who had spent years heading the European Council of Churches, Aleksy was at home among them.

But where, one may ask, is the accord signed between the ROC and the FSB, Russia's successor to the KGB? There is certain to be one. Because the FSB is the secret police, it has kept the agreement secret. There is, of course, no "accord" between the ROC and the moribund CPSU, because its premise was "scientific atheism." Atheism was the god that failed, and for its remnant there can be no compromise. The KGB, however, had no other ideology than its commitment to be the "sword and shield" of the state. For the KGB, patriarchal "conciliation and cleansing" paved the way to the friendliest of accommodations. Indeed, it is noteworthy that at the time of this writing, the Russian Federation seems governed almost entirely by former KGB officials.[16] What is different is that these men no longer attend party meetings; they have joined one of the ROC's Coordinating Committees.

This has meant in practical terms that the patriarch has kept a "hands-off" attitude toward the decisions of the current president of the Russian Federation, Vladimir Vladimirovich Putin, himself a KGB veteran. The one time Aleksy went on record against a Putin decree was to speak (very diplomatically) against the government plan to monetize pensions. Putin went back to the drawing board. The patriarch received fulsome and sincere thanks from pensioners all over Russia—believers and nonbelievers as well. Aleksy did not damage his relationship with Putin because he did not challenge state authority; he merely suggested that the state had not fully realized what hardship this change would bring to its elderly and infirm citizens.

The patriarch has kept a pristine silence about the "Dissenters Marches" sponsored by Garry Kasparov and Mikhail Kasyanov's "Other Russia" party (January–March 2007). Putin ordered in the OMON (Otryad Militsii Oso-bogo Naznacheniya, the Special Forces Police Detachment) troops armed with shields and clubs. Police helicopters whirled overhead.[17] Aleksy's still-ness here contrasts the principled stand he took in January 1991 against the Alpha Unit's storming of the Lithuanian television station, which led to more than twenty dead. However, there is to date no evidence that the ROC has been cheering the Putin response from the sidelines.[18] Aleksy has consis-tently maintained that he wants a "render unto Caesar" relationship with the state. He has forbidden priests to seek public office in the Duma. And Aleksy and Putin seem on the best of terms—they send each other Christmas and Easter greetings. It is a logical inference that they have agreed that the church will stay out of this one. The ROC had a seventy-year track record of saying nothing about Soviet crushing of dissent when it was ROC believers who were getting crushed. It is unlikely that Aleksy feels the need to defend the part-Jewish, part-Armenian Mr. Kasparov. Indeed, what is most surprising about the harsh Putin response is how out of proportion it was to the tiny number of people marching.

As for the future, the crisis would come if a priest in the mold of a Father Gapon should lead such a march. Father Gapon served as a double agent for the Okhrana, but he came to identify with the cause of the workers he was supposed to pacify. The metropolitan of St. Petersburg ordered him not to lead the march on the Winter Palace back in 1905. He did anyway. If there is a Father Gapon in Russia's future, then we will find out how far the ROC is prepared to go to freeze its privileges. The Russian Federation is not a country of laws, though it has a constitution. It is a country of men, and it is the per-sonal relationships that so far have been the "deciders" in the years since the defeat of the coup August 19–21, 1991.

As of today, having won the war of symbols, Orthodoxy remains suspicious of the West, though it has adopted Western-style fundraising and capitalism. Early in the Yeltsin era, the ROC earned the right to export tax-free millions of barrels of Russian crude oil each year.[19] It is a fair inference that this privi-lege continues—just as the Vneshtorgbank account Aleksy opened in 1983 to renovate the Danilov Monastery has not been closed. Aleksy's relationship with the oligarchs has bloomed as well. Much as American billionaires con-tribute to favorite universities or medical research, Russia's super-rich publicly donate to ROC causes. Indeed, the bells of the Danilov Monastery are to be returned from Harvard—a duplicate set are being cast. The entire cost was funded by a private donor.

But while the ROC has adopted capitalism, the faith that emerged from the ashes of "scientific atheism's" funeral pyre was neither purified by rational analysis of its doctrines and theology nor shorn of its myths. It continues to sees itself as the one true Church of the Apostolic Succession as traced from the Gospel of John's account of the calling of Andrew as the first disciple and the first to acknowledge Jesus as the Christ through to the Chronicle of Nestor's story of the saint's putative visits to the future Kiev and Novgorod in the first century. In 1988, the ROC brought out its own authoritative history of the millennium, *Kreschchenie Rusi*, written by Archpriest Lev Lebedev, which forthrightly rejected any doubts on the "historicity" of those events.

Pope Benedict XVI restated Catholicism's claim to be the Church of the Apostolic Succession in a document released to the world July 10, 2007. The document intended to "clarify" disagreement among Catholics about the legacy of the Second Vatican Council, 1962–65. Its end result infuriated Protestants in more than a hundred countries. Patriarch Aleksy II reassured his flock that they are the Church of the Apostolic Succession without angering anyone. He did it through staging another medieval relic pilgrimage.

In June 2006 he organized the return of the hand of John the Baptist to Russia. Orthodox believe it was the very hand that baptized Jesus on that day, circa A.D. 30 in Bethany. Orthodoxy accords John the Baptist, whom it terms the Forerunner (Predtecha), immense importance. His figure, along with Mary the God-bearer and Christ as Pantocrator, forms the *deesis*, an icon of which appears above the "royal doors" on the iconostasis in every Orthodox church. John Predtecha is simultaneously the last of the prophets who prophesied the coming of the Messiah, and the beginning of the era of salvation, because he shows humanity how to recognize Jesus as the Word. He is a witness offering testimony that the "light" of the Scriptures is fulfilled in Christ, the Incarnate Word of God. When John Predtecha baptized Jesus, the Holy Spirit, in the form of a dove, descended on him (cf. John 1:32–34). Thus, the Holy Spirit—the third part of the Trinity—was made manifest in man's affairs. Now, for the first time in history, all three Persons of the Trinity were simultaneously present physically. Jesus was born in Bethlehem, but Christianity itself was born that day in Bethany. Immediately thereafter, Jesus began his ministry by calling to Andrew and an unnamed disciple who followed him, *podite i uvidite* (Come and see). A short time later, Andrew went to his brother Simon Peter and declared "We have found the Messiah." All of this flowed from John's baptism of Jesus that day in Bethany.

The Orthodox believe St. Luke went to the village where John the Baptist was buried. There, he took away John's right hand. That hand was given to the Russian imperial family in St. Petersburg to protect it from Napoleon's advancing armies. When the Russian revolution broke out, it was whisked away to Central Europe. Eighty-nine years later, on June 7, 2006, Patriarch Aleksy II welcomed the hand back at a ceremony conducted at Christ the Savior Cathedral.[20] A beautiful gold reliquary housed it. Aleksy called on all Russian Orthodox to pray before it. Aleksy's selection of the Cathedral of Christ the Savior to begin the hand's translation was no accident. The cathedral has always been linked to Russians' defense of their country. Because the hand itself was originally donated to protect the imperial family during the Napoleonic invasion, and Alexander I had decreed the building of the cathedral to signify Russia's gratitude for its victory in that war, Aleksy's liturgy on June 7, 2006, again affirmed the bond between Russian Orthodoxy and Russian patriotism.

On June 17, 2006, the hand began its translation pilgrimage through Russia, Belarus, and Ukraine. Believers who had seen the hand of John the Baptist only on the *deesis* of their church's iconostasis could now go pray before the hand itself, a neat collapsing of liturgical and temporal time, and a "making present" again of an incident known only in the *New Testament*. In July it returned to Montenegro—now a sovereign state that had severed its ties with Serbia.

The pilgrimage expenses of the hand's translation were financed by a religious foundation chaired by Vladimir Yakunin, head of Russia's state railway network. Russian Railways is a state-owned monopoly that controls both cargo and passenger rail traffic. It will set up soon a new subsidiary to inherit the state-owned company's stock, while still owning the railroad infrastructure—the rail beds. It plans to get some $3 billion for this initial public offering. Yakunin, therefore, will control an entity of enormous wealth and power; the pilgrimage expenses are no challenge for his pocket. Yakunin is being touted as a potential successor to President Vladimir Putin when the 2008 election rolls around.[21] Whereas American politicians go the route of primaries in seeking the presidency, a leading Russian politician positions himself by sponsoring a pilgrimage, and making religious donations.

The hand's pilgrimage confirms James Billington's prediction, cited earlier, that the Russian people were searching for a "new Russian identity that seeks to move forward to a Western-style democracy and backward to the moral roots of their own religious and cultural tradition." If Putin leaves the presidency peacefully and an election picks his successor, then at least a measure of "democracy" will have been achieved. If his successor is Yakunin, or Ivanov, or any of the other oligarchs and politicians who so visibly fund the symbols of Orthodoxy, then the path to that democracy will be directed "backward to the moral roots of their own religious and cultural tradition."

Whether this "democracy" is something Americans would recognize is a difficult question. The ROC supports a universal suffrage for the citizenry. The patriarch urges people to vote for the candidate of their choice. But the ROC is willing to countenance more restrictions on freedom of speech, freedom of the press, and freedom of expression than would the United States. For instance, it thoroughly approved when the mayor of Moscow, Luzhkov, banned a Russian version of a "gay pride" march through the city streets. His words might have been spoken by Aleksy himself: "Our way of life, our morals, and our traditions ... are more pure in all ways. The West has something to learn from us and should not race along in [allowing] mad licentiousness.... Our country is democratic but we live in an organized country and an organized city."[22] This simultaneous projection of Russia as democratic but more "pure" than the West is dear to the ROC's heart.

Given that in 2007 the patriarch is almost eighty, sometime in the coming decade he is likely to die. Another man will put his stamp on the Moscow Patriarchate. But the scene he will face will be diametrically opposed to the one Aleksy saw post August 21, 1991. There will be different challenges ahead, but Aleksy has reached an accommodation with the state satisfactory to both, reunited the ROC with its diaspora children, recovered much of the property and patrimony of the church, and maintained the exceptionalism of the ROC against Catholic feelers toward reconciliation. These are remarkable achievements. When he dies, he will almost certainly be given a state funeral in the Cathedral of Christ the Savior (as was Boris Yeltsin in April 2007.)

Aleksy's passing is likely to be commemorated as well in a whole new series of freshly painted icons. These will depict the events of the early morning of August 21, 1991. They could easily be modeled on the famous three-paneled icon (painted ca. 1475) celebrating Novgorod's miraculous victory under its prince, Mstislav Izyaslavich, against the rival forces of Prince Andrey of Bogolyubovo, grand prince of Suzdal. According to legend, Novgorod's bishop had a revered icon of the Theotokos mounted on the city walls. The top register depicts this icon of the Virgin *Orans* ("praying," i.e., with arms outstretched in the prayer position of the early church). In the middle register, an arrow from the treacherous army of the besieging Suzdal soldiers hits the face of Mary, and tears begin to run down her face. Darkness envelops the besiegers, who panic and begin hacking at each other. In the lower register, the army of Novgorod, having been protected by the Mother of God, now pour across the drawbridge, led to victory by the Archangel Michael flying before them with his sword. Four saints in halos, Alexander Nevsky, Boris, Gleb, and St. George, lead the charge. This miracle averted civil war in medieval times.

The putative icon depicting the *chudo* averting civil war on August 21, 1991, will follow this pattern. The top register will show Aleksy praying before the Virgin of Vladimir in the Cathedral of the Assumption while the tanks assemble before the Russian Parliament Building. In the middle register, people in the crowd will fall to their knees and cross themselves as Aleksy's 1:30 A.M. *obrashchenie* is heard on the radio. The young men in the tanks will be visible in their hatches, for they too respond to Aleksy's prayer-petition to Mater Bozhia, the "Protector" of Moscow. The bottom strip will show the tanks turning around, while the people topple Dzerzhinsky's statue from its plinth in front of the Lubyanka and replace it with an Orthodox cross. Aleksy's death may well put him on the fast track to sainthood. Perhaps as he is buried, the crowd will chant *svyaty seichas!* (Saint now!)—an alliterative Russian equivalent of the Latin *santo subito!* urged by the crowd at Pope John Paul II's funeral. The icons will be a fitting tribute to a man able to operate simultaneously in two time frames—the medieval and the modern—all the while shepherding his flock toward a future where to be Russian and to be Orthodox are one and the same.

Appendix A: Translated Documents

The tragic events that have occurred throughout the night made me turn to you, to reach the nation through you.

There is lawlessness inside the country—a group of corrupt Party members has organized an anti-constitutional revolution. Essentially, a state of emergency has been declared inside the country due to the extreme gravity of the situation, and the laws and constitution of the USSR and of the sovereign republics of the Union have been grossly violated.

It is no coincidence that these events have taken place on the eve of the signing of a new Union Treaty, which would have paved the way to freedom, democracy, and progress and a resolution of the recent crisis.

Our State has been violated and along with it the newly emerging democracy, and freedom of choice for the electorate. There is once again the shadow of disorder and chaos hanging over our country.

At this moment of tragedy for our Fatherland I turn to you, calling on your authority among all religious confessions and believers. The influence of the Church in our society is too great for the Church to stand aside during these events. This *duty* is directly related to the Church's mission, to which you have dedicated your life: serving people, caring for their hearts and souls. The Church, which has suffered through the times of totalitarianism, may once again experience disorder and lawlessness.

All believers, the Russian nation, and all Russia await your word!

Announcement of the Moscow Holy Patriarch of Moscow
and All Russia Aleksy II

An extraordinary event has taken place in the life of our Fatherland. The President of the USSR Mikhail Sergeyevich Gorbachev, elected by the Assembly of Peoples' Deputies of the USSR has retired from supreme power in the country.

Furthermore, the circumstances of his retirement remain unclear.

This situation is troubling the consciences of millions of our fellow citizens, who are concerned about the legality of the newly formed State Emergency Committee which has declared that it has taken supreme power in the USSR.

In this connection we declare that it is essential that we hear without delay the voice of President Gorbachev and learn his attitude toward the events that have just taken place.

We hope that the Supreme Soviet of the USSR will give careful consideration to what has taken place and will take decisive measures to bring about the stabilization of the situation in the country.

We call upon all parts of the Russian Orthodox Church, the whole of our people, and particularly our army at this critical moment for our nation to show support and not to permit the shedding of fraternal blood. We raise the heartfelt prayer to our Lord and summon all true believers in our Church to join this prayer begging Him to dispense peace to the peoples of our land so that they can in future build their homeland in accordance with freedom of choice and the accepted norms of morality and law.

Aleksy II, Patriarch of Moscow and All Russia,
20th August, 1991 Moscow

21 AUGUST, 1991. 1:30 A.M. ADDRESS (OBRASHCHENIE) TO COMPATRIOTS

BROTHERS AND SISTERS!

The delicate civil peace of our society has been rent asunder. According to the latest information, open armed conflict and loss of life have begun. In these circumstances, my duty as Patriarch is to warn everybody for whom the word of the church is dear and carries weight: Every person who raises arms against his neighbor, against unarmed civilians, will be taking upon his soul a very profound sin which will separate him from the Church and from God. It is appropriate to shed more tears and say more prayers for such people than for their victims.

May God protect you from the terrible sin of fratricide. I solemnly warn all my fellow-citizens:

The Church does not condone and cannot condone unlawful and violent acts and the shedding of blood.

I ask all of you, my dear ones, to do everything possible to prevent the flame of civil war from bursting forth.

Cease at once!

I ask soldiers and their officers to remember that no one can set a price on human life and pay it.

I ask the Most Holy Mother of God, the Protector of our city, at this time of the Feast of the Transfiguration, not to withdraw Her protection from us, but to preserve all of us.

O Mother of God, help us to reconcile ourselves to one another, to the truth, and to God!

Aleksy II, Patriarch of Moscow and All Russia

AUGUST 30, 1991. ADDRESS (*OBRASHCHENIE*) OF THE HOLY SYNOD OF THE
RUSSIAN ORTHODOX CHURCH TO THE ARCHPRIESTS, PRIESTS AND
ALL ITS FAITHFUL CHILDREN

[copy sent to Canon Michael Bourdeaux at Keston Institute]
Beloved in the Lord, Most Reverend Archpastors, Pastors and all Faithful
Children of the Russian Orthodox Church!

We all are experiencing the events which were fated to begin on the day of
the Transfiguration of the Lord and which, we believe, end the hard period
in the history of our Motherland and turn over a new page in its history.

History is passing its judgment now. And each of us might present his own
claim to the former ruling party and state circles for those unexampled sufferings which have fallen to our lot or to the lot of our neighbors for the last
73 years. But let this judgment not allow the diabolical seeds of malice and
bitterness to settle in our hearts. Let our minds be transformed and freed
from a totalitarian model of consciousness which had made millions of people in our Fatherland voluntary or involuntary participators in unlawful actions. We do not dare to say anything more in this regard on our own behalf,
but wish to cite the words of St. Tikhon, the great confessor of the twentieth
century and Patriarch of all Russia, which he addressed to his flock in July
1919 in the context of persecutions which came down upon the Church of
Christ at [the] will of the new rulers of our country.

"We implore you,—wrote the Patriarch, "we entreat all our Orthodox children not to diverge from the only salutary property of a Christian, not to move
away from the way of the Cross sent down to us by God to the predatory way
of secular powers or that of revenge. Do not blacken your Christian deeds by
falling back to such a conception of the protection of well-being which could
humiliate the Church of Christ and degrade you to the level of its abusers.
Guard, O Lord, the Russian Orthodox Church against such a horror.

"It is a hard but lofty task for a Christian to keep safe inside the greatest
good fortune of forgiveness and love even when your enemy is overthrown and
when an oppressed sufferer is called to pronounce his judgment over his recent oppressor and persecutor. The Providence of God is already calling some
children of the Russian Orthodox Church to this trial. Feelings are running
high. Revolts are breaking out. New camps are being formed. The fire of settling scores is flaring up. Hostile actions are turning into hatred of mankind.

"Orthodox Russia, let this disgrace pass from you. Let this curse not befall
you. Let your hand not be stained with blood crying out to heaven. Do not
let the Devil, the enemy of Christ, entice you with passions of vengeance,
to disgrace your deed of confession and to belittle the price of sufferings inflicted on you by betrayers and persecutors of Christ."

A new page is turning over in the history of our Church as well. We believe that the last outer chains are being cast off now, the chains which had held back the inner development of the church on the principles of conciliation bequeathed to us by our glorious predecessors who traced them in the resolutions of the Holy Council of 1917–18. We are confident that justice will be restored to all church property which it is necessary to give back to the Church so that it could indeed become national property.

But one should not think that the way lying ahead of the Church will be an easy one. The Church will have to act in the midst of spiritual ravage, this bitter legacy left by the former rulers.

Hard trials are in store for us. We see before us not only millions of our compatriots who were brought up in the spirit alien to Christian ethics and are ignorant of the teaching cherished by the Church, but also those who, using a new "democratic" phraseology as a cover, continue to wage struggle against the Church not balking at direct slander. We see attempts to cast suspicions on our Church and its servants in connection with the recent events and with the historical road the Church has traveled during the last seven decades.

Here we shall touch on the events of the last days and we shall share our vision of the hard legacy, which we have to overcome.

The news of the coup d'état reach His Holiness the Patriarch and members of the Holy Synod who were in Moscow just before Divine Liturgy at the Assumption Cathedral in the Kremlin on the bright day of the Transfiguration of the Lord. Dubious information about the USSR President's withdrawal from power and such an alarming fact as the formation of the "State Committee on a State of Emergency" prompted the Patriarch to repeal remembering the "authorities" and the "army" at the Litany and instead pronounce "for our country protected by God and its people." Later, when Vice President of the RSFSR [the Russian Republic of Soviet times] A. V. Rutskoy conveyed to the Patriarch the message of B. N. Yeltsin, the Patriarch gave his blessing to the legitimate power, and that was mentioned by the RSFSR President at the session of the Russian Parliament on August 21 with gratitude. During the whole day of August 19, the Patriarch discussed the situation with the permanent members of the Holy Synod. Thus an elaborated position in support of the Constitution and law and order was expressed in the Announcement issued on August 20 with the Patriarch's signature. In this Announcement the Patriarch demanded that the voice of the USSR President should be heard and that his attitude to the current events should be found out. The Patriarch appealed to the army not to permit fraternal blood to be shed.

During that night (August 20–21, 1991) when a real peril to the legitimate government of Russia appeared, the Patriarch reiterated his ardent appeal forbidding the shedding of blood.

The Holy Synod declares its unanimous agreement with the Patriarch's actions. The Authorities of our Church cannot take any other stand in the light of the tragic experience which the Church has gained under the burden of the totalitarian system. It is indisputable that it was the many-millions-strong Russian Orthodox Church which suffered most from the prevailing regime in the country. Of course, in carrying out its repressions against certain social groups, such as those of peasants, intelligentsia, workers in science and culture, or the army, the regime did not intend their mass destruction. But as far as the Church was concerned, the aim was for its total annihilation. Millions of believers and almost all Orthodox clergymen perished.

At the same time, the Orthodox faith which has been the spiritual and ethical basis of people's life was purposefully banished from it by various ways and means. A great number of the church and national shrines were defiled and destroyed throughout the country. Towards the end of the war and in the post-war period some opportunities became available for the revival of the church's life, but the Russian Orthodox Church, which for centuries has been a powerful spiritual, cultural and creative force in Russia, found itself in a social ghetto artificially prepared for it where it had to drag out a miserable existence as a "survival of the past." We testify that in those extraordinary circumstances unprecedented in the history of the church's existence, everyone who had a vocation for pastoral ministry had, in this or that way, to take this reality into consideration and to act in compliance with his faith and the voice of his conscience.

By the mercy of God and by the power of His grace, the Russian Orthodox Church has stood fast, kept the faith pure and attracted millions of representatives of new generations who now make up its flock and clergy. At the same time we recognize with humility that not all the servants of the Church were equal to the task of their vocation in the years of trials. Our Lord and Righteous Judge will reward everyone according to his deserts. We get down to the cleansing and reviving of our Church, and in doing this we should be guided by a conciliatory mind, canonical order, and personal responsibility of everyone before God, one's own conscience and the people of God, eschewing temptation to act "according to the elemental spirits of the world."*

---

* [Translator's Note] "*po stikhiyam mira sego*" is not identified as such, but seems to be an allusion to Colossians 2:8, where there is an admonition from Paul to "Beware lest any man spoil you through philosophy and vain deceit, after the tradition of men, *after the rudiments of the world*, and not after Christ."

We are hopeful that our Church will soon be genuinely renewed on the principles of conciliation and that the eucharistic communion will be restored among all its children living in our country and abroad. Therefore we call the archpastors, pastors and all our flock to realize their particular duty before God and His Holy Church, to cleanse their souls and consciences, to overcome today's difficulties and to continue their witness about the eternal salvation which our Lord Jesus Christ has prepared for all who love Him.

We hope that our Church, faithful to its age-long tradition, will revive the forgotten piety and holiness in people, will help save the Fatherland and will educate its children now and in the future in faithfulness to those spiritual principles without which the world cannot exist.

The grace of the Lord Jesus Christ and the love of God the Father and the fellowship of the Holy Spirit be with you. Amen. (2 Cor. 13:13).

Aleksy, Patriarch of Moscow and All Russia.

Members of the Holy Synod:

Philaret, Metropolitan of Kiev and All the Ukraine.

Philaret, Metropolitan of Minsk and Grodno, Patriarchal Exarch of All Belorussia.

Yuvenaly, Metropolitan of Krutitsky and Kolomna.

Kirill, Metropolitan of Smolensk and Kaliningrad, Chairman of the Department for External Church Relations.

Nikolay, Metropolitan of Nizhny Novgorod and Arzamas.

Vladimir, Archbishop of Tashkent and Central Asia.

Yevgeny, Archbishop of Tambov and Michurinsk.

Vladimir, Archbishop of Kishinyov and Moldavia.

Panteleimon, Bishop of Arkhangelsk and Murmansk.

Alexander, Bishop of Kostroma and Galich.

Vladimir, Metropolitan of Rostov and Novocherkassk, Chancellor for the Moscow Patriarchate.

Appendix B: Authors' Letter to the New York Times, May 27, 1990

Some of your readers might think that Irina Ginsburg, the Moscow novelist, was exaggerating when she declared, "We Russian Jews Fear for Our Lives" (Op-Ed, May 5). But as non-Jews who have visited Moscow several times over the past few years, most recently in March, we can confirm that anti-Semitism is indeed on the rise in the Soviet Union and presents a serious threat to Soviet Jews.

The paradox of glasnost is that it has opened up the media not simply to calls for freedom and justice but also to the raw anti-Semitism of members of the ultra-rightwing nationalist organization Pamyat and kindred individuals and groups. Prospective members of Pamyat must submit the names and addresses of five Jews; three names and addresses are sufficient if they belong to Jews "trying to conceal their Jewishness." As a Pamyat leader asserted recently, those "hidden Jews," seeking to attack Russian culture from the inside, are the nation's most dangerous enemies.

There is an obvious parallel between Soviet society today and German society prior to the rise of Hitler. Here again is a weak democracy—really, a democracy in its infancy—where the leadership has no popular support, including Mikhail Gorbachev. Economic collapse seems imminent. Just as Germany went through the hyperinflation of the 1920's, so Russians find their rubles growing increasingly worthless. (In March, we could not find a single cab driver who would take us anywhere for rubles; packs of American cigarettes are the required currency.)

In the midst of the growing corruption, Russians feel frustrated and angry. We listened in Moscow apartments to fears of famine in the countryside within a year, accompanied by street demonstrations and riots in Moscow itself. Such anxieties piled on top of justified exasperation over the denigration of Russian culture during much of the Soviet period makes many Russians give in to the all-too-human desire to find a scapegoat. Inevitably, the old belief in the Jew as the source of the Russians' troubles has reemerged.

Some Russians do condemn anti-Semitism and call upon their compatriots to accept responsibility for the present crisis, but theirs are voices in the wilderness. All too many want to believe that the Jews are guilty, just the Germans eagerly accepted Hitler's claim that they were responsible, in some vague manner, for Germany's defeat in World War I.

What is particularly distressing about the anti-Semitic wave in Moscow is that it is being led by writers and other intellectuals. While conducting interviews for our book "Inside the Soviet Writers' Union" [reviewed April 11] we were treated to the most breathtaking expressions of raw anti-Semitism from privileged members of the organization. Seemingly sophisticated and sensible persons asserted that Jews had been responsible for the terror-famine in the Ukraine, which the Soviet press has now acknowledged starved millions to death. That Lazar Kaganovich, a member of Stalin's Politburo, was a Jew proved the Jews' guilt.

A leading figure in the Russian nationalist, anti-Jewish movement is Igor Shafarevich, a close friend of Alexander Solzhenitsyn and a corresponding member of the Soviet Academy of Sciences. Shafarevich, following Solzhenitsyn's example, has popularized the term "Russophobe" as a codeword for Jew.

The Russian Republic branch of the Writers' Union has as members many well-known Soviet writers who have used the pages of journals under the union's jurisdiction for the worst sort of hatred of the Jews. The journal *Nash Sovremennik* carried the allegation that the Jews themselves were responsible for the murder of Jews at Dachau and Auschwitz. Valentin Rasputin, a respected writer who has just been appointed to Mr. Gorbachev's Presidential Council, stated that the Jews "killed God" and were responsible for the October Revolution and the mass terror that followed it. (*New York Times Magazine*, Jan. 28).

The transcripts of meetings of the Russian Republic branch of the Writers' Union read like accounts of speeches at Nazi rallies in the 1930's. Jews who are major figures in Russian literature, such as Babel, Pasternak, Grossman, are said to belong to "literature in the Russian language," not Russian literature proper. Anyone who opposes these views is condemned as a Jew, whether or not he is Jewish. In other words, the very word Jew has become a term of abuse.

Things *are* falling apart inside the Soviet Union. The center is not holding, and yet another "blood-dimmed tide" is gathering strength. Before its fury is loosed upon the world, let us hope that the intended victims are able to escape.

John Garrard, Carol E. Garrard

Tucson, Ariz. May 12, 1990.

[The writers are, respectively, professor of Russian literature at the University of Arizona and adjunct professor at the University of Phoenix.]

Notes

1. The early Christian church had five areas of jurisdiction: Rome, Antioch, Alexandria, Jerusalem, and Constantinople. Early in the fourth century A.D., Constantine moved the capital to the ancient Greek colony of Byzantium and built a New Rome called Constantinople. The patriarch of Rome was originally seen as a *primus inter pares*, but the holders of that see came to be called popes and claim vastly larger authority over not just Rome but all of Christendom. After the cleavage of Christianity into eastern and western halves in 1054, the "Patriarch of Rome" dropped from the list of five. The visit of Jeremias II to Moscow in 1589 brought the number back up again to five.

2. See "Joint Communique issued by the Ecumenical Patriarch Dimitrios I and Patriarch Pimen of Moscow," *Journal of the Moscow Patriarchate* (hereafter *JMP*), no. 12 (1987): 20.

3. See the complete account in Serge A. Zenkovsky, ed., *Medieval Russia's Epics, Chronicles and Tales*, trans. Nicholas Zernov (New York: Dutton, 1974), pp. 268–69 and 284–85.

4. This extraordinary quotation is from Metropolitan Kirill of Smolensk and Kaliningrad, "Gospel & Culture," in John Witte Jr. and Michael Bourdeaux, eds., *Proselytism and Orthodoxy in Russia: The New War for Souls*, Religion and Human Rights Series (Maryknoll, N.Y.: Orbis Books, 1999), p. 70. The article is a reprint of a speech Metropolitan Kirill gave before the World Council of Churches in November 1996.

5. See Archpriest Lev Lebedev, "Veneration of St. Nicholas in Russia, Conclusion," *JMP*, no. 6 (1987): 71. Lebedev does not mention the Soviet seizure of thousands of ROC churches. The *JMP*'s editor in chief, Metropolitan Pitirim, was one of those "agents in cassocks" the KGB had inserted into the hierarchy.

6. Cyril and Methodius are termed the "apostles to the Slavs"; they created an alphabet, the glagolitic, which was subsequently modified by the Bulgarians, who added more Greek and Latin letters. This became the Cyrillic alphabet, the basis for the creation in the eighteenth century of the Russian literary language. Thus Russians were able to understand a great deal of their liturgy, much more so than Western Christians listening to Latin.

7. As cited in *Welcome to the Orthodox Liturgy*, © 1989, Light and Life Publishing Company, box 26421, Minneapolis, MN 55426. This pamphlet is available for purchase in the kiosks of Russian Orthodox churches in the United States.

8. The Primary Chronicle also includes an argument that probably carried much weight with Vladimir: "If the Greek faith were evil, it would not have been adopted by

your grandmother Olga, who was wiser than anyone." The general reader can find an illuminating account in Robin Milner-Gulland with Nikolai Dejevsky, *Cultural Atlas of Russia and the Soviet Union*, Facts on File (New York and Oxford: Equinox, 1989): 43–44. As summarized there: "Even then Vladimir delayed. He went off to capture the vital Byzantine city of Kherson in the Crimea and demanded the emperor's sister Anna in marriage: all ended happily when he accepted baptism, got his princess and handed back Kherson as the bride price."

9. See the excellent description of the Cathedral of the Dormition in William Craft Brumfield, *A History of Russian Architecture*, rev. ed. (Seattle: University of Washington Press, 2004), pp. 111–12, fig. 134.

10. Ibid., p. 112. See also p. 539, n. 12: "It is now believed that Andrei Rublev painted a number of the original frescoes of the Dormition Cathedral, including two figures (Sts. Flor and Lavr) that have survived on the east (altar) piers. See Lazarev, *Drevnerusskie mozaiki i freski: XI–XV vv.* (Moscow, 1973), pp. 7172, and Plates 393–4."

11. Cited in Helen C. Evans, ed., *Byzantium: Faith and Power (1261–1557)*, catalog of the exhibition at the Metropolitan Museum of Art, New York, March 23–July 4, 2004 (New Haven: Yale University Press, 2004), p. 330. Entry no. 199, pp. 330–31, is an embroidery illustrating the Transfiguration and church festivals, made in Moscow during the second half of the fifteenth century. It was given to the Belozersk Monastery and eventually taken into the state museum in 1923. The *troparion* is embroidered in Old Church Slavonic; the entry notes that a similar altar cloth to this one is from the "Trinity–Saint Sergius Monastery at Sergiev Posad, now in that town's State History and Art Museum-Reserve."

12. As quoted in ibid., p. 303.

13. See ibid., pp. 302–3, for a color plate and analysis of this textile, a masterpiece of ecclesiastical embroidery. Metropolitan Peter was buried in a chapel of the original Cathedral of the Dormition inside the Kremlin. He designed his own tomb. See Brumfield, *A History of Russian Architecture*, p. 84.

14. See the excellent article by Vera Tolz, "Church-State Relations under Gorbachev," in *Radio Free Europe/Radio Liberty*, September 11, 1987 (RL 360/87).

15. At a joint news conference with French president Mitterrand in Paris on July 5, 1989, Gorbachev was asked by a journalist if he had been baptized, and he said yes, "I think that quite normal." He also said his parents were believers. Gorbachev was born in 1931 in the village of Privolnoye near Sevastopol. See *Keston News Service*, July 20, 1989, p. 10.

16. Diarmaid MacCullough, *The Reformation* (New York: Viking, 2003), p. xxviii.

CHAPTER 1. THE END OF THE ATHEIST EMPIRE

1. The Russian word *molodtsy* is stressed on the last syllable. It is often used to mean "Well done!" or "Great job!" The singular form *molodets* (stressed on the last

syllable) is used to praise a single person. For the Western reader, the best single-volume introduction to what happened and how it happened on August 19–21, 1991, is James Billington's memoir, *Russia Transformed: Breakthrough to Hope* (New York: Free Press, 1992). Specialists would also do well to read this book, not only for its enjoyable narrative but also for its analysis of the complexities of the situation coupled with engaging insights into human behavior (see p. 42).

2. *Putsch: The Diary; Three Days That Collapsed the Empire* (New York: Mosaic Press, 1991), p. 85.

3. Ibid., p. 19.

4. Woodrow Wilson library, file "info on the 1991 coup" (Russia 1991 coup). Xerox copy of original fax in Russian. George Kennan Collection, vertical file 1 "Information on coup," Woodrow Wilson International Center for Scholars, Washington, D.C. Translation by Nana Tchibuchian, Woodrow Wilson International Center for Scholars (WWICS) research assistant, and John Garrard.

5. The ROC is proud of this substitution; it is mentioned prominently in the unpublished fax it sent to "the archpastors, pastors and all its faithful children" on August 30, 1991, only days after the failure of the coup. One copy was sent to Canon Michael Bourdeaux at the Keston Institute in Oxford, England, where we consulted the original Russian. See the complete text of John Garrard's translation of this important document in appendix A.

6. The fax, dated August 20, 1991, in the Keston Institute archives. The fax is in Russian; the subsequent quotations are translated by John Garrard.

7. Felix Corley, " Russia: The Patriarch and the KGB," *Keston News Service*, no. 9, 2000, p. 8.

8. Fax, dated August 21, 1:30 A.M., in the Keston Institute archives. The fax is in Russian; the translation is by John Garrard.

9. An English translation of this speech is found in *The Truth about Religion in Russia* (London: Hutchinson & Co., 1942), pp. 47–51; quotations from p. 49. The title page says it was "issued by the Moscow Patriarchate (1942)." English translation under the supervision of Rev. E. N. C. Sergeant. This title page itself speaks volumes. It was "issued by the Moscow Patriarchate," but in 1942, when the post still existed, it was unoccupied. The facing page with a picture of "Sergius, Patriarch of Moscow and All Russia," is a clever piece of disinformation. Sergius did not become patriarch until 1943. The book was intended "for export only" as part of the USSR's World War II propaganda campaign. Pasted on the inside flap of the Keston Institute's copy was a typewritten note from the secretary of the archbishop of Canterbury. In 1942 the Soviet Union was allied with England; the book had been given to the archbishop to distribute. All subsequent quotations are to this text. Among Western historians, few have noted this speech. The exception is Sir Rodric Braithwaite, the former British ambassador to the USSR and Russia from 1988 to

1992, who cites it in his splendid volume *Moscow 1941: A City and Its People at War* (London: Profile Books, 2006), p. 174.

10. Alan Clark, *Barbarossa: The Russian-German Conflict, 1941–45* (New York: Quill, 1965), p. 179. See his chapter, "The Battle for Moscow" (pp. 156–83), for a superb account of this critical battle, based upon German sources.

11. Icons of Mary with the Christ child are divided according to the posture of the mother and the baby. The Vladimir icon is a type known in Greek as *glykophilousa*, that is, "sweetly loving." The Christ child not only sits on her arm but leans his cheek against hers, the most tender of poses.

12. *Russian Orthodoxy on the Eve of Revolution* (Oxford: Oxford University Press, 2004), p. 179. Vera Shevzov's book is well worth reading, combining formerly hard to reach source materials into a coherent and convincing study.

13. G. A. Romanov, "The New Town of New Constantine," in *Moscow: 850th Anniversary*, vol. 1, gen. ed. V. A. Vinogradov (Moscow: Publishing House AO "Moscow Textbooks," 1996), p. 178. This extraordinary book is available in the Russian original and an English translation. Both versions were published in print runs of only 10,000, with funding from the Moscow city government. Though printed on heavy silk paper with hundreds of beautiful four-color illustrations, the book is extremely poorly translated and was apparently never proofread.

14. This semimythic account of Mary as the Protector of Moscow is related from the perspective of faith by Father Thomas Zain, an Orthodox priest, in his account of his visit to the consecration of the lower church of the Cathedral of Christ the Savior in Moscow in September 1997. See "Russia Revisited: Twenty-one Years Later," *Sourozh: A Journal of Orthodox Life and Thought*, no. 71 (February 1998): 19–32. Page 20 deals with his visit to Red Square to see the two churches that were rebuilt after having been blown up by the Soviet regime. One, Our Lady of the Gates, is located at the rebuilt gates at the entrance to Red Square. This church was dedicated to that special icon.

15. Quoted in *Moscow: 850th Anniversary*, 1:151.

16. The Battle of Kulikovo has acquired many of the patriotic connotations for the Russians of an Agincourt for the British or Yorktown for Americans. But just two years later, in 1382, the successor to Mamay Khan, Tokhtamysh, avenged the defeat by assembling a huge army and besieging Moscow, and with Grand Prince Dmitry in the north trying to raise an army, he cleverly persuaded the Muscovites to open the gates so he could "visit" the city. Once inside, the khan's soldiers overwhelmed the welcoming party and other Mongols poured in. The city was thoroughly sacked and burned. But when the Golden Horde withdrew, leaving behind the smoking ruins, it was for the last time. Though they would send punitive expeditions and raids for years to come, never again would the Golden Horde successfully besiege and enter the city. Grand Prince Dmitry rebuilt the wooden Kremlin walls with white stone

battlements. After the city was sacked in 1382, these walls, rebuilt and strengthened, were virtually impregnable as well as fireproof.

17. On August 30, 1991, only a week after the coup's defeat, the Holy Synod of the ROC, with Aleksy II's name at the top of the list of signatures, faxed a magisterial address which gave the Church's spin. It is analyzed in chapter 6, and its text is included in the appendix A. An interesting sentence buried on page 2 addresses the complex relationship between the patriarch, Boris Yeltsin, and Alexander Rutskoy: "when Vice-President of the RSFSR A. V. Rutskoy conveyed to the Patriarch the message of Boris N. Yeltsin, the Patriarch gave his blessing to the legitimate power [i.e., Yeltsin's election as president of the Russian Republic], and that was mentioned by the RSFSR President at the session of the Russian Parliament on August 21 with gratitude." In short, in addition to the radio appeal to the patriarch, Yeltsin sent Rutskoy personally to Aleksy to make his plea.

18. Metropolitan Kirill of Smolensk and Kaliningrad, "The Russian Orthodox Church and the Third Millennium," paper presented at the 7th International Conference on Russian Spirituality, Bose, Italy, September 15–18, 1999. Translated from the Russian by Peter Bouteneff, and reprinted by the *Ecumenical Review* 52, no. 3 (July 2000): 305.

19. As stated in a personal interview at the WWICS, April 22, 2005. The authors are very grateful to Sir Rodric and Lady Braithwaite for sharing their memories and judgments of this momentous time. Sir Rodric was British ambassador from 1988 to 1992, thus spanning the critical transition from the Soviet Union to the Russian Federation. His diary, which he kindly shared with us, was later edited and published as *Across the Moscow River* (New Haven: Yale University Press, 2002).

20. James Billington makes the point that Alexander Borisov had recently reestablished the Russian Bible Society. Thus, for practically the first time in more than seventy years, four thousand brand new copies of the New Testament in Russian were fortuitously available. See his excellent article "Orthodox Christianity and the Russian Transformation," in *Proselytism and Orthodoxy in Russia The New War for Souls*, ed. John Witte Jr. and Michael Bourdeaux, Religion and Human Rights Series (Maryknoll, N.Y.: Orbis Books, 1999), p. 53. Billington's article is exceptionally perceptive. Our account of the crowd and its behavior is drawn from this article (pp. 51–65).

21. See *Putsch: The Diary*, p. 82. The Committees of Soldiers' Mothers made this announcement on August 20, 1991, at 1:53 P.M.

22. Billington, "Orthodox Christianity and the Russian Transformation," p. 58.

23. Boris Yeltsin died April 23, 2007. In "A Bloody Standoff in Moscow," the extensive obituary published in the *New York Times*, April 24, 2007, p. C-15, cols. 2–3, this episode is recounted in detail. General Rutskoy was jailed, but the Parliament pardoned him forthwith.

24. See Billington, *Russia Transformed*, p. 128, n. 63.

25. Eusebius of Ceasarea wrote a *Life of Constantine*, which recounts this vision of the sign of the cross and its exhortation (vol. I, chaps. 27–32). See the translation in *Great Problems in European Civilization*, 2nd ed., ed. Kenneth M. Setton and Henry R. Winkler (New York: Prentice-Hall, 1966), pp. 73–74. As the accompanying article notes, Lactanius, in his *On the Deaths of Persecutors*, describes Constantine as having had this manifestation of divine support in a dream rather than in an actual vision.

26. The British ambassador, Sir Rodric Braithwaite, recorded in his personal diary for Monday, August 26, 1991: "I got to the Kremlin for the extraordinary session of the Supreme Soviet. Deputies are streaming back from the requiem, which the patriarch has just conducted in the Uspensky Sobor. People are milling about in the foyer." The authors are very grateful to Sir Rodric for allowing us to quote from his diary. When John Garrard was a Wilson Fellow at the Woodrow Wilson International Center for Scholars, from September 2004 to the end of April 2005, the ambassador had an adjoining office while he completed his outstanding book, *Moscow 1941: A City and Its People at War* (London: Profile Books, 2006).

27. Billington, "Orthodox Christianity and the Russian Transformation," p. 54.

28. *Izvestia*, July 14, 2000. Oddly, Putin would appear to agree with the former Kremlinologist Stephen Cohen, who proclaimed, "In reality, no anti-Soviet revolution from below ever took place, certainly not in Russia." See the following note.

29. See the roundtable discussion of Stephen Cohen's "Was the Soviet System Reformable?" in *Slavic Review* 63, no. 3 (Fall 2004): 459–554. The discussion is by eminent experts, and a list of their topics is instructive: "Was the Soviet System Reformable?" and "Reply" by Stephen F. Cohen; "The Soviet Union: Reform of the System or Systemic Transformation?" by Archie Brown; "The Reform of the Soviet System and the Demise of the Soviet State," by Mark Kramer; "The Question of Questions: Was the Soviet Union Worth Saving?" by Karen Dawisha; "Reform and Revolution in the Late Soviet Context," by Stephen E. Hanson; and "Alternative Pasts, Future Alternatives?" by Georgi M. Drluguian.

Chapter 2. A New Hope

1. Personal interview conducted at the Woodrow Wilson Center in Washington, D.C., in February 2005. Dr. Glazin in fact stated that he had lived in Tallinn a few blocks away from Ridiger's son.

2. Canon Michael Bourdeaux, "Between Hammer and Anvil," Monday Profile, *Guardian*, September 2, 1991, p. 19.

3. From the Web site of the Russian Orthodox Church, www.russian-orthodox-church.org.ru/. The ROC has operated this Web site since 1994.

4. Oksana Antich, "Pravoslavny monastyr vozvrashchen tserkvi," *Radio Free Europe/ Radio Liberty*, June 27, 1983. All translations by John Garrard.

5. See *JMP*, no. 9 (1983): 7–8.

6. The legislation is printed in the *Gazette of the Supreme Soviet of the USSR* (*Ve-domosti Verkhovonogo Soveta SSSR*). In September 1983 a decree amended article 188 (3) of the Criminal Code of the Russian Republic. The decree went into effect on October 1.

7. *Yuny Kommunist*, no. 7, July 1938, p. 48. All translations are by John Garrard.

8. This had been standard operating procedure for some years under Brezhnev, too. In 1980 John Garrard narrowly missed getting run down by a motorcycle gang when he attended Easter services at a church in Marina Roshcha (Maria's Orchard), now a poor working-class district of Moscow. In 1809 the district's name furnished the title for a sentimental story by Zhukovsky, inspired by Nikolay Karamzin's famous tale, *Bednaya Liza* (*Poor Liza*). The din of the motorcyclists gunning their engines on Easter 1980 eventually died away as the thugs got tired; the liturgy's beauty was thereupon heard uncontested.

9. Ivan IV of Russia, called Grozny, died March 18, 1584. On his deathbed, he ordered the metropolitan to make him a monk. See Stephen Graham, *Ivan the Terrible* (London: Ernest Benn, 1932), pp. 301–2. Ivan's father, Vasily III, who died when Ivan was only three, went through the same bizarre ritual on his own deathbed.

10. On January 11, 1984, the nearly comatose Andropov signed an amendment to the Criminal Code, Article 76 (1) for the RSFSR. It states "The passing or collection with intent of passing to foreign organizations or their representatives of economic, technical, scientific or other 'official-use-only information' by a person to whom this information was entrusted in the course of his duties or work, which he learned by any other means," would become a criminal offense meriting up to three years' deprivation of freedom.

11. Hierodeacon Serafim, "Metropolitan Theodosius Visits the Moscow Monastery of St. Daniel," *JMP*, no. 10 (1986): 11.

12. See *Keston News Service*, May 29, 1986, p. 8. Keston had its own researcher based in Moscow who uncovered this astonishing (at the time) privilege.

13. Personal interview with Dr. William Miller, Woodrow Wilson Fellow and former U.S. ambassador to Ukraine (1994–98), at the Wilson Center, Washington, D.C., on March 10, 2005. Dr. Miller is an enlightened and energetic diplomat. While ambassador to Ukraine, he helped sponsor the preservation of the archaeological site of Chersonesos, the possible location of the original baptism of St. Vladimir on the occasion of his marriage to the sister of the Byzantine emperor Basil II in A.D. 988. See "Legacies of a Slavic Pompeii," *Archaeology*, November–December 2002, pp. 18–25. See especially p. 24, for his successful efforts to mobilize funds from the West to assist Ukraine in preserving the site.

14. See Dimitry V. Pospielovsky, *The Orthodox Church in the History of Russia* (Crestwood, N.Y.: St. Vladimir's Seminary Press, 1998), p. 353. The entire chapter

"The Church under Perestroika and the Agony of Communism" is well worth study.

15. See the ecstatic article describing "Metropolitan Aleksy of Leningrad Elected Chairman of the Council of CEC Presidium and Advisory Committee," *JMP*, no. 12 (1987): 61. This article appears under the subsection title "Oikoumene—The Ecumenical Movement." Both the subsections "Peace Movement" and "Oikoumene" disappeared from the *JMP*'s table of contents once the USSR itself had dissolved.

16. For the photograph, see Paul D. Steeves, *Keeping the Faiths: Religion and Ideology in the Soviet Union* (New York: Holmes & Meier, 1989), p. 214. This excellent book is published as part of the "Beyond the Kremlin" series by the Committee for National Security.

17. This astonishing figure is given by Jonathan Phillips, *The Fourth Crusade and the Sack of Constantinople* (London: Pimlico, 2005), p. 66. The Teutonic Knights contained not only Germans. Geoffrey Chaucer's "Knight" in the *Canterbury Tales* survived his crusading against "Russe and Prusse," we are told.

18. See Wendy Slater, "Russia's Imagined History: Visions of the Soviet Past and the New 'Russian Idea,'" *Journal of Communist Studies and Transition Politics* 14, no 4 (December 1998): 79, n. 44. Slater points out that the words that Stalin chose to describe Lenin's "victorious banner"—*pobedonosnoe znamya*—had religious overtones, "recalling as they did Russia's patron warrior saint, St. George the Victor, or 'Georgy Pobedonosets.'"

19. It is unlikely that the Soviet soldiers were aware that the line itself originates in the New Testament. In Matthew 26:52, Jesus tells an unnamed apostle (John 10:11 identifies him as Peter) who wishes to resist the Roman soldiers who have come to arrest him in the Garden of Gethsemane to "Put up again thy sword . . . for all they that take the sword shall perish with the sword."

20. This was confided to John Garrard in a personal conversation with Yury Nagibin at his dacha outside Moscow in the spring of 1980. Nagibin, a well-connected writer with close friends in the Russian elite, said that it was party policy to play down these casualties. And, indeed, the party did draw a veil over Red Army losses for the duration of the war.

21. Pospielovsky, *The Orthodox Church*, p. 366, n. 8.

22. Metropolitan Pitirim of Volokolamsk and Yuriev, ed., "The Second Invention of St. Serafim of Sarov's Relics," *JMP*, no. 12 (1991): 26.

23. On November 3, 1988, as part of the millennial year celebrations, *Izvestia* reported the miraculous rediscovery of the bones of St. Amvrosy—the ascetic monk who is the original of Fyodor Dostoevsky's Father Zosima in *The Brothers Karamazov*.

24. Phillip Walters discusses the Orthodox monastery explosion in his perceptive article, "The Russian Orthodox Church and Foreign Christianity: The Legacy of the Past," in *Proselytism and Orthodoxy in Russia: The New War for Souls*, ed. John

Witte Jr. and Michael Bourdeaux, Religion and Human Rights Series (Maryknoll, N.Y.: Orbis Books, 1999), pp. 31–50. These statistics are cited on p. 39.

25. The occurrence of phantom pregnancy is known in obstetrics. Another queen who suffered not one but two hysterical pregnancies was Mary Tudor, who married Phillip II of Spain.

26. *Nicholas and Alexandra: The Last Imperial Family of Tsarist Russia*, ed. Mark Sutcliffe, from the State Hermitage Museum and the State Archive of the Russian Federation, catalogue of the exhibition at the State Hermitage Museum, 1998 (New York and London: Harry N. Abrams and Booth-Clibborn Editions, 1998), p. 291.

27. Mikhail Iroshnikov, Liudmila Protsai, and Yuri Shelayev, *Sunset of the Romanov Dynasty*, trans. Paul Williams and Juri Pamfilov (Moscow: Terra, 1992), p. 247.

28. Pitirim, "The Second Invention of St. Serafim of Sarov's Relics," p. 28. The journal printed excerpts from previously secret Soviet documents concerning the government's filching and hiding of the relics.

29. Quoted by Chris J. Chulos, *Converging Worlds: Religion and Community in Peasant Russia, 1861–1917* (De Kalb: Northern Illinois University Press, 2003), p. 109.

30. Pitirim, "The Second Invention of St. Serafim of Sarov's Relics," p. 27. As the editor Metropolitan Pitirim notes in the foreword, "The documents published not only reveal the formal sequence of events which took place in Tambov Gubernia in 1920–1921 but give a picture of the unprecedented mockery and persecution of Orthodox clergy and laity." The journal concurs with the peasantry's explanation for the horrors of these years: "The uncovering of relics, desecration of national shrines could not pass without leaving a trace: Russia was living through the years of unprecedented famine."

31. The parish was founded in 1741 as the chapel of the Russian Embassy. The cathedral moved to its current building, formerly the Anglican parish Church of All Saints, in 1956. The building was an ideal fit for Orthodox worship, because its basilica was already modeled on the eleventh-century basilica of San Zeno Maggiore in Verona, Italy. The beautiful iconostasis dates from the eighteenth century. It was removed from the Russian Embassy chapel in 1917 and now glows in the cathedral.

32. Personal interview with the deacon, July 24, 2003. This sensational event was reported in *Izvestia*, January 11, 1991, p. 7. *Izvestia* was an organ of the Soviet state, as opposed to the official mouthpiece of the Communist Party, *Pravda*.

33. See the report in *Izvestia*, January 11, 1991, p. 7.

34. B. Kolymagin, "Translation of the Relics of St. Serafim to Moscow," *JMP*, no. 5 (1991): 7.

35. "Oration by His Holiness Patriarch Aleksy II at the Ceremony Marking the Return of the Holy Relics of St. Serafim of Sarov to the Church," *JMP*, no. 4 (1991): 29.

36. Dennis Nineham, "The Iffley Millennium History Lecture," in *Life around the Time of the First Millennium*, Iffley Local History Society, Publication No. 4 (October 2000), p. 10.

37. Venice, however, lost out to the city of Bari (Italy) for the bones of St. Nicholas, who happens to be one of the special saints dear to Russia. St. Nicholas's bones are still an object of veneration in Bari. And their theft still rankles Orthodox believers.

38. See *Age of Chivalry: Art in Plantagenet England 1200–1400*, ed. Jonathan Alexander and Paul Binski, catalog to the exhibition, Royal Academy of Arts, London, 1987 (London: Weidenfeld and Nicolson, 1987). Examples are shown on pp. 219–22. The accompanying article "Pilgrim souvenirs" (pp. 218–19) analyzes the emotions of pilgrims to the Becket shrine; they can be paralleled with the emotions of nineteenth- and twentieth-century peasants toward St. Seraphim and his relics. Ordinary doctors are seen as expensive "failures."

39. Personal interview, Oxford, England, June 14, 2005.

40. Kolymagin, "Translation of the Relics of St. Serafim to Moscow," p. 7.

41. A. Victorov, "Translation of the Relics of St. Seraphim of Sarov from Moscow to Diveyevo," *JMP*, no. 12 (1991): 22.

42. We flew to Moscow July 1, 1991, but were focused on revelations about the experience of the Red Army during World War II. A conference in Leeds, England, had marked the fiftieth anniversary of Barbarossa, the German invasion of the USSR on June 22, 1941. Concentrating on previously unseen documents on *shtrafbaty* (punishment) battalions, we paid no attention to the St. Seraphim translation.

43. Aleksy II, Patriarch of Moscow and All the Russias, *Tserkov i dukhovnoe vozrozhdenie Rossii* (Sofrino: Moscow, 1999), p. 684.

44. Igor Simonov, "State Church Cooperation No Threat to Freedom," *Centennial. Birzha* (Nizhny Novgorod), July 28, 2003. This article was issued on the centennial anniversary of the canonization of St. Seraphim.

45. Ibid. Our interviews with the Moscow congregation of St. Vladimir's Orthodox Church confirm that believers had a vague yet fervent conviction that St. Seraphim had predicted the general course of events for Russia, which would terminate in the country's return to the true faith of Orthodoxy. One believer told us that St. Seraphim's prophecies were coming true "one by one," though she didn't say what each "one" was.

46. "Excerpts from the Sermons and the Speeches of His Holiness Patriarch Aleksy II," *JMP*, no. 12 (1991): 24.

47. Victorov, "The Translation of the Relics of St. Serafim of Sarov from Moscow to Diveyevo," p. 22.

48. See *Current Digest of the Soviet Press* 43, no. 31 (August 1991): 29–30. This contains a condensed version of the original article by A. Vasinsky and A. Yershov that appeared in *Izvestia*, July 31, 1991, p. 6. Yershov and Vasinsky were the two correspondents assigned by *Izvestia* to cover the pilgrimage. For their report on the beginning of the pilgrimage, see *CDSP* 43, no. 29 (1991): 27.

49. James Billington, "The True Heroes of the Soviet Union," *New York Times*, August 30, 1991.

50. The gullible Ambassador Davies wrote an unintentionally comic memoir, *Mission to Moscow*, which became a painful movie of the same name, about his tenure during the 1930s. While famine was sweeping the country, the movie shows peasants eating bread laced with caviar as a normal snack. A "useful idiot," indeed, to quote Lenin's dismissive comment on Western supporters of the USSR.

51. *The Diveyevo Chronicle* was reprinted by Gorad Kitezhe. We are grateful to Dr. Ann Shukman, of Oxford, England, for a long interview in which she explained the checkered publication history of both the Diveyevo Chronicle and the Prophecies of St. Seraphim (July 2, 2005). Dr. Shukman's unpublished paper, "'The Conversation between St. Seraphim and Motovilov': The Author, the Texts, and the Publishers," was invaluable.

52. *Sobornost* in the late nineteenth century was a term widely used to indicate the specific quality of Russian Orthodoxy and Russian consciousness.

Chapter 3. Rebuilding Holy Moscow

1. January (no year), second edition, cost three rubles. Keston Institute provisionally dates it to 1923–24. The image of the New Soviet man climbing a ladder to "build Communism" became a standard motif even before the official formulation of "socialist realism." Serafima Riangina painted a "classic" of socialist realist art, *Ever Higher* (1934), showing the *novy chelovek* in overalls, smiles on their chubby faces, climbing an endless ladder, presumably to heaven. It is in the collection of the Tretyakov Gallery, Moscow. A statue of an idealized pair is at the entry of the Exhibit of National Achievement (VDNKh) near the Cosmos Hotel.

2. The Nazis stole across Europe and the Soviet Union for Hitler's *Führermuseum*, a super-showcase designed to be the largest art collection in the world. When the Red Army occupied Berlin in 1945, the USSR stole Nazi loot back. During the Soviet period, the authorities denied the existence of stolen books. Then, in 1990, a researcher revealed that several million "rare German imprints" had been left to rot under pigeon droppings in the Uzkoe church outside Moscow owned by the Academy of Sciences of the USSR. See Patricia Kennedy Grimsted, "Tracing 'Trophy' Books in Russia," in *Solanus: International Journal for Russian & East European Bibliographic, Library & Publishing Studies*, n.s., 19 (2005): 131–45. This quotation occurs on p. 134. In 1992, a joint Russian-German Round Table on trophy books revealed that a 1948 Soviet document detailed shipments of about ten million books to the USSR. It is impossible to say which books were German and which were themselves stolen by the Germans from Occupied Europe. Grimstead (p. 134, n. 11) states that a list of

these books is available electronically. For those readers with Russian, see http://www. libfl.ru/restitution. There is also an extensive bibliography on this conflicted subject there as well.

3. See *New York Times*, March 7, 2005.

4. Cited from his entry dated Tuesday, May 5, 1992.

5. Ibid.

6. See *Keston News Service*, no. 332, August 24, 1989, pp. 6–7.

7. Archpriest Lev Lebedev, "Veneration of St. Nicholas in Russia, Conclusion," *JMP*, no. 6 (1987): 72, n. 9.

8. Brigit Farley and Ann Kleimola, "The Church of the Icon of the Kazan Mother of God on Red Square: A Symbol of Unity for Russian Society," in *Burden or Blessing? Russian Orthodoxy and the Construction of Civil Society and Democracy*, ed. Christopher Marsh (Brookline, Mass.: Boston University Institute on Culture, Religion and World Affairs, 2004), p. 71.

9. Both versions of the book are part of the collection at the Keston Institute, Oxford, England. The Russian version was published by Publishing House AO "Moscow Textbooks ," 1996. When quoting from the Russian, all translations are by John Garrard.

10. *Moscow: 850th Anniversary*, gen. ed. V. A. Vinogradov (Moscow: Publishing House AO "Moscow Textbooks," 1996), 1:149–64, for short articles on each of these topics.

11. Ibid., p. 80. The reader will notice that the English is very labored and crude. The meaning of "insicie" is evidently a misprint for "inside."

12. Ibid., pp. 149–64, for short articles on the medieval city's mystical features.

13. Ibid., p. 94. This first Cathedral of the Assumption was replaced by a new one begun in 1475 by the Italian architect Aristotle Fioravanti. This opened the way for the reconstruction of virtually all the Kremlin's buildings, mostly by Italian architects.

14. The Savior Gates and Tower were built in 1491 by the Italian architect Pietro Antonio Solari together with Marco Russo. Ibid., p. 97.

15. See Abraham Ascher, *The Kremlin*, Wonders of Man Series (New York: Newsweek, 1972), p. 165.

16. See the *Herald of the Russian Student Christian Movement*, no. 1 (1974): 220–32. It was published by the Action Chrétienne des Étudiants Russes, rue Olivier de Serres, Paris 15e, France. This is from a typescript extract found in the Keston Research Archive.

17. From the official Web site of the Moscow Patriarchate, www.xxc.ru/english/. March 10, 2005.

18. William Craft Brumfield, "The 'New Style' and the Revival of Orthodox Church Architecture, 1900–1914," in *Christianity and the Arts in Russia*, ed. William Craft Brumfield and Milos Velimirovic (New York: Cambridge University Press, 1991), p. 105.

19. Alexander Solzhenitsyn, *The First Circle*, trans. Thomas P. Whitney (Evanston, Ill.: Northwestern University Press, 1997), p. 125. The entire chapter, "The Church of St. John the Baptist," is well worth reading. The description of the church makes it clear it is in the style known as Naryshkin baroque, a seventeenth-century favorite.

20. Kathleen E. Smith, "An Old Cathedral for a New Russia: The Symbolic Politics of the Reconstituted Church of Christ the Saviour," *Religion, State & Society* 25, no. 2 (1997): 163–72. See p. 165 for her discussion of "The Death of a Cathedral."

21. Fred A. Bernstein, "The End of 1960's Architecture," *New York Times*, October 31, 2004, p. AR 28.

22. William Craft Brumfield, *A History of Russian Architecture*, 2nd ed. (Seattle: University of Washington Press, 2004), p. 485. At a book launch held at the Kennan Institute of the Woodrow Wilson International Center for Scholars, Washington, D.C., Professor Brumfield spoke forcefully about the need for Western Slavists to address the important discipline of Russian secular and religious architecture.

23. Stalin chewed into the Moscow skyline seven monstrous skyscrapers, known as the "the ugly stepsisters" to the inhabitants. He ordered each wedding cake of concrete and steel topped by a spire. The cramming of a component of ancient Russian architecture on top of a modern structure left the Western tourist with the sense he had entered the city of Flash Gordon comics.

24. *World War 2 and the Soviet People*, ed. John and Carol Garrard (New York: St. Martin's Press, 1993), pp. 125–46. All details of the entries and the popular responses to them are taken from this article.

25. When Yeltsin died, Monday, April 23, 2007, his posthumous reward was a state funeral inside the cathedral conducted by Aleksy himself. The last time such an occasion was celebrated was the service conducted inside the original cathedral for Tsar Alexander III, who died in 1894.

26. As stated by Inga Pagava, director of the Development Department, Charities Aid Foundation, Russia, at a seminar on Russian fundraising hosted by the Kennan Institute on Wednesday, April 6, 2005.

27. Ms. Pagava headed Khodorkovsky's foundation, which now is on its last $13 million—an allocation he made before his arrest and incarceration. She stated further that she expected his foundation to fold when these funds were expended, as he had gone from owning $15 billion to being, in his own words, "middle class." Khodorkovksy's company, Yukos, was nationalized at the insistence of President Vladimir Putin, and Khodorkovsky himself was imprisoned on what appear to be spurious charges of tax evasion. On May 31, 2005, he was sentenced to nine years in prison.

28. For a lively account by a Western eyewitness of the parade and light show, see Matthew Brzezinski, *Casino Moscow: A Tale of Greed and Adventure on Capitalism's Wildest Frontier* (New York: Simon & Schuster, 2002), pp. 153–58, and 166.

Brzezinski was not in Moscow at the time of the reconsecration of the rebuilt Cathedral of Christ the Savior.

29. From Father Thomas Zain, a member of the North American delegation that accompanied Metropolitan Phillip, from the Antiochan diocese. "Russia Revisited: Twenty-One Years Later," *Sourozh: A Journal of Orthodox Life and Thought*, no. 71 (February 1998): 25. Father Zain's account was originally published as the lead article in the journal of the archdiocese, *The Word*, December 1997, pp. 5ff. The entire delegation, as guests of the patriarch, stayed in the lavish Danilovskaya Hotel, which is owned by the Orthodox Church and overlooks the Danilov Monastery.

30. See the ecstatic account by tsar Nicholas II in a letter to his mother dated September 10, 1912, in *Nicholas and Alexandra: The Last Imperial Family of Tsarist Russia*, ed. Mark Sutcliffe, from the State Hermitage and the State Archive of the Russian Federation, catalog of the exhibition at the State Hermitage Museum, 1998 (New York and London: Harry Abrams and Booth-Clibborn Editions, 1998), pp. 347–48. Nicholas was very moved at the procession of the same icon. For a photograph of Nicholas inspecting the troops on the field of Borodino, see the catalog no. 571.

31. "Oil firm Seeks Divine Help," *BBC News*, November 2001, http//news.bbc.co.uk/hi/English/business/newsid.

32. See "Soviets Eager to Save Historic Buildings," *Christian Science Monitor*, August 22, 1974, p. A-3.

33. Ibid. There is a fine photograph of this church taken by Jonathan Gray.

34. Personal interview between John Garrard and VOOPIK staff, June 1980. The experience of walking into a bright, clean space occupied by a Soviet enterprise was unusual then. Soviet maintenance was notoriously slovenly, even in state hospitals, where it was particularly noticeable and dangerous.

35. For those interested in the phenomenon of the "creative unions" of the Soviet Union, see the authors' book, *Inside the Soviet Writers' Union* (New York: Free Press, 1990). While it focused on the Writers' Union, all the creative unions were like *matroyshka* dolls: of virtually identical shape and structure. The party was the ultimate authority.

36. *Pravda*, August 21, 1974, p. 2.

37. See "Soviets Eager to Save Historic Buildings," p. A-3. 1974.

38. See ibid.

39. L. A. Morozova, "The State and the Church," *Russian Social Science Review* 38, no. 1 (January–February 1997): 40–55. Translation by Michel Vale. See subheading: "Types of Legal Status of the Church." This information is cited in *Rossiiskaya gazeta*, 10 February 10, 1994, n. 8.

40. See "Two Approaches to the Problem of Ancient Monuments," *Radio Liberty Research*, January 5, 1976. The article contains a complete and balanced assessment of the entire controversy. All subsequent quotations to the debate are to this text.

41. *Sovietskaya Rossiya*, October 2, 1975, p. 4. Translation by John Garrard.

42. See "Churches-into-Factories Plans Rouse Russians," Overseas News, *London Times*, August 1, 1966, sec. 2, p. 7.

43. This institute operated departments of ancient sculpture, and their restorers were expert. The church began agitating for the return of its building in 1991, but the restorers did not have any place to go. This epic struggle was finally resolved on August 17, 2004, when Aleksy's personal appeal to the Federal Agency for Federal Property (formerly the Ministry of Property) paid off. An order was given that the Grabar restorers would be granted premises of a former factory shop on Radio Street. Thus the director, Aleksey Vladimirov, recognized that he was beaten and made the best of it by saying that that he was actually grateful to the ROC: "Since 1991 we have written letters to Moscow city hall and to the government and we asked to be resettled from the churches." This ended a quarrel that had seen Orthodox believers seize the church building forcibly and close off access to its grounds; both sides hired attorneys to argue their cases. See "Resolution of Church Seizure Nears," *Russian Religion News Current News Items*, August 18, 2004, translated by Paul Steeves, Sedmitza.ru.

44. *Molodyozh Estonii*, December 14, 1979, p. 4.

45. Smith, "An Old Cathedral for a New Russia," p. 168. See her note 25 for the rant of Vladimir Zamansky, who published them originally as "Pod klyuch? Net, pod krest!" *Literaturnaya Rossiya*, no. 38 (September 28, 1989): 4.

46. See John Garrard, "The Challenge of Glasnost: *Ogonek's* handling of Russian Anti-Semitism," *Nationalities Papers*, Fall 1991, pp. 228–50. For an analysis of VOOPIK'S connection with Pamyat, see especially pp. 229–31.

CHAPTER 4. ACCURSED QUESTIONS: WHO IS TO BLAME?

1. Translated by Dr. Howard Spier, and cited in John Garrard, "A Pamyat Manifesto: Introductory Note and Translation," *Nationalities Papers*, Fall 1991, p. 134.

2. Mikhail Iroshnikov, Liudmila Protsai, and Yuri Shelayev, *Sunset of the Romanov Dynasty*, trans. Paul Williams and Juri Pamfilov (Moscow: Terra 1992), p. 184.

3. See *Newsweek*, May 7, 1990, pp. 34–44. This quotation occurs on p. 35. The reporter for the Moscow segments of this long and interesting article is listed as Carroll Bogert.

4. Garrard, "A Pamyat Manifesto," pp. 228–50. John Garrard passed his translation along to the United Jewish Appeal, together with the number of the group's bank account. His translation of this Manifesto is what motivated us to volunteer for Operation Exodus, an international effort to sponsor Soviet Jews for emigration to Israel or the United States.

5. The vivid details of this "war to the knife" between the patriarch and the museum curators of the Kremlin cathedrals are taken from Sir Rodric Braithwaite's personal

diary. Braithwaite attended these services and was harangued by Rodimtseva herself on the issue.

6. See *New York Times Magazine*, January 28, 1990.

7. In a December 5, 1991, interview in the *Arizona Daily Star*, pp. 1C and 3C, we urged Soviet Jews to leave the USSR, with the help of Operation Exodus.

8. There is some confusion as to the date of the *Ur* edition of this book. In 1994 the editors of a Russian reprint in Novosibirsk say it went through "four" editions, but they reproduce only three prefaces. One is to the 1903 edition; "Preface to the Second Edition" is reproduced as from the 1905 edition. A third preface, which is entitled "Preface to the Third Edition," is dated 1911. It is this 1911 edition that is reprinted in 1994 in Novosibirsk, edited by A. N. Lyulko and D. G. Sushkov.

9. Binjamin W. Segel, *A Lie and a Libel: The History of the Protocols of the Elders of Zion*, ed. and trans. Richard S. Levy (Lincoln, Nebraska: University of Nebraska Press, 1955), pp. 108, 110, 110.

10. See Sergey Nilus, *Velikoe v malom: Spiritual Instructions*, Little Russian Philokalia Series, vol. 1, trans. Fr. Seraphim Rose (Platina, Calif.: St. Herman of Alaska Brotherhood, 1996), p. 108.

11. We are deeply grateful to Dr. Ann Shukman who shared with us her unpublished essay, "'The Conversation between St. Seraphim and Motovilov': The Author, the Texts, and the Publishers" (personal interview, July 2, 2005, Oxford, England). She cites these sources as taken from Michael Hagemeister, "Il problema della genesi del "Colloquio con Motovilov,"" in *San Serafim: da Sarov a Diveevo*, ed. V. Kotelnikov, S. Senyk, N. Kauchtschischwili, et al. (Monasterio di Bose, 1998), pp. 157–74.

12. There is no way to check any of this. Did Nilus decode Motovilov's handwriting correctly? Is Motovilov himself telling the truth about his conversation with Seraphim and all the other sayings of Seraphim? Nothing can be proved through either logic or rationality.

13. As quoted (with a photograph of the 1854 dossier "from the Third Department of His Imperial Majesty's Office: Titular-Councillor N. A. Motovilov's Report on the Prophecies of St. Seraphim of Sarov") in *Nicholas and Alexandra: The Last Imperial Family of Tsarist Russia*, ed. Mark Sutcliffe, from the State Hermitage and the State Archive of the Russian Federation, catalog of the exhibition at the State Hermitage Museum, 1998 (New York and London: Harry N. Abrams and Booth-Clibborn Editions, 1998), catalog no. 561, p. 340.

14. Nilus, *Velikoe v malom*, p. 124.

15. *Nicholas and Alexandra*, p. 340.

16. Seraphim's prophecies are scattered through the Chronicles of the Diveyevo Monastery—a very, very long text. A new edition in Russian was supposed to appear in 2005 published by Palomnik. There his prophecies relate to the future visit of the royal family—which did indeed occur in July 1903. He also speaks of the coming of

the Antichrist, who will not be able to cross the sacred moat surrounding the convent, and the future expansion and glory of the Diveyevo Monastery. There is nothing explicit about Jews. We thank Dr. Ann Shukman for these insights (personal letter, July 24, 2005).

17. In his preface to the 1905 edition (cited from the 1994 Novosibirsk reprint), Nilus says that the book was a success. It sold out in one year, and this has encouraged him to add new essays, "Service of the Mother of God and Seraphim," "One of the Secrets of Divine Construction," and "What Awaits Russia." He says that he will now include some essays that have appeared separately in the press, "Heavenly Inhabitants," "The Anti-Christ as an Immediate Possibility." These new articles show the "coming triumph of Christian hopes but also the imminent threat of the Devil which we must all fight." (Translation from original Russian by John Garrard.)

18. The tsarist secret police, the Okhrana, had its headquarters in St. Petersburg, but it also maintained an international headquarters in Paris, France, to oversee its European agents. Fortunately for historians, the archive of the Paris Okhrana passed intact into Western hands. It is today located at the Hoover Institute, Stanford University. The last tsarist ambassador to France gave it to Herbert Hoover, who agreed that only after the ambassador's death would its existence be made public. The Hoover's file on *The Protocols*, however, does not reveal the name of the agent.

19. For Harting's posts, see file xlllb (2) folder 5, 6, Okhrana Archive, Hoover Institution.

20. See Index xxivh. Folder 4-c, Okhrana Archive, Hoover Institution.

21. For a detailed discussion of the creation of this forgery and its worldwide impact, see *Anti-Semitism: A History Portrayed*, ed. Janrense Boonstra et al. (Amsterdam: Anne Frank Foundation, 1989), pp. 71–73. The time, place, and perpetrator of this fabrication remains an issue. In 2004 an English translation of Cesare G. De Michelis's exhaustive examination of all variants of *The Protocols* was published as *The Non-Existent Manuscript: A Study of the Protocols of the Elders of Zion*, trans. Richard Newhouse (Lincoln: University of Nebraska Press, 2004). De Michelis believes that *The Protocols* was fabricated in "1902–1903" (p. 74) and that they "were compiled on Krusevan's [the same man active in the Kishinyov pogrom and the serializer of them in his newspaper] initiative with the complicity and perhaps the help of other representatives of the antisemitic Right" (p. 81). De Michelis, however, dismisses the idea of an Okhrana forgery in Paris.

22. Boonstra et al., *Anti-Semitism: A History Portrayed*, p. 71.

23. Michael Hagemeister, whose research on *The Protocols* has now superseded the work of Norman Cohn's fine *Warrant for Genocide: The Myth of the Jewish World Conspiracy in the Protocols of the Elders of Zion*, Brown Judaic Studies (Chico, Calif.: Scholars Press, 1981), states that while the authorship of the forgery is still unclear, "Piotr Rachkovsky (1853–1910), chief of the foreign affairs department in Paris, and

his collaborator Matvey Golovinsky (1865–1920), were involved in their creation around the turn of the century, but the manner and extent of their contribution has never been clarified or proven." See his entry "The Protocols of the Elders of Zion," in *The Holocaust Encyclopedia*, ed. Walter Laqueur (New Haven: Yale University Press, 2001), p. 503. Hagemeister does not see a causal relationship between publication of *The Protocols* and the pogroms of 1905–7. He states, "The *Protocols* were discovered only in the wake of the Bolshevik revolution of 1917" (p. 501.) We have given great weight to the fact that they were appended to the 1905 edition of Nilus's *The Great in the Small*, a Russian Orthodox best seller. Subsequent prerevolutionary editions of *The Great in the Small* published *The Protocols* as well as the St. Seraphim "Conversation." The saint's cult merged popular anti-Semitism among the peasantry with the state anti-Semitism encouraged by the autocracy.

24. Steven G. Marks, *How Russia Shaped the Modern World: From Art to Anti-Semitism, Ballet to Bolshevism* (Princeton: Princeton University Press, 2003), p. 152.

25. See the newsletter printed by the Jewish Bund, *Poslednie izvestiya (Latest News)*, for eyewitness accounts of the complicity of the authorities and the police in this pogrom. Original copies are available at the Okhrana Archive, Hoover Institution.

26. See Ioann, "Bitva za Rossiyu," *Sovetskaya Rossiya*, February 20, 1993, pp. 1, 4; reprinted in *Sobesednik pravoslavnykh khristian* 1, no. 3 (1993): 19–22; extract translated as "The West Wants Chaos," in *Christianity after Communism*, ed. Niels C. Nielsen (Boulder: Westview Press, 1994), pp. 107–12.

27. See "Judge Rules on 'Protocols,'" *Arizona Jewish Post*, December 3, 1993, p. 3.

28. See Wendy Slater, "A Modern Day Saint? Metropolitan Ioann and the Postsoviet Russian Orthodox Church," *Religion, State & Society* 28, no. 4 (2000): 313–24, for a comprehensive overview of Father Ioann's career. This citation occurs on p. 316.

29. See Maria Kamenkovich, "Myth in the Making," in *Frontier*, published by Keston Research, January–February 1994, pp. 9–10.

30. Cited by Slater, "A Modern Day Saint?" p. 316, n. 16. The letter was signed by K. Dushenov and Sokolov, a man we knew as an influential member of the Russian Writer's Union. The letter, "Peterburgsky vladyka v bor'be...," appears on p. 3 of the newspaper.

31. Slater, "A Modern Day Saint?" p. 316, n. 17. Ioann's piece was entitled "The Building of Statehood," *JMP*, no. 2 (1993): 26–30. This article had originally appeared in *Sovetskaya Rossiya*, November 14, 1992, reprinted in *Sobesednik pravoslavnykh khristian* 1, no. 3 (1993): 9–12.

32. Quoted by Slater, "A Modern Day Saint?" p. 316. The text of the entire interview can be found in *Moskovskiye novosti*, no. 16 (April 17–24, 1994): 21.

33. Edited by A. N. Lyulko and D. G. Sushkov (Novosibirsk: *Blagovest* regional Orthodox press, 1994). The editors, in a giveaway as to their own bias, in their brief one-page preface, print this epigraph from Moscow Metropolitan Filaret (1782–1867):

"Love your enemies, hate the enemies of Christ and beat the enemies of the Fatherland." "Fight the enemies of the Fatherland" (*bei vragov Otechestva*) repeats the same verbal construction, *bei*, in the old tsarist call to arms for the pogroms, *bei zhidov*—or "*Beat the Yids!*" All translations from this text are by John Garrard.

34. Slater, "A Modern Day Saint?" p. 320. Like Banquo's ghost, Father Ioann refuses to go away. He still has fervent admirers within the ROC laity and hierarchy, who as of this writing (2007) are clamoring for his canonization. Father Ioann's sudden demise is eerily reminiscent of other puzzling deaths, such as that of Alexander Litvinenko, a defector from the FSB, who came to London, became a British citizen, and was poisoned by polonium in the spring of 2007. He too, had become a nuisance to the power brokers of Russia.

35. In his excellent book *Russia in Search of Itself* (Washington, D.C.: Woodrow Wilson Center Press, 2004), p. 86, James Billington describes how Oleg Platonov, a reactionary and anti-Semite, has continued the same line of Father Ioann. Platonov told Billington that Father Ioann was the inspiration for his own unpublished magnum opus, "Holy Rus," which sees the Jewish-Masonic conspiracy trying to destroy the true faith and its believers today. Platonov claims that ten days before his demise, Metropolitan Ioann gave him a manuscript, a "kind of last testament, 'Overcoming the Time of Troubles,'" which affirms how *The Protocols of the Elders of Zion* is evidence for the conspiracy. Billington also notes that Metropolitan Mefody of Voronezh speaks for the xenophobic and nationalistic side of the ROC, and the radio station of Radonezh spouts the same. Billington draws attention (p. 186, n. 53.) to Metropolitan Kirill's arguing against religious pluralism in "Rossia—pravoslavnaya, a ne mnogokonfessionalnaya strana," as quoted in *Radonezh*, no. 8, 2002.

36. See "Russian Orthodox Church to Canonize Persecuted Christians," *Lutheran World Information* 25 (1990). All subsequent citations are to this text.

37. See Yakov Krotov, *Moscow News*, no. 27 (1992).

38. G. P. Fedotov, *The Russian Religious Mind: Kievan Christianity from the Tenth to the Thirteenth Centuries* (New York: Harper Torchbooks, Harper & Brothers, 1960), p. 109. This is a paperback reprint of the original 1946 volume. Fedotov also made the following analysis of this category: "Saints Boris and Gleb created in Russia a particular, though liturgically not well defined, order of 'sufferers,' the most paradoxical order of the Russian saints. In it are included some victims of political crimes among the princes or simply victims of a violent death. Among them one finds many infants, the most famous, Prince Demetrius of Uglich in the sixteenth century, in whom the idea of innocent death is blended with the idea of purity. In most cases it is difficult to speak of voluntary death; one is entitled to speak only of the nonresistance to death" (pp. 104–5).

39. *Ogonyok*, nos. 42–43 (1992). Translated by John Garrard. All quotations from Alexander Nezhny's article are to this text. These two contrasting pieces are from a series *Proshu slovo*, "I Want to Be Heard."

40. Edward I's decree of expulsion has never been officially revoked. However, Cromwell, as Lord Protector, allowed Jews to open three synagogues in London during the Commonwealth. Prior to the restoration of the monarchy, Charles II signed a "stand fast" agreement with representatives from Parliament. This meant that those three synagogues were allowed to stay; Jews subsequently drifted back during the seventeenth century and thereafter.

41. The complete documentation of the trial has newly become available. It consists of nine reels of 35-mm microfilm, which makes up 6,200 + pages. The collection is offered by East View Information Services, 3020 Harbor Lane North, Minneapolis, MN 55447, USA. The list price is $1,260.00.

42. See Jeffrey Taylor, "Escape to Old Russia," *Atlantic Monthly*, October 2006, pp. 129–33. The author, traveled the Golden Ring circuit and writes sensitively of how such a visit "surrounds one with the artistic and spiritual treasures of Old Russia" (pp. 129–30).

43. This lady fooled many people. Upon her death, she was cremated by her husband. It would have seemed that final dispensation of the mystery was impossible until DNA researchers found that she had had an operation in Charlottesville, Virginia. Her surgeon, Dr. Shrum, had preserved a section of her colon. DNA research conclusively proved she had no relationship to the imperial family. John Garrard had noted very early on in the controversy that "Anastasia" refused to speak Russian.

44. See Andrei Zolotov Jr., "The Last Tsar: Sainthood Issue May Split Church," *St. Petersburg Times*, July 17, 1998, p. 8.

45. See Robin Lodge, "Russian Bishops Begin Final Steps to Canonise Last Tsar," *The Times*, February 19, 1997, p. 15.

46. See the SEIA *Newsletter on the Eastern Churches and Ecumenism*, no. 57 (Washington, D.C., June 27, 2000).

47. *Nicholas and Alexandra*, p. 17. Nicholas's fatalism was well known in the court. Maria Pavlovna, the wife of Grand Duke Vladimir Aleksandrovich, put it more directly: "He is weak. . . . He is a fatalist. When things go wrong, instead of making a decision one way or another, he convinces himself that it is what God has decreed, and so submits himself to God's will!"

48. Iroshnikov, Protsai, and Shelayev, *Sunset of the Romanov Dynasty*, p. 341. The editors fail to note that Grand Duchess Olga is quoting St. Paul's letter to the Romans here (12:21): "Be not overcome of evil, but overcome evil with good." The grand duchess's citation is particularly appropriate, as it occurs where Paul specifically abjures us from taking revenge. Verse 19 states forthrightly: "Dearly beloved, avenge not yourselves, but rather give place unto wrath: for it is written, Vengeance is mine; I will repay, saith the Lord."

49. See Wil van der Bercken, "The Canonization of Nicholas II in Iconographic Perspective: Political Themes in Russian Icons," in *Orthodox Christianity and*

Contemporary Europe: Selected Papers of the International Conference held at Leeds June 2001, ed. Jonathan Sutton and Wil van der Bercken (Leeds, 2002), pp. 187–209. This quotation occurs on p. 202.

50. For the transcript of this meeting see "For the First Time the Church Carries Out Her Service Free and Unfettered," ROC Web site, http://www.mospat.ru/, for October 4, 2004. All subsequent quotations are from this transcript.

51. Personal interview, anonymous, March 1992, Moscow.

52. See "Words of His Holiness Patriarch Aleksy II of Moscow and All Russia at the Opening of the All-Russian Scientific and Theological Conference 'Heritage of St. Serafim of Sarov and the Destinies of Russia,'" ROC Web site, http://www.mospat. ru/printe_news/id/7384.html, for October 4, 2004. All subsequent quotations to this speech are from this text.

53. The restoration of the monastery in Sarov was finally finished in the fall of 2006. "The Russian Orthodox Church has reopened the famed monastery in the town of Sarov, Nizhny Novgorod region. The 300-year old monastery was closed for 80 years and is one of Russia's most sacred sites. Sarov, formerly known as Arzamas-16, is also the home to the first Soviet nuclear bomb, built in 1949." *Russian Life* 49, no. 5 (2007): 11.

54. Evgeny Zamyatin, *We*, trans. Mirra Ginsburg (New York: Avon Books, 1983), p. 61. The actual speaker of these words is the Poet, R-13, a sensitive and perceptive man who has been forced to write a verse praising the Benefactor's execution of a malefactor, at a public ritual attended by all subjects of the One State. D-503 praises his trochees; R-13, who acts as a voice for Zamyatin, despises himself and everything about the One State, though his weapon is heavy irony. He sarcastically says, "all this is good, all this is sublime, magnificent, noble, elevated, crystally pure. Because it protects our unfreedom—that is, our happiness" (p. 62). Only by keeping its subjects in an artificially prolonged state of childish innocence can the One State preserve its hegemony. The minute the Numbers think for themselves, all the structures of the state's power will crumble.

55. Of course, the general tenor of the patriarch's approach to Russian Orthodox anti-Semitism has been clear through what has been published—and not published—inside the *JMP*. Apart from the one time the infamous Father Ioann managed to slip in some rant, not once in its many post-1991 articles detailing the loss of its churches and its sufferings at the hand of the Soviet state, has there ever been a call for revenge, or trials to identify and punish the evildoers. Instead, the *JMP* has consistently empha-sized that it is not a question of who but why. And it answers that question by glossing a phrase from the book of Isaiah: "When we received double for our sins," which deserves to be quoted: "Speak ye comfortably to Jerusalem, and cry unto her, that her warfare is accomplished, that her iniquity is pardoned: for she hath received of the Lord's hand double for all her sins" (40:2) The *JMP*'s citation derives its power from the ancient

belief of Orthodox Russians that they are the people of the Second Jerusalem, the "Chosen" of the New Testament, just as the Jews were the Chosen of the Old. These words, come directly from the mouth of the Lord, "Comfort ye, comfort ye my people, saith your God," are read as meant for them. The church's official position, then, is that seventy years of Soviet power was God's punishment for Russia's own sins. As for why Divine Power should have chosen to hand out a double portion, well, God's will cannot be comprehended but only obeyed. Here the ROC falls back on its thousand-year theological stance with respect to theodicy: the ways of God are mysterious to men.

56. Canon Michael Bourdeaux, a distinguished Anglican churchman, wrote in his exceptionally prescient profile of Aleksy, "Such a statement could do much good." "Between Hammer and Anvil," *Guardian*, September 2, 1991, p. 19.

57. It is true that he has not intervened when publications outside the purview of the ROC have printed anti-Semitic rant. It seems he feels he has his hands full with the anti-Semites within his own church. The *Dallas Jewish Week* reported on January 25, 2001, in a short article entitled "Kudos to Anti-Semites," that "The Patriarch of the Russian-Orthodox Church congratulated the editorial staff of *Russkie Vestnik*, a Russian-Orthodox newspaper known to be openly anti-Semitic, on the 10th anniversary of its publication. Patriarch Aleksy II thanks the newspaper, which has published articles about the Jewish 'fifth column' and the 'fascism of the Jewish Bourgeoisie' in Russia, for upholding the traditional values of the Russia people, and he wished its staff success in their future work." The *Dallas Jewish Week*, however, is wrong that *Russkie Vestnik* (*Russian Herald*) is an official organ of the ROC.

58. Dr. James Billington to no avail appealed personally to President Putin to show mercy to Khodorkovsky. By July 2006, the assets of Yukos were being sold off by the Russian government, and Western capitalists were among the eager bidders. The only Western voice raised against this scramble over the pickings was that of the philanthropist George Soros. We met Khodorkovsky in 1994, at his father's apartment in Kiev. His father introduced him as a *biznesmen*.

59. Vjekoslav Perica, *Balkan Idols: Religion and Nationalism in Yugoslav States* (Oxford: Oxford University Press, 2002), pp. 166, 166, 167, 163. This is the most detailed and objective study of this complex subject and deals impartially with the role religion played in those tormented years.

60. See ibid., p. 293, n. 164, for his own translation of this statement, which was originally printed in *Vijesnik*, March 6, 1991.

61. See "Videotape Forces Serbs to Face War Crimes," *New York Herald Tribune*, June 11, 2005, p. 3, col. 1. The videotape was submitted as evidence in the trial of the former Yugoslav leader Slobodan Milosevic at the International Criminal Tribunal for the former Yugoslavia in The Hague.

62. Michael Sells, "Kosovo Mythology and the Bosnian Genocide," in *In God's Name: Genocide and Religion in the Twentieth Century*, ed. Omer Bartov and Phyllis

Mack (New York: Berghahn Books, 2001), p. 184. This excellent volume is part of the Studies on War and Genocide Series, the general editor of which is Omer Bartov.

63. Michael Sells, "Religion, History and Genocide in Bosnia-Herzegovina," in *Religion and Justice in the War over Bosnia*, ed. G. Scott Davis (New York: Routledge, 1996), p. 24.

64. Sells, *In God's Name*, p. 196.

65. Unpublished diary of Sir Rodric Braithwaite, April 12, 1992. The ambassador quotes Aleksy as declaring that "the Russian Orthodox Church is not anti-Semitic, for we share the Old Testament and its prophets with the Jews."

CHAPTER 5. IRRECONCILABLE DIFFERENCES: ORTHODOXY AND THE WEST

1. All citations are to the New Testament, the King James version.

2. Visitors to Hillwood, the home of Marjorie Post in Washington, D.C., may see the original set.

3. See p. 41 of the article by Archpriest Simeon Solovyev, "On the Feast of the Apostle St. Andrew the First Called," *JMP*, no. 12 (1987): 41.

4. Ibid.

5. See a photo of the monument, dated to "early 1910s" in Mikhail Iroshnikov, Liudmila Protsai, and Yuri Shelayev, *The Sunset of the Romanov Dynasty*, trans. Paul Williams and Juri Pamfilov (Moscow: Terra, 1992), p. 10.

6. Quoted by Edward V. Williams, "Aural Icons of Orthodoxy: The Sonic Typology of Russian Bells," in *Christianity and the Arts in Russia*, ed. William Craft Brumfield and Milos Velimirovic (New York: Cambridge University Press, 1991), p. 5.

7. How does the actual Acts of the Apostles fit with this? It is worth remembering that, from the outset, the Russian Orthodox had only the Four Gospels translated into Old Church Slavonic (OCS). A Russian printing of Acts of the Apostles into OCS did not occur until the sixteenth century during the reign of Ivan the Terrible, who established the first printing press. This book, *Apostol*, was desperately needed by the Orthodox for the Easter liturgy, as it is read in its entirety on Holy Saturday. Russian copies of this exceedingly rare book had fallen to tatters by the twentieth century. It was the librarian of the Codrington, John Simmons, who found a pristine and uncut copy in an Anglican bishop's library in Dublin—he had been given it on a visit to Ivan's court, and, unable to read the Cyrillic, had misfiled the copy in his library under "Greek." Needless to say, Russian historians and theologians were thrilled when Simmons ensured the return of an immaculate copy to them.

8. As quoted by George P. Fedotov, *The Russian Religious Mind: Kievan Christianity from the Tenth to the Thirteenth Centuries* (New York: Harper Torchbooks, 1960), p. 89.

9. Hilarion was soaked in the Gospel of John, as is attested by his text for the most

famous sermon of medieval Russian history, "On the Law and the Grace." This draws a contrast between the Old Testament, which says man is saved through the law (i.e., Moses), and the New Testament, which declares that man is saved through Grace. The key verse comes from the Gospel of John: "For the law was given by Moses, but Grace and Truth came by Jesus Christ" (John 1:17).

10. The *JMP*, no. 6 (1987), had for its inside frontispiece a color reproduction of Rublyov's masterpiece, and a selection of how church fathers have interpreted it: St. John Chrysostom: "The Trinity is existing before all ages, and is without beginning, unoriginate, eternal, ageless, deathless, endless, unwaxing, indestructible and inviolable." St. Athanasios the Great: "The catholic faith consists in our worshipping One God in the Trinity and the Three in One, without merging the Hypostases and without splitting the essence. ... The Father is not created by anyone, and is not made or begotten; the Son is begotten of the Father, and is not made or created; the Holy Spirit is not made, created or begotten, but proceedeth from the Father. Within this Holy Trinity ... all the three Hypostases are co-eternal and equal." Not one word of these learned disquisitions mentions Abraham, or the source of the incident in Genesis.

11. As quoted by Mara Kozelsky, "Ruins into Relics: The Monument to Saint Vladimir on the Excavations of Chersonesos, 1827–57," *Russian Review* 63 (October 2004): 655–72. The citation occurs on p. 655.

12. Personal interview, Oxford, England, 1991.

13. The illustrations are by K. K. Kuznetsov, *Kreshchenie Rusi: 988–1988* (Moscow, 1992). The borders were borrowed from the well-known tsarist illustrator Bilibin, whose work was still familiar even in Soviet times because of his famous books illustrating Russian folk tales. The original publisher of *Kreshchenie Rusi* was Zaria Publishing Inc., 73 Biscay Road, London, Ontario, Canada. We thank Serge Sauer, president of Zaria, for his permission to reprint from this fascinating booklet.

14. Personal interview, Moscow, March 1992.

15. On July 14, 2006, the *Guardian's* magazine "G2" featured an intriguing article by Natasha Walter, "On a Wink and a Prayer," pp. 6–11. The cover illustration was clasped hands praying, with the fingers crossed. The subtitle was "How Parents Lie to Get Their Children into Church Schools." According to the article there are approximately seven thousand "faith schools" in the state education system in England. Of these the vast majority are Christian, and nearly two thousand of them are "voluntary-aided" (i.e., fee-paying) Church of England primary schools. As the piece made clear, these are two thousand near clones of the Orthodox primary school of St. Vladimir's in Moscow—that is, parents who are not believers of the Church of England vie to get their children into them because the quality is higher, and the discipline is better. Some English parents resort to even attending the local Church of England to ensure a place for their offspring. This should be a salutary reminder that

parents everywhere simply want the best for their children. Some of the volunteers we saw helping restore St. Vladimir's church were doing so to get their child into its excellent preschool.

16. Natalya Baranskaya, "A Week Like Any Other," trans. Pieta Monks, in *A Week Like Any Other and Other Stories* (London: Virago Press, 1989). Baranskaya's short story, originally published in Russia *Novy mir* (1969), tells of a married working mother with two small children having to patch together child care using state day care centers. A CNN documentary, *Soviet Women*, shown in late Soviet times, illustrates how nothing had changed. One of the mother's interviewed boarded her child from Monday to Friday at a center a full two-hour train journey from her job in central Moscow.

17. The pantheon of *Ravnoapostolnye* begins with Constantine, the Roman general and emperor. Then come Cyril and Methodius, two ninth-century monks who created the special alphabet that allowed the translation of the Gospels into a language for the Eastern Slavs. This eventually became Old Church Slavic and was accorded the status of a "sacred language" by the church prior to the 1054 split. Grand Princess Olga of Novgorod converted to Christianity in 954 but failed to persuade her son to follow suit. St. Vladimir, her grandson, "Equal to the Apostles," brought Christianity to the Slavs.

18. According to *Atlas of the Christian Church*, ed. Henry Chadwick and G. R. Evans (New York: Facts on File Publication, 1987), p. 74, "At Constantinople and at Antioch, in the period of Byzantine rule there from 969 until the 1070s," the emperors, because they were charged with the duty of safeguarding the faith, also bore the epithet "equal to the apostles." We have not been able to ascertain if the title was retained by the dynasty of the Palaiologoi after the city was retaken for Orthodoxy in 1261.

19. Quoted in *Moscow: 850th Anniversary*, gen. ed. V. A. Vinogradov (Moscow: Publishing House AO "Moscow Textbooks," 1996), 1:151. This reference occurs in a chapter entitled "The Second Jerusalem," by M. P. Koudriavtsev and G. Ya. Mokeev. No translator is named from the original Russian. We are grateful to Malcolm Walker, the librarian of Keston Institute, for letting us use his personal copy.

20. See "Children's Games," *Russian Life*, November–December 2006, pp. 50–51, for a color picture of manly Prince Vladimir from the film. The cartoon was a hit in Russia; it was withdrawn after being shown for two weeks in Ukraine—its call for "brothers to unite" against foreign enemies was read by the Ukrainians as a pitch for "brotherly states" to unite—that is, for Ukraine to join with its Big Brother Russia.

21. See Paul Abelsky, "Redrawing Russian History," *Russia Profile* 3, no. 4 (May 2007): 45. *Prince Vladimir*, as the article notes, is part of a trilogy of big budget, Disney-style action cartoons concerning Russia's medieval heroes. Next year will be the third installment, describing the heroics of Ilya Muromets.

22. *Atlas of the Christian Church*, ed. Henry Chadwick and G. R. Evans (New York: Facts on File Publication, 1987), p. 58.

23. The Orthodox cite the Gospel of John as being God the Son's own statement about the procession of the Holy Spirit. In John 15:26 Jesus speaks authoritatively: "But when the Comforter [*Paraclete*] is come, *whom I will send unto you* from the Father, even the Spirit of truth, which *proceedeth from the Father*, he shall testify of me" (emphasis added). According to Orthodox theology, this verse is the precise revelation of Scripture: Christ sends the Spirit, but it proceeds from the Father. To add "and the Son" to the Procession of the Holy Spirit makes for double procession. This would contaminate the Holy Ghost by confusing the inner relations of the Persons of the Trinity. Those puzzled by all this (and that includes the authors) must take at face value the Orthodox assertion that they are the only ones who understand the Trinity correctly.

The issue is so opaque that the brilliant historian Diarmaid MacCullough in his authoritative work *The Reformation* (New York: Viking, 2003) reprints the Nicene Creed, which he correctly labels an "Eastern Creed," yet unaccountably adds the words "and the Son" to the statement on the procession of the Holy Spirit.

24. We thank Bishop Kallistos (known previously as Timothy Ware) for an extensive interview after his informative seminar "The Council of Florence (1438–39): Success or Failure?" held at All Souls College, Oxford, on May 23, 2005. The seminar itself was part of a series on Byzantine Church History hosted by All Souls College.

25. *The Historical Road of Eastern Orthodoxy*, trans. Lydia Kesich (Crestwood, N.Y.: St. Vladimir's Seminary Press, 2003), p. 14. For those interested in a fuller discussion of this topic, see Afanassiev et al., *The Primacy of Peter in Orthodox Thought* (London, 1963).

26. This forthright summation of the Great Schism is found in Archpriest Lev Lebedev, "Veneration of St. Nicholas in Russia (Concluded)," *JMP*, no. 6 (1987): 69.

27. Anon., *Door to Paradise: Jesus Christ in Ancient Orthodoxy* (N.p.: St. Herman Press, n.d.), p. 13. Also see its accompanying "Time Line of Church History."

28. As quoted by Jonathan Phillips, *The Fourth Crusade and the Sack of Constantinople* (London: Pimlico, 2005), p. 299. The original citation is to Innocent III, "Letters," *Contemporary Sources for the Fourth Crusade*, trans. A. J. Andrea (Leiden, 2000), pp. 116–17.

29. Phillips, *The Fourth Crusade*, p. 299.

30. Quoted by George Herring, *An Introduction to the History of Christianity: From the Early Church to the Enlightenment* (London: Continuum, 2006), pp. 173–74. Herring is generally an apologist for the papacy.

31. Of course, the ROC is not the only faith that does not look back upon the Crusades with pleasure. Their legacy looms very large in the Muslim psyche as well.

President Bush's doubtless instinctual reference to "a crusade against terrorism" sent furious shock waves through the Islamic world, and he had to drop the image forthwith, switching to the phrase "war on terrorism."

32. The Inquisition itself lasted much longer than the extermination of the Cathars and the crusades against the Russians. It continued until 1820, when it was replaced by an organization called Congregation for the Doctrine of the Faith. The current pope, Benedict XVI, headed this organization when he was Cardinal Joseph Ratzinger. His July 2006 visit to Spain illustrated his extreme irritation at the liberal social laws transforming that country.

33. Solovyev, "On the Feast of the Apostle St. Andrew the First Called," p. 42. This theft occurred in 1208, and the relics were translated to the Cathedral Church of Amalfi, Italy. Under Pope Pius II, the head itself was translated to the Cathedral of St. Peter the Apostle in Rome. Andrew was martyred in Patras (Achaia) by its ruler, Aegeatos.

34. See Janet Martin, *Medieval Russia, 980–1584* (repr., Cambridge: Cambridge University Press, 2004), p. 155.

35. See *Byzantium: Faith and Power (1261–1557)*, ed. Helen Evans, catalog to the exhibition at the Metropolitan Museum of Art (New Haven: Yale University Press, 2004). See the essay by Alice-Mary Talbot, "Revival and Decline: Voices from the Byzantine Capital," pp. 20-21, for interesting examples of these unfortunate young women (one was a girl of five) who were pawns in the dynastic game.

36. Fedotov, *The Russian Religious Mind*, p. 383.

37. The Council of Lyon, which met in 1274 trying to rejoin the church halves, failed. After the Council of Florence, the Greek East was invited to the Council of Trent but did not go. Representatives were again invited to Vatican I and did not go. They were invited to the Second Vatican Council, but only in the status of observers, the same footing accorded Protestant clerics. It was finally at Vatican II that the mutual anathema Eastern and Western Christianity visited upon each other back in 1054 was officially revoked.

38. See N. P. Tanner, ed., *Decrees of the Ecumenical Councils* (London: Sheed & Ward, 1990), p. 523.

39. Ibid., pp. 523–28. See Session 6, held on July 6, 1439. Though the allusion is not referenced either in the decree or by Tanner, citing First Chronicles 16:31, was a deliberate and appropriate step by the Council of Florence: it comes from David's psalm to "thank the Lord" as the Israelites deliver the Ark of the Covenant "in joyful procession" to the City of David—that is, Jerusalem. The council thought its work would go to building a "new" Jerusalem of reunited Christianity.

40. See *Moscow: 850th Anniversary*, 1:178. The reference given for the quotation is cited (p. 193, n. 44) as A. V. Kartashev, *Essays on the History of Russian Church* (Paris: YMCA Press, 1959; 1991), 1:369.

41. The Russians were not alone in this astringent view of the Turkish victory. The theologian Gennadios II Scholarios (1400/5-1472) had been enslaved during the chaos of the sack of the city, but Mehmed II freed him and made him the patriarch of the Orthodox Church. Gennadios had attended the Council of Florence 1938–39, and he retrospectively very much regretted the Decree of Union. The contemporary historian Doukas (ca. 1400–ca. 1462) quoted Gennadios "as allying himself with Grand Duke Loukas Notaras (r. 1449–53), who is supposed to have said, as the Turkish army massed before the walls of Constantinople before its fall, 'It would be better to see the turban of the Turks reigning in the center of the City than the Latin mitre.'" These details are taken from the introductory essay to *Byzantium: Faith and Power (1261–1557)*, p. 13.

42. Of course, secular historians might wish to point to the fact that the same Grand Prince Vasily II who threw Isidore into prison and rejected the Unity Accord had already won from the Horde in 1432 the patent to collect the taxes paid by the Russians as tribute. This meant that hereafter no rural princes could become grand princes.

43. As quoted by Abraham Ascher, *The Kremlin*, Wonders of Man Series (New York: Newsweek, 1972), p. 29.

44. *Byzantium: Faith and Power (1261–1557)*, contains catalog no. 4, "Reveted Icon with the Virgin Hodegetria" (pp. 28–30), which it identifies as the very icon given to the Trinity–Saint Sergius Monastery by Sophia. This monastery was under the protection of the city's grand princes. Sophia prayed for an heir at the monastery, and her son, the future Vasily III, was born in 1479. He was declared the heir after a dynastic struggle. It seems that the original icon was damaged, and it is theorized that Dionysius, the most famous icon painter of the time, painted it over. This attribution is apparently becoming acceptable to art historians, who have analyzed its pigments, which are similar to works securely attributed to him (see p. 30, n. 9).

45. As cited in *The Russian Chronicles: A Thousand Years That Changed the World; From the Beginnings of the Land of Rus to the New Revolution of Glasnost Today*, ed. Tessa Clark (London: Garamond Publishers with Random Century, 1990), p. 128. See also Cyril Toumanoff, "Moscow the Third Rome: Genesis and Significance of a Politico-Religious Idea," *Catholic Historical Review* 40, no. 4 (January 1955): 438. For the dating and purpose of Filofey's epistle, see N. Andreyev, "Filofei and His Epistle to Ivan Vasilievich," *Slavonic & East European Review* 38 (1959–60): 1–31. The "Appolonian heresy" Filofey alludes to derives from "Apollinaris, Bishop of Laodicea (d. 392), [who] in his efforts to demonstrate his anti-Arianism [a heresy that Christ was not coequal to the Father because there was a time when he was not "begotten"] emphasized the divinity of the Lord at the expense of his manhood and ended by creating a heresy of his own which denied that Christ had a human mind." From Paul Johnson, *A History of Christianity* (London: Penguin Books, 1990), p. 90.

46. See Stephen Graham, *Ivan the Terrible* (London: Ernest Benn, 1932), pp. 198–99, for an exciting account of the duel between Metropolitan Phillip and the half-mad Ivan.

47. Ibid., p. 305. See the chapter "Tsar and Jesuit Debate the Faith" (pp. 319–23) for both the Jesuit's and Kremlin's versions of this verbal duel.

48. Ibid., p. 320.

49. As quoted by Paul D. Steeves, *Keeping the Faiths: Religion and Ideology in the Soviet Union*, Beyond the Kremlin, a publication of the Committee for National Security (New York: Holmes & Meier, 1989), pp. 42–43.

50. Ibid., p. 46. See also pp. 43–46, for a document-based assessment of Avvakum, the most famous of Patriarch Nikon's victims.

51. This excerpt from *The Spiritual Regulation of Peter the Great* (Seattle: University of Washington Press, 1972), pp. 60–61, is reprinted in ibid., p. 47.

52. See Ascher, *The Kremlin*, p. 79.

53. This discrepancy had profound historical consequences for the Battle of Austerlitz: no one on the staffs of either the Russians or the Austrians noticed they were on different calendars when they were synchronizing their plans. The Russians simply showed up too late to be of real help. Napoleon won one of his greatest victories.

54. The interested reader may consult the *Cultural Atlas of Russia and the Soviet Union*, ed. Robin Milner-Gulland with Nikolai Dejevsky (New York: Facts on File, 1989), pp. 92–93, for a succinct and perceptive analysis of this bizarre side to Peter's personality.

55. Father Artyom, quoted by Anita Deyneka, "Stepping Back from Freedom," *Christianity Today*, November 17, 1997, p. 10.

56. See Geraldine Fagan, "Will Moscow Salvation Army's Rights Be Restored?" March 29, 2007, p. 2, Forum 18 Web site, http://www.forum18.org/. The Council of Europe's Convention for the Protection of Human Rights and Fundamental Freedoms entered force for Russia in 1998. The Salvation Army filed its case in Strasbourg under Article 46 of the convention. The Russian Council of Ministers paid the judgment. The official at the Federal Registration Service of the Ministry of Justice, one Viktor Korolev, has made the Moscow Salvation Army's existence as difficult as possible. Out in the provinces, it has been able to function much more easily.

57. The Web site of Forum 18 News Service, located in Oslo, Norway, can be located at: http://www.forum18.org/. See August 26, 2007, p. 5, for the story's latest permutations.

58. Anita Deyneka, "Stepping Back from Freedom," p. 10.

59. This entire interview is recounted at http://www.mosnews.com/commentary/2005/04/05/churchstory.shtml. All subsequent quotations are to this text.

60. The Russians still remember that during the breakdown of negotiations in Brest Litovsk between Germany and Trotsky for an armistice, Germany invaded Russia all

the way through the Crimea and beyond the Don. The Germans actually reached more deeply into the country than did Hitler's Panzers in the winter of 1941–42.

61. The two prelates met at the Patriarchal Cathedral of St. George, in Istanbul. The Order of St. Andrew/Archons of the Ecumenical Patriarchate in America, who owe allegiance to the patriarch of Constantinople, took out a full-page ad in the *New York Times*, December 21, 2006, p. A13, ecstatically hailing this visit as support by the pope for his "Fellow Apostle of Peace, … Bartholomew." The purpose of the ad is to let the West know that Turkey is confiscating churches, orphanages, cemeteries, and schools of the Ecumenical Patriarchate. The eight-column picture of the two prelates describes them as "joining hands in solidarity." Bartholomew is described as the "269th successor of St. Andrew, the First Called Apostle," while Benedict is the 265th successor of St. Peter.

62. On November 2, 2000, the English edition of *Pravoslavie.ru* (Web site of the Moscow Patriarchate) had this as its headline: "The Scandalous Visit of Patriarch Bartholomew to Estonia Is Over." Without letting Aleksy know in advance, Demetrios's successor, Bartholomew, showed up in Estonia—the canonical territory of the Moscow Patriarchate. It is also, of course, the home turf of Aleksey Ridiger, former altar boy for the Tallinn's Cathedral of St. Prince Alexander Nevsky. Aleksy had proclaimed Bishop Platon of Revel as a "New Martyr," at the Cathedral of Christ the Savior on August 20, 2000. Platon was bishop of Revel (the future Tallinn) and vicar of the diocese of Riga. The Bolsheviks murdered him in January 1919. Bartholomew claimed he wanted to visit Estonia to canonize Platon as a New Martyr for the Russian Orthodox Church of Constantinople. However, Platon had not been Constantinople's cleric. Bartholomew's actual agenda was that he wanted to abrogate the decision reached earlier that the Constantinople Patriarchate would hand over the legal deeds to eighteen churches to the ROC, which already administered and used the properties, and had done so for years.

63. Father Ronald Robertson, CSP, "East & West: Healing the Rift," in *John Paul II*, ed. Sister May Ann Walsh, RSM (Lanham, Md.: Sheed & Ward, 2003), p. 200.

64. See Kate Connoly, "Pope Says Sorry for Crusaders' Rampage in 1204," World News, *Telegraph*, June 30, 2004, p. 13. The article notes that John Paul also apologized to the Greek Orthodox and asked God's forgiveness for Catholic misdeeds against their faith. He also said "sorry" to the Muslims for the Crusades.

65. See Jeffrey Gros, FSC, Eamon McManus, and Ann Riggs, *Introduction to Ecumenism* (New York: Paulist Press, 1998), p. 167.

CHAPTER 6. THE BABYLONIAN LEGACY: EXILES, MARTYRS, AND COLLABORATORS

1. Felix Corley, "Russia: The Patriarch and the KGB," *Keston News Service*, no. 9 (2000): 8.

2. Grossman never attempted to publish this work in his lifetime; he knew it was treason. On his deathbed he entrusted it to the love of his life, Mme. Yekaterina Zabolotskaya. In 1993 she gave the original manuscript to John Garrard for transmittal to the West. He donated it to the Andrey Sakharov Archive, now at Harvard University's library, where it is readily available to other researchers.

3. The *obrashchenie* puts this phrase in quotations, but then does not give the address of the verse. It seems to refer to Colossians 2:8, where Paul admonishes the flock to follow the example of Christ and not behave according to the ways of men: "Beware lest any man spoil you through philosophy and vain deceit, after the tradition of men, *after the rudiments of the world, and not after Christ [po stikhiyam mira, a ne po Khristu].*" This fits very well with the *obrashchenie's* message.

4. Unpublished diary of Sir Rodric Braithwaite, entry for April 12, 1992.

5. Braithwaite revealed this part of his vita himself at the end of his article, "Heated Words Have No Place in a Post–Cold War World," Op-Ed, *Financial Times*, May 2, 2007.

6. The biographical details of Sergy, the history of the Local Council, Sergy's role in the early Soviet period, his election as patriarch in 1943, and the account of the meeting with Stalin are taken from Dr. Ann Shukman's informative article, "Metropolitan Sergy Stragorodsky: The Case of the Representative Individual," *Religion, State, and Society* 34, no. 1 (March 2006): 51–61.

7. As cited in ibid., p. 55. The original citation is to M. Vostryshev, *Patriarch Tikhon* (*Zhizn zamechatelnykh lyudei, Seriya biograficheskaya*, no. 726) (Moscow: Molodaya Gvardiya, 1997).

8. The best discussion of the iconostasis is found in Leonid Ouspensky, *Theology of the Icon*, vol. 2, trans. Anthony Gythiel (Crestwood, N.Y.: St. Vladimir's Seminary Press, 1992). This discussion of the icon of the Good Thief and its placement occurs on p. 278. Leonid Ouspensky was also a well-known icon painter; his students painted many of the icons for the iconostasis of the Cathedral of the Dormition of the Theotokos and All Saints, the cathedral for the Sourozh Diocese located in London.

9. James Billington has discussed the incredible emotions of the Moscow crowd at the funeral procession of the three young men with great sensitivity in *Russia Transformed: Breakthrough to Hope* (New York: Free Press, 1992), pp. 122–38.

10. Dimitry Pospielovsky argues in his excellent study, *The Orthodox Church in the History of Russia* (Crestwood, N.Y.: St. Vladimir's Seminary Press, 1998), that Yakunin was defrocked because he ran for Parliament. The Synod ordered all priests running for election, whether locally or nationally, to withdraw as candidates. All did but Yakunin. See pp. 357–58 for an in-depth analysis of his case.

11. *Frontier*, September–October 1991, p. 15.

12. See "Father Gleb Yakunin Readmitted to Priestly Duties," *Radio Liberty*, no. 213, June 5, 1987.

13. See Popielovsky, *The Orthodox Church*, p. 397, n. 28.

14. This letter is known only through *samizdat*. During Soviet times, it was censored out of collections of Lenin's works published in the USSR. This citation occurs in a perceptive article by Dr. Vera Tolz, the granddaughter of the distinguished Russian historian Dmitri Likhachev, a full member of the Soviet Academy of Sciences, and an expert on old Russian culture. See "Church-State Relations under Gorbachev," *Radio Free Europe/Radio Liberty Research Bulletin*, September 11, 1987 (RL 360/87), p. 10.

15. The English translation of this address is printed in a book entitled *The Truth about Religion in Russia* (London: Hutchinson & Co., 1942). The selection from Sergy's address of June 22, 1941, is found on p. 9.

16. Shukman, "Metropolitan Sergii Stragorodsky," p. 58. All details of the meeting in the Kremlin are taken from this article.

17. This extremely valuable remark is quoted on p. 11 of the text of an interview with Archpriest Georgy Mitrofanov, who participated in the All Diaspora Pastoral Conference in Nyack, N.Y. (December 8–12, 2003). An English edition, entitled "New Martyrs Unify Us," was posted on the ROC Web site at http://www.pravoslavie. ru. The man who interviewed him was Maxim Massalitin. See also www.russian-orthodox-church.org.ru.

18. See Alexander Solzhenitsyn's superb chapter 21, "Old Age," in his novel *The First Circle* (New York: Harper & Row, 1968), pp. 112–16, for a fascinating view of Stalin's personality and mind-set. The chapter acts as virtual interior monologue for the dictator.

19. Personal interview conducted on August 4, 2006, at Keston Institute in Oxford, England, with Yevgeny Ostanin, a professor from the Vyatka State University of Humanities in Kirov, Russia. Professor Ostanin possesses the archive of Boris Talantov. Ostanin stated he is himself an atheist, but he believes that the ROC has returned to its former subservience under Soviet power. His view of those officials in the patriarchate is that, because they called themselves Christians, they should have been willing to take up their Cross and follow Talantov's path to martyrdom. When we mentioned the statement of Jesus that occurs in each of the Synoptic Gospels, "Judge not, that ye be not judged," he looked uncomprehending.

20. Gregory Mitrofanov, *Istoriya russkoi pravoslavnoi tserkvi 1900–1927* (*History of the Russian Orthodox Church, 1900–1927*) (St. Petersburg: Satis, 2002). Mitrofanov is on record as stating that he wrote this book at the request of Metropolitan Ioann (Snychev) of St. Petersburg—that is, the same Ioann who had encouraged the publication of *The Protocols of the Elders of Zion*. Mitrofanov makes no mention of this part of Father Ioann's past and simply states that parishes from the Russian Orthodox Church Abroad (ROCA) were springing up in the fatherland in post-Soviet Russia. They called themselves the "Free Russian Orthodox Church" (FROC). ROCA had created these FROC parishes, on May 16, 1990, alleging that God's grace was absent

from the sacraments performed by clergy of the Russian Orthodox Church who had collaborated with the regime. However, grace would be present in the services and sacraments given by those priests who had not collaborated. (Exactly how believers were to determine whether their priest had collaborated was unclear.) Therefore, Ioann asked Mitrofanov to publish an "objective" study of the history of this émigré church.

21. Mitrofanov, *Istoriya*, p. 2.

22. Ibid., p. 10.

23. See the Web site of the Moscow Patriarchate, www.mospat.ru, for an account of the visit along with a photograph of Putin, Laurus, and Aleksy.

24. There is an excellent discussion of the Tikhvin icon, and others painted like it, in Leonid Ouspensky and Vladimir Lossky, *The Meaning of Icons*, trans. G.E.H. Palmer and E. Kadloubovsky (Crestwood, N.Y.: St. Vladimir's Seminary Press, 1999), p. 85. This is the fifth printing of the original 1952 edition. All of this superb book repays careful study.

25. See the *Telegraph*, July 8, 2004, for a vivid account and photo of the return.

26. See Steven Lee Myers and Erin E. Arvedlund, "In Russian Church, Still an Undercurrent of Animosity to the Vatican and the Pope," *New York Times*, April 7, 2005.

27. Shukman, "Metropolitan Sergi Stragorodsky," p. 51.

28. *Russian Life* 49, no. 6 (November–December 2006): 8. See "Note Book," for the entry "Almost There: Two Russian Orthodox Churches Approaching Reunification." The article quotes Aleksy pointing out that ROCOR had only 280 parishes while the ROC has more than 27,000. Under the tentative agreement, ROCOR will retain a considerable amount of autonomy from the Russian Orthodox Church. On November 30, 2006, the "Act of Canonical Communion" was published on the ROC Web site.

29. See Sophia Kishkovsky, "2 Russian Churches, Split by War, to Reunite," *New York Times*, International section, Thursday, May 17, 2007. A nice black-and-white photo of worshipers praying accompanies the article. All subsequent quotations to this event are from this article.

30. See "His Holiness Patriarch Alexy [*sic*] meets with President of Russia Putin," www.mospat.ru for May 29, 2007.

31. Mikhail P. Kudryavtsev, *Moskva, Trety Rim* (*Moscow, the Third Rome*) (Russia: Sol Systems Ltd., 1994). We were able to obtain the Russian version of this book at the Keston Research Institute in Oxford, England.

32. Aleksy's approval almost certainly translated into a considerable subvention. Its heavy silk paper and hundreds of full-color reproductions make this a Russian equivalent of an opulent coffee table book. Readers in the West who are familiar with the seminal works of William Brumfield on Russian Church architecture may find the self-conscious encomiums by Kudryavtsev a bit jarring, but he writes from the perspective of faith. Ibid., chap. 4.

33. Kudryavtsev's analysis of the monk Filofey's "Third Rome" identification of Moscow begins by carefully laying out the origin of this trinity of cities: it began as a Troy-Rome-Constantinople linkage. At that time, Constantinople was seen as the final culmination of the series, the Christian capital of the world. The Slavs abandoned Troy and saw Constantinople as the center of the true faith. Kudryavtsev argues that the search for a "Third Rome" to carry the true faith forward began in 1204, with the sacking of Constantinople by the Venetian-led Fourth Crusade. This fatally weakens the Byzantine Empire, though it predates the final taking of the city by almost 250 years.

34. Kudryaytsev, *Moskva, Trety Rim*, top of column 2, p. 254. Translation by John Garrard.

35. Ouspensky and Lossky, *The Meaning of Icons*, p. 15. It is intriguing that Vladimir Lossky quotes the same verse from Colossians 2:8 that the August 30, 1991, Appeal from Aleksy and the Holy Synod does. The verse makes a distinction between living according to the "tradition of men, after the rudiments of the world, and not after Christ."

36. The continuation of this prayer is equally moving:

By Thine all-powerful might,
Mercifully deliver all of us and Thy holy church
From ever evil circumstance.
Free our Russia Land
From the cruel godless ones and their power
And raise the holy Orthodox Russia;
Hearken unto the painful cry of thy faithful servants
Who cry unto Thee day and night
In tribulation and sorrow ...
Grant peace and tranquility, love and steadfastness, and
Swift reconciliation to Thy people,
Whom Thou has redeemed by Thy precious Blood.
But unto them that have departed from Thee and seek Thee not,
Be Thou manifest,
That not one of them perish,
But all of them be saved and come to the knowledge of Thy truth,
That all in harmonious oneness of mind and unceasing love
May glorify Thy most holy name,
O patient-hearted Lord Who art quick to forgive,
Unto the ages of ages. Amen.

37. See http://www.compromat.ru/main/rpc/a.htm.

38. See Craig S. Smith and Ian Fisher, "Second Church Official Resigns in Poland," *New York Times*, January 9, 2007, p. A6.

39. This story is ongoing. See the "Poland Reels at New Wave of Charges Against Clerics," *New York Times*, International section, January 10, 2007, p. A6. See also Serge Schmemann, "A Bishop's Fall Provides a View on Soviet era Collaboration," editorial page. *New York Times*, January 16, 2007. Of course, not just the clergy was collaborating. The revelations from the archives have ensnared more than 700,000 Poles, including journalists, teachers, and company directors, as well as priests and politicians. See "Poland Must Stop the Witch-hunt," editorial, *Financial Times*, April 30, 2007, p. 10.

CHAPTER 7. FAITH-BASED ARMY

1. At the conclusion of our research for *The Bones of Berdichev: The Life and Fate of Vasily Grossman* (New York: Free Press, 1996), we visited the town of Berdichev in Ukraine. The massacre pits where the bodies of approximately twenty thousand Jewish men, women, and children lie in mass graves (murdered by the SS along with the help of Ukrainian *politsai*, September 15–16, 1941) straddle the barbed wire fence of the military airport. Once off-limits to the populace, now Ukrainians garden up to the fence itself. We stood at the fence and looked at the hangar, and saw enormous helicopters—identical to the U.S. Sea Stallion—parked around it. The USSR had copied the Sea Stallion, and these helicopters were inherited by the newly sovereign Ukrainian Air Force. We thank John Garrard's research assistant at the time, a former U.S. Navy submariner, Phil Hammond, for this identification.

2. Yury Nagibin confided this to John Garrard at his dacha in Peredelkino, the famous Writers' Union village outside Moscow in May 1980. The elite were extremely bitter.

3. The dispatch of the missiles had an unanticipated result: the victory of the Afghani "freedom fighters" over the mighty Soviet Union turned one of their commanders, Osama bin Laden, a Saudi, into a legend. The network he founded in the caves of the Khawak Pass eventually matured into Al-Qaeda, a terrorist organization that would attack his former benefactor, the United States, on September 11, 2001.

4. He stated this to Sir Rodric Braithwaite, at his first meeting with the then British ambassador to Russia, in March 1992 at his private residence at Chisty Pereulok. Personal interview, WWICS, Washington, D.C., April, 2005.

5. Mark 16:12–13 does not give the place name, but Luke 34:13–35 gives a very full description of Jesus' appearance, on the third day after he was laid in the tomb, to two of the disciples as they walked to Emmaus, about three furlongs out of Jerusalem. They were joined by a man, "But their eyes were holden so they should not know him." After walking with them to the town, he joins them for supper and takes bread,

and breaks it, and gives it to them, whereupon "And their eyes were opened, and they knew him; and he vanished out of their sight."

6. The most important work on this subject is by A. Bogoliubov, *Ocherki iz istorii upravlenyia voennymi i morskim dukhovenstvom v biografiiakh glavnykh sviashchennikov ego za vremya s 1800 po 1901 god* (*Studies on the History of the Management of Military and Naval Clerics in the Biographies of Leading Priests over the period from 1800 to 1901*) (St. Petersburg, 1901).

7. Robert L. Nichols, "The Friends of God: Nicholas II and Alexandra at the Canonization of Serafim of Sarov, July 1903," in *Religious and Secular Forces in Late Tsarist Russia: Essays in Honor of Donald W. Treadgold*, ed. Charles E. Timberlake (Seattle: University of Washington Press, 1992), pp. 207–29. This quotation occurs on p. 223.

8. As quoted in ibid., p. 227. The original citation occurred in *Pribavleniya k tserkovnym vedomostyam* (*Additions to Church News*), no. 12 (1902): 426–27.

9. Cited in Nichols, "The Friends of God," p. 228. The original citation is to Edward H. Judge, *Plehve: Repression and Reform in Imperial Russia, 1902–1904* (Syracuse: Syracuse University Press, 1983), p. 167.

10. See Mikhail Iroshnikov, Liudmila Protsai, and Yuri Shelayev, *The Sunset of the Romanov Dynasty*, trans. Paul Williams and Juri Pamfilov (Moscow: Terra, 1992), p. 306, for this quotation, as well as a picture of Nicholas and the grand duke on maneuvers at Krasnoye Selo in 1913.

11. Philippe informed the tsarina, before he was packed out of Russia, that she would conceive a son if she prayed to "St. Seraphim." The rolls of the Orthodox Church were canvassed: there was no such saint. But there was a monk, Prokhor Moshnin, who had taken the name "Seraphim" when he was tonsured.

12. Alison Weir, *Eleanor of Aquitaine: A Life* (New York: Ballantine Books, 1999), pp. 43, 44.

13. Both ceremonies bore fruit. Queen Eleanor did give birth but, alas, to a girl. As for Alexandra, already the mother of four daughters, just a year and a few weeks after Nicholas had carried the solid silver reliquary, her prayers were answered. On July 30, 1904 o.s., a boy, a tsarevich, was born. Eleanor and Louis VII, who detested one another, could get a divorce from the obliging clergy on the grounds of "consanguinity." Alexandra and Nicholas, who were sincerely, passionately in love, did not have this option, and so sought the ministrations of the corrupt monk, Rasputin.

14. Weir, *Eleanor of Aquitaine*, p. 69.

15. As quoted in ibid., p. 72.

16. Iroshnikov, Protsai, and Shelayev, *Sunset of the Romanov Dynasty*, p. 158.

17. Ibid.

18. Constantine Pleshakov, *The Tsar's Last Armada: The Epic Journey to the Battle of Tsushima* (New York: Basic Books, 2002), p. 170. This entire book is well worth

reading for insights into how Nicholas conducted war at land and sea according to what can only be charitably described as "faith-based" policy.

19. Vera Shevzov, *Russian Orthodoxy on the Eve of Revolution* (Oxford: Oxford University Press, 2004), p. 180 and n. 46, which notes, "On this icon, see A. M., 'Prebyvanie ikony Torzhestvo Presviatyia Bogoroditsy v gorode Vladivostoke i otpravlenie eia v Port Artur,' *Vladivostokskie eparkhialnye vedomosti* 2 (1905): 31–36; 3 (1905): 64–67; 4 (1905): 88–92; 5 (1905): 112–13; V. N. Malkovskii, *Skazanie ob ikone*; A. Andersin-Lebedeva, *Skazanie ob ikone Port Arturskoi*; RGIA, f. 796, op. 201, 6 ot. 3 st., d. 298." Her book includes (p. 180) a black-and-white picture of this icon, taken from V. N. Malkovskii, comp., *Skazanie ob ikone "Torzhestvo Presviatyia Bogoroditsy" izvestnoi po imenem Port-Arturskoi Bozhiei Materi* (Tver, 1906).

20. Pleshakov,*The Tsar's Last Armada*, p. 64.

21. Ibid., p. 85.

22. This extraordinary statement is quoted from Witte's *Memoirs* (*Vospominaniia*, 1: 345) by Nichols, "The Friends of God," p. 223.

23. Pleshakov, *The Tsar's Last Armada*, p. 89.

24. Iroshnikov, Protsai, and Shelayev, *The Sunset of the Romanov Dynasty*, p. 141.

25. David G. Rowley, *Exploring Russia's Past* (Upper Saddle River, N.J.: Pearson Education, 2006), p. 81.

26. It would annex Korea in 1910; the tsar would be impotent to do anything.

27. See the full text of the manifesto in Elisabeth Heresch, *The Empire of the Tsars: The Splendour and the Fall (Pictures and Documents 1896 to 1920)*, trans. Paul Williams (Moscow: Stroitel, 1991), p. 146.

28. Vera Shevzov, *Russian Orthodoxy on the Eve of Revolution* (Oxford: Oxford University Press, 2004), p. 179.

29. Pavel Felgengauer, *Segodnya*, March 3, 1994, p. 1.

30. The account of this conference is taken from George Evans (a retired military chaplain), "The Russian Army and Religion," *Contemporary Review* 264, no. 1537 (February 1994): 67–70. All subsequent citations to the conference are from this text.

31. From *Russian Life* 50, no. 4 (July–August 2007): 11. The figure for civilian dead is still given as 26.7 million dead; this figure was originally floated in 1989.

32. Evans, "The Russian Army and Religion."

33. "Russian Border Troops Will Henceforth Serve 'God and Fatherland,'" *Segodnya*, March 17, p. 2. Reported in *Current Digest of the Post-Soviet Press*, April 12, 1995. News of the Week for the Russian Federation, *Military Affairs* 47, no. 11 (1995): 20. All subsequent quotations are to this text.

34. See E.N.I., "Russian Church Reaches Accord with Government," *Christian Century* 112, no. 20 (June 21, 1995): 635–36.

35. Evans, "The Russian Army and Religion."

36. As reported by Vladimir Isachenkov, Associated Press, in "Russian Military a Mess; Generals Resist Reform," *Arizona Daily Star*, December 3, 2001, p. A.21, col. 2.

37. Valentin Hibutin and Fr. Mark (Smirnov), "The New Saints Come Marching In," *Moscow News*, June 1988, pp. 1–2.

38. Having created the Order of St. Prince Daniel in 1988, for several years the church handed it to ROC clerics—a fairly elastic interpretation of the provision that it is to go to an individual who has distinguished himself in the "defense" of the Fatherland. Similarly, the Order of St. Sergius Radonezh—which had been created on December 26, 1978 by Pimen and the Synod—was accepted only by ROC hierarchs.

39. This typescript was located at the Keston Institute, Oxford, England, file folder Ort/7/1. The report of Metropolitan Juvenaly is appendix 4. This citation is from p. 3. In 2007, the Keston Archive was transferred to Baylor University.

40. This startling fact was revealed in Maureen Orth's vivid article, "Russia's Dark Master," *Vanity Fair*, October 2000, p. 222. The entire piece (pp. 200–24) is well worth reading.

41. Hegumen Feofilakt, "The Orthodox Prince Dimitriy [*sic*] Donskoi: For the 600th Anniversary of His Blessed Demise (1389–1989)," Theology Section, *JMP*, no. 3 (1989): 59. See p. 60 for a full color reproduction of a 17th century portrait.

42. Ibid., p. 59. This is the opening paragraph of a Feofilakt's fascinating article.

43. Ibid., p. 60, n. 10. Hegumen Feofilakt gives the original citation: V. Klyuchevsky, *Kurs russkoi istorii* (*Course of Russian History*) (Moscow: Gosizdat, 1957), vol. 2, part 2, p. 8.

44. Ascher, *The Kremlin*, pp. 17–18.

45. From *Tserkov i dukhovnoe vozrozhedenie Rossii* (*The Church and the Spiritual Revival of Russia*) (Moscow: Sofrino, 1999), pp. 847–73. This particular quotation occurs on p. 860 in a speech by the patriarch entitled "The Role of Moscow in the Defense of the Fatherland," "Rol Moskvy v zashchite Otechestva" (pp. 860–67), given March 22, 1995. Translation by John Garrard. This book of Aleksy's speeches is critical to understanding what is happening inside the ROC and Russia today. Sadly, the only two copies we have ever been able to find are located in the Library of Congress and the specialized collection of Keston Institute, Oxford, England.

46. Ibid., pp. 860–61. Translation by John Garrard.

47. The patriarch has been highly selective in his reading of the Chronicles. Other Chronicles relate quite a different story. The Rogozhsky Chronicle, which "apparently escaped later Muscovite censorship," relates a different point of view on the fate of the prince of Ryazan whom Daniel had defeated: "Ever since 1301, when Daniil of Moscow had defeated the Ryazanites at the battle of Pereyaslavl' Ryazansky, Prince Konstantin Romanovich of Ryazan' had been held in virtual captivity in Moscow." This is rather a different picture from the "fraternal peace and love" Aleksy claims Prince Daniel displayed to his foe.

The patriarch claimed that when his nephew Ivan Dmitrievich died childless, he "bequeathed [his patrimony] to Daniel Pereyaslavl." The patriarch is citing the Trinity Chronicle which claims that the nephew "… gave his blessing to Prince Daniil of Moscow to rule in his place in Preyaslavl', for he loved him more than all others." But John Fennell, in his authoritative book, *The Emergence of Moscow, 1304–1359* (London: Secker and Warburg, 1968), compared all the Chronicles' tale of this event and concluded: "Of course the information of the tendentiously pro-Moscow compiler of the Trinity Chronicle must be taken with a pinch of salt. The sober and factual Laurentian Chronicle makes no mention of any testamentary bequest; and it is probable that Daniil was in fact obliged to seize Pereyaslavl' by force" (p. 49). The patriarch is doing no more than the church has done in answering the two questions of who is the first apostle to be called by Jesus, and who is the first to acknowledge Jesus as the Christ. Aleksy is picking a source, according it sacred status, and proclaiming it alone the "Gospel truth."

48. *Moscow: 850th Anniversary*, gen. ed. V. A. Vinogradov (Moscow: Publishing House AO "Moscow Textbooks," 1996), Russian version. p. 7. Translation by John Garrard.

49. Ibid., p. 151.

50. Ibid., p. 10.

51. Ibid.

52. See Wil van den Bercken, "The Canonization of Nicholas II in Iconographical Perspective: Political Themes in Russian Icons," in *Orthodox Christianity and Contemporary Europe: Selected Papers of International Conference held at Leeds June 2001*, ed. Jonathan Sutton and Wil van den Bercken (Leeds, 2002), pp. 187–209. This quotation occurs on p. 187.

53. See reproduction of Tree of the State of Moscow" as frontispiece to Ascher's *The Kremlin*. There indeed are John "Moneybags" and St. Hierarch Peter at the roots of the tree, behind the walls of the Kremlin, with the Savior Tower and Savior Gate next to them. The Cathedral of the Assumption is behind them. The Vladimir icon is in center, with Christ above. See G. G. Belyaev and G. A. Torgashev, *Dukhovnye korni russkogo naroda* (Moscow, 2002), who see "Russian spirituality relinking earth with heaven as the 'world tree' did in ancient Slavic mythology." Quoted in "Bibliographical Postscript" to James Billington, *Russia In Search of Itself* (Washington, D.C., and Baltimore: Woodrow Wilson Center Press and the Johns Hopkins University Press, 2004), p. 216.

54. This was reported on the Web site www.pravoslavie.ru of the *Orthodox Encyclopaedia*, December 21, 2004, as background for the main story.

55. Cited by Lawrence A. Uzzell, "Centralization of Power, Fragmentation of Belief: Statist Relativism in Post-Soviet Russia," in *Burden or Blessing?*, ed. Christopher Marsh (Brookline, Mass.: Institute on Culture, Religion, and World Affairs, 2004),

pp. 45–52. This statement occurs on p. 49. The source is his note 5 to Sergei Mozgo-voi, *"Siloviki blagochestiya," Otechestvennye zapiski* 1 (2003).

56. See the e-mail newsletter maintained on the Web site of David Johnson, at http://www.cdi.org/Russia/Johnson/7016-12. On January 14, 2003, it featured an ar-ticle "Russian Soldiers' Mothers Work Together to Help Deserters," from the Moscow AP.

57. Dr. Glazin was also a Fellow at the Woodrow Wilson International Center for Scholars during the time when John Garrard was. Personal interview, January 12, 2005, Washington, D.C.

58. Leonid Brezhnev, whose contributions to the war effort had been extremely modest as a political officer serving in the Caucasus, had written a lavish memoir de-tailing his experiences. The closest he ever got to danger apparently was when a boat he was sitting in was shelled and overturned. Other than getting wet, however, he suf-fered no crippling injuries. This did not prevent the obliging Union of Soviet Writ-ers giving this particular veteran's journal its highest prize. Brezhnev's memoir was printed in a beautiful leather binding; many Soviet readers bought the book, whose price was heavily subsidized, and ripped out the pages, thus possessing a very nice binding that could be filled with better reading material.

59. Lazar Lazarev, "Russian Literature on the War and Historical Truth," in *World War 2 and the Soviet People*, ed. John Garrard and Carol Garrard (New York: St. Mar-tin's Press, 1993), pp. 28–37. See p. 33 and pl. 9 for an example of this theme song.

60. The Holocaust on the soil of the Occupied Soviet Union took at least one mil-lion lives, where Jewish civilians were shot by four enormous killing squads, the *Ein-satzgruppe*, often in full view, and sometimes with the help, of their Soviet neighbors of non-Jewish ethnicity. We discuss one episode of this immense and divisive tragedy in *The Bones of Berdichev: The Life and Fate of Vasily Grossman* (New York: Free Press, 1996). We also researched the fate of one other city on occupied Soviet soil, Brest-Litovsk, in "Barbarossa's First Victims: The Jews of Brest," *East European Jewish Affairs* 28, no. 2 (1998–99): 3–48. We donated a database of the names of 12,600 vic-tims murdered in the Brest Ghetto, October 1942, to the Jewish Genealogical Society Web site. It may be searched at www.jewishgen.org/databases/html.

61. This fact is stated by Army General Nikolay Pankov, head of the Human Re-sources and Personnel Support Service of the Russian Ministry of Defense. He told the "Novosti" News Agency on June 10, 2005, that "We will actively work with all traditional religions." In fact, given that Buddhism is officially listed as one of the "tra-ditional religions" of Russia in the 1997 Law on Conscience, General Pankov said that "training conferences with the participation of Buddhists would take place in the Siberian Military District in July."

62. See Seth Mydans, "From Village Boy to Soldier, Martyr and, Many Say, Saint," International Section, *New York Times*, November 21, 2003. Mydans quotes

one representative Web site: "Nineteen year old Yevgeny Rodionov went through un-thinkable sufferings, but he did not renounce the Orthodox faith but confirmed it with his martyr's death. He proved that now, after so many decades of raging atheism, so many years of unrestrained nihilism, Russia is capable, as in earlier centuries, of giving birth to a martyr for Christ, which means it is unconquerable."

63. We have not seen this booklet, printed in Moscow, 1999, but it was cited by Billington, *Russia in Search of Itself*, p. 213, n. 51.

64. The visit of Rodionov's mother to the area where his body had been buried in Chechnya had been facilitated by Russian military officers. These men were also awarded medals. Passing them out was Dmitry Smirnov, *protoierei*, president of the Synodal Department of the Moscow Patriarchate Department for Cooperation with the Military Forces. This was taken from the Web site, pobeda.ru, and also appeared on the Russian Orthodox Web site, www.pravoslavie.ru/news (Moscow, March 27, 2006): "Yevgeny Rodionov Awarded *Slava Rossii* Posthumously."

65. Within the capital of Chechnya, this view is expounded by the highest ranking Russian military officer within the Interior Ministry. (That is, the action is taking place within the borders of the Russian Federation.) In 2005 Nikolay Rogozhkin arrived in Grozny to take command of the "46th Separate Operational Brigade of the North Caucasian District of the Interior Ministry's Internal Troops." He declared the army was not at war with Islam but only the terrorist variant known as "Wahhabism." That, he reiterated, had to be stopped. Commander Rogozhkin emphasized that "young people are listening to their hearts and reaching out to the church. We welcome rep-resentatives of all denominations and are cooperating in all areas with representatives of other religions, not only Christianity." There were more than fifty working churches and chapels in the Internal Troops, he added.

66. No one knows when that will be. Demographers predict that, given the high birthrate among Muslims in the Caucasus, within seventy-five years, this area of the Russian Federation may become autonomous. The ROC thinks in terms of centu-ries; Evgeny Rodionov's canonization will occur someday.

67. *Russian Life*, September–October 2006, p. 10. The "Statistical source" quoted for this figure comes from *Vedomosti* (News), August 7, 2006.

68. As reported in *Russian Life*, July–August 2006, p. 9, under the column heading "In Brief," Army Reality TV.

69. Several years before this momentous event, the ROC had already begun al-lowing tourist vessels to visit along with the pilgrims who stream there. The mon-astery is reached by overnight trip on a cruise ship north from St. Petersburg across Lake Ladoga. In 1980 there were eighteen Orthodox monasteries open in all the vast reaches of the USSR. By 2001 there were more than four hundred. Valaam is offi-cially known as the monastery of the Holy Transfiguration of the Savior. Valaam was founded in the middle of the tenth century by saints Sergey and Gherman. It remains

Russian Orthodoxy's oldest existing monastery. See "A Cruise to the Soul of Russia," *New York Times*, April 29, 2001, pp. 8–9, 25.

70. K. Logachev, "Metropolitan Aleksy's Birthday Celebration," *JMP*, no. 8 (1989): 11–13. This quotation occurs on p. 12. A black-and-white picture of the sixty-year-old Aleksy is on p. 11, wearing around his neck the new crosses he had just been given.

71. See the Web site of the ROC, http://www.mospat.ru/index, for April 6, 2006.

72. See "Celebration of 625th Anniversary of the Battle of Kulikovo." *JMP*, no. 10 (2005): 7. All translations from this article are by John Garrard. The *JMP* is now printed online exclusively in Russian.

73. See Ascher, *The Kremlin*, pp. 26–27, for vivid color depictions of the battle and the thanksgiving afterward.

74. Tula was almost encircled by November 22, 1941. See John Erickson, *The Road to Stalingrad* (Boulder, Colo.: Westview, 1984), p. 259. However, the commander of the 50th Army, Boldin, continued to hold on, and a small corridor to the north was kept open. The Red Army launched its counteroffensive on December 5, 1941, by widening this corridor. See ibid., p. 275.

EPILOGUE. TWENTY YEARS AFTER: FROM PARTY TO PATRIARCH

1. This is taken from the official Web site of the ROC, http://www.mospat.ru.

2. Immediately after accepting this award from President Putin, wherein he also declares that the church would not meddle in politics, the patriarch left to greet a round table conference on "Culture, Education of Youth, and Religion" held at St. Daniel's Monastery. Once again, the subject of *vospitanie*—translated variously as education or nurturing in morality, or character, or ethics—was brought under the church's wing. The Russian military had sought aid in *vospitanie* for its recruits back in 1994. In both cases, those in power saw a moral vacuum in young people. (In 1991, the Russian Ministry of Education had thrown out the CPSU state-ordered courses on atheism.) The conference was dedicated to his "jubilee"—that is, his seventy-fifth year. Given that it was Aleksy who had gotten the monastery returned to the church back in the bad old days of Andropov, it was a fitting tribute.

3. Anatoly Krasikov, "Russia: A Country of Religious Freedom?" *European Legacy* 3, no. 2 (1998): 39.

4. In an important speech, "The Church as the Mystical Body of Christ," delivered at the annual conference of the Diocese of Sourozh, which we attended at Oxford in May 2004, Bishop Basil of Sergeyevo, a diocese that acknowledges the authority of the Moscow Patriarchate, stated the theological rationale behind the new dispensation of a separation of church and state in contemporary Russia. He drew a distinction between the world, which is in darkness, and the Light that Christ brings humanity. The church is created to expand the light, and in the Liturgy of the Russian

Orthodox Church the believer sees and experiences how Light came into the world. But he emphasized, "The Church is part of the world; [therefore] the Church must always be in tension with the world around it. If it is at one with the world, then the darkness of the world has entered the Church itself ... The Church as the mystical body of Christ carries on His work, but there will be a darkness inside the Church, a human darkness." The bishop's inference is clear: the Orthodox Church has no desire to be a state church, because then it would allow the darkness of the world to overcome the Light of Christ. Bishop Basil is himself, at the time of this writing, in a kind of limbo, because his attempt to take the Sourozh Diocese away from allegiance to the Moscow Patriarchate to the Patriarchate of Constantinople is being strenuously forbidden. However, his description of the role of the church vis-à-vis the state is a succinct summation of what seems to be the official ROC position.

5. The full text is posted on the Moscow Patriarchate's Web site: "Bishops' Council Bases of the Social Concept of the Russian Orthodox Church," August 15, 2001, http://www.russian-orthodox-church.org.ru/sd00e.htm.

6. But the modern observer may be somewhat disconcerted that the list begins with "peacemaking" when the ROC now chooses to move to "deep background" its former zealous endorsement of "peacemaking" as conducted through the World Council of Churches. The WCC is now seen as too "ecumenical." As soon as the USSR itself disappeared, so did the section entitled "*Oikoumene*" (the Greek root of "ecumenical" meaning the "inhabited world," from *oikein*, "to inhabit," from *oikos*, "house") in the *Journal of the Moscow Patriarchate*. For the ROC, "ecumenism" became a code word used as an insult. It was hurled as a slur against Mitrofanov and the other ROC delegates to the December 2003 Nyack Conference with ROCA and ROCOR in the United States. Mitrofanov rejected it forthrightly. As the ROC and the diaspora churches reunified, ecumenism came to be seen more and more as antithetical to Russian Orthodoxy's exceptionalism. Whether ROC membership in the World Council of Churches will outlive Aleksy is an open question. It is likely that, given his decades of work in the organization, he will not withdraw during his lifetime, but a new patriarch would be free to maneuver.

7. If it is possible to "model" anything so complicated and emotional as church-state relations in the new Russia, the emerging model might be the Republican Party in the United States with George W. Bush in the White House. The United States enshrines separation of church and state in its constitution, yet religion and politics are intimately integrated. The "evangelical" block of voters turned out overwhelmingly for George Bush and the Republican Party in the elections of 2000 and 2004. Time will tell if this block remains as dedicated. But the Republican Party's success in marketing itself as the party of God and country mirrors precisely what Orthodoxy has achieved in Russia—the uniting of faith and patriotism under its banner. As revealed by Garry Wills in a devastating article, "A Country Rule by

Faith," Bush's first attorney general, John Ashcroft, told an audience at Bob Jones University "we have no king but Jesus," and called the wall of separation between church and state a "wall of religious oppression." See *New York Review of Books* 53, no. 18 (2007): 8–12.

8. This astonishing set of statistics comes from the research of Dmitri Furman and Kimmo Kaariainen, "Orthodoxy as a Component of Russian Identity," *East-West Church and Ministry Report* 10, no. 1 (2002): 12–13 .

9. See "Religion in the Society as a Whole," *SOVA*, December 28, 2004. Translated by Nana Tchibuchian, research assistant for John Garrard at the Woodrow Wilson International Center for Scholars, Washington D.C., January–May 2005.

10. For the text of this chilling exchange, we are indebted to Sir Rodric Braithwaite, Great Britain's ambassador to what was then the USSR, diary entry for "Sunday, 16 July, 1989." This detailed and lively journal is an "inside" view from the perspective of one of the West's most informed diplomats. His excellent book, *Moscow 1941: A City and Its People at War* (London: Profile Books, 2006), testifies to the wide knowledge of this remarkable man.

11. As reported by the Associated Press in the *Arizona Daily Star*, December 31, 2000, p. A19.

12. The groundwork for this change in the secular almanac had been laid the preceding year. On August 23, 2004, the ROC added a new holiday to the ecclesiastical calendar, The "Day of Mercy and Charity." Orthodox Christianity holds that no believer can "earn" salvation. Because salvation is granted only through the merciful forgiveness of Christ, believers themselves are called to imitate divine mercy to each other.

13. See Paul Richardson, "Film Flam: Kremlin Backs a Resurgent State-Friendly Film Industry," *Russian Life* 50, no. 4 (July–August 2007): 7. Ten million dollars in financing has been allocated to Kremlin ally Nikita Mikhalkov's TRITE studio. Nikita Mikhalkov is the son of the same Sergey Mikhalkov who wrote the lyrics to the Stalinist and to the contemporary Russian anthem.

14. This quotation is cited by Michael Grant in his excellent biography *Constantine the Great: The Man and His Times* (New York: Charles Scribner's Sons, 1994), p. 154.

15. By 2004 the elite of Moscow society were happily accepting the Order of St. Prince Daniel of Moscow. The Rector of St. Petersburg State Technical University, Yury Vasilyev, added it (third degree) to his Order of the Red Banner. The vice-president of Lukoil got his from the patriarch on October 23, 2004. As this mini-list of awardees illustrates, the "service to the Fatherland" that entitles one to the order would be interpreted broadly.

16. Dzerzhinsky is back too—not his statue, but in the form of a bronze bust on a pedestal in the Interior Ministry. See Eleanor Randolph, "Ultimate Soviet Henchman Returns to His Pedestal," op-ed, *New York Times*, November 20, 2005, p. 12.

17. See "Russian Protests: Democracy à la Russe," *Economist*, April 21–27, 2007, pp. 60–61. The article shows the troops; one can make out the OMON letters on their backs.

18. Forum 18, whose people monitor religious freedom in Russia, has not identified the ROC as having anything to do with Putin's harsh response.

19. Andrew Meier, *Black Earth: A Journey through Russia after the Fall* (New York: Norton, 2003), p. 25.

20. See "Orthodoxy Revisited: Hand of John the Baptist in Russia," International section, *Guardian*, June 10, 2006, p. 13. Accompanying the article is a color photograph of Aleksy, clad in a gorgeous gold robe, elevating the hand in its solid gold reliquary.

21. *Russian Life*, July–August 2006, p. 15. This information is reported from *Vedomosti* (*News*).

22. Ibid, p. 10.

Select Bibliography

Aleksy II, Patriarch of Moscow and All the Russias. *Tserkov i dukhovnoe vozrozhdenie Rossii (The Church and the Spiritual Revival of Russia)*. Moscow: Sofrino, 1999. [This volume contains speeches made by the Patriarch.]

Alexander, Jonathan, and Paul Binski, eds. *The Age of Chivalry: Art in Plantagenet England, 1200–1400*. Catalog of exhibition held at the Royal Academy of Arts, London. London: Weidenfeld and Nicolson, 1987.

"Almost There: Two Russian Orthodox Churches Approaching Reunification." Notebook, *Russian Life* 49, no. 6 (November–December 2006).

Anon. *Door to Paradise: Jesus Christ in Ancient Orthodoxy*. N.p.: St. Herman Press, n.d.

Antich, Oksana. "Pravoslavny monastyr vozvrashchen tserkvi." *Radio Free Europe/Radio Liberty*, June 27, 1983.

Ascher, Abraham. *The Kremlin*. Wonders of Man Series. New York: Newsweek, 1972.

Bartov, Omer, and Phyllis Mack, eds. *In God's Name: Genocide and Religion in the Twentieth Century*. New York: Berghahn Books, 2001.

Belyaev, G. G., and G. A. Torgashev. *Dukhovnye korni russkogo naroda*. Moscow, 2002.

Billington, James H. "Orthodox Christianity and the Russian Transformation." In *Proselytism and Orthodoxy in Russia*, edited by John Witte Jr. and Michael Bourdeaux, pp. 51–65. Religion and Human Rights Series. Maryknoll, N.Y.: Orbis Books, 1999.

———. *Russia in Search of Itself*. Washington, D.C., and Baltimore: Woodrow Wilson Center Press and the Johns Hopkins University Press, 2004.

———. *Russia Transformed: Breakthrough to Hope*. New York: Free Press, 1992.

Boonstra, Janrense, et al. *Anti-Semitism: A History Portrayed*. Amsterdam: Anne Frank Foundation: 1999.

Bourdeaux, Canon Michael, "Between Hammer and Anvil," The Monday Profile, *Guardian*, September 2, 1991, p. 19.

Braithwaite, Sir Rodric, "Heated Words Have No Place in a Post-Cold War World." Op-ed, *Financial Times*, May 2, 2007.

———. *Moscow 1941: A City and Its People at War*. London: Profile Books, 2006.

Brumfield, William Craft. *A History of Russian Architecture*. Rev. ed. Seattle: University of Washington Press, 2004.

Brzezinski, Matthew. *Casino Moscow: A Tale of Greed and Adventure on Capitalism's Wildest Frontier*. New York: Simon Schuster, 2002.

Chadwick, Henry, and G. R. Evans, eds. *Atlas of the Christian Church*. New York: Facts on File, 1987.

Chulos, Chris J. *Converging Worlds: Religion and Community in Peasant Russia, 1861–1917*. DeKalb: Northern Illinois University Press, 2003.

Clark, Tessa, ed. *The Russian Chronicles: A Thousand Years That Changed the World; From the Beginnings of the Land of Rus to the New Revolution of Glasnost Today*. London: Garamond Publishers with Random Century, 1990.

Corley, Felix. "Russia: The Patriarch and the KGB." *Keston News Service*, no. 9, 2000.

Davis, G. Scott, ed. *Religion and Justice in the War over Bosnia*. London: Routledge, 1996.

De Michelis, Cesare D. *The Non-Existent Manuscript: A Study of the Elders of the Protocols of Zion*. Trans. Richard Newhouse. Lincoln: University of Nebraska Press, 2004.

Evans, Helen C., ed. *Byzantium: Faith and Power (1261–1557)*. Catalog of the exhibition at the Metropolitan Museum of Art. New Haven: Yale University Press, 2004.

Fedotov, G. P. *The Russian Religious Mind: Kievan Christianity from the Tenth to the Thirteenth Centuries*. New York: Harper Torchbooks, 1960.

Furman, Dmitri, and Kimmo Kaariainen. "Orthodoxy as a Component of Russian Identity." *East-West Church and Ministry Report* 10, no. 1 (2002): 12–13.

Garrard, Carol, and John Garrard. *The Bones of Berdichev: The Life and Fate of Vasily Grossman*. New York: Free Press, 1996.

———. *Inside the Soviet Writers' Union*. New York: Free Press, 1990.

———, eds. *World War 2 and the Soviet People*. New York: St. Martin's Press, 1993.

Graham, Stephen. *Ivan the Terrible*. London: Benn, 1932.

Grant, Michael. *Constantine the Great: The Man and His Times*. New York: Scribner's, 1994.

Gros, Jeffrey, FSC, Eamon McManus, and Ann Riggs. *Introduction to Ecumenism*. New York: Paulist Press, 1998.

Heresch, Elizabeth, ed. *The Empire of the Tsars: The Splendour and the Fall (Pictures and Documents 1896 to 1920)*. Moscow: Stroitel, 1991.

Herring, George. *An Introduction to the History of Christianity: From the Early Church to the Enlightenment*. London: Continuum, 2006.

Iroshnikov, Mikhail, Liudmila Protsai, and Yuri Shelayev. *The Sunset of the Romanov Dynasty*. Translation by Paul Williams and Juri Pamfilov. Moscow: Terra, 1992.

Johnson, E. N. "The Crusades of Frederick Barbarossa and Henry VI." In *A History of the Crusades*, 6 vols., edited by K. M. Setton, 2:87–122. Wisconsin, 1969–89.

"Joint Communique Issued by the Ecumenical Patriarch Dimitrios I and Patriarch Pimen of Moscow." *Journal of the Moscow Patriarchate* 12 (1987): 20.

Judge, Edward H. *Plehve: Repression and Reform in Imperial Russia, 1902–1904*. Syracuse: Syracuse University Press, 1983.

Kartashev, A. V. *Essays on the History of the Russian Church*. Paris: YMCA Press, 1959.

Kirill, Metropolitan of Smolensk and Kaliningrad. "Gospel & Culture." In *Proselytism and Orthodoxy in Russia: The New War for Souls*, edited by John Witte Jr. and Michael Bourdeaux. Maryknoll, N.Y.: Orbis Books, 1999.

———. "The Russian Orthodox Church and the Third Millennium." Paper presented at the 7th international conference on Russian Spirituality, Bose, Italy, September 15–18,1999. Translated from the Russian by Peter Bouteneff, and reprinted by the *Ecumenical Review* 52, no. 3 (July 2000): 300–309.

Kishkovsky, Sophia. "2 Russian Churches, Split by War, to Reunite." International Section, *New York Times*, May 17, 2007.

Klyuchevsky, V. *Kurs russkoy istorii*. Reprint, Moscow: Glosizdat, 1957.

Krasikov, Anatoly. "Russia: A Country of Religious Freedom?" *European Legacy* 3, no. 2 (1998): 39–43.

Kudryavtsev, Mikhail P. *Moskva, Trety Rim*. Moscow: Sol Systems Ltd., 1994.

Kuznetsov, K. K. *Kreshchenie Rusi: 988–1988*. Moscow, 1992. [This is a rogue imprint from the second edition, published in 1992 by Zaria Publishing, London, Canada. The first edition was published by Zaria in 1988.]

Lacqueur, Walter, ed. *The Holocaust Encyclopedia*. New Haven: Yale University Press, 2001.

Lebedev, Archpriest Lev. "Veneration of St. Nicholas in Russia, Conclusion." *Journal of the Moscow Patriarchate*, no. 6 (1987): 61–73.

MacCullough, Diarmaid. *The Reformation*. New York: Viking, 2003.

Marsh, Christopher, ed. *Burden of Blessing? Russian Orthodoxy and the Construction of Civil Society and Society*. Brookline, Mass.: Boston University Institute on Culture, Religion and World Affairs, 2004.

Martin, Janet. *Medieval Russia, 980–1584*. Reprint, Cambridge: Cambridge University Press, 2004.

Meier, Andrew. *Black Earth: A Journey through Russia after the Fall*. New York: Norton, 2003.

Milner-Gulland, Robin, with Nikolai Dejevsky. *Cultural Atlas of Russia and the Soviet Union*. Facts on File. New York and Oxford: Equinox, 1989.

Mitrofanov, Georgy. *Istoriya russkoi pravoslavnoi tserkvi 1900–1927 (History of the Russian Orthodox Church, 1900–1927)*. St. Petersburg: Satis, 2002.

Nicholas and Alexandra: The Last Imperial Family of Tsarist Russia. Edited by Mark Sutcliffe. From the State Hermitage Museum and the State Archive of the Russian Federation. Catalog of the exhibition at the State Hermitage Museum, 1998. Translated by Frank Althaus and Darya Lakha. New York and London: Henry N. Abrams and Booth-Clibborn Editions, 1998.

Nilus, Sergey. *Velikoe v malom: Spiritual Instructions*. Little Russian Philokalia Series, vol. 1. Translated by Fr. Seraphim Rose. Platina, Calif.: St. Herman of Alaska Brotherhood, 1996.

"Orthodoxy Revisited: Hand of John the Baptist in Russia," *Guardian*, June 10, 2006.

Ouspensky, Leonid. *Theology of the Icon*. Translated by Anthony Gythiel. Iconostasis, vol. 2. Crestwood, N.Y.: St. Vladimir's Seminary Press, 1991.

Perica, Vjekoslav. *Balkan Idols: Religion and Nationalism in Yugoslav States*. Oxford: Oxford University Press, 2002.

Phillips, Jonathan. *The Fourth Crusade and the Sack of Constantinople*. London: Pimlico, 2005.

Pleshakov, Constantine. *The Tsar's Last Armada: The Epic Journey to the Battle of Tsushima*. New York: Basic Books, 2002.

"Poland Must Stop Witch-hunt." Editorial, *Financial Times*, April 30, 2007.

Pospielovsky, Dimitry V. *The Orthodox Church in the History of Russia*. Crestwood, N.Y.: St. Vladimir's Seminary Press, 1998.

Putsch: The Diary. Three Days That Collapsed the Empire. New York: Mosaic Press, 1991.

Rowley, David G. *Exploring Russia's Past*. Upper Saddle River, N.J.: Pearson Education.

Schmemann, Serge. "A Bishop's Fall Provides View on Soviet Era Collaboration [in Poland]." Editorial page, *New York Times*, January 16, 2007.

Sells, Michael. "Religion, History and Genocide in Bosnia-Heregovina." In *Religion and Justice in the War over Bosnia*, edited by G. Scott Davies, pp. 23–43. London: Routledge, 1996.

Serafim, Hierodeacon. "Metropolitan Theodosius Visits the Moscow Monastery of St. Daniel." *Journal of the Moscow Patriarchate*, no. 10 (1986): 11.

Setton, Kenneth M. *A History of the Crusades*. 6 vols. Madison: University of Wisconsin, 1969–89.

Setton, Kenneth M., and Henry R. Winkler, eds. *Great Problems in European Civilization*. 2nd ed. New York: Prentice-Hall, 1966.

Shevzov, Vera. *Russian Orthodoxy on the Eve of the Revolution*. Oxford: Oxford University Press, 2004.

Shukman, Ann. "Metropolitan Sergi Stragorodsky: The Case of the Representative Individual." *Religion, State, and Society* 34, no. 1 (March 2006): 51–61.

Slater, Wendy. "Russia's Imagined History: Visions of the Soviet Past and the New 'Russian Idea.'" *Journal of Communist Studies and Transition Politics* 14, no. 4 (December 1998): 69–86.

Smith, Craig S., and Ian Fisher. "Poland Reels at New Wave of Charges against Church." *New York Times*, January 16, 2007.

———. "Second Church Official Resigns in Poland." *New York Times*, January 9, 2007.

Solovyev, Archpriest Simeon. "On the Feast of the Apostle St. Andrew the First Called." *Journal of the Moscow Patriarchate*, no. 12 (1987): 40–43.

Steeves, Paul D. *Keeping the Faiths: Religion and Ideology in the Soviet Union*. Beyond the Kremlin, a publication of the Committee for National Security. New York: Holmes & Meier, 1989.

Sutton, Jonathan, and Wil van der Berken, eds. *Orthodox Christianity and Contemporary Europe: Selected Papers of the International Conference Held at Leeds, June 2001*. Leeds, 2002.

Tanner, N. P., ed. *Decrees of the Ecumenical Councils*. London: Sheed & Ward, 1990.

Timberlake, Charles E., ed. *Religious and Secular Forces in Late Tsarist Russia: Essays in Honor of Donald W. Treadgold*. Seattle: University of Washington Press, 1992.

Tolz, Vera. "Church-State Relations under Gorbachev." *Radio Free Europe/Radio Liberty Research Bulletin*, September 11, 1987 (RL 360/87).

The Truth about Religion in Russia. Produced by the Moscow Patriarchate. Edited by Nicholas (Yarushkevich), the Metropolitan of Kiev and Galicia; Gregory Petrovich Georgievsky, Professor of Bibliology [sic], Cathedral of the Epiphany in Moscow; Alexander Pavlovich Smirnov, Archpriest of the St. Nicholas (Kuznetsky) Church in Moscow. English translation by the Reverend E.C.C. Sergeant from *Pravda o religii v Rossii*. London: Hutchinson & Co., 1942.

Vinogradov, V. A., gen. ed. *Moscow: 850th Anniversary*. Jubilee edition in two volumes. Vol. 1. Moscow: Publishing House AO "Moscow Textbooks," 1996.

Vostryshev, M., *Patriarkh Tikhon (Zhizn zamechatelnykh lyudei, Seriya biografickeskaya*, no. 726). Moscow: Molodaya Gvardiya, 1997.

Weir, Alison. *Eleanor of Aquitaine: A Life*. New York: Ballantine, 1999.

Williams, Edward V. "Aural Icons of Orthodoxy: The Sonic Typology of Russian Bells." In *From Christianity and the Arts in Russia*, edited by William Craft Brumfield and Milos Velimirovic. New York: Cambridge University Press, 1991.

Wills, Garry. "A Country Ruled by Faith." *New York Review of Books* 53, no. 18 (2007): 8–12.

Witte, John, Jr., and Michael Bourdeaux, eds. *Proselytism and Orthodoxy in Russia: The New War for Souls*. Religion and Human Rights Series. Maryknoll, N.Y.: Orbis Books, 1999.

Zain, Father Thomas. "Russia Revisited: Twenty-one Years Later." *Sourozh: A Journal of Orthodox Life and Thought*, no. 71 (February 1998): 19–32.

Zamyatin, Yevgeny. *We*. Translated by Mirra Ginsburg. New York: Avon Books, 1983.

Zenkovsky, Serge A., ed., *Medieval Russia's Epics, Chronicles and Tales*. Translated by Nicholas Zernov. New York: Dutton, 1974.

Index

315

Fioravanti, Aristotle, 274n13
First Circle, The (Solzhenitsyn), 84, 275n19, 294n18
Fisher, John, 168
Forever Flowering ... (Vse techyot) (Grossman), 183, 293n2
Forum 18, 307n18; Web site of, 291n57
Frederick I (emperor), 49
Frederick III (emperor), 166
FSB (Federativnaya Sluzhba Bezopasnosti; Federal Security Service), 184, 249
Führermuseum, 273n2

Gapon, George (priest), 250
Garbett, Cyril (archbishop), 192
Garrard, Carol, 276n35
Garrard, John, 104, 268n26, 269n8, 276n35, 277n4, 293n2
"Gathering of New Russian Martyrs and Confessors, The," icon, 126
Gennadios II Scholarios, 290n41
Gibbon, Edward, 248
Glazin, Igor, 29, 37, 233, 268n1, 302n57
Glinka, Mikhail, 246–47
Glory to Russia! (*Slava Rossii!*) award, 236
Godunov, Boris, 121
Golotyuk, Yury, 221
Golovinksy, Matvey, 279–80n23
Gorbachev, Mikhail, 2, 12, 14–16, 17, 44, 45, 52, 56, 219; baptism of, 13, 264n15
Gorbachev, Raisa, 45
Gospels (New Testament): the Gospel of John, 285–86n9, 288n23; on the primacy of Peter versus Andrew, 142, 144–45
Grabar All-Russian Artistic Scientific Restoration Center (VKhNRTs), 97, 277n43
Grachev, Pavel, 217, 219, 220
Graham, Stephen, 291nn46, 47
Great in the Small, The; or, The Advent of the Antichrist and the Approaching Rule of the Devil on Earth (Nilus), 108–9, 113, 203–4; inclusion of *The Protocols* and St. Seraphim's "Conversation" in prerevolutionary editions of, 280n23; various editions of, 109–10, 111, 115–16, 278n8, 279n17

Great Schism (1054), 13, 157–58; ROC view of, 158–59
Gregory IX (pope), 161
Gregory XIII (pope), 169, 176
Grigoriev, Dmitry, 9
Grimstead, Patricia Kennedy, 273–74n2
Gros, Jeffrey (priest), 179
Grossman, Vasily, 183, 293n2
Guderian, Heinz, 241

Hagemeister, Michael, 279–80n23
Halloway, Christopher, 81
Harting (ARTAK), 112
"Heated Words Have No Place in a Post–Cold War World" (Braithwaite), 293n5
Helsinki Accords, 38
Henry II (king), 59
Henry VIII (king), 168
Herring, George, 288n30
Hilarion (metropolitan), 147, 156, 285–86n9
history, Russian approach to, 225–26
History of Russian Architecture, A (Brumfield), 264n9
Hitler, Adolf, 49, 108
"Holy Rus" (Platonov), 281n35
"Holy Trinity" (Rublyov), 148
Holy Trinity Cathedral, 47
Honecker, Erich, 15
Hoover, Herbert, 279n18
How to Win Friends and Influence People (Carnegie), 224
Humbert (cardinal), 157
Husar, Lubomyr (cardinal), 178

icons, 6; *glykophilousa* icons of the Theotokos, 266n11; icon painting technique, 5; the iconography of bells, 146–47; and the iconostasis, 5–6, 9, 85, 251; and the *krasny ugol* ("beautiful corner"), 77, 222. *See also various icons listed under* Mary; "Gathering of New Russian Martyrs and Confessors, The" icon; "Implantation of the Tree of the Russian State" icon
"Implantation of the Tree of the Russian State" icon, 229, 301n53

Kremlin, 81; reconstruction of buildings of by Italian architects, 274n13; Savior Tower (Spasskaya Bashnya), 81, 274n14
Kreshchenie Rusi (Lebedev), 251
Kreshchenie Rusi (*The Baptism of Rus*) coloring book, 148–51, 154–56; illustrations in, 286n13; original publisher of, 286n13
Krivov, Mikhail, 118
Krotov, Yakov, 117
Krushevan, Pavolachi, 113
Kryuchkov, Vladimir, 14, 30
Kudryavtsev, Mikhail P., 202, 295n32, 296n33
Kulakov, Alexander, 101–3, 114, 134, 136
Kutuzov, Mikhail, 47

Lactanius, 268n25
Laurus (metropolitan), 196–98
Law on Freedom of Conscience and Religious Associations (1997), 173–74; Article 14, 174
Law on Freedom of Conscience and Religious Organizations (1990), 68, 72, 172–73
Lazar (king), 138
Lazarev, Lazar, 234
Lebed, Alexander, 17
Lebedev, Alexander, 201
Lebedev, Lev (archpriest), 7, 79, 251, 263n5
Lenin, Vladimir, 6, 7, 79, 185; and hatred of the church, 191; and the murders of the Romanovs, 103, 185; on Western supporters of the Soviet Union, 273n50
Leonid (archimandrite), 146–47
"Letter to the Future" (St. Seraphim), 63, 110
Life of Christ, The (St. Nicholas of Cabasilas), 8
Life of Constantine (Eusebius of Caesarea), 268n25
Litvinenko, Alexander, 281n34
Lossky, Vladimir, 204, 295n24
Louis VII (king), 211, 298n13
Lukichev, Boris, 218
Lukijan, Pantelic, 137
Lukoil, 92–93

Luzhkov, Yury, 80, 89–91, 122, 174, 227, 253

MacCullough, Diarmaid, 13, 288n23
Major, John, 17
Makary (Bulgakov) (metropolitan), 148
"Manifest Destiny," 226
Markov, Sergey, 201
Marx, Karl, 172
Marxism, 172
Marxism-Leninism. *See* "scientific atheism"
Mary: Hodegetria (Guide) icon of the Theotokos, 91–92, 161, 166, 290n44; Kazan icon of the Theotokos, 25–26, 199; as "Protector of our city [Moscow]," 24, 25, 30, 91; "Victory of the Blessed Mother of God, The," icon, 213; "Virgin of the Don" icon, 26, 241; Virgin *Orans* icon, 253; Virgin of Tikhvin icon, 198–99; Vladimir icon of the Theotokos, 24–25, 216, 229, 266n11
Mary Tudor, 271n25
Mazur, Igor (archpriest), 238
Meaning of Icons, The (Oupensky and Lossky), 295n24
Mefody (metropolitan), 281
Men, Alexander (priest), 194
"men of '38," 40, 183
Methodius, 7–8, 263n6, 287n17
"Metropolitan Sergy Stragorodsky" (Shuman), 293n6, 294n16
Michael VIII Palaiologus (emperor), 161
Mikeshin, Mikhail, 146
Mikhailovich, Alexander, 124
Mikhalkov, Nikita, 306n13
Mikhalkov, Sergey, 247, 306n13
Miller, William, 43, 269n13
Milosevic, Slobodan, 139
Minin, Kuzma, 247
Mission to Moscow (Davies), 273n50
missionaries, in the Soviet Union, 68–69
Mitrofanov, Georgy (archpriest), 122–23, 124–25, 194, 195–96, 201, 294–95n20, 305n6
"Modern Day Saint, A?" (Slater), 280n28
Mokva, Trety Rim (*Moscow, the Third Rome*) (Kudryavtsev), 202; Aleksy II's approval of, 295n32